Not Under My Roof

Parents, Teens, and the Culture of Sex

AMY T. SCHALET

University of Chicago Press
Chicago and London

Amy T. Schalet is assistant professor of sociology at the University of Massachusetts, Amherst.

The University of Chicago Press, Chicago 60637
The University of Chicago Press, Ltd., London
© 2011 by The University of Chicago
All rights reserved. Published 2011.
Printed in the United States of America

20 19 18 17 16 15 14 13 12 11   1 2 3 4 5

ISBN-13: 978-0-226-73618-1 (cloth)
ISBN-13: 978-0-226-73619-8 (paper)
ISBN-10: 0-226-73618-0 (cloth)
ISBN-10: 0-226-73619-9 (paper)

Library of Congress Cataloging-in-Publication Data
Schalet, Amy T.
    Not under my roof : parents, teens, and the culture of sex /
Amy T. Schalet.
        p. cm.
    Includes bibliographical references and index.
    ISBN-13: 978-0-226-73618-1 (alk. paper)
    ISBN-10: 0-226-73618-0 (alk. paper)
    ISBN-13: 978-0-226-73619-8 (pbk. : alk. paper)
    ISBN-10: 0-226-73619-9 (pbk. : alk. paper)   1. Teenagers—Sexual
behavior—Netherlands.   2. Teenagers—Sexual behavior—United
States.   3. Parent and teenager—United States.   4. Parent and
teenager—Netherlands.   I. Title.
    HQ27.S2567 2011
    306.70835—dc22   2011003357

♾ This paper meets the requirements of ANSI/NISO Z39.48-1992
(Permanence of Paper).

CONTENTS

ACKNOWLEDGMENTS

Looking back on the almost epic journey from the inception to completion of this book, I am filled with gratitude for the mentors, colleagues, and friends who contributed in ways large and small. I want to start by recognizing three people who were especially important at different points along the road: at the very beginning, during the long haul, and in the final stretch of the research and writing process. In the Social Studies Concentration at Harvard College where I conducted my earliest research on adolescence in Holland and America, Suzanne Kirschner gave generously of her time and insight to guide me through the uncharted territory of gathering and interpreting my own data. At the University of California at Berkeley, where I conducted the bulk of the research for this book, Ann Swidler was a fantastic advisor. Unwavering in her enthusiasm, commitment, and, dare I say, love, Ann welcomed my intellectual autonomy *and* turned out to be right about every bit of important advice she gave. Finally, as I completed the book at the University of Massachusetts Amherst, Robert Zussman's excellent judgment, gentle insistence, and generosity of spirit have been true and precious gifts.

At Berkeley, I benefited greatly from additional mentorship from Raka Ray, who deftly combined the roles of skeptic and fan, and from Kristin Luker, who provided astute observations and, together with Jane Mauldon, helped solidify the research design. Jorge Arditi and Gil Eyal gave valuable suggestions about how to best think through the project's theoretical framings. Everywhere, my friends have been among my greatest teachers. In the early phases of the project, Justin Suran did me the tremendous favor of taking his unrelenting red pen to drafts, leaving me forever the better as a writer. Fellow Berkeley graduate student and friend, Teresa Gowan, joined my intellectual quest, offering a wellspring of insights which have become an organic part of my own thinking. Hilary Abell, Phillip Fucella, Anna Korteweg, Greggor Mattson, Rachel Sherman, Millie Thayer, and Ann Marie Wood also shared their thoughts generously and have left imprints on the book.

I want to thank my Dutch friends Floor Bouhuijs, Marina Millington-Ward, and Annelou de Vries for helping me find housing and make research contacts during fieldwork in the Netherlands. I am also grateful to my Dutch colleagues Christien Brinkgreve, Sanderijn van der Doef, Godfried Engbersen, Evert Ketting, Trudie Knijn, Olga Loeber, Ariana Need, Janita Ravesloot, Ali de Regt, and Paul Schnabel for helpful comments and enlightening conversations. Geert de Vries and Cas Wouters both went above and beyond the call of collegiality. At many points, Geert was extraordinarily engaged, intellectually and practically, and Cas tirelessly provided thoughtful comments from across the ocean.

I am very grateful to the late Charlotte Ellertson, Sarah Holcombe, Cynthia Harper, and Philip Darney for institutionalizing the Charlotte Ellertson Postdoctoral Fellowship in Abortion and Reproductive Health at the University of California at San Francisco's Bixby Center for Global Reproductive Health, which was designed to advance interdisciplinary research and help social science researchers become better public intellectuals. At UCSF, I learned a great deal from Carole Joffe, Jillian Henderson, and Tracy Weitz about the politics of abortion and about the significant barriers to young people's access to abortion and contraception services in the United States. Through the fellowship, located at the School of Medicine, I learned how to relate my research on adolescent sexuality and culture to questions and concerns of health researchers, policymakers, advocates, and professionals, which has made it possible for me to participate in broader sets of academic and public conversations about adolescent sexual health.

I have had the privilege of presenting my research at a range of seminars and conferences where I received and integrated input from many different audiences. I enjoyed exchanges with Dutch colleagues in seminars at the Royal Tropical Institute and the universities of Amsterdam, Utrecht, and Nijmegen. In the United States, I benefited from opportunities to present this research at, among others, the Comparative Research Workshop at Yale University, the Center for German and European Studies at the University of Wisconsin–Madison, the American Sociological Association, the Pacific Sociological Association, and, closer to home, the Five College Women's Studies Research Center and the University of Massachusetts Amherst's Center for Public Policy and Administration. I also benefited a great deal from interprofessional exchanges during presentations at, among others,

Emory University's School of Medicine, the University of California at San Francisco's School of Medicine, the Society for Adolescent Medicine, the Centers for Disease Control and Prevention, CDC's National STD Prevention Conference, Columbia University's Mailman School of Public Health, the Massachusetts Department of Public Health, the National Coalition for STD Directors, and the Teenage Pregnancy Prevention Conference.

Crossing boundaries in research—whether between countries or between disciplines—usually requires outside financial support, and my experience has been no exception. I am grateful for fellowships and grants from the National Science Foundation, the University of California at Berkeley, the Woodrow Wilson Foundation, the Berkeley Chapter of Sigma Xi, the Center for German and European Studies at Berkeley, and the anonymous donor who supported several cohorts of Charlotte Ellertson Postdoctoral Fellows. I want to express special thanks to the Ford Foundation for grants which have made it possible for me to disseminate my research among medical professionals and educators, and to learn more from them about youth populations other than the ones I had studied, as well as to ask questions about the practical tools necessary to improve adolescent sexual health outcomes. These opportunities for interprofessional exchanges have yielded several extremely fruitful collaborations with, among others, Veenod Chulani, Kaiyti Duffy, and John Santelli, who have each shaped my thinking about adolescent sexual health, especially as it is impacted by health and education professionals.

It has been a great pleasure to work with editors at the University of Chicago Press—specifically with Doug Mitchell, Timothy McGovern, and Richard Allen, who all command such an impressive way with words. Communicating with humor and grace, Doug's e-mails have invariably been feasts for the eye and ear, and Richard's engagement and precision have been sources of joy and comfort in the final editing. I want to thank Chicago's anonymous reviewers whose challenges and enthusiasm for the book's potential have strengthened it in equal measure. Thanks also to Jo Ellen Green Kaiser, who helped me think about how to organize a book so that it could speak to academics and nonacademics alike. Finally, I have been lucky to have had two outstanding research assistants, whose roles in editing and manuscript preparation cannot be overemphasized: talented and dedicated, Paula Partee and Sarah Miller have been dream assistants, and I hope that they will receive similar support when they write their own books.

All good things must come to an end. And as I neared the finish line, my colleagues at the University of Massachusetts, Amherst, Naomi Gerstel, Joya

Misra, and Don Tomaskovic-Devey—all of whom read the entire manuscript at least once—helped me figure out how to put on the right finishing touches. I am deeply grateful to friends, family, and those who have been like family—Dana Blackburn, Anna Branch, Sally Curcio, Jillian Henderson, Greg Jones, Mariette Leufkens, Arden Pierce, Robin Prichard, Melissa Rodgers, Kate Thurston, Ben Schalet, Melissa Wooten, and James Wilson—for their confidence and company in moments of doubt and jubilation.

My final words of thanks go to the parents and teenagers who allowed me to interview them about such intimate parts of their lives—and to the teachers, counselors, and community members who made it possible to reach them. I have lived with their company for many years, poring over transcripts and marveling each time at how much I love working with this material. Listening to their words over and over, I have learned so much, not just about culture and difference, but about love, growth, and letting go. I hope that as I release this long labor of love, youth, parents, and parents-yet-to-be will find it a resource for insights of their own.

Some of this research first saw the light of day in an article entitled "Sex, Love, and Autonomy in the Teenage Sleepover" (*Contexts* 9, no. 3 [2010]: 16–21).

ONE

Raging Hormones, Regulated Love

Karel Doorman, a soft-spoken civil servant in the Netherlands, keeps tabs on his teenage children's computer use and their jobs to make sure neither are interfering with school performance or family time.[1] But Karel would not object if his daughter Heidi were to have a sexual relationship: "No," he explains. "She is sixteen, almost seventeen. I think she knows very well what matters, what can happen. If she is ready, I would let her be ready." If Heidi were to come home and say, "Dad, this is him," he says, "well, I hope I like him." Karel would also let Heidi spend the night with a steady boyfriend in her room, provided he did not show up "out of the blue." But Karel thinks that he would first "come by the house and that I will hear about him and that she'll talk about him and . . . that it really is a gradual thing." That said, Karel suspects his daughter might prefer a partner of her own sex. Karel would accept her orientation he says, though he grants, "the period of adjustment might take a little longer."

Karel's approach stands in sharp contrast to that of his fellow parent, Rhonda Fursman, a northern California homemaker and former social worker. Rhonda tells her teenage son and daughter that premarital sex "at this point is really dumb." It is on the list with shoplifting, she explains, "sort of like the Ten Commandments: don't do any of those because if you do, you know, you're going to be in a world of hurt." It comes as no surprise therefore that Ronda responds viscerally when asked whether she would let her fifteen-year-old son spend the night with a girlfriend. "No way, José!" She elaborates: "That kind of recreation . . . is just not something I would feel comfortable with him doing here." She ponders her reaction: "I tried to be very open and modern . . . but I am like, no, I'm not comfortable. I don't think I want to encourage that." She has a hard time imagining changing her position on permitting the sleepover, although maybe "if they are engaged or about to be married . . ."

Karel and Rhonda illustrate a puzzle: both white, middle class, and secular or moderately Christian, they belong to the one hundred and thirty Dutch and American parents and teenagers, mostly tenth-graders, whom I interviewed between the early 1990s and 2000.* Despite the fact that both groups of parents are similar in education, religion, class, and race— features that often influence attitudes toward sexuality and childrearing— the vast majority of American parents oppose a sleepover for high-school-aged teenagers, while most Dutch parents permit it or consider doing so under the right circumstances. This book seeks to solve the puzzle of this striking difference, which is all the more surprising given the liberalization in sexual attitudes and practices that took place throughout Europe and the United States since the 1960s. Given similar trends, why do the Dutch and American parents respond so differently? How do the parental approaches affect teenagers' experiences of sexuality and self? To answer these questions, we must look beyond sexuality at the different cultures of individualism that emerged in American and Dutch societies after the sexual revolution.

Not Under My Roof will take us beyond our usual perspectives on adolescent sexuality.[2] Medical and public health literatures conceptualize adolescent sexuality primarily in terms of individual risk-taking and the factors that augment or lessen such risks.[3] American developmental psychologists tend to view adolescent sexuality as part of adolescents' separation from their parents and as an aspect of development that is especially perilous given the disjuncture between teenagers' physical and cognitive development.[4] American sociologists have generally bypassed the parent–teenager nexus to focus on relationships and networks *among* teenagers—in romance and peer groups. They have examined how peer cultures and networks and the status hierarchies within them impact adolescent sexuality.[5] Finally, gender scholars have examined how teenage girls' and boys' experiences of sexuality are profoundly shaped by gender inequalities—including the sexual double standard.[6]

This book takes a different approach. It focuses on the negotiation of adolescent rights and responsibilities within the parent–teenager relation-

---

* To promote narrative flow, I will often refer to "Dutch" and "American" parents and teenagers rather than specify the socio-demographic characteristics of the groups I studied. But since there are many sources of cultural variation within each country, care must be taken in generalizing from the findings and analyses to the larger Dutch and American populations.

ship as a particularly fruitful, and often overlooked, site for illuminating how youth come to relate to sexuality, themselves, and others. This cross-national comparison shows how much of what we take for granted about teenage sexuality—in American folk, professional, and academic wisdom—is the product of our cultural constructs and institutions. Indeed, the apparently trivial puzzle Karel Doorman and Rhonda Fursman introduce is not just a puzzle but a window onto two different ways of understanding and shaping individuals and social relationships in middle-class families and in the societies at large, which constitute nothing less than two distinct cultures of individualism. Each culture of individualism comes with freedoms and sacrifices: the Dutch cultural templates provide teenagers with more support *and* subject them to deeper control, while the American cultural templates make the experience of adolescent sexuality particularly conflict-ridden.

Adolescent Sexuality in America after the Sexual Revolution

Today most adolescents in the United States, like their peers across the industrial world, engage in sexual contact—broadly defined—before leaving their teens, typically starting around age seventeen.[7] Initiating sex and exploring romantic relationships, often with several successive partners before settling into long-term cohabitation or marriage, are normative parts of adolescence and young adulthood across the developed world.[8] In the Netherlands, as in many countries of northwestern Continental Europe, adolescent sexuality has been what one might call *normalized*—treated as a normal part of individual and relational development, and discussible with adults in families, schools, and health care clinics.[9] But in the United States, teenage sex has been *dramatized*—fraught with cultural ambivalences, heated political struggles, and poor health outcomes, generating concern among the public, policymakers, and scholars.

In some respects, it is surprising to find adolescent sexuality treated as such a deep problem in the United States. Certainly, age at first intercourse has dropped since the sexual revolution, but not as steeply as often assumed. In their survey of the adult American population, *The Social Organization of Sexuality: Sexual Practices in the United States*, Edward Laumann and colleagues found that even in the 1950s and 1960s, only a quarter of men and less than half of women were virgins at age nineteen. The majority of young men had multiple sexual partners by age twenty.[10] And while women especially were supposed to enter marriage as virgins, the majority of those who came of age in the late 1950s and early 1960s had sexual intercourse before they married.[11] Still, a 1969 Gallup poll found that two-thirds of Americans said it was wrong for "a man and a woman to have sex relations before marriage."

But by 1985, Gallup found that a slim majority of Americans no longer believed such relations were wrong.[12] Analyzing shifts in public opinion following the sexual revolution, sociologists Larry Petersen and Gregory Donnenwerth have shown that among Americans with a religious affiliation, only fundamentalist Protestants who attended church frequently remained unchanged. Among all other religious groups acceptance of premarital sex grew.[13] This growing acceptance of premarital sex did not, however, extend to teenagers: in their 1990s survey, Laumann and colleagues found that almost 80 percent of the American population continued to believe sex among teenagers was *always* or *almost always* wrong. Since then, two-thirds of Americans have consistently told interviewers of the General Social Survey that sex between fourteen and sixteen is always wrong. Interestingly, disapproval has remained widespread even among youth themselves: six in ten fifteen- to nineteen-year-olds, surveyed in the National Survey of Family Growth, said it was not right for unmarried sixteen-year-olds who have "strong affection for each another" to have sexual intercourse.[14]

Part of the opposition to, and discomfort with, adolescent sexuality is its association with the high prevalence of unintended consequences, such as pregnancy and sexually transmitted diseases. In the United States, the rate of unintended pregnancies among teenagers rose during the 1970s and 80s and started dropping only in the early 1990s.[15] However, despite almost a decade and a half of impressive decreases in pregnancy and birth rates, the teen birth rate remains many times higher in the United States than it is in most European countries. In 2007, births to fifteen- to nineteen-year-old girls were eight times as high in the United States as they were in the Netherlands.[16] One reason for the different birth rates is that while condom use has improved among American teenagers, they remain far less likely to use the most effective methods of birth control, such as the pill.[17] Another reason is that, once pregnant, American girls are far more likely than their Dutch peers to carry their pregnancies to term.[18]

Nor are high rates of unintended pregnancies the only problems. Many American teenagers have positive and enriching sexual experiences, yet researchers have also documented intense struggles. Sharon Thompson found that only a quarter of the four hundred girls she interviewed about sexuality talked about their first sexual experiences as pleasurable. Among the girls Karin Martin interviewed, puberty and first intercourse decreased self-esteem. Psychologist Deborah Tolman found that most of the girls she interviewed struggled to fully own their sexual desires and experiences in the face of cultural constructs such as the double standard and the "slut" label that stigmatize and deny girls' desires. Laura Carpenter illuminated another side of the double standard, finding that many of the young men she interviewed experienced their virginity as a stigma which they often sought to cast off as rapidly as possible. And in her ethnographic study *Dude, You're a Fag*, C. J. Pascoe found that teenage boys were encouraged to, treat girls as sex objects and risked social derogation if they openly expressed affection for their girlfriends.[19]

These qualitative studies are corroborated by national surveys that show that American teenagers feel widespread ambivalence and misgivings about their first sexual experiences, which suggests that they do not feel control over, or entitled to, their sexual exploration. In a national survey, a minority of young women and a small majority of young men in their early twenties reported that their first heterosexual intercourse was "really wanted." Almost half of the women and a sizable minority of the men surveyed said they had mixed feelings.[20] In another poll, a majority of American girls and boys said they wished they had waited longer to have sex.[21] Research has also found that if girls are young relative to their peers when they first have sex, they are more likely to experience negative emotions afterward, especially if their relationship breaks up shortly thereafter. But even without intercourse, first romance can bring girls "down" because their relationship with their parents deteriorates.[22]

American teenagers have received uneven, and often very limited, support in navigating the challenges of sexuality and first relationships from adult institutions outside the family. Despite rising pregnancy rates, in the early 1970s American policymakers and physician organizations lagged in making contraception easily available to teenagers, and even today American youth face multiple barriers in accessing contraception, including confidentiality concerns.[23] With few other venues for discussing sexuality, the media has been an important, although often unrealistic, source of sex education for many American teenagers. Describing the 1960s and 1970s when sex permeated the media, historians D'Emilio and Freedman write, "From everywhere sex beckoned, inciting desire, yet rarely did one find reasoned presentations of the most elementary consequences and responsibilities that sexual activity entailed."[24] Since then, researchers have noted that some media including magazines and Internet sites provide good sexual health information but not the interactive dialogue with adults that teenagers seek.[25]

Teenagers have been unlikely to find such dialogue in the classroom.

Along with fights over the legal age to consent to contraceptive and abortion services, battles over sex education have been among the most heated sexuality-related political struggles in America.[26] Politically organized religious conservatives succeeded in institutionalizing a federal sex education policy that has required the schools it funded to teach "abstinence only until marriage." Initiated in the early 1980s, federal support for abstinence-only policy was institutionalized in the 1996 welfare reform bill. Generously funded for many years, this policy dictated that schools teach that sex outside of heterosexual marriage is likely to be damaging, and it prohibited them from teaching about the health benefits of condoms and contraception.[27] Even in school districts not funded by this federal policy, sex education about contraception, pleasure, sexual diversity, and relationships has often been greatly constrained.[28]

Few survey findings have been as consistent as the finding that the general public supports sex education in schools.[29] In keeping with surveys of the past three decades, a 2004 national survey by NPR, the Kaiser Family Foundation, and Harvard University found that most parents wanted their children to learn about contraception and condoms. Yet, the same survey also gives some insight into why the abstinence-only policy nevertheless prevailed: while most parents did want their children to learn the information they needed to protect themselves, most respondents also wanted students to be taught that they should not engage in intercourse or other intimate sexual activities. And they accepted the "marriage only" framework: two-thirds of parents of middle and high-school students agreed that teenagers should be taught that abstaining from sexual activity outside of marriage is "the accepted standard for school-aged children."[30] Abstinence, most agreed, includes refraining from oral sex and intimate touching—sexual activities that most American youth, in actuality, start experimenting with in their mid-teens.[31]

Adolescent Sexuality in Dutch Society after the Sexual Revolution

In a late 1980s qualitative study with one hundred and twenty parents and older teenagers, Dutch sociologist Janita Ravesloot found that in most families the parents accepted that sexuality "from the first kiss to the first coitus" was part of the youth phase. In middle-class families, parents accepted their children's sexual autonomy, though lingering embarrassment kept them from engaging in elaborate conversations. Working-class parents were more likely to use authority to impose their norms, including that sex belonged only in steady relationships. In a few strongly religious families—Christian or Muslim—parents categorically opposed sex before marriage, which meant "no overnights with steady boy- or girlfriends at home."[32] But such families remain a minority: a 2003 national survey by *Statistics Netherlands* found that two-thirds of Dutch teenagers, aged fifteen to seventeen, who had steady boy- or girlfriends, said that their parents would allow their boy- or girlfriend to spend the night in their bedrooms; girls and boys were just as likely to say that they would be granted permission for a sleepover.[33]

The situation could hardly have been predicted in the 1950s. Then, women *and* men typically initiated intercourse in their early twenties, usually in a serious relationship if not engagement or marriage.[34] In a national survey in the late 1960s, the Dutch sociologist G. A. Kooij found that the majority of the Dutch population still rejected premarital sex if a couple was not married or was not planning to be married very shortly. After repeating the survey in the early 1980s, he noted a "moral landslide" had taken place in the interim, as evidenced by the fact that six out of ten of those surveyed no longer objected to a girl having sexual intercourse with a boy as long as she was in love with him.[35] Dutch sociologist Evert Ketting spoke of a "moral revolution": Not just a reluctant acceptance of sex outside of the context of heterosexual marriage, this revolution involved serious deliberation among medical professionals, the media, and the public at large—the result of a widely felt need to adjust the moral rules governing sexual life to real behavior.[36]

Many groups in Dutch society played a role in this transition. In the 1950s and '60s, Dutch religious leaders had begun questioning traditional definitions of morality. The Dutch Catholic Church—which represented the nation's largest religious group—was early to embrace the use of oral contraception as a method of birth control.[37] The Dutch media played a key educational role.[38] With television and radio time partially funded by, and divided among, groups with different religious and political perspectives, discussions about sexuality were widespread.[39] Remarking on such discussions throughout the 1970s, researchers for the Guttmacher Institute noted in 1986, "One might say the entire society has concurrently experienced a course in sex education."[40] From these public deliberations resulted, Evert Ketting has argued, new moral rules that cast sexuality as part of life to be governed by self-determination, mutual respect between sexual partners, frank conversations, and the prevention of unintended consequences.[41]

Notably, these new moral rules were applied to minors and institutionalized in Dutch health-care policies of the 1970s, which removed financial and emotional barriers to accessing contraceptives—including the require-ment for parental consent and a pelvic examination.[42] Indeed, even as the age of first sexual intercourse was decreasing, the rate of births among Dutch teenagers dropped steeply between 1970 and 1996 to one of the lowest in the world. With their effective use of oral contraception, what dis-tinguished Dutch teens from their Swedish counterparts, for instance, was that in addition to a very low fertility rate they also had a low abortion rate. Despite the AIDS crisis, by the mid-1990s—just when American policy-makers institutionalized "abstinence only until marriage"—Dutch funding agencies were so confident that, in the words of demographer Joop Gars-sen, youth were doing "wonderfully well," they decided that further study of adolescent sexual attitudes and behavior was not warranted.[43]

Dutch researchers at that time noted similarities in boys' and girls' expe-riences of sexuality. Ravesloot found that the boys and girls she interviewed were equally as likely to feel controlled by their parents. Large-scale surveys from the early and mid-1990s found that boys and girls were approximat-ing one another in combining feelings of being in love and lust as they pursued romantic relationships and initiated sexual experimentation.[44] At the same time, researchers found evidence of the double standard and sex-stereotyping—including the notion that boys were supposed to be more active and girls more passive in sexual interactions.[45] To counteract these "traditional" gender beliefs and roles, researchers recommended teach-ing negotiation or "interaction" skills, including the expression of sexual wishes and boundaries.[46] A 2005 national survey found high levels of such skills among both girls and boys, which include "letting the other person know exactly what feels good" and not doing things that one does not want.[47]

Indeed, the same study, which surveyed youth aged twelve through twenty-four, suggests Dutch adolescents feel more in control of their first sexual experiences and decision-making than their American peers, or al-ternatively, that the former feel more entitled or obliged than the latter to describe themselves as empowered sexual actors: four out of five Dutch youth described their first sexual experiences—broadly defined to include different activities—as well timed, within their control, and fun. About their first intercourse, 86 percent of girls and young women and 93 percent of boys and young men said, "We both were equally eager to have it." At the same time, there were some notable gender differences. For instance, girls were much more likely to report having ever been forced to do some-thing sexually. They were also more likely to regularly or always experience pain (11 percent) or have trouble reaching orgasm (27 percent) during sex than were boys. Nevertheless, the vast majority of both Dutch females and males were (very) satisfied with the pleasure and contact they felt with their partner during sex.

Emphasis on the positive aspects of sex and relationships—within the context of respect for self and others—is a key feature of Dutch sex education. Although they set national "attainment targets," Dutch policymakers avoided political controversy over sex education by delegating the task of reaching agreements on the content and delivery of sex education to professionals.[48] Sociologists Jane Lewis and Trudie Knijn have argued that like Dutch policymakers, Dutch sex educators have accepted teenage sexual exploration, viewing it as the result of societal changes. They teach students to view such issues as sexual diversity and diverse family formations in broader societal contexts as well. Sex education typically covers anatomy, reproduction, STDs, contraception and abortion. But in addition, sex education curricula often interweave the emotional and physical aspects of sex, emphasize relationships and developing mutual understanding, and openly discuss masturbation, homosexuality, and sexual pleasure.[49]

Investigating the Puzzle

The previous sections show how across an array of social institutions, adolescent sexuality has been viewed as a problem to be prevented in the United States, while in the Netherlands it has been accepted as part of teenage maturation to be guided by new moral rules. Why do adults in the two countries have such different approaches? This question is especially puzzling given that, in both countries, the generation in question lived through an era when attitudes toward sexuality outside the confines of heterosexual marriage changed rather dramatically. Indeed, of the two, the country in which it had been more common for teenagers to engage in sexual intercourse during the 1950s became, several decades later, the country in which teenage sexuality remained controversial.

Two factors immediately spring to mind when considering why adults in these two countries who lived through the sexual revolution—in which many themselves participated—would embrace such different approaches to the sexual socialization of the next generation. The first is religion. Americans are far more likely to be religiously devout than their Dutch counterparts, many of whom left their houses of worship in the 1960s and 1970s. As Laumann and colleagues found, Americans who do not view religion as a central force in their decision-making are much less likely to categorically condemn sex among teenagers. By the same token, devout Christians and Muslims in the Netherlands are more likely to hold attitudes towards sexuality and marriage that are similar to those of their American counterparts. That a larger proportion of the American population than the Dutch population can be categorized as religiously conservative explains some of the difference between the countries.[50]

A second factor is economic security: as in most European countries, the Dutch government provides a range of what sociologists call "social rights" and what reproductive health advocates call "human rights."[51] These include the rights to housing, education, health care, and a minimum income. These rights ensure youth access to quality health care, including, if need be, free contraceptive and abortion services. Such supports—from universal children's allowances to college stipends—also make coming of age less perilous for both teenagers and parents, and they might make the prospect of sex derailing a child's life less haunting. Ironically, it is the lack of such rights in the United States, along with rates of childhood poverty that exceed those of most of Europe, that contributes to high rates of births among teenagers. Without adequate support systems or educational and job opportunities, young people everywhere, not just in the United States, are much more likely to start parenthood early in life.[52]

And yet, as Karel Doorman and Rhonda Fursman illustrated at the start of this chapter, there is more to the story: both parents are economically comfortable and neither attends church regularly, yet their answers to the question of the sleepover could not be more different. To understand why parents such as Rhonda and Karel reached such opposing conclusions about the sleepover, and how their different household practices affected teenagers, I interviewed one hundred and thirty members of the American and Dutch white, secular or moderately Christian middle classes—fifty-eight individual parents or couples, thirty-two boys, and forty girls, with most of the teens in the tenth grade. To avoid only studying professionals, I included a spectrum of lower- and upper-middle-class families, and interviewed parents and teenagers living in households where the breadwinners ranged from salespeople and bank clerks with little or no postsecondary education, to nurses and managers with four-year degrees, to psychotherapists and doctors with advanced degrees.

In both countries, most interviewees came from one of two locations: In the Netherlands, they lived in or around the medium-sized cities of Western and Eastern City, which are located in the more cosmopolitan, densely populated Western region and in the less cosmopolitan, less densely populated Eastern region respectively. In the United States, most interviewees lived in and around Corona, a medium-sized city in northern California, and Tremont, a small town in the Pacific Northwest. An additional group of American interviewees resided in Norwood, a New England suburb.[53] Avoiding the most cosmopolitan urban centers and liberal hotspots, as well as the most conservative regions and remote rural areas, the two samples represent what I would call the "moderate middle" among the white middle class in the two countries. Comparing these population segments cannot illuminate important cultural differences *within* either nation—between classes, races, regions, ethnicities, and religions. But the comparison does illuminate differences between the two countries in the family cultures of two particularly influential groups—differences that are not accounted for by our prevailing theoretical perspectives on adolescent sexuality.

Medical, Social Science, and Historical Perspectives

In the United States, the prevailing perspective in the field of public policy and health has been that teenage sexual intercourse is a health risk—a potential sickness, which is to be ideally prevented altogether.[54] The primary focus of research in this field is on the various factors that increase and decrease the risks of adolescent sexuality—defined narrowly as acts of intercourse. This risk perspective is corroborated by one view from developmental psychology which sees adolescents as inherently risk-prone and subject to impulses that they are not yet able to handle, given their stage of cognitive development.[55] Classical developmental psychology also conceptualizes sexuality as part of young people's separation process from parents.[56] This process, however, produces discord—between teenagers' impulses and their brains' capacities, between early onset of sexual feelings and their later proclivity for emotional intimacy, and between teenagers and parents whose job it is to communicate their values and to monitor and limit their children's opportunities for sex.

These perspectives from medicine and psychology do not explain the puzzle posed by the differences in approach to and experience of adolescent sexuality in two developed nations. If anything, the puzzle challenges their assumptions. While Dutch teenagers, like their American counterparts, must certainly navigate the potential health risks of sex, the variation between the two nations in negative outcomes of sexual activity shows that neither the level of sexual activity itself nor adolescents' inherent biological or psychological capacities are responsible for such outcomes. The normalization of adolescent sexuality in Dutch middle-class families challenges, moreover, the notion that teenage sexuality—and adolescence as a phase of life—causes a schism between parents and teenagers that is often assumed in the United States to be an inevitable part of development. Indeed, normalization suggests an alternative model of adolescent development, one in which parents and teenagers remain more closely connected and able to negotiate the potential disruptive elements of adolescent maturation.

A third perspective comes from American gender scholars who argue that adolescent sexuality—conceived broadly, to include feelings, actions, and identities—is a premier arena for the expression, transmission, and challenging of gender inequality. While some scholars see girls gaining power vis-à-vis boys in heterosexual relationships,[57] others have pointed out the myriad factors that impede an empowered sexual development in girls—including the sexual double standard that, according to Karin Martin, results in "antagonistic gender strategies" between girls and boys.[58] Especially troubling to many American gender scholars is what Michelle Fine has poignantly called "the missing discourse of girls' desire."[59] Without recognition in sex education curricula, the media, and the social sciences that girls have their own sexual desires, it is difficult for them to develop "sexual subjectivity": the capacity to feel connected to sexual desires and boundaries and to use these to make self-directed decisions.[60]

But the gender inequality perspective also does not solve the puzzle, for while it helps explain why many girls in the United States experience a lack of physical pleasure as well as negative emotions about sex, especially when sex happens outside of a steady relationship, it does not account for the ambivalence and misgivings that many American boys also report. Nor does it account for the similarity in Dutch surveys in boys' and girls' reports of wanting, feeling control over, and enjoying first sexual experiences. Moreover, it offers no explanation for why, unlike the American parents interviewed for this book, the Dutch parents do not talk about gender as a salient feature of teenage sex and relationships, and why they are just as likely to permit daughters as sons to spend the night together with steady boy- and girlfriends. In fact, as we will see, gender plays a role in both countries—more overtly in the United States and more covertly in the Netherlands. But the perceptions and experiences of boys and girls in each country often approximate one another more than those of their same-sex peers across the ocean.

A final perspective on adolescent sexuality places it in the context of historical change. French philosopher Michel Foucault has argued that in the modern era, governments are no longer able to rule large populations through repression and punishment alone. However, they have found in official discourses about "normal" heterosexual identities and reproductive behavior effective methods for social control. Originating in religious, medical, scientific, and penal institutions, disciplinary practices and discourses encourage self-disclosure, differentiate people into categories, and goad them into new self-conceptions. Unlike the "sovereign" power of authorities who impose harsh punishments, the power of discipline and discourse is harder to detect, which makes it effective. Modern power is "productive" rather than repressive, Foucault argues, because rather than forbid, it exhorts individuals to voluntary shape their subjective sense of themselves according to confining understandings of what is normal, healthy, and desirable.[61]

Foucault's argument that, in the modern era, conceptions and practices around sexuality have been power-ridden and often serve the interests of authorities is useful but incomplete. Indeed, as we will see, the dramatization and normalization of adolescent sexuality are imbued with forms of social control. But Foucault's account does not help us understand why different discourses of adolescent sexuality have come to prevail in the institutions of two equally modern, post-sexual-revolution societies. Nor does it provide an explanation for why these different discourses—of adolescent-sexuality-as-risk in the United States, and of adolescent sexual self-determination in the Netherlands—resonate as they do among lay people. Finally, Foucault's argument about the effectiveness of modern power misses key ingredients.

The successful use of contraception among Dutch girls appears a prime example of disciplinary power. But, I argue, this power "works" because girls remain connected to and supported by adult institutions and are able to develop self-mastery—parts of the puzzle Foucault bypasses.[62]

Defining and Identifying Culture

To solve the puzzle left unaccounted for by existing literatures, we must turn to culture. But as the British sociologist Raymond Williams famously noted, culture is one of the most complex words in the English language.[63] Even sociologists have meant very different things with the concept, ranging from cultural products—books, music, and art—and the institutions that produce them, to assumptions and practices so taken for granted that they are largely invisible.[64] They have debated whether cultural meanings form a coherent "system" or an assemblage of potentially contradictory cultural tools that people use as their circumstances and goals warrant.[65] Moreover, sociologists have questioned the extent to which meanings are shared, given the social and economic inequalities that divide people.

Cultural forms—both cultural products and less tangible assumptions and practices—are used to signal and draw status distinctions.[66] Socially marginalized groups, in turn, often construct alternative meanings and subcultures.[67]

Mine is a synthetic approach to culture.[68] As an analytic category, I use the concept of culture to refer to three different processes—the three C's. The first pertains to the way people *conceptualize* themselves, each other, and the world at large using language, concepts, and frameworks. These interpretative, descriptive, and communicative tools create what the late anthropologist Clifford Geertz poetically called the "webs of significance" that give meanings to bare facts. A second process pertains to the potentially *controlling* component of culture. Cultural tools not only interpret and describe. They also implicitly or explicitly prescribe individual behavior and relationships, and they thus serve as covert or overt vehicles for the exercise of power, especially by those who possess the resources to impose their will. Finally, culture is *constitutive*. Cultural concepts and practices get inside people's skin, shaping their sense of themselves and of others by encouraging certain proclivities, capacities, and "emotion work."[69]

Central to my conception of culture is the notion that we live through shared "structures of meaning" which help us filter the myriad possibilities of being human. Such structures of meaning operate as preconscious, taken-for-granted interpretive frameworks that help us understand what aspects of the human potential are plausible and desirable, what we must do to develop those aspects as individuals, both within relationships and as communities of individuals, and what experiences are to be sought or avoided and what sacrifices are required to do so. Structures of meaning can interrelate to create a "cultural logic" that can give certain decisions and practices the appearance of cognitive, emotional, moral, and practical commonsense. This does not mean that cultures are uniform, static, or that everyone agrees with one another. Even within the same cultural community, people draw on multiple "cultural languages," struggle with one another about how to apply cultural concepts, and confront experiences that contradict those concepts.[70]

As challenging as defining culture analytically is "finding it" empirically, for as cultural sociologist Ann Swidler has pointed out, "when culture fully takes, it merges with life as to be nearly invisible."[71] The merging of culture with experience makes the former invisible not only to lay individuals but also to the researchers studying phenomena that are shaped by culture. One way to illuminate cultural processes is to compare them cross-nationally, for exposing cultural differences denaturalizes them and provides an entry into their internal dynamics. The highly charged emotional terrain of child-rearing and sexuality lends itself well for capturing and examining cultural differences. Asking people to make and justify a decision with regard to a hypothetical question, such as about a sleepover, encourages them to articulate culture, often inadvertently in the language they use, the metaphors they choose, and the modes of reasoning that make most sense to them. But people's articulations are not to be taken at face value. Rather, they must be used as clues to reconstruct the cultural processes in which they often inadvertently participate.

Culture is, at least in part, national.[72] Nations provide people with distinctive conditions and resources for shared meaning-making. Transnational economic and political processes notwithstanding, cultural processes are still shaped by nation-specific political, economic, and cultural institutions. National policies draw on cultural ideals and categories and, in turn, inform perceptions and experiences.[73] Cultural products—elite and popular—both reflect and shape broader national cultures. But national differences in culture are not just products of current conditions. More important are cultural concepts and practices that originate in, among others, formative geo-political events, geographic conditions, and religious traditions, and that persist after their original impetus has either mutated or been lost.[74] Language and rituals—everyday and exceptional—are both repositories of cultural concepts and means to communicate and enact them.

To argue that there are meaningful and systematic cultural differences across nations is not to suggest that those cultures are timeless.[75] National cultures do change, but they usually do so in ways that build on their pasts. Indeed, the topic of this book—the management of adolescent sexuality in Dutch and American families in the 1990s—results from processes of change that played out differently in two different national contexts. And one of the book's central contentions is that parents, policymakers, and intellectuals in the two countries have mobilized different cultural templates to come to terms with the challenges to the sexual, gender, and authority relations that existed before the 1960s. The cultural resources on which the generation of white middle-class Dutch adults who came of age during the 1960s and 1970s drew gave them reason to trust social bonds and self-restraint even as their attitudes toward sexuality, individuality, and authority changed profoundly. Meanwhile, their American peers drew on a model for individualism that made self-control and social bonds—intimate and societal—fragile when left unsupported by the traditional precepts that kept men and women, teenagers and parents in their respective places.

If cross-national comparisons are fertile territory for the excavation of cultural meanings, they also pose challenges. One such challenge is that there are, of course, multiple cultural communities within any given nation. Recognizing that people's social class, race and ethnicity, and religion can profoundly shape their cultural processes, I avoid comparing apples and oranges by focusing on two white, secular or moderately Christian middle-class cultures. But even within this segment of the population there are differences—between spouses, parents and teenagers, girls and boys, lower- and upper-middle class families, and between liberal and conservative families. Some of these differences cut across nations: girls and boys in the two countries confront similar constraining gender constructs. Parents in both countries face challenges in exercising control, and teenagers face challenges in developing independent selves. But, as we will see, cultural forces mediate gender, parental power, and adolescent maturation.

There are ways in which the position of the white secular or moderately religious middle class vis-à-vis other social groups in the two societies impacts the power of their cultural forms. Members of the white middle class have a disproportionate influence on the institutions of politics, education, and health care. Consequently, their cultural language, concepts, and frameworks are often presented as universal. Equally important, members of the white middle class have used conceptions of sexuality, as well as the cultural assumptions and ideals that inform them, to distinguish themselves from members of other social groups deemed inferior. The United States has, for instance, a long history of defining white middle-class girls as nonsexual in opposition to the over-sexualization of low-income girls of color.[76] Although the normalization of teenage sexuality in the Netherlands preceded the largest influx of immigrants in the 1980s and 1990s, normalization, which has also included homosexuality, has taken place in opposition to members of religious and ethnic minorities—especially Muslims.[77]

But while it is important to recognize how cultural forms can be used to impose norms and draw social distinctions, culture should not be reduced to its uses in the exercise of power. The challenge is to at once recognize that cultures allow people to make meaning and communicate *and* that such meanings can be used to draw boundaries against outsiders and exert control. As we will see, cultural concerns and ideals about the state of "complete freedom" shape the management of adolescent sexuality in American families, as do concerns and ideals about the state of *gezelligheid* or cozy togetherness in Dutch families. Genuinely treasured, these states of being are sources of pleasure and communion. At the same time, attaining "complete freedom" to do as one pleases is more accessible to certain segments of the American population than to others. And while the ideal of *gezelligheid* exerts control over those inside a given social circle, it can make it difficult for outsiders, especially new arrivals, to enter it.

Dramatization and Normalization

The first step to solve the puzzle of the sleepover is to see that Dutch and American parents engage in different cultural processes as they interpret and manage teenage sexuality. Culling words, expressions, and modes of reasoning from interviews shows how the American parents engage in *dramatization*: highlighting difficulties and conflicts, they describe adolescent sexuality, first, as "raging hormones," individual, potentially overpowering forces that are difficult for teenagers to control and, second, as antagonistic heterosexual relationships in which girls and boys pursue love and sex respectively. Finally, parents see it as their obligation to encourage adolescents to establish autonomy—and gain the potential for financial self-sufficiency or marriage—before accepting their sexual activity as legitimate. And viewing sex as part of a process of separation in which parents must stand firm ground around certain key issues, the response to the question of a sleepover, even among many otherwise liberal parents is, "Not under my roof!"

The Dutch parents, by contrast, engage in a cultural process of normalization. Theirs is a conception of "regulated love": that is, the Dutch parents speak of sexual readiness (*er aan toe zijn*), a process of becoming physically and emotionally ready that they believe young people can self-regulate, provided that they have been encouraged to pace themselves and prepare adequately by using the available means of contraception. But readiness does not happen in isolation. The Dutch parents talk about sexuality as emerging from relationships, and they are strikingly silent about gender conflicts. And unlike their American counterparts, who are often skeptical about teenagers' capacities to fall in love, they assume that even those in their early teens do so. They also permit the sleepover for those in their mid- and late teens, even if it requires an "adjustment" period to overcome their feelings of discomfort, because they feel obliged to accept the changes and to stay connected as relationships and sex become part of their children's lives.

The interplay of cultural frames that parents use to interpret adolescent sexuality, the capacities of young people, and the responsibilities of adults gives parents' responses to the question of the sleepover their cognitive, emotional, and moral common sense. These "webs of significance" thus create a more or less coherent cultural universe of meanings in which certain decisions and practices make intuitive sense while others do not. At the same time, there are holes in the webs: as significant as the cultural languages that parents have readily available are the silences, lacunae, and the ways in which dramatization and normalization do not adequately address aspects of parents' and teenagers' experiences. And although there are dominant tendencies in each middle-class culture, not everyone is on the same page. Indeed, as we will see, rather than constitute seamless wholes, dramatization and normalization often involve negotiations—between different people and between expectations and realities.

Adversarial and Interdependent Individualism

The second step in solving the puzzle is to see that the normalization and dramatization of adolescent sexuality are embedded within different cultures of individualism and control that have come to prevail in Dutch and American societies. These different cultures of individualism and control build on longstanding traditions within each country. At the same time, they are also nation-specific responses to the changes in sexual, gender, and authority relations of the 1960s and 1970s: In the United States an "adversarial individualism" has prevailed, according to which individual and society stand opposed to each other, which leaves uncertainty about the basis for social bonds between people and for self-restraint within them. In the Netherlands an "interdependent individualism" has prevailed in which individual and society are conceptualized as mutually constitutive. Interdependent individualism makes social bonds and the mutual accommodations necessary to maintain them more of a matter of course.[78]

Each version of individualism has been accompanied by a distinct form of social control: Adversarial individualism permits, encourages even, individuals to attain autonomy by breaking away from social ties and dependencies, and only after that break form intimate relationships. However, because this definition of autonomy necessitates a disruption of social connectedness, it makes it difficult to envision social cohesion and self-restraint without some higher authority. Thus ironically, adversarial individualism calls for the use of overt external control, especially against those who have not (yet) attained full autonomy. Interdependent individualism, by contrast, encourages individuals to develop their autonomy in concert with ongoing relationships of interdependence. Because such relationships require, by their nature, a certain amount of mutual accommodation and self-restraint, the use of external controls appears less necessary. But while overtly egalitarian, interdependent individualism can obscure inequality and the fact that the less powerful parties in relationships are expected to make the greater accommodations.

The premises of adversarial and interdependent individualism—their assumptions about the relationship between self and other, and the relationship between different parts of the self—create cultural logics that undergird the dramatization and normalization of adolescent sexuality. Hence, American middle-class parents encourage adolescents to pursue individual interests and passions, break away from home, and establish themselves as emotionally and financially self-sufficient beings. At the same time, during the teenage years, American parents also view it as their responsibility to fight back, sometimes forcefully, against the passions that they at the same time encourage as signs of individuation but doubt that their teenage children are able to control. This template for adversarial individualism makes parents wary of adolescents' establishing intimate bonds. It also makes domesticating such bonds by permitting a sleepover out of the question.

The Dutch template of interdependent individualism provides a way for adolescents to develop their autonomy within relationships of interdependence. Such ongoing interrelatedness is not viewed as a matter of choice as much as an inherent human need and proclivity. Thus, adolescence does not bring the same rupture in the relationships with parents or in the self. An assumption of interdependent individualism is that even as they develop autonomy, individuals—parents and children alike—must demonstrate interpersonal attunement, which requires from adolescents the development of self-regulation. Within this framework of interdependent individualism, teenagers' intimate relationships do not pose a threat to the acquisition of autonomy, nor does their sexual component threaten parental authority within the home. By negotiating the sleepover, parents model the very interdependent individualism—integrating the needs of the self and the social—they encourage in their children.

Connection through Control and Control through Connection

Intergenerational cultural transmission takes place not just through cultural narratives but also through methods for maintaining control and connection that psychologically encode them. As part of a new generation, young people's cultural universe only partially overlaps with that of their parents: they consume different media, are subject to different technological fluencies, participate in different institutions—school and peer culture—and are recipients of different formative "zeitgeists." Having not been fully socialized and yet subject to multiple sources of socialization, young people are often "rawer" in their desires and tendencies than their parents. For all these reasons, one cannot assume that just because a cultural logic makes sense to parents, it will make sense to their children as well. Yet, as we will see, even as they are in the process of forging their independent selves, young people do, in fact, reproduce through the interpretation and construction of their own experiences many of the same cultural categories their parents use.

Such cultural reproduction between the generations is not a matter of course. In both countries, adolescent experimentation with sexuality and alcohol are sources of potential parent-adolescent conflict. However, the methods by which parents establish control and connection shape how those conflicts are experienced. Most American teenagers describe a parental strategy of *reestablishing connection through control*. Many American teenagers encounter parental policies much like those in the Fursman household—no sex or alcohol. And while most young people start their teenage "careers" as rule followers, sooner or later they start "sneaking around" to engage in forbidden activities, which in turn become vehicles through which they engage in a *psychology of separation*. But this secrecy also creates a disjuncture in the connection between parents and children. To reestablish that connection, parents must exert overt control and young people must "get caught."

In most Dutch families, by contrast, teenagers are subject to parental strategy of *maintaining control through connection*: With the belief widespread that it is not possible to keep young people from engaging in sex and drinking if they decide they want to, few teenagers find such exploratory activities outright forbidden. At the same time, they are expected to continue participation in family rituals that keep them connected to their parents, even as they begin to experiment with sex, alcohol, and venturing into the world of nightlife. The "domestication" of their experimentations creates bridges between the world of adults and the world of peers that their American counterparts lack, and it encourages in Dutch teenagers a *psychology of incorporation*. Those bridges are two-way streets: young people are able to integrate their experiences outside the home more easily with their roles as family members, but they are also subject to a deeper form of social control. This "soft" power is particularly effective when young people stay genuinely connected to their families not just out of duty but out of desire.[79]

Individualism and Gender

The different cultural templates for individualism and control also shape interpretations and experiences of gender. The American parents often mention differences and conflicts of interest between girls and boys. In fact, in some, though certainly not most, families, the American boys report receiving implicit or explicit encouragement from fathers to pursue sexual interests. And while the interpretation and management of sexuality in American middle-class families led both girls and boys to use sex as a vehicle to engage in a psychology of separation, bifurcating sexuality and family life, this process tends to take a greater psychological toll on girls. While boys are expected to be "bad," girls are encouraged to be "good." But with "good girl" status and sex viewed as incompatible, American girls often experience, or anticipate experiencing, difficulty reconciling their sexual maturation with good daughterhood.

Interdependent individualism shapes the language and experience of gender in Dutch middle-class families. As noted, the Dutch parents do not speak about adolescent sexuality in terms of girls' and boys' different positions of power or of their "antagonistic gender strategies." Nor do they give evidence of treating sons and daughters differently with regard to sexuality and relationships. In keeping with national statistics and qualitative research, they suggest that daughters and sons are equally likely to receive permission for sleepovers. Like their female counterparts, most Dutch boys are subject to a "soft control" that socializes them into a relationship-based experience of sexuality and self and that encourages negotiations within, rather than separation from, the household. But there are subtle gender differences: such negotiation tends to be more fraught for girls, and while few Dutch boys express reservations about actually bringing their girlfriends home for the night, a number of Dutch girls say that they would rather spend the night elsewhere, suggesting that they do feel more closely supervised by their parents.

Adversarial individualism and interdependent individualism also provide cultural templates with which the American and Dutch girls and boys navigate sex and sense of self within peer cultures. The different assumptions about people's inherent relational needs and proclivities—at the root of the two versions of individualism—shape teenage girls' and boys' dilemmas of gender. In both countries girls are confined by the potential slander of being called a slut, but that label is much more prominent in the interviews with American girls. One reason is that American girls encounter adult and peer cultures skeptical about teenagers' ability to sustain meaningful sexual relationships. This skepticism means that American girls lack the indisputable certainty that the Dutch girls possess about whether and when sex is culturally legitimate. But while Dutch adult and peer cultures validate sexual experience in relationships, uncritical validation of relationship-based sexuality can obscure conflicts of interest and power differences in heterosexual relationships.

To different degrees, the notion that boys want sex but not relationships has some currency in both American and Dutch peer and popular culture. But in both countries, the vast majority of boys describe themselves as quite romantic in their orientation, wanting to experience sex with someone with whom they are in love. The American boys tend to see themselves as unique for their romantic aspirations, calling to mind the icon of the lone cowboy opposing the crowd of hormone-driven boys and a peer and popular culture of soulless sex. Indeed, some American boys set the bar for love very high—defining it as a heroic relinquishing of self—thus distancing themselves not only from other boys but from sexual pleasure itself. The Dutch boys describe themselves as normal in their pursuit of a combination of sex and relationships. Without the stark oppositions—between male and female, love and lust, and pleasure and responsibility—they evidence a more integrated experience of ideals and realities.

Coming Full Circle

Having set out to solve a puzzle, in the end *Not Under My Roof* reveals a comprehensive picture of coexisting processes occurring at the intrapsychic, interpersonal, familial, and societal levels. For, as we will see, there are striking parallels between policies governing the household and the polity itself. The premises of adversarial individualism inform the organization of government and economy in the United States, pitting different political parties and economic actors against one another in winner-take-all political battles and in often highly contentious economic negotiations. Within such adversarial political and economic climates, people are encouraged— and when they have the necessary resources are able—to pursue individual ambition relatively unfettered. The flipside of such unfettered opportunities, however, is that post-1960s American society has had an unusually punitive penal system which imposes heavy sentencing for minor infractions to control people, including teens, not deemed able to exert sufficient control over their impulses.[80]

Meanwhile, the premises of interdependent individualism have structured the organization of government and economy in the Netherlands:

building on a longstanding tradition of the "politics of accommodation," decision-making, including about contentious issues, has long been resolved through a process of consensus-seeking between the different political parties.[81] A similar consensus orientation informs the regulation of economic negotiations, requiring all parties partaking in negotiation—management, unions, and government representatives—to broker mutually agreeable arrangements that are sensitive to the needs of, and acceptable to, all.[82] Such a politics of accommodation can often preempt social disruption and successfully elicit compliance. At the same time, public authorities in post-1960s Dutch society have approached "vices," including sex work and drugs, much as have the Dutch parents, through a regulated legalization or tolerance of activities that are subject to "harsh justice" in the United States.[83]

There are multiple relationships between what sociologists call the "micro-sociological" teenager-parent interactions and the "macro-sociological" political and economic structures. The prevailing legal climate, for instance, places clear constraints on the forms of adolescent experimentation that can be legally negotiated between parents and teenagers. With sexual intercourse before the age of eighteen illegal in the Northern California field site, permitting a sleepover is a potential legal liability, as is permitting teenagers to drink alcohol. Using drugs, engaging in sex before the age of consent, or drinking alcohol before the legal age also puts American teenagers at risk of a criminal record. That neither consensual adolescent sexual experience nor teenage alcohol and soft drug use are subject to criminalizing procedures in the Netherlands gives Dutch parents a great deal more leeway to determine their own household policies.[84]

At the same time, the management of adolescent sexuality in the middle-class family is a cultural process through which parents model and induce competencies that are useful given the organization of the societies for which they are preparing their children. Indeed, normalization and dramatization encourage young people to acquire proclivities, engage in emotion work, and develop self-conceptions that allow them to thrive in their respective societies. Learning to experience oneself as autonomous from social ties and free from ongoing interdependencies, for instance, makes it easier for young Americans to navigate the geographic mobility typical for American middle-class educational and occupational trajectories. By the same token, developing a strong sense of one's autonomy in the context of ongoing yet shifting relationships of interdependence allows Dutch young adults to hold their own and exhibit flexibility in institutions that will require them to engage in a great deal of negotiation to reach consensus.

The above does not mean that we can reduce the cultural processes at work in the management of adolescent sexuality to the organization of political and economic institutions. Rather, the management of adolescent sexuality proves to be a sensitive prism that allows us to see core cultural ideals and contradictions that structure social institutions throughout society. "Raging hormones" symbolically represents the potential and the problem of unlimited drive, not held back by dependencies or internal brakes. But such a vision denies people's inherent dependencies and relational needs and legitimates external control for the maintenance of order. "Regulated love" is premised on an ideal of an adaptive yet stable co-constituted sociality, in which people adjust themselves in such a way as to prevent intractable conflicts of interest. Yet this ideal denies that some conflicts and differences do not lend themselves to accommodation, and that in the course of creating togetherness some parties make greater sacrifices than others.

Culture's Costs

At the same time that interpretation and management of adolescent sexuality are "functional" in that they prepare adolescents to function within the institutions they will enter, especially for American teenagers and their parents these cultural processes also take a toll: teenagers do better emotionally when they can remain connected to their parents during adolescence.[85] But with sexuality culturally coded as a symbol of, and a means to attaining, separation between parents and children, an important developmental experience becomes cause for disconnection in the parent-teenager relationship. This disconnect makes it more difficult for parents to serve as support when adolescents start their first sexual experiences during their mid-teens. And when teenagers must keep their sexual behavior a secret or know it is a disappointment to their parents, it becomes more difficult to seek assistance from adults—to obtain contraception, assess their readiness, or discuss the qualities of a romantic relationship.

The ways in which the American culture of individualism conceptualizes autonomy and intimacy also do not serve adolescents well. The cultural narrative which dictates that one must attain financial and emotional autonomy before being ready for sex and emotional commitment leaves youth with a conception of autonomy they cannot attain until their mid-twenties, if ever. Such a conception does not provide the cultural tools to develop the *internal* discernment and regulation necessary to exercise psychological autonomy within teenage sexual and romantic relationships.

As important, this narrative leaves young people and their parents without cultural templates for validating and assessing adolescent intimate relationships on their own terms. Strikingly, many American parents as well many American teenagers—girls *and* boys—use marriage as the ultimate measure of love. But this ideal may lead teenagers to diminish the forms of intimacy that they are capable of and to strive for commitments they are not yet able to make.

The Dutch culture of interdependent individualism does not lead to the same psychological disconnect between parents and teenagers. Though the negotiation of adolescent sexuality is not tension-free, especially when it concerns the sexuality of girls, ultimately most of the Dutch girls and boys can integrate their sexual development with their relationship with their parents. This continued connectedness makes it easier for Dutch teenagers to draw on the support of parents and other adults as they move through their adolescent sexual and emotional explorations. With autonomy conceptualized as a matter of exercising self-direction within relationships, and with interdependence viewed as a matter of necessity rather than choice, Dutch teenagers also receive more cultural validation for their intimate relationships. At the same time, the cultural template of interdependent individualism makes it more difficult for Dutch teenagers and their parents to recognize and address conflicts of interest within relationships than it is for their American counterparts, who speak readily of conflicts and battles.

The Book's Organization

Chapters 2 and 3 illuminate normalization and dramatization as cultural processes, respectively. Analyzing the interviews with the Dutch and American parents, they highlight the cultural frames on which parents draw to interpret adolescent sexuality and make sense out of their decision to permit or to not even consider a sleepover. The chapters show, moreover, how normalization and dramatization each operate as active cultural processes through which parents constitute themselves as well as their children as distinct types of individuals. At the same time, the two chapters illuminate the "holes in the webs": the silences in the cultural languages that parents use, the ways in which they negotiate differences between themselves and their children, and between cultural expectations and lived experience. Finally, the chapters show how the interpretation and management of adolescent sexuality are grounded in experiences of history.

Chapter 4, "Adversarial and Interdependent Individualism," delves into the dilemmas faced by parents and public authorities in the post-1960s

and 1970s era, namely, how to make space for the autonomy of subordinates while inculcating restraint and maintaining social order. With
the fixed hierarchies and social roles that had previously structured family life and other social institutions challenged, if not entirely eradicated,
middle-class parents in the two countries use the cultural tools available to
them to handle gray areas of the adolescent parenting project—the inculca-
tion of self-restraint, the exercise of legitimate authority, and the fostering
of autonomy. How parents in the two countries interpret and handle the
three dilemmas differently illuminates the two different models of individualism on which they are drawing. These different models—of adversarial
and interdependent individualism—create the cultural logics that give the
normalization and dramatization of adolescent sexuality their common
sense.

Chapters 5 and 6, "'I Didn't Even Want Them to Know': Connection
through Control" and "'At Least They Know Where I Am': Control through
Connection," show how the American and Dutch teenagers, respectively,
view and experience the negotiation of sexuality, alcohol, and other potentially contentious issues within the parent-teenager nexus. In Chapter 5, we
see that despite sometimes radically different parental responses to their
sexuality, American girls and boys engage in a psychology of separation
from home. Encouraged to make their adolescent experimentation furtive,
when they do, teenagers often lose partial or complete connection with
their parents, despite an earlier closeness in the relationship, making it
necessary for their parents to exercise overt control to reestablish that connection. In Chapter 6, we see that Dutch girls and boys receive more similar treatment, and that the parental strategy of exercising control through
maintaining connection induces a psychology of incorporation. Nevertheless, we see evidence of tension, especially among girls, some of whom say
they want to keep their sexuality and the parental home at arm's length.

Just as chapter 4 compares parents in the two countries with regard to
their shared dilemmas of autonomy and authority, chapter 7, "Romantic
Rebels, Regular Lovers," compares teenagers in the two countries with regard to their shared dilemmas of gender. This chapter shows that in the
United States, the construction of sex as risky, promulgated in the home
and school, makes sex appear by definition dangerous to boys and not just
to girls, as folk wisdom and gender theorists assume. In the Netherlands,
by contrast, girls and boys assume that the risks of sex can and should be
controlled. However, in practice, it is teenage girls on whom much of the
work of prevention falls. The bulk of the chapter focuses on the teenagers'
negotiation of sex, gender, and relationships in relation to peer and popu-

lar culture. It shows how in both countries girls and boys encounter the double standard, but that the meaning and experience of this gender construct are mediated by culture-specific conceptions of love and lust.

Chapter 8, "Sexuality, Self-Formation, and the State," demonstrates the parallels between the conception, control, and constitution of individuals in the family and in the polity. It shows how the interpretation and management of adolescent sexuality express core cultural ideals and contradictions about individual and collective well-being. It also shows how economic and political institutions in the two countries support and constrain parents in their childrearing choices. We see how concerns about sexuality are vehicles through which parents and teenagers engage in processes of self-formation—processes through which they develop capacities that serve their participation in society at large. In the book's concluding chapter, I address the problem of culture's costs and the potential for cultural creativity. With sexuality a symbol of, a means for, and a potential threat to attaining autonomy, teenagers in the United States do not receive the support they need to navigate sexual and emotional maturation. To change this situation, we must engage in processes of cultural and institutional innovation.

TWO

Dutch Parents and the Sleepover

"A Matter of Course?"

Few aspects of mothering two teenage daughters seem to faze Jolien Boskamp, a casually dressed, part-time secretary who lives with her daughters and her husband, Mark, a salesman, on the outskirts of Eastern City. That their eldest daughter Natalie regularly spends the night together with her boyfriend Rob in their modest middle-class home is not something that Jolien regards as problematic. Jolien told Natalie long before she met Rob: "If you are ready (*er aan toe*), say it honestly and use the pill—in any case." Jolien had been very clear: "If you are ready—not with the first person who comes along—you can only give it away once. Give it to someone about whom you think, 'this is the one.'"

Jolien knows that Rob might not turn out to be Natalie's *only* one. But she trusts her daughter and has confidence in the relationship. "Natalie is just the kind of child that is so open and honest and sensible—almost like an adult—that, when Rob slept over . . . well . . . for me it was really a matter of course that they would sleep together." But that Rob would spend the night in his home was not a matter of course for her husband, Mark.

Natalie was sixteen and had been in courtship (*verkering*) with Rob for a couple of months when her father asked her, "Are you going to bed with Rob?"[1] Natalie was indignant, "What do you think of me? I need to have been in a courtship (*verkering*) a little longer to do that." At that time, Natalie had started spending the night at Rob's house. But for a while Natalie and Rob just slept together, "sleeping, literally," her mother knows. Jolien was impressed. "You would think, [as] she'd been crazy about him for years, that the first best time—as a figure of speech—you'd say 'let's do it,' but no, it really took a few months," but "at a certain point you can't hold back those feelings, and then it goes further."

At a certain point, things did go further. Natalie wanted Rob to spend the night with her at home. "Absolutely not," was Mark's first response. Jo-lien played a mediating role. She told Natalie, "Rob is your boyfriend, you two want to sleep together. It's all right with me. It's not all right with papa. Therefore you will need to talk about it with papa." Natalie questioned her father's objections. She didn't let him off the hook when he claimed that Rob's presence would make it impossible for him to feel free in his own house. "You don't have a problem with a girlfriend sleeping over."

Mark had to fight the battle on two fronts. When he told his wife, "I wasn't allowed to sleep with you either when we were younger," she re-torted, "Are they supposed to do penance for that—you know, if you put it that way—that you weren't allowed to sleep with me?" At the same time Jo-lien sympathized with her husband. "He was confronted with a fact that he was not really thinking about yet or ready for. He saw Rob as an intruder, which he did not feel with her girlfriends, because Rob was a boy who had a relationship with HIS daughter," Jolien explains. "Well, it is his daughter, his honor, his oldest." But that is history. For the past nine months, Rob has spent the night in their house and "Mark doesn't have any problems with it anymore. No, no."

No "Go-as-You-Please Situation in My House"

A few miles further out of town, in one of the bedroom communities south of the city, lies the home of Marga Fenning, a part-time nurse, her second husband, a small business owner, and Marga's children Thomas (18) and Rachel (16). A few years older than Jolien Boskamp and dressed more formally in a calf-length skirt, Marga Fenning makes a stately impres-sion. Nevertheless, like Jolien Boskamp, Marga Fenning has permitted her sixteen-year-old daughter Rachel to spend the night with her boyfriend.

When Rachel's boyfriend visits, he sleeps on a mattress next to her bed. The arrangement is not entirely to Marga's liking. She thinks her daughter is too young to have sexual intercourse.

> Yes, last week she came to me, "Mama, I kind of want to go on the pill." You know, I think that is sensible. I am glad about that. I say, well then you have to go to the doctor. And then we talk about that, of course. [Rachel asked] "Do you think it's all right. I'm a little scared." I say, "The doctor will give it to you." "But what if he thinks I'm too young?" I say, "Rachel he'll definitely give it to you. That is totally not a problem." So we went over there together and I stayed in the waiting room. . . . But I did tell her that I think she is much too young.

Although Marga thinks Rachel is much too young, she did not say, "You may not do it." The doctor, whom Marga had visited for another matter a little while ago, had strongly recommended this approach. "Never say that they are not allowed to do it," he had told her. "Because then it will definitely go wrong." Forbidding is not Marga's style anyway: "I don't tell them very quickly that they can't do something. I always try to talk about things and then usually it works out, you work it out together. And I have to say my daughter is pretty sensible." And indeed Rachel seems to be steering a cautious course. "I am totally not ready (*er aan toe*) yet," Rachel told her mother. "But, you know, just imagine that [at some point] I am." To underscore Rachel's sensibility, Marga relates a story of Thomas, Rachel's older brother, teasing her: "When she's about to go out, he'll take a condom and say, 'Here Rachel, take this just to be safe.' And then she laughs and blushes a little and we also laugh about her, because she won't take it with her."

Although Marga doesn't usually put her foot down, recently she did. Thomas asked whether a male friend and two girls could spend the night. One of the girls would sleep in his room, the other with his friend in the guest room. After thinking his request over for a few days, Marga decided: "I just don't want to have such a go-as-you-please kind of situation in my house. So I told him, 'No, I would not like it if you do that. I won't feel comfortable in my own house.'" Marga added that she would feel differently if the request concerned his girlfriend:

> I can't have such an old-fashioned reaction that the girlfriend has to sleep somewhere else. Then I would be fooling myself, because at night they'll sleep together anyway. [Insisting on two bedrooms] would feel childish. But, if it's just a girl he's going out with and next time it's another girl, and then another girl. No. I don't find that pleasant. No, I don't want that.

The Sleepover and the Normalization of Adolescent Sexuality

In permitting their sixteen-year-old teenage daughters to spend the night in one room with a steady boyfriend, Jolien Boskamp and Marga Fenning are hardly unique. Of the twenty-six Dutch parents interviewed, only two are certain they will not permit a sleepover. The other Dutch parents say that under the right circumstances, they will permit, or consider permitting, a sixteen- or seventeen-year-old teenager to spend the night with a romantic partner. Six have indeed permitted such a sleepover already. How are we to understand this openness among Dutch parents to minors' spending the night together? This chapter starts answering this question by examining three powerful frames parents use to understand adolescent sexuality and their own responsibility as parents—*normal sexuality, relationship-based sexuality*, and *self-regulated sexuality*.

In the process of illuminating those frames, we gain insight into the workings of normalization as an active cultural process—which involves conceptualizing, controlling, and constituting both teenagers and parents: we will see that the three cultural frames construct adolescent sexuality as a nonproblematic, non-emotionally disruptive, and decidedly relationship-based phenomenon. They help parents describe and interpret teenage sexuality. At the same time, parents may use these cultural frames to exercise control—Marga Fenning, for instance, uses the frame of relationship-based sexuality not only to describe her children's sexuality but also to communicate a distinction between the relationships of which she approves and the fleeting encounters of which she does not. Finally, the sleepover serves as a means to constitute teenagers and parents as people who rationally discuss a potentially disruptive topic and jointly integrate it into the household.

But if the normalization of adolescent sexuality involves conceptions, control, and the constitution of individuals, it does not constitute a seamless cultural process. Implicit and sometimes explicit in the Dutch parents' efforts at normalization are references to "other" times and "other" social circles in which sexuality was or continues to be not approached normally. And as Jolien's account of her husband's initial protest and eventual acquiescence illustrates, parents can disagree with one another and with their children. Even when they agree to permit the sleepover, they may be left, as is Marga Fenning, with mixed feelings. Nor is there a perfect fit between cultural language and people's actions and experiences. Indeed as we will see, parents struggle when they run up against situations for which normalization does not provide adequate frames—instances of adolescent sexuality that are not the product of self-regulation or embedded in egalitarian relationships, and other instances in which teenage sexuality has become *too* normal.

Contestation and contradiction notwithstanding, the normalization of teenage sexuality in middle-class Dutch families—and in the institutions of education and health care that support them—runs counter to the management of adolescent sexuality, as described in the American scholarly literature. Not only do Dutch parents generally articulate an acceptance of adolescent sexuality, under the right conditions. They underscore that boys *and* girls must develop and use their inner resources and relationships to determine their readiness and sexual identities. They describe teenagers as moving along a continuum of sexual and emotional development, not as categorically different from adults. Although this generation of parents was, for the most part, raised with a very different dominant sexual ethic, they can normalize adolescent sexuality because they have both the cultural and material resources to do so: they possess the ideal of an interdependent individualism, which recognizes self-determination as a key feature of modern life—but always within cultural practices that maintain continuity, connection, and control—and they can rely on economic safeguards that have made changes in adolescents and society less threatening.

Normal Sexuality

Like Jolien Boskamp, Marga Fenning, and Karel Doorman (in chap. 1), most Dutch parents make an effort to demonstrate both their capacity to talk normally about sexuality with their teenage children and their capacity to regulate the emotions of shame or discomfort that sexuality might evoke between family members. The word *gewoon* communicates this capacity. The dictionary translates *gewoon* as commonly, normally, simply, or plainly. It is important to note, however, that "normally" in this context means "ordinarily" but also contains an intensely, if obfuscated, normative component: to say something is "normal" implies that it is acceptable and right.[2] Moreover, *gewoon* used in relation to sexuality denotes especially the absence of its antonyms: friction, discomfort, anxiety, secrecy, or conflict, as well as the capacity to exert self-regulation over potentially unruly emotions.[3]

Hannie and Dirk de Groot, parents of seventeen-year-old Elizabeth, have been talking with their daughter about sexuality in a *gewoon* manner ever since she was young. As Hannie puts it, "If I can talk *gewoon* about playing at a girlfriend's house, then I should be able to talk *gewoon* about sex. It should happen the same way as other things that you talk about with each other. You should not think: 'Oh that is scary' or 'I don't dare to talk about that' or 'I have to make a special time for that.'" To underscore her point, Hannie adds, "Yes, it should be *gewoon* to talk about it during dinner." Why? "Because it is *gewoon*," Hannie explains. "Because it is natural, isn't it," Dirk adds. Similarly, Anneke Schutte thinks that sex should be a *gewoon* topic of conversation in school: "I think that it is good that they don't only talk about it in the home, but that it becomes very *gewoon* to talk about it and that the school is an excellent institution to promote that."

Indeed, Dutch sex education curricula encourage teenagers to talk in a *gewoon* way about sexuality, including topics such as masturbation, homosexuality, and pleasure.[4] These topics are integrated into a broader discussion of the emotional, relational, and larger societal forces that shape experiences of sexuality. One textbook explains, "Your own experiences with sex start with yourself. . . . Thus, you can have sex with yourself, but also with others. You make love because you and the other person enjoy it." But, it continues, "There are valid reasons not to make love to someone yet," including not wanting it, not being ready, or one's religion.[5] Another textbook addresses same-sex experiences in a chapter entitled, "With whom would you like to wake up?"[6] And a third textbook states that "making love takes patience. Your whole body is full of places that want to be caressed, rubbed, licked, and bitten softly."[7] Notably, this passage teaches that self-restraint is a prerequisite for the enjoyment of the full range of sexual pleasures.

For parents, one marker of being able to normalize is the lack of bodily shame in the household. Some Dutch parents seek to demonstrate the normality of bodily matters by noting, often with a certain amount of pride, that nudity among family members has always been a matter of course, even if culturally it is a relatively recent phenomenon.[8] Corinne van Zanden explains, "When [the children] were younger, they also went under the shower with us. So as far as that is concerned, we have few secrets here." Anne van Wijngaarde echoes a similar sentiment. She explains, in response to questions about the sex education her children received, that discussion of reproduction and contraception "start[ed] at an early age, not unusual at all. They know everything." Communicating the cultural significance of bleaching bodies from their potential to embarrass, she continues:

> Everyone always walked around in their bare bottoms and went to nudist camps if we wanted that. They still walk around in their bare bottoms and we are very grateful for that. Because then it is so childlike and innocent. You think, as father and mother, 'We did a pretty good job' . . . that they turned out so candid.

Parents like it when their children give evidence of being able to talk about sex in a normal, nonconflicted way. Loek Herder's younger son Paul is quite open. "It's not that he is always talking about it, but. . . . Well, when [Paul] sees a cute girl on the television, then he immediately says, 'Oh, that's a good-looking girl.' And then he talks about her beautiful breasts and so forth. . . . Yes, he definitely notices all of that." How does Loek feel about the way he talks about sex? "The way he talks about it? I think that is fine, I quite like it." Anne van Wijngaarde says she knows exactly how far

her son has gone: "Harm tells me, 'now I French-kissed' and then we become weak with laughter because he tells me what he did with them. That
is nice. It's so innocent and open."

In illustrating the normality of sexuality in their family, Dutch parents
often make an explicit comparison with the way they were raised themselves. Doing so, they demonstrate that normal sexuality is as important
for what it is not as it is for what it is. Normal sexuality is *not* secretive
(*stiekem*). Marga Fenning thinks it is a very good thing that young people
these days "ask and tell everything at home": "You know, I did not think
that was good at all about the way it used to be, that everything had to be
done so *stiekem*." Hannie de Groot agrees: "I experienced it as very unpleas-
ant in the past, that it was all so impossible and that it was all so mysteri-
ous (*geheimzinnig*). It was really something dirty, disgusting. That is how it
was conveyed. I don't think that was conscious, but that is how things used
to be." It is a good thing, Karin Meier believes, that sex is becoming more
"*gewoon*, less secretive." [9] In Dutch society today, "there are very few taboos
you know, in that area," says Trudy van Vliet. "It is very open."

But parents are not always as at ease with talking about sexuality as the
mandate to make sexuality *gewoon* suggests they ought to be. Indeed, Ada
Kaptein was reluctant give her daughter Madeleine sex education: "About
condoms and stuff . . . we haven't really talked about that." In fact, when
her daughter went on the pill to regulate her menstruation, Ada told her, "I
hope you don't yet see the pill as contraception." But when it came time to
educate Madeleine's younger brother, her daughter took the lead. In doing
so, she cajoled her mother into a more normalized approach. Madeleine
explained menstruation to her brother and then called over her mother to
tell him "the rest." So, "there I sat telling him the rest," Ada recalls. And in
spite of having given evidence to the contrary, she concludes saying: "Really it never was a problem. We can talk *gewoon* about that."

Normal sexuality dictates that parents accept their children's sexual relationships. Parents are wise to adjust themselves to their children's pace of
development, so a common line or reasoning goes, lest they lose touch with
the reality of their children's lives. Corinne van Zanden says she hopes her
children's relationships progress gradually, but "it is going to happen anyway at some point. We're pretty open about that." And even Ada Kaptein,
who told her daughter not to treat the pill as a contraceptive method too
early, believes that "you can't forbid it. Then they will start to do it *stiekem*.
We used to do it *stiekem*." That kind of secretiveness Ada wants "to avoid
that at any cost." Should her son Laurens request to sleep together with a

girlfriend at home, Christien Leufkens says she would definitely acquiesce. "I'd rather have them do it here," she explains, "when I am here, than that they do it *stiekem*. Because when you start to forbid, it doesn't mean that they don't do it. It just means that they don't do it under your eyes."

Relationship-Based Sexuality

At the heart of the relationship-based conception of adolescent sexuality lies the assumption, taken for granted by all Dutch parents, that teenagers can be in love. Unlike the American concept of "falling in love," which is usually thought of as distinct from "sexual attraction," the Dutch concept of *verliefd zijn*, which means "being in love," blurs, rather than sharpens, the line between love and lust. *Houden van*, in turn, describes the more stable and long-term love for romantic partners, parents, siblings, and friends. Dutch parents communicate this relationship-based view of teenage sexuality by the words they use to describe their children's feelings and attachments. Like Jolien Boskamp, parents typically refer to romantic relationships as *verkering* (courtship). And they describe their children, even young teens, as capable of experiencing being "in love."

Loek Herder remembers that her son was "interested in girlfriends at a very early age and then he was also often intensely in love." Helen de Beer says her daughter is ready to have a boyfriend, for after all a person "is never too young for romantic love." Mariette Kiers, the *only* Dutch parent to mention the role of hormones in relation to adolescent sexuality, synchronizes rather than opposes physicality and emotionality. Considering what makes a person ready for sex, Mariette Kiers says: "At a certain moment those hormones begin to rage and, who knows, it may be the love of your life." In other words, hormones may rage but love lights the fire. Notable amidst Mariette's description of the interweaving of biology and emotionality is her recognition of female sexual pleasure:

> Look hormones start raging, that starts at age ten. . . . At a certain point, a person becomes more adult and then sexuality also acquires a more adult character. . . . Yes, and then you don't just kiss. But something *happens* to you. I mean [something happens] with your emotions too. . . . There is a biological component, of course: it starts with kissing, that is preparation and then if you are making love the right way, then you become wet . . . that is biological yes. But in addition to [the biological] there is something very emotional. . . . Of course, at sixteen you can . . . you do really love. Of course, you can [love] when you are ten years old.

Outside the family, the frame of relationship-based sexuality and the language of love also prevail. One popular sex education curriculum is, for instance, entitled "Long Live Love," which conveys the notion that teenagers can fall in love and that sex is (ideally) about love. Government-sponsored safe-sex campaigns have also built on a relationship-based model of sexuality. One such campaign dictates, for instance: (1) you fall in love; (2) she feels the same; (3) you kiss; (4) you use a condom.[10] In sex education, relationship-based sexuality translates into a general emphasis on relationship skills. The Dutch government delegates decisions about the specific content of sex education to local civil society groups. It does however dictate "target goals," including teaching students "that they can apply their own thoughts, attitudes, and feelings and make them clear to others, and that they can empathize with the feelings, attitudes, and situations of others."[11]

Among the interviewees, a subtle but significant intra-class difference emerges in how parents discuss their wishes that teens develop their sexuality in an emotional and relational context. Lower-middle-class Dutch parents are particularly eager to see their children form monogamous and long-lasting relationships. Hannie de Groot and her husband believe that "you have sex with someone when, in any case, you know that person quite well. We hope that it isn't when you meet someone in a disco that you go to bed with him the same evening." But Hannie won't quantify "knowing quite well" because, she says "it also has to do with the [kind of] being in love. Is it superficial or are you totally crazy about the person." Loek Herder thinks neither of her sons has had intercourse. She hopes that when the time comes, it will be "more than only that." If it were "like in a brief contact with a girl or boy, then that would trouble me. Because I hope that for them it means more than a brief fling, that it is more than that. But if they really have something special with someone and then it happens, well then who am I?"

Parents who belong to the upper-middle class typically draw distinctions based on the *quality* of the interaction between partners rather than on the duration of the relationship. In fact, as we will see later on, some professionally employed mothers have misgivings about relationships that are too steady. Daphne Gelderblom supports sex education at school as long as it is about relationships and not "sex pure . . . I think the relationships—learning to interact with each other, learning to understand each other—that I think is excellent." Christien Leufkens is more liberal than most: had her son or daughter wanted to start such experimenting in their mid-teens, Christien would have let them "as long as they think that they can do it in a good way." She explains that a "good way" means: "You are careful with each other. That is really important, that they simply take each other into account, and that it is not the case that one of them has a painful experience."

"A good way" of relating not only determines whether parents approve of their children's sexual activities. It also determines whether or not they will permit the sleepover. Granting her daughter such permission depends, Corinne van Zanden says, on "who it is and what [the relationship] is and how he is. Where he comes from doesn't matter a bit to me." What does matter to her is "how they behave toward one another." Notably, like Marga Fenning at the start of the chapter, several mothers apply the same criteria of relationship-based sexuality to their sons: Jacquelien Starring would have serious objections if her son Hans were to "do it with that one and then that one and. . . . But if it is a girlfriend that he has known a bit longer . . . and she comes over to our house, and she sleeps over. I don't think I would have problems with that." Nienke Otten experiences the sleepover as a bit of a stretch, but she explains "you permit it when you see that they really care about each other, that it isn't just a passing fancy."

But while parents like Nienke Otten are heartened to see their children form relationships which are not just "passing fancies," they do not necessarily expect those relationships to last forever. Dutch parents do not want to see teenagers form "mini marriages." They want to see sex embedded in connections that are mutually nourishing. And before permitting the sleepover, most want to have formed a relationship with the partner in question. But they recognize that young people often learn to relate well through a succession of romantic relationships before they are ready to settle into a life-long romantic attachment.

(Self)-Regulated Sexuality

A third frame that recurs through the Dutch interviews is that of self-regulation. Parents describe their teenage children as capable of being self-regulating sexual actors. They illustrate this confidence in their children's capacity for self-regulation with their use of the term *er aan toe zijn*, which translates as "being ready." Their use of the term demonstrates an assumption that young people are the best judges of when they are ready, although it is the job of parents to remind their children, especially daughters, not to do anything before they *feel* ready as well as to take the precautions necessary to *be* ready.

Katinka Holt believes being ready is "whenever they feel it themselves, 'I am *er aan toe*.' And really feel 'Now I dare do it.'" She told her sixteen-year-old daughter Marlies not to do it because "the other person wants it, but because you want it yourself." For a while, Marlies was very insecure about her body. She told her mother, "I dare to show my breasts but down there, I don't want them to touch it." Katinka's response was, "Well, Marlies, if that is the case, then you are not yet *er aan toe*. And then you should not do it." Han de Vries believes his sixteen-year-old stepdaughter was ready because "she herself indicated that she was ready." Illustrating how he recognizes what scholars call "sexual subjectivity" in his daughters, Han recounts having told them:

> I will never have any objection to [a sexual relationship] when they—really out of their own free will, and never because they have to do it or because of coercion or because they feel that they have to belong, or because otherwise the boyfriend won't like them anymore—but only when they themselves feel the desire for it, and when they are themselves ready for it. And when that is, I don't know.

As Karel Doorman suggested in the book's first chapter, the premise of self-regulated sexuality also applies to same-sex adolescent sexuality. With the interview questions about sexuality framed in a gender-neutral language, four Dutch parents volunteered that their son or daughter might desire a same-sex partner.[12] About that possibility, Karel says: "You are choosing the harder route. I still think that is true. It is not like thirty years ago, but it remains the harder route." Were Heidi to be a lesbian, Karel says, "Yes well . . . then let it be so. I do not believe that you can change their [sexual] orientation by talking it through with them. . . . You cannot persuade a person with regard to [their sexual orientation]. So, I think that you will come to accept it."

Yet, even as many parents describe becoming *er aan toe* as a self-generated process, they suggest also that it occurs not in isolation but in the context of specific attachments. Being *er aan toe* is for many parents the product of a particular relational or emotional configuration. Piet Starring expects he will start to notice that his "sons are becoming ready when they bring home girls regularly." "Yes, when they start getting a bit of a courtship," his wife adds. Karin Meier believes a child is ready as soon as that child is "him- or herself curious about it." Yet Karin does not value "sex for sex's sake." She believes sex "has a value within a communication, within a relationship." Christien leaves her children free to explore. As long as "they relate to one another with respect, that is so important. If they both want it, then it does not concern me in the least."

Being *er aan toe* is not just a matter of feeling ready and relating well. It requires taking precautions against the potential dangers of sex. Parents play a crucial role in solidifying this capacity in their children. Hannie and Dirk de Groot believe it is "stupid" to try to avoid giving teenagers opportunities to have sex. "They need to determine it themselves," says Dirk. "They can do that. They can [be in charge], provided that you have spoken about it with them, and that you pointed out the dangers and the consequences to them. And if they know all that, they can handle it well." Concerned about AIDS, Marga Fenning has warned her son repeatedly about using condoms. "Now he makes a joke . . . if I say something [about condoms]. Right now I really don't need to tell him, 'You've got to be careful.' He certainly knows where Abram gets the mustard [how it works]. I don't need to say anything anymore. That would sound really silly."

In urging their children to use contraception, Dutch middle-class parents are bolstered by education and health policies that strongly support educating teenagers about contraception and giving them easy and stigma-free access to birth control. "The approach in the Dutch [sex education] materials," write sociologists Jane Lewis and Trudie Knijn, "is to encourage the student to think about what he or she wants before the situation arises and then to act responsibility." In other words, acquiring self-regulation means developing not just the capacity for sexual self-knowledge—knowing what one wants and does not—but also exercising foresight and engaging in planning. Knowing one's responsibilities, a Dutch expression, means carrying condoms and making timely appointments to see the family doctors, who provide the bulk of primary care in the Netherlands, and who, as a matter of policy, provide contraception to adolescents.[13]

Even when teenagers have all the pieces of being ready in place—they recognize the desire for sex inside themselves, have established the right relational context, and have taken the right preventative action—parents require a fourth component to permit the sleepover. Parents say they themselves need to be ready. What enables adolescent sexuality to become "normal" in the sense of being non-emotionally disruptive seems to be less a matter of age, or any other absolute criterion, than a matter of proper process. For parents to trust that a child is *er aan toe*, they say they need to witness the gradual progression of his or her desires and attachments. Loek describes the process that she thinks will enable her to become ready to recognize when her children are ready: "When they get a relationship . . . I think as a parent you anticipate . . . [Sex] is going to happen. . . ." And once you know that they are going to bed together. . . . Well, then it doesn't seem such a problem to let them spend the night together." Parents are much more inclined to accept the sleepover when they know that a relationship, and the sexual component of that relationship, have built gradually over time.

Marlies de Ruiter says her daughter Frieda developed sexually "step by step" in the relationship with her boyfriend until they eventually had sexual intercourse. But that only happened after they had spent "many a night together that they did not go to bed with each other." If Barbara Koning's son were to have a girlfriend, she would let them sleep together. But permission is not unqualified. Barbara hopes her son's first experience is "as innocent as in our time." Such "innocence" means *not* doing what she has heard about: "That they just have a girlfriend and it is just a love of a few weeks, and then boom, they dive into bed. That is a bit exaggerated. Get to know each other first."

Normalization as a Cultural Process

We have seen that three cultural frames interact to create a web of meaning and feeling that gives the practice of the sleepover its cognitive, emotional, and moral sense.[14] The first is *normal* sexuality: the sexuality of teenagers can and ideally should be talked about and dealt with in an open, frictionless, and matter-of-fact manner. Things sexual, including bodies and their functions, should inspire as little discomfort or turmoil as talk about what and when to eat. The second is *relationship-based* sexuality: sexual desire and sexual acts grow out of a teenager's feelings for and relationship with another person. Finally, *self-regulated* sexuality dictates that readiness for sex is a moment when emotional and physical desires are united and sensible preventative measures are taken.

On the one hand, the three cultural frames lead parents to interpret adolescent sexuality, and their own role as parents, in such a way that the sleepover makes sense. On the other hand, the sleepover itself is a practice through which parents normalize. Conversations about when the sleepover is allowed and breakfasts where boyfriends and girlfriends join other family members give an everyday quality to adolescent sexuality. When parents permit only serious boy- and girlfriends to spend the night, they encourage a relationship-based sexuality. And when adolescent sexual development happens gradually over time, as it can when the prospect of sexual activity is openly discussed, rather than engaged in furtively and suddenly, it becomes easier for teenagers to plan and take precautions against dangers. With the conversations they have, the rules they enforce, and the rituals they institute, parents create conditions under which adolescent sexuality can be experienced as a normal, nondisruptive part of childrearing and coming of age.

While many Dutch parents do worry about AIDS, and some worry about pregnancy, these concerns do not swell into sources of strong parental anxiety.[15] Fact and faith, experience and expectation, largely corroborate one another. Rates of pregnancy, birth, abortion, and HIV among youth are much lower for Dutch teens than they are for their American counterparts.[16] And, unlike their American counterparts, few Dutch parents know teenagers who become pregnant.[17] Just how rare it is for Dutch middle-class parents to be confronted with pregnancies among teenagers becomes evident when Piet Starring tells of his shock after hearing from acquaintances about a girl who became pregnant at age sixteen: "My God, can you imagine that happening to you, [your daughter] comes home saying, 'I'm pregnant.'"

At the same time, as a cultural process, normalization also evidently takes place in opposition to examples of non-normalized adolescent sexuality. Several Dutch parents clearly construct their own capacity to normalize in opposition to "other" times and "other" people. They oppose their own normal ways to the secretiveness and shame they experienced in their own upbringing. Nienke Otten explains overcoming reservations because "you do not want to do it the way you were raised yourself. That you just don't want. You want to try to keep up with the times." Mariette Kiers remembers being told, "You must save yourself because men are only looking for [sex]." She did not want to teach her daughter, as she had been taught, that men are predators. Mariette has made a point of not teaching her daughter that her virginity is something that should "be saved."

It is not only their own parents to whom the Dutch interviewees oppose themselves. While none of the parents are explicit about which "other" groups in Dutch society treat sexuality in non-normal ways, they imply that these others have a lower class status. Some interviewees—usually those who came of age earlier and experienced the most notable shift in attitudes during their own youth and young adulthood—express pride, seeing themselves as especially progressive frontrunners in a historical trend. Anneke Schutte and Daphne Gelderblom think that in their circle parents are open about sexuality. "I don't think we are average," says Anneke. Moreover, Daphne believes, in certain (lower) milieus, "[sex] does not get talked about." Barbara Koning also sees herself as different from most parents who are, she believes, stricter than she and her husband are. They are not representative. "No, my husband and I are pretty open for all kinds of new developments and we try to go along with those as much as possible."

Holes in the Web

Yet, even within the middle-class family, there are signs that sexuality is not without the taboos, secrets, and feelings of shame that were characteristic of the past. Sometimes, teenage children are not as eager to normalize sexuality as are their parents. The Starrings found Hans not terribly cooperative when they wanted to educate him: "You know we had all the [sex education] books at home, and I think he read things and talked about things, but if you really wanted to start talking about something, then he didn't really care for that, no." About her daughter's first time, Mia Klant says, "They never tell you. . . . They never told me." Mariette Kiers also bumped up against the limits of normalization when she tried to initiate a conversation with her daughter about when might be a good age at which to have sex. Marjolein responded, "'A, I don't feel like talking with you about that'—I could understand that—'but B, not anytime soon.'"

To overcome tensions and inhibitions, and to bring the potentially uncomfortable aspects of sexuality into language, many Dutch parents use humor. Mia Klant was not pleased about her daughter's first boyfriend. She did not feel she could really influence her daughter's choice, but she tried: "You can talk about it, you know generally. Like, 'Is he really the best . . . you know the guy is nice but why don't you look around a bit more.' And then sure, you make jokes, you make jokes, until that little light in their head goes on." Corinne van Zanden was relieved when her son Anton finally told her that his friend Johan was gay. Sensing that Anton had been troubled for a while, Corinne asked him what was wrong. Later Anton remarked that he should have told her earlier. "We have no problems about [his being gay] because he is and remains Johan. I mean we can say Johanna, now, just for a joke, but he remains *gewoon* Johan to us."[18]

And when there are tensions between what parents want and what happens, humor is a way to manage conflicts and discomfort. Daphne Gelderblom and her husband Peter joke about everything with their children—life, death, and sex. Their fourteen-year-old has just had the "sex project" at school, the term Daphne and Peter use jokingly to refer to the officially entitled "relationship lessons." Although she and her husband joked by giving their children golden colored condoms for Christmas—which they had purchased on a visit to Berkeley, California—Daphne would not like her daughter to become sexually active at age sixteen. Were that to happen, however, she would permit the sleepover, she says, because she finds it "extraordinarily hypocritical" to say not under my roof when you know it is happening elsewhere. But tellingly, Daphne adds, "I am not going to jump up and down with joy in front of their bedroom either."

Another source of tension is sex that is *too* normal—that is, sex that is too easy. A number of Dutch parents suggest that sex has become a matter that young people take too lightly and that it has lost its "specialness." Mieke Aalders tells her sons "sexuality is not [part of] the consumption society." Trudie van Vliet believes that "it has become very normal, if you have been out a few times with someone, and sometimes even the first time, which is what I am hearing. Well, that I don't think is normal yet. . . . That scares me. Because I think sex is something that can be very beautiful and it should not become so regular as saying goodbye or hello." Marga Fenning thinks "it is good that [young people today] are able to tell and ask everything at home." But sometimes she wonders whether freedom has gone too far. "My mother would turn over in her grave" if she could hear "all the things [my children] talk about during dinner. There are words that I have never heard of. . . . Well by now, I know them all, but I had never heard of them."

A final source of tension is sex which takes place *too* early. When their children are seventeen, most Dutch parents do not "have problems" with their sexual activity. Parents are divided over whether sixteen is too early or just right for sexual initiation. But most agree that at age fourteen and fifteen, teenagers are too young. When sex does happen, or threatens to happen, too early, the framework of normalization provides only limited tools to account for, or deal with, the reasons for and results of this experience. Han de Vries and Mia Klant were confronted with their daughter Irene's early sexual initiation. At fourteen, Irene was too young, in Han's opinion. "For parents, it is by definition too young," Mia adds. Irene's sexuality sits more comfortably with her parents now that she is a happy and healthy seventeen-year-old and in a relationship with a boy they like very much. In retrospect, they don't think Irene's early initiation harmed her.

In short, some of the parents acknowledge that sex is not always easy to discuss normally, that sometimes sex becomes too normal, and that sex can sometimes happen too early. Still, they firmly believe talking openly about adolescent sex is better than keeping it secret, that young people can and do form relationships of mutual care and respect, and that they can and should be in charge of determining when they are ready and of preventing any unwanted consequences. Worries about sexuality constitute discordant notes against the main tune of their expectation that all will go smoothly and turn out well. But as the following two vignettes demonstrate, the dominant frames of normalized adolescent sexuality—as normal, relationship-based, and self-regulated—sometimes fail to account for real experience. Both vignettes expose a silence in normalization, namely, about the conflicts of interest, inequalities, and use of power that can shape relationships.

A Troubling Revelation

When Marga Fenning's son Thomas was in elementary school, two boys in the neighborhood took him into the bushes and "told him something, they said things and did things, nothing serious luckily." After that she noticed that "Thomas suddenly, and he was still very young, suddenly he had a lot of interest in those things. When I stood in the bathroom, and it even embarrassed me really . . . and you know, we have always washed ourselves *gewoon* and walked around at home, nothing with bathrobes and being *stiekem*. [But] then he would start sitting like this [bending over to look up] and start to look at me. And oh, I did not feel good about that at all [laughing]. . . . But I would think, behave *gewoon*, behave *gewoon*. But really it was terrible, he just kept on looking."

Thomas became very interested in sexual play. At one point, a friend, Marcel, told Marga, "'Our kids need to get married with each other now because they have examined each other thoroughly and . . . in the bathroom you know.' And I say, 'Oh.' But I was sort of . . . he really had to laugh about it. He's a teacher, so I'm sure he is used to a lot. A really nice guy. . . ." Marcel's daughter Madelief would come over to play often. And when Marga would come home in the afternoon, she could look up from her car and see through Thomas's bedroom window that the two of them were "messing around" on the bed. "Well, nothing could happen because they were really too young for that, but still." After that, Thomas's sex education took off in quick tempo: "He started asking questions and later . . . well, we talked a lot about it. But really, I was very unhappy that those kids had done that with him, because then it became for him such a revelation that he kept on going on with it and asking about it and acting on it. Well, I really did not like that at all, I really did not like it at all. But I did always answer [his questions]."

Marga felt angry at the older boys for initiating Thomas prematurely. She felt embarrassed by his behavior in the wake of the incident and uncertain about how to respond to that behavior. Yet, all along, she opted for a response that played down her own discomfort and carefully accommodated his questions and play, even though this course of action required considerable emotional restraint and adaptation on her part.

Only when Thomas was older and was becoming interested in girls again in his mid-teens did his approach to sexuality lead to an open conflict with his mother. She started cautioning him against getting a girl pregnant. But his attitude, she felt, was much too cavalier. "He was like, 'Oh well, then she can just have it taken away [an abortion]'. And then I said: 'Well, that is no way of behaving,' I said, 'to get someone pregnant and then to say 'take it away'. I say, '[If that happens] you are equally responsible.' I say, 'Not just the pleasures, but also the burdens'. I say, 'You've got to remember that.'"

"Such a Little Couple in My House"

A fifteen-minute train-ride away from Eastern city lies the formerly agricultural town turned bedroom community of Kers. In an upscale section of town, substantial stretches of green surround large, uniquely styled freestanding houses, including the home of Ria and Maarten van Kampen, and their children Fleur, sixteen, and Jasper, fourteen. Their occupations—he is a senior administrator and she works as a psychotherapist in private practice—put the van Kampens in the upper-income bracket of the middle class. In addition, Ria is one of the few Dutch mothers interviewed who works full-time in a professional capacity, leaving her more pressed for time than most and caught, more often than she would like, juggling contradictory demands.

When Fleur first started her courtship with Vincent, her mother was quite happy. Vincent is her first, at least the first she told her mother about: "I think there were other boyfriends before, but I don't know that." Yet, Ria is of two minds. "I like that boyfriends come into her life. I think that is a very healthy development. But I think it is too bad that it is taking such steady forms." Having been together for a year and a half,

> The courtship [between Fleur and her boyfriend] has grown into a full-fledged partner relationship. And I just think she is too young for that. I think, 'Gee, why don't you sniff around here, sniff around there'. That sniffing around would not have been easy for me either. But I mean that is what I think you need when you are young and not . . . to have such a lengthy

relationship with the first person who comes along. But okay, that is not something [as a parent] you can control.

Ria had told Fleur before, "If you are ready, then you need to say it honestly and then you also need to take precautions." When Fleur said she was *er aan toe*, Ria first hoped, "Who knows, maybe the relationship will be over in a month. But you know, gradually I thought to myself, 'He's a nice, very pleasant, friendly, and calm boy, so. . . .' So that makes you say at a certain point, 'Okay she is *er aan toe* and he is a nice boy so what can you do?'" Still, despite the fact that Fleur feels ready, has a steady boyfriend, and uses the pill and condoms, her parents do not let Vincent spend the night at home. They have told her: "We are not there yet." Fleur does not accept their point of view: "Why not, I'd like it so much." The boyfriend also objects: "What a ridiculous situation, how old-fashioned." Fleur has asked: "Would you rather I had multiple, short-lived relationships?" Ria sees Fleur getting stuck in between her parents and Vincent, who is nineteen: "She understands us, but she would rather have had it differently."

Ria admits that she is ambivalent. She has been influenced by her own upbringing, which was, in her own words, "very authoritarian." Looking back, she says:

> My opinion was not important. My parents decided a lot of things for me. The distance between [us] was also much greater. . . . I want to do things differently, but that does not always make it easier for me. . . . I think it is better for [Fleur]. At least I hope it is better for children today to learn to feel what they want and think.

But giving her daughter the space she did not have requires, Ria says, adjustment. "When you look at the development around her boyfriend, then I think, in the end, you constantly have to yield. . . . As a parent, I feel that I have to keep adding water to the wine [compromising] because I think the relationship [with my daughter] is more important." Ria and her husband have for instance let Fleur and her boyfriend go away for a weekend and camp together on a family vacation. But the sleepover is still a no-go: "I just don't want to have such a little couple in my house. . . . I have the feeling that if we were to say yes to that, he would practically be living here. [It would be] coming a little too close, the sexuality, our feeling is that that just doesn't feel right."

What Does Inequality Have To Do With It?

These two final vignettes are instances of conflict. As such, they defy the dominant cultural categories of adolescent sexuality and bring into view a matter left almost entirely unspoken in the Dutch interviews: power. In relaying their own conversations about sex with their children or discussing the relationships their children have with others, Dutch parents rarely talk about the inequalities, antagonisms, and power differences that those relationships may entail.[19] When confronted with what appears to be an instance of sexual violation, Marga Fenning struggles to find words and responses that make sense out of her son's experience and behavior. Yet, Marga remains strikingly attached to the language and practices of normalization, prodding herself, despite shock and discomfort, to respond to Thomas's experiences as were they *gewoon*.

Fleur van Kampen's sexual development tests the limits of normalization in another way. Although confronted with a textbook case of "normal" adolescent sexual development, Ria van Kampen has nonetheless forbidden her daughter's boyfriend to spend the night. Her notable articulation of discomfort and exercise of parental power may well be an expression of two concerns that typically remain unarticulated in the Dutch interviews. Gender, conceptualized as an unequal or power-ridden relationship, is a rare theme in the Dutch interviews. If Dutch middle-class parents speak at all of the inequalities of gender and the disadvantages girls face, they do so in reference to other times or the other social classes. A few Dutch parents acknowledge being more worried about, or protective of, daughters given their capacity for childbearing. But unlike their American counterparts, the Dutch parents do not tend to talk about adolescent sexuality and relationships as an arena in which girls are at a gender-specific disadvantage.

Concerns about gender and power may, however, be hidden in Ria's refusal to permit the sleepover. Without explicitly addressing gender inequality, like Ria, several other professionally employed mothers of daughters hint that in relationships that are prematurely stable, girls may have more to lose than their boyfriends—who are often a few years older. Anneke Schutte, for instance, is "fine with [my daughters'] having a boyfriend as long as he doesn't last." She is wary of the "really steady relationships," ones that could entail losing contact with other friends. If Mariette is honest, she too would rather that her own daughter wait until later. "But that has nothing to do with sex," Mariette explains. "It has to do with being free. You're getting yourself into such a bind. . . . You limit yourself. If you have a steady relationship, you need to start adapting. . . . [Sixteen] is a bit young to start adjusting yourself to another person."

Status anxiety may be another reason Ria and her husband do not want to grant their daughter's relationship full recognition. Although there are subtle hints that the social class of their children's boyfriends and girl-friends matters—and is a basis for deciding whether the partner in question is a suitable candidate for the sleepover—Dutch parents never say that "a good way of relating" requires the right class. Many do not need to. Dutch secondary schools are tracked by academic level, which largely matches a student's social class.[20] Children from middle- and upper-middle class families often attend the upper-level tracks, resulting in relatively homog-enous school-based peer groups. Schools are, however, only one place to meet boyfriends. That at nineteen, Vincent lives in a town, rather than hav-ing moved to a city, as university students often do, suggests that his class trajectory may not make him a suitable sleepover partner.

But if concerns about gender and class drive Ria's resistance to the sleep-over, they will not, she says, outweigh her desire to eventually move be-yond a state of conflict:

> It is also our life's process, and every time we too shift a little. . . . At a certain
> point you can no longer hold it back. We feel we have been able to prolong
> [our resistance] a bit, [thinking] it could be that the relationship breaks up. . . .
> But okay, if the [courtship] stays strong, then [as a parent] you also get more
> accustomed to the boy, become more familiar with him. . . . I won't say, [the
> conflict over the sleepover] is going to stay like this. I hope not. No [having
> this conflict stay] wouldn't be good. . . . You know, you need to move with
> your time.

Moving with Your Time

Accepting the sleepover is, for Dutch parents, a sign that one has moved with the times: with the historical time—since the prevailing norms re-garding adolescent sexuality have changed dramatically in the course of a generation—and with personal time—since a child that was once little is now on the way to becoming an adult. To navigate these changes, and the tensions they produce, Dutch parents draw on distinct cultural tools—cultural frames, forms of reasoning, and everyday practices that help them to smooth out most of the wrinkles of discomfort and disarray. The cultural frames, as we have seen, are *normal* and *nonsecretive* sexuality, *relationship-based* sexuality, and *self-regulated* sexuality. Together, these cultural frames create an understanding of adolescence and of parenting in which permitting the sleepover, under the right conditions, makes cognitive, emotional, and moral sense to the Dutch parents.

As a cultural process, normalization contains a cultural logic: its conceptual components reinforce one another to make the sleepover seem reasonable and right. However, this does not mean that parents do not struggle—with one another, with their children, and with themselves: Jolien Boskamp exhorted her husband Mark not to make their daughter "do penance" for the limitations imposed on them when they were young. Natalie Boskamp and Fleur van Kampen use the frame of normal sexuality to turn the tables and win over reluctant fathers and mothers by arguing that their sexuality should not provoke such an "overblown" emotional response. Finally, confronted with potentially uncomfortable elements of children's sexuality—whether in providing run-of-the-mill sex education or in responding to sexual violation—Ada Kaptein and Marga Fenning both had to struggle to make their actions and reactions match the mandates of normalization.

Indeed, the controlling and constituting components of normalization apply as much to adults as they do to youth themselves.[21] Permitting the sleepover under the right conditions is part of a strategy for exercising control through connection: with teenage sexuality open to discussion, parents can maintain oversight and are thus able to encourage youth to engage in "good ways of relating" and to "know their responsibilities."[22] By allowing sleepovers at home, the Dutch parents provide young people both the opportunity and the incentive to experience sexuality as part of life that can be discussed, rationally planned, and experienced in harmony with, rather than in opposition to, the social fabric of the household. But providing such opportunities requires substantial emotional work on the part of parents. Indeed the sleepover exacts from parents the same qualities they hope to induce in their children—self-restraint, interpersonal attunement, and the capacity to keep reservations and embarrassment from creating alienation in the family.

Notably, this process of normalization differs significantly from patterns observed by American sexuality and gender scholars. Unlike their American peers, Dutch parents do not describe girls and boys as engaged in "antagonistic gender strategies." Insisting that girls listen to and act on their sense of readiness, several Dutch parents clearly recognize their daughters' capacity for sexual subjectivity and agency. And with regard to the sleepover, many Dutch parents hold their sons to the same standards of self-regulated and relationship-based sexuality as they do their daughters. But when parents run up against sexual behavior that is not self-determined or embedded in egalitarian relationships, they can be at a loss for words. Indeed, for all the desire to have sex not be a source of words left unspoken, normalization entails notable silences about the internal conflicts, conflicts of interest, and conflicts over power that can shape sexuality.

Both the premises and the silences embedded in normalization are products of a distinct experience of the transition from the pre-1960s to the post-1960s social order. As we will see in chapter 4, the Dutch parents interviewed for this book are part of a generation—born roughly between 1945 and 1955 and adolescents during the 1960s and 70s—who have drawn on a particular model of individualism in raising their own children. One reason that this generation of parents was able to embrace the falling away of old taboos is because they had at their disposal cultural templates for understanding and instilling self-restraint and social cohesion within the family and within society at large. Striking is the faith that underlies not just normalization but this model of individualism: faith in the self-regulatory capacities of teenagers, faith in teenagers' aptitude to form healthy relationships, and faith in parents' own ability to overcome shame and embarrassment—and control their own emotional impulses—so they can accept change.

A more tangible disposition than faith underlies this normalization: trust.[23] Parents convey that they trust their children—and their children's judgment about when they are ready and about whom to (learn to) love. They also express trust in the relationships they have with their children and an expectation that the relationship will continue despite the shocks and shifts wrought by the inevitable changes of maturation. Trust extends beyond the intimate sphere to institutions outside the family. Unlike their American peers, the Dutch parents do not describe themselves as under assault by a commercial media culture that overstimulates their children and takes away their control as parents.[24] And concerns about sexuality becoming *too* normal notwithstanding, they take for granted that professionals in health care and education will assist them when necessary in making adolescent sexuality the normal experience that they want it to be.

THREE

American Parents and the Drama of Adolescent Sexuality

"The Next Thing You Know It Will be Too Late"

One afternoon, a few months after her daughter, Stephanie, started dating a new boyfriend, Cheryl Tober, a dental hygienist, met Stephanie for lunch in a café outside of Tremont. Their talk quickly turned intimate. Cheryl and Stephanie had always been close, and Cheryl prided herself on raising her daughter with an understanding of all her options in life. Cheryl is "pro-abortion," for instance. "I think that every woman has the right to make that decision in her life," she confides. "And my daughter has been raised in a household where she knows that's one of her choices." Her relatively liberal position on abortion notwithstanding, Cheryl was unprepared for the turn their conversation took.

"Mom, I think I'm ready," Cheryl recalls her daughter telling her. Cheryl disagreed. "I don't think so Stephanie. I think you're too young. You are, I know, sixteen, but I don't think you're really aware of what the consequences will be." Cheryl recalls Stephanie countered her, saying, "I've researched this about the morning-after pill and the birth control pills." But Cheryl did not buy it. First of all, "Before you can go on birth control you have to go and have the exam. Are you ready to face that?"[1] Second, Cheryl argued, "sex is not really important for young people. I mean I don't think you're going to get a whole lot out of it because you're too young and whoever it is you're going to make love with is going to be too young to make it good for you either." Cheryl did not want Stephanie to have to go through what she did when she was a young woman:

> I was just in a position where by the time it happened I really didn't even realize it had gone that far. . . . [I told Stephanie] "Guard yourself against being put in that position because the next thing you know it will be too late. . . .

You can't get that close to it without having it happen. One of the times it will go further than you thought it was going to."

Cheryl asked Stephanie to put her decision on hold for a while. But shortly thereafter, Stephanie got some unwelcome news. The previous night, when Charles, Stephanie's boyfriend, joined the family for a weekend getaway, Stephanie and Charles had had their first sex and it was unprotected. Cheryl was glad that Stephanie confided in her, but she wanted her to face the "consequences of her actions." She was almost "grateful that we had this experience" so that Stephanie could learn about the consequences without "getting really burned": "[Stephanie] stood there in front of the pharmacist and she explained to them what she needed and what she had done. . . . We had a very teary-eyed girl standing there facing the music. I thought that was an important part of it."

One of the lessons Cheryl wanted Stephanie to learn was that teenage girls and boys face different physical and social consequences when they have sexual intercourse:

> [Stephanie] learned a lot from that experience because it was her, not Charles, who was facing that pharmacist and it was her, not Charles, having to take that medication and being sick from it and [having] the worry of it. . . . You're looking at a very small town here. Everybody knows everybody . . . and I think that word does get around. And I am concerned about Stephanie's reputation.

All in all, Cheryl has no doubt that Stephanie's untimely first intercourse taught her several valuable lessons, including that it is "important for teenagers to wait on sex" until they are "financially able to handle the consequences." Tying sexuality to the ability to make a living, Cheryl explains how having sexual intercourse during high school is different from doing so during college: "[Then] I think that they are adults. They've graduated from high school. They can get a job if that's what needs to be [done]." In keeping with this philosophy, Cheryl does not let her son spend the night with a girlfriend even though, at eighteen, he is a legal adult. Her opposition to a sleepover would change, Cheryl explains, once her son is "self-sufficient." Then he "could do whatever he wanted to do." His sexuality would be his business: "If he comes to stay with me for some reason and he sleeps with somebody, has a relationship with someone, I don't think I'd have a problem with that."

"Getting Laid at Any Cost (but Not at Home)"

Harold Lawton, a retired engineer and social libertarian, knows one thing for sure: "Teenage boys want to get laid at all times and at any cost. I certainly did." The same might be true for girls: "Traditionally they say that girls are not that interested in getting laid . . . but I'm not too sure if that is really true." Harold draws a line between sex and relationships. "Sex is one thing, relationships another altogether. It's kind of a strange thing . . . because you've got sex drives in there . . . and out of it grows relationships that really need to be beyond all that . . . [And] I don't know how it happens."

Neither Harold nor his wife Doreen have communicated much with their son Jesse about sex. "What it really boiled down to was checking to make sure he knew what . . . and he already knew all that stuff already, so it was a short conversation. But beyond that, into the dynamics of male-female relationships beyond sex, I haven't had many discussions about that." Nor does Harold think more talk was necessary. He believes:

> As long as they can protect themselves against having children or getting diseases, then they're ready to have sex. . . . How that affects relationships is something else. . . . Whether they're ready to have a relationship, well they have to practice doing relationships. So as soon as they start practicing, that's cool.

But Doreen, a clothing designer, has a very different opinion about sex and relationships. To begin with, she does not think teenage girls are interested in sex. Some girls, she says, "give in to having sex . . . for fear of losing a guy." Besides, "guys don't think much about that they could get pregnant." But, Doreen notes, boys too can get duped. Not long ago she had an in-depth conversation with her twenty-two-year-old son Darren, who is seeing a woman Doreen does not like: "I just wanted him to make sure," she explains, "he was careful that he didn't become a father before his time, by accident."

Doreen is firmly opposed to sex before marriage. Doreen grew up, she says, "without any discipline," which she regrets, and was in her husband's words, "a bad girl." When her fifty-year-old sister comes to visit with her boyfriend, Doreen assigns them separate bedrooms. "We're at odds on the issue, actually," says Harold. He would consider permitting a sleepover for Jesse, who is eighteen (though not when he was sixteen). Given his wife's strong feelings, however, Harold has decided that taking an explicit position on the matter "would only cause problems." Hence Doreen is in charge of deciding their guests' sleeping arrangements. And she speaks with considerable pride about the "old-fashioned" rules that she imposes in her home:

> I'm adamant about it because I think that it's very important to instill that in the kids. . . . That's just my rule. I don't want to project that it's okay not to be married and sleep together. Even though I know that they're doing that. But they're not doing it in my house. It's kind of an old-fashioned thing, but I think that the boys get it. They know that it's not okay, and it just won't happen.

The Drama of Adolescent Sexuality

There are many differences in the interviews with the American parents—between fathers and mothers, between liberal and conservative parents, between past behavior and current approaches, and between cultural languages: Harold, sympathetic to teenage boys' desires to get laid "at any cost" and not unwilling to consider sleepovers for adults, is married to Doreen, once a "bad girl" who now opposes all premarital sex. Cheryl Tober, who knows from personal experience that sexuality can easily get out of control, seeks to give her daughter tools to prevent feeling as out of control as she did. And Rhonda Fursman, who in the book's first chapter describes teenage sex as mere "recreation," also embraces, as we will see in this chapter, the view that the kind of love that justifies sex can happen to her fifteen-year-old son "in one year or in fifteen years."

But if the differences and contradictions that characterize the American parents' conceptions of teenage sexuality and romance are easy to identify, a less apparent shared narrative of sequence unites them: adolescent sexuality starts early with impulses, leads to battles, but becomes only fully legitimate once young people have successfully navigated these trials by fire and established autonomous households, an accomplishment both deeply desired and dreaded. Three frames structure that narrative. The first is *hormone-based adolescent sexuality*. The second is the *battle between the sexes*, according to which boys and girls pursue antagonistic interests. Finally, until youth establish their autonomy—through financial self-sufficiency or marriage—the principle of *parent-regulated adolescent sexuality* applies, leading twenty-nine out of thirty-two parents to respond to the sleepover question, much as Rhonda does: "No way, José."

Ironically, while legitimating a more blatant exercise of parental control, the dramatization of adolescent sexuality is built around the premise of a more radical separation between parents and their adolescent children than is the Dutch notion of normalization. As we will see, the American parents are most at ease relegating their children's sexuality to times (adulthood) and places (not at home) when and where they have no say over their choices. And for now and at home, most parents have no trouble telling teenagers what they should *not* do. But they are less prone and able than their Dutch peers to influence the nature of their adolescents' actual sexual and romantic experiences—which like those of Dutch adolescents typically start during the mid-teenage years.[2] More willing to accept conflict over sex between parents and adolescents, few American parents exact from themselves or from their children the emotional work necessary to create the physical and emotional space to negotiate teenage sexuality within the home.

If American parents do not exert as deep a control as their Dutch peers, they are also more constrained in the support they can offer by cultural templates that construct sex as a battle between parents and teens, girls and boys, and different parts of the self. Such battles have been amply noted by American gender and sexuality scholars, who often mistakenly assume that these experiences have been shared across nations.[3] In fact, elements of the dramatization of adolescent sexuality, like the missing discourse of teenage love in parental accounts as well as in education and health policy, suggest a particular experience of the transition between the pre- and post-sexual revolution orders:[4] An adversarial individualism, according to which people must struggle with one another and with themselves to attain autonomy and intimacy, has left parents uncertain about the basis for self-restraint and social bonds—intimate or societal—in post-1960s America.

Hormone-Based Sexuality

"Raging hormones" metaphorically represent the notion of teenage sexuality as an individual, overpowering force that is difficult for teenagers to control, a notion present throughout the American interviews.[5] "Hormones" was one of the first words that the Tremont high-school sex educator mentioned when she heard about this study comparing adolescent sexuality in the United States and the Netherlands. "I am sure," she said, "Dutch teenagers have as many hormones as the American ones." Indeed, for many American parents, adolescent sexuality brings to mind first and foremost hormones. Sometimes, parents connect hormones and sex drive to a young person's zest for life, as does Harold who speaks with glee about the insatiable urges of teenage boys. But as often, hormones are associated with dangers youth cannot fully protect against.

Rhonda Fursman can see her son's "testosterone bubbling." That does not surprise her. She expects teenagers to be interested in the opposite sex, and to want to date as soon as they are allowed to—which in her son's case is not until he is sixteen. Thus, it concerns her that her daughter, a high-school senior, has not thus far shown much interest in boys. Fathers like Harold Lawton may go further than assuming sexual interest in boys. They may actively sympathize or identify with their sons' hormones. Calvin Brumfield had no doubt that his son Adam's hormones were "kicking in early." But Calvin also has his concerns, as Adam is somewhat overweight and has trouble finding dates. By the time Adam turned sixteen, Calvin was hoping his son would have a chance to have a sexual relationship because "the poor kid, his hormones were just raging, they're still raging. I was hoping that he would because his friends were dating."

Yet, if raging hormones propel youth outward toward the opposite sex—no American parent mentions observing same-sex desires in their teenage children—those hormones can also lead the young to inadvertently go further sexually than they should. Like Cheryl Tober, several parents believe that teenagers have difficulty controlling their own sexual progression, and that they must therefore guard against things getting out of control. In fact, to prevent sex, Jennifer Reed does not allow her son and his girlfriend to be home alone. "Maybe it would never happen, maybe they're just good friends but I just think 'raging hormones syndrome.'" She remembers being that age and worries things will go too far: "Kissing is all right but I think it can get carried away. It can lead to other things. That's the hard part. . . . Fondling is starting to get a little, it gets mistier because it's harder to stop what you're doing and have it lead to something else." The something else is not sex as much, says Jennifer Reed, "as what could happen, the babies and all that."

Deborah Langer too fears the "raging hormones" that have taken her daughter into "the dark ages" because of the possibility of pregnancy and its repercussions. Like many American parents, Deborah is intimately familiar with those repercussions, having seen her two nieces make "some poor choices in life" and have babies in high school. Accounts of lives seriously disrupted through the consequences of sex haunt the American parents' discussions of teenage sexuality.[6] "Pregnancy you can live through, some of the STDs you can't," says Donald Wood. But Frank Mast views pregnancy as almost "life-threatening." He believes that early pregnancy is one of those "huge mistakes" that can result from "the decisions you see kids make that they're not able to handle the consequences [of] and it ruins them for five, ten, fifteen years, maybe the rest of their life."

The dangerous consequences of teenage sex loom particularly large because parents see a disjunction between the onset of hormones and the development of the cognitive and emotional capacity to handle them. Jany Kippen thinks her son Neil is definitely not ready to have a sexual relationship because he lacks "a real clear picture of the consequences." She just cannot "see Neil remembering to use a condom." He "is not ready to take responsibility for what he does. I mean not that he doesn't know that there are consequences but they're always not going to happen to him. He's the invincible fifteen-, sixteen-year-old and nothing could go wrong." Rhonda Fursman's son Sam "has all the adult equipment, he's got the desires. . . . [It's] just a question again of perhaps learning how to channel them." She wants to avoid putting him in "situations where he can't make a decision, or a more reasoned decision."

A sleepover with a girl- or boyfriend would be the kind of situation in which American parents believe teenagers might be unable to make a "more reasoned decision." While sexual interest is expected and to a certain extent even welcomed, parents see their own role as containing and directing, rather than giving full range to, their children's raging hormones. Theirs is a delicate role, for while many parents institute rules against dating before sixteen, or keeping the door open when girl- or boyfriends are visiting, none go as far as to prohibit dating altogether, an acknowledgement that some amount of romantic and sexual exploration should be part of the adolescent maturation process.

Yet, that exploration should be kept within certain parameters. And given the assumption that when offered the opportunity, teenagers may not be able to control themselves against the forces of their hormonal urges, permitting a sleepover of the kind that is common in Dutch middle-class families strikes many American parents as ludicrous.

The Battle between the Sexes

The second cultural frame that structures discussions of teenage sexuality among the American parents is that of the *battle between the sexes*. While the Dutch parents talk about teenage sexual desire in relation to being in love and forming a relationship with another person, the American parents are more likely to talk about teenage sexuality in the context of internal hormonal urges and external peer pressures than as the result of a strong romantic connection with a girl- or boyfriend. Indeed, many American parents express extreme skepticism about the possibility of falling in love as a teenager; several suggest that while teenagers, particularly girls, may think they are in love, they are not actually in love. Instead, the American parents emphasize the ways in which girls and boys have opposing, even antagonistic, desires and interests, and the ways in which girls and boys pay a different price when they do engage in sexual activity during high school.

Harold Lawton believes that boys want to get laid at any cost, while his wife Doreen believes that girls have sex grudgingly, only to hold on to their boyfriends.[7] Like Doreen Lawton, many American parents assume that boys are much more active than girls in pursuing sex. Helen Mast believes that if her daughter Katy decides to become sexually active, it will not be because she herself wants to, but because "she's only doing it because [her boyfriend] wants her to." Dierdre Mears believes that boys *and* girls are hormonally driven, but "most teenage boys would fuck anything that would sit still. And some things that wouldn't. . . . And I don't believe girls would do that." Donald Wood was anxious about his daughter's recent dating debut. He explains why: "I'm a parent of a teenage cheerleader. I'm very concerned: 'Dirty little boys! Get away! Get away.'"

Like Doreen, many American parents argue that girls make an emotional investment in their sexual partners that boys do not. Jennifer Reed believes women "perceive sex as something very permanent and lasting where I don't know, I don't think, this is hearsay, because I am not a man but I think a man can definitely have sex just for the night." Pamela Fagan says, "Teenage girls have so much more of a romantic fantasy, and emotional involvement [than boys] and all-encompassing kind of emotions with it and think, 'I am so in love and this love will last forever.' It's not likely it will." Helen Mast also sees girls, not their boyfriends, "emotionally distraught over a broken relationship." To remind her sixteen-year-old daughter that her relationship will probably not be the last one, she will ask her, "Are you guys going to get married or something?"

If different investments are one part of the story, different costs are another. Parents stress both the emotional and economic costs of sex. Dierdre Mears thinks that "when we got rid of the double standard and had the 'sexual revolution' someone forgot to say, 'Excuse me, it appears that the emotional cost is higher for women than men.'" And Frank Mast is trying to teach his daughter Katy:

The ultimate shouldering of the responsibility of making a mistake, having a boy/girl relationship, is on the girl. The boy can say, "Sorry, it didn't work out," walk away, "See ya later." . . . They [have to] feel mentally responsible for what they did, or have some deep inward feeling that "I'm responsible," . . . to step up and say, "I'm financially responsible." . . . Ultimately girls don't have that choice.

One of the costs of sex for American high-school girls is the loss of symbolic resources. What it takes to acquire a "bad reputation" differs in different social locations. A good reputation is fairly precarious in small-town Tremont. But even in Northern California's Corona, "the old double standard is still there," Flora Baker knows. "As much as we would like to think not, if a girl has sex with a couple of different people, she gets a reputation." She recalls the words her daughters use: "They call someone a slut, whore . . . She's a . . . yeah, she'll do anybody. She'll go to a party, she'll do anybody. To some degree that's [a bit unfair]. But that is something that women have to deal with."

But parents also suggest that, in today's world, sometimes girls are aggressors. Deborah Langer was dismayed when she intercepted a number of notes boys had written her daughter. The sexual acts they described convey an "astounding" lack of respect for women. She tells herself, "Boys are boys and I have two of them myself. And I'm not saying that some of these boys won't turn out to be nice young men some day, but they're going to have daughters too." Deborah wonders whether perhaps girls have become more like boys: "I just feel that there's just a lack of modesty and I think that some of the girls are almost just as forward as the boys and perhaps my own daughter included."

More socially liberal than Deborah, Rhonda Fursman thinks "boys will be boys" is a "piece of crap." She believes that in the post-sexual-revolution battle over sex's costs, boys too can become victims. Rhonda worries that her son might fall prey to a girl who wants sex only to get back at her mother. By not letting her son date until he is sixteen, she is protecting him, she explains, against becoming a victim of a girl's pressure "to bring her flowers and stuff." Now her son can just say, "My mom won't let me do this." Bonnie Oderberg wants her son to understand "the vulnerability of both himself and of girls." But like Rhonda, Bonnie worries about (ab)use: "I don't want [Alan] to be a user of women. He's a real good-looking young man and he has a lot of girls that call him all the time, so I want him to be respectful and responsible with their feelings as well as his."

With sex at adolescence conceptualized as a battle where there are costs and benefits, winners and losers, it is not only the power of biology that makes adolescent sex such a risk-ridden territory. The battle between the sexes and the different types of pressures boys and girls exert on one another are also cause for parental concern. Not just "hormones" but "love," or what especially girls might mistakenly call love, is easily out of control, and parents encourage their children to consider the costs of both. Given these concerns, the American parents view it as their job to rein in romantic relationships during the high-school years. Not wanting their children to fall prey to dangerous and premature relational entanglement, placing external parameters on their romantic relationships—for instance, by not permitting a sleepover—is one way to protect adolescents against relationships that they are not yet equipped to successfully negotiate.

Parent-Regulated Adolescent Sexuality, or "Not Under My Roof"

Since they envision young people as easily carried away by their hormonal urges or by emotions they mistake for love, American parents view it as their responsibility to prevent their teenage children from having the opportunity to engage in sexual activity, at least within the domain that parents ought to control: the parental home. Such *parent-regulated adolescent sexuality* stands in tension with another mandate, namely, to respect and promote the development of autonomy, and to provide adolescents space to explore their emerging independent identities outside the home. Indeed, parents expect and even encourage young people to experience themselves as driven by sexual interest—in fact, they are sometimes concerned when they see no evidence thereof—but they also believe it is vital for parents to place clear external parameters on that interest.

The often visceral opposition to a sleepover—even for older teenagers who are still living at home—is one parameter on which almost all of the American parents agree, even when they appear reconciled to the fact that sex will likely become part of their children's lives during their adolescent years. Henry Martin is a divorced father with full-time parenting responsibilities who has gone farther than most in providing his son with sex education. He has instructed his son Steve on the details of female anatomy and sexual pleasure, so that his son will know how to be a good lover. But when asked whether he would permit his seventeen-year-old daughter to have her boyfriend spend the night, Henry recoils. There is "no justification for any of that, in whatever sense," he says. "It goes completely against the things I believe in. For one, religiously, I don't believe that type of relationship would be good, but I don't live that kind of life."

The belief that permitting a sleepover under one's own roof is inappropriate is particularly noteworthy in American parents who may be liberal in other ways. Iris DiMaggio, for instance, has openly discussed sexuality and contraceptives with her children. She does not, however, let her son Phillip sleep with his girlfriend at home. Why? "Maybe it is my own comfort," she says. "It's like giving them license to do as they please, and I am not ready to do that." Neither would she let her nineteen-year-old daughter spend the night with her boyfriend. "That's not an example I want my [son] given," she says. What example does she want him given? "There is a time and a place. And it's not at home." Bonnie Oderberg has spoken openly with her stepson Alan about sex, and she has left condoms for him in the bathroom. Still, she cannot imagine letting him spend the night with his girlfriend at home. "It would be uncomfortable for me."

Relative to their Dutch counterparts, American parents are very upfront about their emotional discomfort with teenage sexuality. They experience and express it strongly, without apparently feeling a social pressure to moderate their emotional reaction. About the prospect of a sleepover, Bonnie Oderberg says, "It's not necessarily that I would feel it would be wrong for him. It would be very uncomfortable for me" because "it's right in your face that they're having an adult type of relationship." Kirsten Rickets does not like the idea of permitting a sleepover, now or in the future:

> It's better not to have it so blatant, to do things a little more secretively like I was raised. We were on the sly and in secret. It seems a little better that way, rather than blatant in front of your parents about it. . . . If my [adult] son wanted to bring a girlfriend home he can rent a hotel room. . . . I'm not going to have some adults in my house screwing away in the bedroom and I can hear them. Forget it.

In addition to emotional recoiling at the thought of a sleepover, the American parents also oppose a sleepover because it would violate their notion of proper sequencing in the adolescent developmental trajectory. Like Cheryl Tober, Iris DiMaggio believes her son's continued dependency on her makes a sleepover inappropriate. Once her son Phillip is "really on his own," and is "making his own decisions," Iris says she would no longer object to a sleepover: "When you are still living in this house you are still financially dependent on us. To some degree you are emotionally dependent on us. You are dependent on us for almost everything, day to day." Self-sufficiency makes the sexuality of children their own business: "To be honest with you, when they are gone, they will be living their own lives, and I don't have a say. So if they come home and they choose to share a bed with someone, that's their choice."

In other words, Iris would accept the sleepover *not* because she wanted to make sure that, as a parent, she continues to be connected to her son's development, or because she is willing to accept his girlfriend as a (temporary) member of the family. Rather, Iris would accept the sleepover out of respect for Phillip's hard-won autonomy and out of recognition that she no longer had the right to "have a say" over what he does. Like Iris, Calvin Brumfield would not permit a sleepover until his son has attained full financial autonomy—which Calvin defines in legal terms. In the meantime, Calvin sympathizes with, even encourages, his son's "raging hormones," chuckling when he found fifty condoms in his drawer. But a sleepover is out of the question until age twenty-one: "Twenty-one is the magic number. You're not a teen anymore, you're an adult, you can be sued, you can be, you know, [you're] super-adult, you know, there is no more."

Yet, for another set of parents, self-sufficiency in and of itself is not enough. Like Rhonda Fursman, some parents say that only marriage, or near-marriage, will make it possible for them to permit their children such a sleepover in good conscience. Frank Mast says, "If they want to stay over here, there's a couch. We'll find a place to put you up. It would even be difficult after they were married to be honest with you. You have to do it, but it's still difficult." Flora Baker also ties full acceptance of adolescent sexuality to (near) marriage. She insisted, against her husband's wishes, that her daughters be allowed to use contraceptives. But she puts her nineteen-year-old daughter's boyfriend on the couch. To her daughter's protests, she responds, "You can have your intimate relationship when you want. We don't have to broadcast it to the family. We don't have to share in that. Should you decide to live together or get married some day, that's a decision we will respect. But when you are in my house, these are my rules."

Dramatization as a Cultural Process

Three frames—like those that contribute to the normalization of adolescent sexuality in the Netherlands—form an interrelated cultural logic: young people, who cannot regulate their impulses and are prone to emotional entanglements that hinder rather than help their developmental process, require external controlling authorities. At the same time, parental control over adolescent sexuality is not, nor is it supposed to be, total. For sexual interest, springing from adolescent drives and desires, is to be expected and given some measure of leeway, as part of adolescent maturation and exploration. Consequently, even the most conservative of the American parents do not prohibit dating altogether, but, instead, they use rules to place parameters around the practice. Conversely, even liberal American parents exert external control over adolescent sexual exploration by prohibiting teenage couples from spending the night together at home.

At the heart of dramatization as a cultural process are notions of autonomy. Parents should, the cultural logic dictates, not recognize their children's sexuality before they have established themselves as autonomous beings. At the point that children have attained such absolute autonomy—whether by way of financial self-sufficiency or by way of marriage—parents simply lose their say over their children altogether.[8] It is not necessary, in other words, to find a common ground on matters of sexuality and relationships, but just to recognize that, as adults, one's children choose their own way. Until that point, however, letting children make their own sexual choices at home compromises not only the adolescent maturation process but the integrity of the family. Indeed, within the household, adolescent sexual activity and parental authority are conceptualized as a zero-sum game—the former's presence diminishes the latter.[9]

Ironically, dramatization as a cultural process involves more overt control than normalization but less deep control over teenagers, their sexuality, and their relationships. The cultural frames that they have available to discuss teenage sexuality give American parents only limited tools with which to help their adolescent children navigate their entry into sexual exploration. The metaphor of "raging hormones" may explain why, in Harold Lawton's words, "teenage boys want to get laid at all times and at any cost," or why, as Cheryl Tober puts it, "the next thing you know it will be too late." But the frame of hormone-based sexuality does not give parents cultural tools with which to understand or teach teenagers about how to pace and exert control over their sexuality. Likewise, the concept of the battle of the sexes explains why young people become burned by sex and love and teaches them to mistrust one another. It does not offer tools to form relationships. "How [that] happens," Harold Lawton admits, "I don't know."

Conceptualizing adolescent sexuality through the lens of raging hormones and the battle between the sexes makes parent-regulated sexuality appear necessary and the sleepover of a teenage couple seem like the abrogation of one's parental responsibilities. But the criteria that make their children's sexual activity legitimate to parents—full financial self-sufficiency or marriage—are ones most middle-class Americans cannot meet until their mid- or late twenties, as much as a decade after typical sexual initiation. Financial self-sufficiency and marriage constitute, moreover, endpoints on the adolescent and young adult developmental trajectory, rather than the middle point when young people are still living at home and beginning their sexual and romantic careers. During that period, the American parents are often at a loss about how to guide teenagers other than by issuing prohibitions and warnings against the dire consequences of sexual activity.

Second Thoughts, Second Languages

As we have seen, the vision of adolescent sexuality as a drama, the product of raging hormones, the battle between the sexes, and the struggle between the generations seems to leave little room for a positive conception of adolescent sexuality, particularly for teenage girls who lack the tacit approval to roam that boys sometimes receive from their fathers. There is, moreover, a real disconnect between the ideal life-course trajectories—according to which sexual activity coincides with the attainment of full independence—that parents envision for their children and the more likely trajectory. Finally, while the cultural logic dictates parental regulation during adolescence, ironically, American parents have fewer tools to intervene than their Dutch counterparts. The very autonomy parents seek to foster before recognizing a child's sexual activity makes it difficult for them to help teenagers navigate sexual maturation and relationships.

One way parents address these lacunae and disconnects is by drawing on what sociologist Robert Bellah calls "second" cultural languages.[10] These might appear to contradict but in fact coexist alongside the primary cultural languages. One such secondary language is that of romantic love which defies limitations of age. As we saw in the book's first chapter, Rhonda Fursman told her teenage children that not having premarital sex as teenagers is part of her "Ten Commandments." In threatening that they would be "in a world of hurt" if they did not abide, she applies the frame of parent-regulated sexuality. But she also says she is "enough of a romantic to believe that for sex, some love [should be] involved." Her fifteen-year-old son could, she says, find love "in a year or in fifteen years." Deborah Langer also believes that love could come beckoning at any time. She wants her daughter to wait for marriage to have sex:

> But I'm not going to put my head in the clouds either. I'm hoping it's something that she really thinks long and hard about. . . . She's already saying, "I don't want to get married until I'm twenty-three or twenty-six. . . . [But in] the real world when you fall in love or you think you're in love, I don't know.

Sometimes parents describe love as so powerful that it wipes away rational consideration. Other times, they talk about falling in love as a state of being so difficult to attain that one might have to settle for lesser forms of relating. Flora Baker wants her children to "know themselves" before having sex "because it is a commitment." They "need [not] be truly in love" to be ready, she explains. But they do need to "care for that person deeply and trust them and not to take it lightly." Iris DiMaggio says "commitment of some sort" is necessary. And it has "to be a commitment to the other person. It has to be a mutual commitment. It would be nice if there was love, but there isn't always." Like love, mutual commitment can, Iris explains, happen "at any wide variety of ages."[11]

A second cultural language is that of "staying safe." While the question of the sleepover elicits parents' disapproval and prohibition, questions about conversations parents have had with teenagers about contraception and condoms tend to elicit their pragmatism, especially among Corona and Norwood parents. The topic of sexual safety—how and where children should receive sexual education and access to contraception—brings out most clearly regional differences in sexual culture. Iris DiMaggio is among the most committed to an atmosphere of openness. She has "had some really interesting dinnertime conversations" with her children. "We've been very open. . . . Because nowadays with AIDS and a lot of the STDs . . . they have to know that a condom is something you use, not something you carry in your pocket." And Flora Baker explains how her realism led her to go against her husband's wishes and provide her children with contraception:

> There is no reason in this world for you to have a child at your age, and there
> is no reason for you to contract any STDs. . . . Even though deep down, in a
> perfect world, you would want everyone to choose your mate and that would
> be the person you decide to lose your virginity to, I think that is unrealistic.

Relative to their generally more liberal Corona and Norwood counterparts, Tremont parents tend to approach the topic of contraception in a more tentative fashion and with more misgivings. Jany Kippen's son "probably knows more than he should: He has a good knowledge of the mechanics" from sex education at school. Jany discussed contraception and condoms in the context of a nephew who has AIDs, but "not maybe as much as I should." And Carole and Donald Wood, social conservatives, have not broached the topic. Discounting that contraception and condoms might protect their daughter against pregnancy and disease, Donald Wood explains the message he has communicated: "You need to think about it because if you make this decision now and you get pregnant, this is where you're going. If you make this decision and you get a venereal disease, this is where you're going." Were her daughter to have sex before marriage, Carole's position would be:

> She would have to support herself. I would not be able to support her finan-
> cially, maybe emotionally but not financially. . . . If she decided that she was
> going to have a child or she was going to take the risk of having a child, I
> wouldn't be able to have her live here and have the child and just have a free
> ride. I couldn't do that because my warning to her was . . . the consequence
> for doing it is probably the worst. You're on your own. You make a decision
> and you live by it.

"When You Smell Trouble, Just Get Out of There"

At the other end of the political spectrum from the Woods is Dierdre Mears. Having come of age in the San Francisco Bay area during the 1960s and still a Northern California resident, Dierdre remains more radical than many of her friends. Her parents were pretty liberal. "We were in Planned Parenthood," explains Dierdre's mother, Molly, who lives with Dierdre's family today. When Dierdre became sexually active at sixteen, Molly wasn't thrilled about it, but, she says, "I didn't freak out like my friends were." When Dierdre's boyfriend got kicked out of his own house, he even moved in with the family: "He had the room upstairs. And the way I was looking at it, at least she was getting some needs met, and at least they could focus on their studies. They didn't have to do this silly adolescent stuff." The good thing about the arrangement, says Molly, is that her daughter was not running around and that at least she knew where she was.

Dierdre feels the same way and would permit her son and daughter a sleepover: "I think that parents frequently live in an illusion that they can control their kids' behavior and certainly they can influence it, and I believe that they should. But it is actually extremely difficult to control." She knows her experience and position are not common: "It was extraordinarily unusual then, but it is still unusual now. . . . I think that parents are terrified of their kids' sexuality, mostly because they realize how little control they have over it. I think that adolescents really are completely hormonally driven." Dierdre opposes sexual intercourse during the early teens, but she is more approving of teenage sexual relationships "somewhere around sixteen or seventeen, somewhere around junior or senior year . . . [when]

people kind of start pairing up and have a steady relationship and kind of start practicing those skills, [then] it is not necessarily a bad idea."

Dierdre also gives more credence than many American parents to teenagers' feelings of being in love. She knows they "absolutely believe they are in love" and they are "capable of phenomenally intense feelings." And she says, "their direct experience is unbeatable and ungovernable and a riot in the heart." At the same time she wonders whether these feelings are hormone-based. She thinks that "culturally we cloak [hormonal forces] within the context of the romantic, so we dress it up and I mean, the question is, is love really biochemical?" She is, moreover, wary of teenagers' relationships with each other: "I think that is very easy for girls to manipulate boys and vice versa." She also sees costs: "You got a girl who's sixteen, seventeen, and is kind of doing okay, makes going to the JC, doesn't have any really good plans, and then she gets a boyfriend. And then they fall in love and then her life becomes his life. . . . Why do I know that? Because I did that."

Nor is it just girls she sees being easily derailed by their hormones and emotions. Like Doreen Lawton, who was concerned about her twenty-two-year-old son becoming a father before his time with a girlfriend she did not like, Dierdre is more concerned about her son than her daughter. Were the latter to come home pregnant at sixteen, Dierdre says, "I could put a gun to her and say you don't want to continue this pregnancy, though I mean that only emotionally." But what really frightens her is that, she admits, "I cannot exert that same kind of control over whoever Matthew interacts with." She is acutely aware that whether or not teenage girls become mothers has to do with their educational opportunities and aspirations. Therefore, to exert as much control as she can, Dierdre would not let Matthew go on a date without answers to the "who, what, where" questions. As she explains the questions she asks, she is more upfront than any parent interviewed about her concern that romance could take her son over to the wrong side of the track:

> I wanted to know her last name and . . . her home phone number. That's the minimum. You can't get out the door without the minimum. The other things I would like to know are things like were her parents ever married to each other, are they still together? . . . That has everything to do with socio-economics. Things I want to know are . . . what does her father do? . . . Tiffany was the first girl that I knew about that Matthew was truly was interested in. I hate the name Tiffany . . . because in my book you can't get a trashier, white trash name than Tiffany.

In addition to voicing concerns about out-of-control hormones and emotions and mixing between classes, Dierdre worries about her children inadvertently becoming involved in sexual assault. When Matthew attended an unsupervised event, she told him:

> I said let me tell you how it happens: six guys go to a motel room with three girls to get drunk, two guys leave because they need to get home, one girl leaves when she gets scared, one girl pukes her guts out in the bathroom, and one girl pulls a train (becomes the victim of a group rape), and even the guy who didn't do anything is also culpable. I said when you smell trouble, just get out of there.

Although, she admits, it might sound strange coming from her, she thinks girls may have become more likely to fall victim to sexual violence because the sexual revolution loosened sexual constraints: "I am not sure we benefited ourselves a lot by throwing out the double standard." There was something to be said, she believes, about the old dorm rules that made girls keep both feet on the ground. Nor does she want her children to follow her footsteps: "I would not like them to have as many one night stands or casual relationships as I had, because I don't think they were valuable in retrospect. I think in many ways they were not valuable [and] in some ways they were damaging."[12]

What Does History Have to Do with It?

Having been permitted to spend the night with her boyfriend as an adolescent, Dierdre Mears is among the few American parents who say that as parents they have or would permit their own children such a sleepover during the high-school years. Dierdre also validates teenagers' experiences of being in love more than most of her American counterparts. And yet in several notable ways, Dierdre's language, tone, and reasoning in talking about teenage sexuality are similar to those of other American interviewees. She speaks recurrently of the overwhelming power of hormones, and she emphasizes girls' and boys' antagonistic interests. Finally, although she recognizes the limits of her control when it comes to her children's sexuality and romances, Dierdre uses the language and the strategies of parent-regulated sexuality. She speaks of holding a metaphoric gun to her daughter and of unabashedly intervening to prevent her son from "downward" dating.

But what stands out perhaps most from the interview with Dierdre

Mears is the ambivalence she expresses about the 1960s and their after-math. By no stretch of the imagination a social conservative, Dierdre nevertheless articulates the belief that the loosening of the old restrictions has done damage to intimate relations and girls' safety. In this regard, she is hardly unique. Unlike their Dutch counterparts who, reservations about sexuality becoming too *gewoon* notwithstanding, tend to embrace the gains of normalization, the American parents speak with greater ambivalence about the changes in sexuality and society that have taken place during and since their youth. Their accounts show how the drama of adolescent sexuality in the United States, like its normalization in the Netherlands, is constituted in relation to personal and societal histories.

Several American parents welcome the greater openness they observe around sex in society. Calvin Brumfield sees an "open awareness" of things like homosexuality, Internet sex, and STDs, which used to be taboo. Looking back, he says, "Those were oppressive times whereas now that stuff is open and discussed." He is open with his son about sexuality-related issues: "If he sees something or has an issue, we'll talk about it. It's not like you better talk to your mother about that or we don't want to be talking about that." Iris DiMaggio has made a conscious effort to raise her son and daughter more openly than she was: "I was not taught anything about sexuality . . . about my own, about anybody's. I swore that that was not an area that I was going to miss in raising my kids because I got the clinical level, but not the emotional level, and that's important."

But others question whether greater openness about sex is a positive development. They describe the emphasis on sex in the media as disempowering parents and adding to the pressures teenagers face. Mark DiMaggio questions the greater exposure to sex in the media because "it puts an awful lot of pressure on young people." Frank Mast is not an "anti-media" person, but he is disturbed by the blatant sexual references in songs on the radio: "You get bombarded with it in the news, newspapers, and magazines." Jennifer Reed believes more attention to homosexuality has made her sons "paranoid . . . about the idea of being gay." Pamela Fagan sees the effect of the media on teenage girls:

> The kids have learned a lot more about sex and sexuality and the emphasis on it at a much younger age than I was ever exposed to or knew about. . . . I think that's very sad. [Exposure] to all these images of young, beautiful, sexy women who have boob jobs . . . just takes away from their childhood. . . . They have this pressure to have this supposed ideal that's not real.

It is not just sex that inspires nostalgia. Several parents say authority and gender relations were more hierarchical in the past, but growing up was easier and more fun. Kristin recalls growing up in a "more rigid structure than exists today." But she thinks that "in a way that was a lot easier because I knew what the expectations were." When Frank Mast was growing up in the rural Midwest, it was "Yes sir, no sir, yes ma'am, no ma'am." Frank also had adventures that "people wouldn't think twice about back then, but now you could go to jail [for them]. And a lot of things were harmless fun." Calvin Brumfield thinks "the kids aren't having as much fun" as in the past. Back in the late 1960s, "There was money, the country was flush, and so there were funds for all this extracurricular stuff." He recalls: "Every church, every synagogue, every school, every community center on a given Friday or Saturday night, there was something going on."[13]

But there are also plenty of recollections of fun getting out of hand. Jany Kippen recalls: "My lab partner was stoned out of her mind and we flunked our project in Home Ec because she forgot to turn the oven on." The oven incident turned Jany off drugs, but, she says: "I must admit that I was drunk more than once. I broke the rules." The daughter of a divorced mother who worked evening shifts to make ends meet, Jany did not have a lot of supervision. "Consequently, my kids sometimes have a little more than they'd like to have." Flora Baker had multiple abortions and does not want her daughters "to go through having to be pregnant." Deborah Langer remembers having "really rowdy friends and growing up in the '70s, you sat next to kids that came to class stoned." In college she experimented a lot with alcohol and was in an alcohol-related car accident. Looking back she thinks, "Oh my God, thank God I survived." Deborah does not tell her children about her experiences, because she does not want to give them the green light.

Several of the most conservative American parents draw implicit or explicit linkages between the excesses of the past and their embrace of a stricter sexual ideology. As we saw, Doreen Lawton, who in her own words lacked "discipline" growing up, and who was, according to her husband, a "bad girl," opposes premarital sex even for adults. Donald Wood, who describes his own background as "dysfunctional," is relieved that the country returned to a more conservative sexual ideology after the "free sex" of the past: "If you follow the trends of say the '50s and the apple pies, in the '60s the war protests and free love and the women's movement and equalization from the '50s to the '70s. . . . We saw sex becoming free sex in the '60s and '70s and what came of that wasn't very good." In response, people started thinking: "Gee, maybe there is more to this family value or this family unit and this commitment to one another or commitment to yourself."

Cheryl Tober also describes the 1960s and '70s as a chaotic period. She remembers "sitting around the family table and . . . seeing Vietnam on the TV and looking at the body count." At that time, "there was so much unrest: The college, Kent State, with those kids being mowed down by the National Guard. People were just at odds with each other. The generations were at the furthest gap that you can possibly imagine." About sex, Cheryl says, "Boy, I'm telling you, it was fast pace. . . . It was sleep around." With her pro-choice position and embrace of gender equalization in the workplace, Cheryl is no social conservative. But like Donald Wood, Cheryl is glad "things are going back a little bit more conservative." Intentionally departing from the past, she says: "With my children, I try not to be too liberal. I know that my husband had multiple partners and I did too. They don't know that. And I don't think they can live the same way that my husband and I did because of . . . AIDS and the problems there. . . . It's scary."

Like Cheryl Tober, the general public and researchers in the United States tend to attribute the conservative turn at least in part to AIDS.[14] That in the Netherlands the epidemic deepened rather than undermined a commitment to normalization demonstrates that the disease cannot explain how policymakers and lay individuals respond to it.[15] Instead, to understand the backlash against the 1960s and 1970s in the United States, we must understand how the generation that came of age during those decades experienced change. As Cheryl Tober and Dierdre Mears demonstrate poignantly, even many who wholeheartedly participated in the changing times came to look back in ambivalence. Having experienced the costs of change, Cheryl and Dierdre join their conservative peers like Doreen Lawton in embracing in part the "old fashioned" rules because they lack other templates that would help them to envision restraint in individuals and safety in intimate relationships.

Swimming Against the Tide

Unlike their Dutch counterparts who describe adolescent sexuality as *gewoon* or normal—a cultural frame that dictates the behavior of parents as much as it describes the behavior of youth—the American parents have no unified narrative about the positive place of sexuality in adolescence and about parents' role in facilitating its constitution. Instead, the American parents view adolescent sexuality as a multifaceted drama—in which hormonal drives outdo reason, boys are pitted against girls and parents against teenage children, and in which unwanted consequences are all too often the result. Lacking a shared cultural frame such as *normal sexuality* through which Dutch parents both describe and prescribe a positive—and controlled—place for sexuality in the adolescent experience, the American parents find it difficult within the context of the interview to speak of teenage sexuality in terms other than the drama and its drives, divisions, and disasters.[16]

Thus, for most American parents it goes without saying that one does not permit a high-school-aged child to spend the night with a boy- or girl-friend. For while parents expect that teenagers—especially boys—are driven by hormones and girls pursue an often misguided quest for love, they also believe that such impulses easily lead young people astray: doubting teenagers' capacity to exercise self-control and common sense in sex, the American parents are genuinely frightened for their children's physical and emotional safety. Assuming that instrumentality, rather than intimacy, guides adolescent heterosexuality, they fear that teenagers will be burned by the battle between the sexes, and that an STD or an unintended pregnancy will derail them from their intended trajectories. Hence, they believe parents should sanction their children's sexual activity only when the latter have attained—or possess the capacity for—autonomous adulthood.

At the same time, many American parents convey that taking a firm stand against teenage sexual activity is like swimming against the tide. The sources of parents' ultimate powerlessness are multifold. The drives and desires that they imagine propel their teenage children away from parental protection inspire fear and awe. Although they discuss teenage sexuality mainly in terms of hormones and fantasies that are mistaken for love, when parents do talk about adolescents falling in love, they suggest love could derail a child's trajectory every bit as much as hormones could. Finally, given that sexuality culturally symbolizes the drive for autonomy from parents, and that parents are supposed to recognize their children as sexual actors only when they are adults, it is difficult for them to talk with teenagers about the realities of sex and intimacy and help them acquire the psychological skills to navigate their challenges.

What makes the sexual socialization of adolescents especially challenging for American parents, and what embroils the parents in the drama of adolescent sexuality, are not only the cultural frames of hormones and battles between the sexes which portray teenagers as unable to exercise the control and forge the intimacy to make sex safe. Also challenging are the criteria for the attainment of autonomy and legitimate sexuality that parents seek to instill—financial self-sufficiency, and, alternatively, marriage. Those criteria—and the definitions of adult personhood they communicate—propel young people into the world outside the parental home with gusto while cordoning off sexuality and romance as arenas in which parents have little or no actual input. These criteria, moreover, leave a lengthy gap between the time when young people start their sexual careers and the time when that part of their life can be fully recognized by parents.

This disconnect is partially historically constituted. Unlike the Dutch, who responded to the sexual revolution with a normalization of adolescent sexuality, grounded in and predicated on a shared ethics of self-regulation and interpersonal attunement, many American parents, even those who partook in the sexual revolution wholeheartedly, seem to have emerged from the pivotal decades of 1960s and 1970s more lost than found. Amidst a society that was becoming painfully reconfigured, many American parents experienced or saw the pursuit of pleasure—sexual and otherwise—run amok. And without having apparently found a new, post-sexual-revolution basis for social bonds, they became skeptical of adolescent intimacy and the institutions that shape it. In the absence of faith in new forms of self-mastery, intimacy, and societal cohesion, parents draw in their moment of need—when asked about what makes sex right for youth—on narratives more suited to a 1950s biography than to the lives their children are living.[17]

FOUR

Adversarial and Interdependent Individualism

The Puzzle

The previous two chapters have left us with a puzzle: the American and Dutch white middle-class parents I interviewed—who resemble one another closely in terms of age, occupation, and education—nonetheless differ dramatically in how they understand and respond to the sexual maturation of their teenage children. Dutch parents construct a nonproblematic, non-emotionally disruptive, and decidedly relationship-based adolescent sexuality. American parents, by contrast, construct adolescent sexuality as dangerous, conflicted, and deeply polarized. The difference between the American drama and the Dutch "normality tale" crystallizes around one striking contrast: a high-school-aged teen spending the night with a boy- or girlfriend at home is potentially permissible to nine out of ten Dutch parents, while this practice strikes nine out of ten American parents as beyond the pale, and even, quite frankly, as ludicrous.

What explains this dramatic difference between two otherwise similar groups? Are Dutch teenagers so different from American teenagers? This is part of the story. American girls are more than four times as likely to become pregnant and more than two times as likely to have abortions as their Dutch counterparts, even though they first have sex at comparable ages. Sharp differences remain even if we compare only white girls.[1] It also appears that Dutch teenagers are less likely to have sex outside of the context of monogamous romantic relationships.[2] In other words, when the American and Dutch parents talk about adolescent sexuality, they are referencing a different set of realities. But as we will see in later chapters, the experiences of American and Dutch teenagers are not as different as their parents would lead us to expect. The behavior of teenagers often—though not always—reinforces parents' expectations and approaches, but it does not explain them.

To understand why American parents dramatize and Dutch parents normalize, we must look at the two cultures of modern individualism that emerged out of the pivotal decades of the 1960s and '70s and that became embedded in both private and public institutions, including the welfare state, in the two countries during the last quarter of the twentieth century. These different cultures of individualism constitute distinct responses to the challenges to traditional authority relations and sexual morality. The common currents of technological, political, and cultural change that swept through the advanced industrial world, unsettling the existing patterns of power and possibility, were interpreted through country-specific cultural and political traditions and were filtered through country-specific historical contingencies. What resulted were different conceptions of how individuals come to control themselves, attain autonomy, and assert and accept authority.

The first section of this chapter examines cultural traditions that shaped the perception and experiences of the changes of the 1960s and '70s in the United States and the Netherlands. Out of the confluence of different cultural traditions, the social policies they influenced, and the different experiences of the upheavals of the unruly decades emerged what might be called an "adversarial" and an "interdependent" individualism. Using the interview material from parents who lived through these decades and began raising children in their wake, I then unfold the different individualisms by examining three "gray" areas parents confront as they guide their children through adolescence: the fostering of self-control, the attainment of adulthood, and the exercise of authority. Finally, we see how the individualism on which each set of parents draws sets up a logic that makes their approaches to teenage sexuality possible and plausible, in part because adversarial and interdependent individualism not only control but also constitute youth.

Concepts of Self and Social Change

The parents I interviewed—most of whom were born between the mid-1940s and mid-1950s—have seen the norms that govern behavior for adolescents and adults change dramatically in their lifetimes. The societies into which they were born dictated rigid gender roles between men and women and strict authority relations between parents and children.[3] But when, in the late 1970s and early 1980s, Dutch and American parents began raising their own children, a more egalitarian and individualistic childrearing ethic had come to prevail, especially among the middle classes.[4] In the 1990s, with their children poised at the cusp between childhood and adulthood, the American and Dutch parents said that they wanted their teenage children to become independent, self-determining individuals. Yet what it means to encourage these traits differs between countries, for parents in the two countries were referencing two different kinds of modern individualism.

A key difference between the two individualisms pertains to the relationship between the self and others. In their 1985 classic *Habits of the Heart: Individualism and Commitment in American Life*, sociologist Robert Bellah and his colleagues assert that "individualism lies at the very core of American culture."[5] Such individualism celebrates the sacredness of individuals and their judgment, self-reliance, and self-expression. But inherent in American individualism is also a tension between autonomy and society.[6] Indeed, write Bellah and colleagues, American individualism includes a fear that "society may overwhelm the individual and destroy any chance of autonomy unless he stands against it."[7] That fear is accompanied by the belief that, to attain full autonomy and to commit to others and contribute to society, "one must be able to stand alone, not needing others, not depending on their judgments, and not submitting to their wishes."[8]

Given that Americans view social ties as matters of individual volition rather than necessity, Bellah and colleagues worry that with the waning of cultural languages that have long encouraged Americans to make commitments to family, religion, and civic life, their social fabric is fragile. One cultural vocabulary that allows Americans to reconcile their conception of themselves as free agents with their need for union is, Ann Swidler argues, the ideal of love (in the context of marriage) because "it describes a relationship so right that it can be simultaneously perfectly free and perfectly binding."[9] But, argues family scholar Andrew Cherlin, Americans have ended up on a "marriage-go-round." Being both more individualistic and more attached to marriage as an ideal than their European counterparts, they are more likely to marry, divorce, and remarry again.[10]

If in the private sphere American individualism is accompanied by an exceptionally strong attachment to the institution of marriage, in the public sphere American individualism has gone hand in hand with an exceptionally punitive justice system. On the one hand, the celebration of self-reliance—and the stigmatization of dependency—have inhibited the institutionalization of income replacement programs that have made day-to-day living since the 1960s more secure in Europe.[11] On the other hand, the United States has long imposed harsh justice on those deprived of freedom.[12] Lacking a notion of membership in a wider society apart from individual volition, Americans see no alternative to punishment when individual volition proves insufficient to regulate behavior. Following the 1960s, the tradition of harsh justice grew into what David Garland has called "a culture of control": the divestment from public welfare accompanied by rapid growth in incarceration rates, especially since the start of the War on Drugs, which has imprisoned a large segment of population, often on minor charges.[13]

In contrast to a conception of the self as ideally completely self-reliant and unencumbered by social ties other than commitments that he or she has freely chosen, the Dutch conception of self situates the individual within the sociality of which he or she is part. Writing in 1987, North American anthropologist Peter Stephenson observes that "the concept of self with respect to others in the Netherlands is simultaneously intensely egalitarian and highly individualistic." Noting the expression, "One Dutchman a belief, two Dutchmen, a church, three Dutchmen, a schism," Stephenson argues that Dutch culture is characterized by a high degree of differentiation among individuals.[14] And yet, an equally pervasive cultural value is that of functioning and living in close interaction and cooperation with others, a potential contradiction that is resolved by a particular conception of the self as "a discrete individual who can nonetheless work well with others."[15]

The cooperative yet individualistic concept of self that Stephenson observes has multiple antecedents. Citing British historian Simon Schama, Stephenson traces it back to the seventeenth-century floods in the Netherlands, which instilled an understanding of interdependence and interreliance in Dutch citizens.[16] And the Dutch scholar Walter J. M. Kickert has argued that consultation and cooperation, aimed at consensus between leaders of different interest groups, are "centuries-old characteristics of the Dutch state." During the twentieth century, Kickert argues, this tradition informed Dutch industrial practices—including collective labor agreements between employers, unions, and government—and what political scientist Arend Lijphart has termed the Dutch "consensus democracy," whereby the elite representatives of interest groups—including religious groups—broker mutually acceptable compromises.[17] In the post-1960s era, this "politics of accommodation" was democratized to include new interest groups.[18]

Indeed rather than view equalization and individualization as a threat to the social fabric, prominent Dutch sociologists of the 1970s and 1980s argued that people were becoming more dependent upon one another, leading to the "emancipation" of previously subordinate groups—children, workers, women, and homosexuals.[19] They saw a new mode of regulating social relations in private and public life—negotiations between more or less equal parties who exercise self-restraint and willingness to consider each other's needs.[20] Theory reflected public policy. Following the expansion of the welfare state in the 1950s and '60s, Dutch society of the 1970s and '80s underwent one of the strongest equalizing trends in the industrial world.[21] And the assumption that people would, under controlled circumstances, self-regulate their impulses was reflected in a lenient penal policy, including the tolerance of soft-drug use, which was institutionalized in 1976.[22]

The cultural traditions—most notably about the self in relation to others—filtered the experience of the 1960s and 1970s and their aftermath in the two countries. Many scholars and lay individuals in the United States harbored misgivings about the changes wrought by shifts in sexual and authority relations in part because, ironically, the conception of the self, celebrated and feared in middle-class culture, does not provide tools to conceptualize and foster self-restraint and social bonds without institutions that can hold individuals in check: marriage, religion, and the justice system. In the Netherlands, by contrast, lay individuals, scholars, and policymakers embraced the gains of "modernization" because they could draw on cultural resources to reconcile growing self-determination with strengthening of social bonds: traditions of inter-reliance and cooperation between elites lent themselves as means for exerting "soft" control and maintaining stability at home and in the polity in a more democratic society.[23]

Notable is that order *was* in fact maintained in the Netherlands.[24] As we saw in the previous chapter, few Dutch parents describe their own coming of age as out of control.[25] Nor do they describe a fundamental uprooting of the mutual obligation between men and women noted by many American interviewees and by American feminist scholars who argued that the sexual revolution enabled the "flight of hearts" among men.[26] At the same time, interdependence between the sexes came at a price: until the 1990s, Dutch mothers were usually full-time homemakers.[27] In the 1970s and '80s, their participation in the labor force was a fraction of that of their American counterparts, even if the latter often worked by economic necessity rather than choice.[28] Finally, lacking the intergenerational battles over Vietnam and struggles over racial oppression, the Dutch did not confront the violence on their own soil that Americans did.[29]

Adversarial and Interdependent Individualism

Out of the confluence of nation-specific cultural traditions, historical trajectories, and policies emerged two different versions of modern individualism in the two countries. Asked to address three gray areas in the fostering of autonomy—the acquisition of self-control, the attainment of adulthood, and the exercise of authority—parents in the two countries illuminate what I call "adversarial" and "interdependent" individualisms. Presuming the antinomy between autonomy and social relationships of dependency, the former celebrates the capacity to leave the collectivity and establish full self-sufficiency, while at the same time it requires external control of adolescents' drives, using blatant force if necessary. The latter presumes mutual dependence of individual and relationships, which makes fostering autonomy a matter of encouraging self-determination and self-regulation within ongoing but changing relationships of interdependence, maintained through consultation.

I gauge the conception and management of autonomy in three areas. The first pertains to parents' perceptions of self-control. I gauge those perceptions by asking them about their conceptions of and approach to alcohol consumption. Because alcohol can enhance emotionality and impulsiveness, the question of when and how young people ought to be permitted to drink invites parents to articulate assumptions about teenagers' capacity to control their emotions and impulses. We will see that American parents articulate notions about alcohol that are similar to those about sexuality—the adolescent self who is not yet equipped to control the strong inner passions or peer pressures and whose potentially out-of-control drinking must be held in check by adult supervision. Dutch parents, by contrast, assume that young people can and will control their alcohol intake and place their drinking in the context of their participation in sociality.

The second topic is adulthood. While young people become legal adults at age eighteen in both countries, many middle-class youth remain financially tied to their parents for years thereafter. In both countries parents name independence as a criterion for adulthood. However, how they measure independence is quite different. American parents from across the political spectrum tend to agree that becoming an adult requires attaining economic and emotional self-sufficiency—which is measured by the ability to have made one's parents superfluous. Moving away from home is an important step in attaining such self-sufficiency. By contrast, Dutch parents do not conceptualize adulthood in terms of financial and emotional self-sufficiency or their own redundancy. Moving out of the home, while expected, is also not viewed as a radical break.[30] Instead, Dutch parents measure adulthood by the capacity for financial and emotional self-regulation and by the ability to hold one's own and express oneself *within* a sociality.

The exercise of authority is a third gray area. Since fostering autonomy involves granting teenagers increasing self-determination, and yet full autonomy is neither possible nor desirable for sixteen- or seventeen-year-old children, parents in both countries must occasionally exert their power as parents to keep their children on the right track. Doing so can cause conflict, especially since neither set of parents thinks unquestioning obedience is desirable, or even healthy, in adolescents. Parents reconcile respect for their children's growing autonomy with their need to use authority in different ways. The American parents describe "letting go" of the small things but "winning" the big battles, thereby validating overt conflict and power more than most of their Dutch peers, many of whom describe a process of what I call "continuous consultation" to reach "agreements" even on matters American parents do not describe as in need of regulation, such as eating.

Table 4.1   Two cultures of modern individualism

	American adversarial individualism	Dutch interdependent individualism
Alcohol	Impulse-driven teenager requires external control	Socially embedded teenager develops internal control
Adulthood	Requires financial and emotional self-sufficiency	Requires financial and emotional self-regulation
Authority	Winning important battles, letting go of small things	Continuous consultation to reach mutual agreements

In considering the cultural processes that American and Dutch parents bring to bear on these three dilemmas of the middle-class "adolescent-parenting project," it is important to recognize how these processes interact with the legal and economic opportunities and constraints young people and their parents encounter in the two countries. The consumption of alcohol, for instance, is more dangerous in the United States than it is in the Netherlands. Drinking beer and wine—but not harder liquors—is legal for Dutch sixteen-year-olds and illegal for their American peers. When youth drink outside the home in the Netherlands, they typically do so in established settings, like cafés and clubs to which they commute by bicycle, while in the United States, youth are relegated to illicit, age-segregated spaces to which they commute by car. Parents, moreover, can be charged for serving alcohol to teenagers.[31]

Achieving independence, like drinking alcohol, takes place in the context of a particular set of political and economic conditions and opportunities. Government supports for families and youth shape the process of attaining middle-class adulthood. For instance, all Dutch college students receive a modest government stipend to help pay for living expenses, and, if they chose, for housing away from the parental home.[32] American college students receive no such guaranteed grants. Moreover, those American students who attend private academic institutions face much greater expenses than do their Dutch counterparts. They remain more directly financially dependent on their parents than are Dutch young adults.[33] American parents who support their children through college have a financial leverage to "win" the battles they deem important. Adult autonomy *is* thus more contingent on financial self-reliance in the United States than it is in the Netherlands.

"Like Gasoline on a Bonfire"

The vast majority of Americans believe sixteen-year-olds are not ready to drink, other than at special family occasions, such as Thanksgiving.[34] They describe the adolescent self as operating without the capacity for self-restraint, leaving it at the mercy of strong internal and external impulses. Sixteen-year-olds are not ready, knows Jennifer Reed: "There are enough things that impair their judgment—their peers, their zest for life—that they don't need another thing [to do that]." Sixteen-year-olds lack the "brains" to control alcohol, Jany Kippen explains: "Too often young people don't have the ability and they don't think of the consequences of anything because they're immortal. They have this protective shell around them, and it's impenetrable, and there's nothing that is going to harm them." In Rhonda Fursman's words:

> [Teenagers] are living close enough to the surface of their skin emotionally that adding alcohol to it is like throwing gasoline on a bonfire. I don't think they can handle the mental and physical changes that alcohol produces at that stage. I see the normal, kind of, the stupid things they do when they are not drunk and I can only imagine that that would go to a power of ten if they are drunk.

The image of the reckless, drunken youth is thus at the forefront of American parents' imagination when they discuss alcohol use among teenagers.[35] They recount stories of alcohol-related (near) disasters among teenagers, not unlike the tales of doom they tell about out-of-control teenage sex. Deborah Langer learned about alcohol "the hard way." She wonders why "some of us choose to go through these silly things with alcohol. I'm glad I went through it and got on with it. I hope my kids don't. It's not something I want for them." But not everyone "gets on with it," Brad Fagan knows:

> There was a girl at our high-school class who started out drinking and then she smoked a little marijuana, pretty soon she was on cocaine. Ultimately her life ended as a prostitute in San Francisco and she got run over by a truck. [By then] her family had basically—tough love sort of—divorced her. They couldn't deal with her. She was burned out. Her brain was fried from various drugs. This girl was cute, perky, smart, and was on the rally squad. She was one of us.

It is not that all abandon is wrong. But as is true for sex, there is a time and a place for drinking. That time and place, says Helen Mast, is after turning twenty-one and moving out: "You go through that phase where you have to be wild and reckless and do whatever you want to just because you need to experience it and you're told so many times by your parents, 'Don't do that.' And so you go, 'Now I can do it because I'm old enough to do it and they're not around to tell me "No" because I live by myself and now I can do it and get away with it.'" After that period, Helen explains, follows one in which a person attains a balance between letting go and being in charge:

> You can still be crazy and everything else but you don't let it rule you. At that time, sometimes the alcohol rules you for a while. You have to be so cool, so you have to get smashed every Thursday, Friday, and Saturday night at the bar, but after that you reach [a point] that you go, "Oh, that's dumb. Been there, done that. Let's move on to something better."

But during the high-school years, drinking alcohol is wrong. Parents say they would have strong reactions if they found out their children were drinking, even though many did so themselves. Calvin Brumfield, who experimented with drugs as a teenager himself, has told his son, "No drinking, no drugs, no smoking." Jany Kippen drank as a teenager, but if her sons were to do so, "they're probably going to get grounded because I still think they need to know that's not acceptable. It wasn't acceptable for me, it's not acceptable for them." If his fifteen-year-old daughter Lisa were to come home and say, "I had a couple of beers at a party," Brad Fagan would take radical action:

> Her life would be rearranged rapidly. . . . She would lose some of her independence. Depending on why—and that's sort of in the category of letting her make mistakes. Depending on what came out of that, if that was a one-shot-deal, maybe not a lot. But if it was like, "Yeah, I like that and I might do that again," major things would start happening, maybe with counselors, family counseling. . . .

But rules, punishments, and counseling are not the whole story. Many American parents employ an additional, "secondary" approach to alcohol which is more lenient.

In Jennifer Reed's household, the "party line" has been "don't [drink] under any circumstances." At the same time, she is not "naïve enough to think that they're not going to have any experience with alcohol until they are twenty-one." She went to parties, "So I probably wouldn't have a conniption fit as long as I knew that they weren't putting themselves or someone else at risk." Jennifer does not, however, tell her sons about her experiences. "I would be worried that they would take that as the green light," particularly right now. "I mean if they want to enjoy alcohol later in life that's fine. I just think it's just a little too risky right now." Instead, she has told them:

> If they're ever in a situation that they need to get out of, and they don't want to tell us why—if it's drugs or alcohol or they're just uncomfortable—they're always free to make the phone call and say, "Come get me," especially when they can't drive, and we won't ask. We'll just let it go by.

Rather than provide an unofficial escape clause to the official no-drinking rule, other American parents openly permit some drinking under their direct supervision. Even as they firmly oppose teenagers' drinking on their own, such parents believe in letting their children try alcohol in "controlled situations." Alicia Groto permits her sons to drink on special occasions, though they are not allowed to do so "independently." But as Henry Martin illustrates, parents who permit alcohol in certain circumstances must be very careful, given that drinking before age twenty-one is illegal, while driving is legal at age sixteen. Hence, American teenagers who drink are at serious physical and legal risk:

When we go to the beach or something, I've given [my sons] a beer.... When we go out, they like to have a drink of my drink just to see what it's like. But I don't want them being social drinkers. Number one, it's illegal and, if they get caught with a DUI, it will really affect their lives. I want them to know what alcohol is about, but I don't want them to use it as something social.

"It's a Part of *Gezelligheid*"

The majority of Dutch parents say sixteen-year-olds are ready to drink in moderation, either at home or in the cafés and discos they frequent on the weekends.

Helen de Beer, for instance, believes her sixteen-year-old daughter Lorena is ready to drink "in moderation." After all, alcohol is "part of life, it is a part of *gezelligheid*." There are few words with more of an unequivocally positive cultural connotation than the word *gezelligheid* in the Dutch language. Literally translated as "togetherness," "sociability," or "conviviality," *gezelligheid* has no comparable counterpart in English. Used to describe moments of pleasant togetherness with family, friends, or colleagues—moments which can range from the everyday and ordinary to the specifically festive—*gezelligheid* for the Dutch connotes one of the most treasured states of existence.

The Dutch parents view the wish to participate in *gezelligheid* through drinking alcohol as a legitimate and respectable motivation for adolescents as well as for adults. Since drinking is legal at age sixteen while driving is illegal until age eighteen, Dutch parents have fewer acute dangers to worry about than do their American counterparts. Still, it is striking that few worry about the dangers of drinking. Marlies de Ruiter says alcohol has become "so much part of our society. . . . They see it at home, and then I think that as a sixteen-year-old, you are allowed to participate in that. I would hope though that as a sixteen-year-old, that they mainly drink at home and now and then when they go out." Christien Leufkens uses a similar line of reasoning. It is perfectly reasonable to offer sixteen-year-olds something to drink at home, Christien says, since "for us, having a glass of wine at dinner on the weekend is part of the culture. . . . Also [it is all right for them to drink outside the home], given that they want to partake in the nightlife."

In addition to validating their teenage children's wish to partake in sociability, Dutch parents express confidence that their children will moderate their alcohol intake. Jolien Boskamp, who expressed complete confidence in her daughter's capacity for sexual self-regulation, "just know[s Natalie] will also drink in moderation: She will drink one, two, maybe once she'll drink three beers, but then that will be enough." Similarly, echoing his confidence in his sixteen-year-old daughter's ability to use contraception effectively, Karel Doorman is comfortable with the fact that his daughter Heidi drinks a glass of wine "now and then." She is "ready for that," Karel explains: "Because she has [drunk] herself, and I know that she is very moderate in how she drinks. So given the way she drinks, she is really ready." Ria van Kampen also never "had problems" with Fleur drinking alcohol from time to time because "she is such a smart gal."

Not all Dutch parents express that level of confidence in their children's self-regulatory capacity. Parents of boys express more concern about too much drinking. Nevertheless, Dutch parents expect their sons also to learn to drink with acceptable levels of self-restraint. Karin Meier says her son Berend is ready to drink because "he wants to live a healthy life and drinking too much is not part of that [kind of life]." Jan Gaaij believes his son is old enough to drink now and then "in moderation" since Jan himself also drinks in moderation. Nienke Otten expresses more concern than most Dutch parents about teenage drinking, and she admits she would rather not have her seventeen-year-old son drink. Still, she does not take a hard line:

> If they really want to, you cannot keep them from the beers, but sometimes it goes of course beyond just one, that is the problem. [I won't say,] "Never do it." After all, they have to experience it. So I think even if they drink at sixteen, they need to have that experience. [They need to figure out answers to questions like,] How far do I want to go? Do I want to go along? They want to be together.

Like Nienke Otten, most Dutch parents believe learning to moderate oneself is something that young people need to and will learn, be it with a mistake here and there.

Hannie de Groot's son once drank too much. But "it is not like I thought 'now I really need to watch him.' No, I more or less trusted that it would turn out all right." Her husband Dirk agrees: "Because you had that experience yourself once too—that you drank and then the next day you thought, 'never again.'" By the time a person turns sixteen, he or she should have gained the ability to drink sensibly, Mariette Kiers believes: "At fourteen, you start tasting it secretively, you learn from that. By the time you're sixteen you should be able to sensibly drink a beer. . . . If you don't [drink], you can't know what it is." Corrine van Zanden also does not worry about her teenage children:

> I think they will discover that themselves [how far they can go]. I am not afraid of that. I think they can find those limits themselves. And they must experience it themselves once anyway, I say. If it ever happens, then I guess they must have that experience. I don't worry about that. [Laughing] And if they go too far one time, as long as they clean up the mess themselves if they are going to throw up.

Even when Dutch parents are confronted with evidence of excessive behavior, they still resort to the self-regulatory model for teaching about how to control it. When Marga Fenning's son came home drunk at age fifteen, she was angry but she did not tell him, no alcohol: "It's ridiculous to forbid it; it's not like he needs to drink soda all night. [But] I told him, 'It is fine if you drink something but at a certain point, you have to stop.'" It worked, she says, "After that it never happened again." When her fourteen-year-old son told his father that he recently drank ten beers while socializing at the club where he plays sports, Ria van Kampen was taken aback, but not alarmed:[36]

> We don't say, "You are not allowed to do that." Instead we say, "Wow, that takes us by surprise that you are so far [along]. We didn't think you were that far." [I think that a person] has to experiment [with alcohol]. So you get sick once or you need to throw up the next day. . . . It is kind of funny if that happens once.

Passing the Trial by Fire

There are no two ways about it. To be an adult, you need to be earning your own living, American middle-class parents across the political spectrum agree. To be an adult, earning a living is "very important, a major criteria," says Jennifer Reed, a social conservative. "That's the goal you would shoot for." She expects her son to "be a responsible citizen and self-sufficient." Cheryl Tober's daughter Stephanie will be an adult "when she's self-sufficient. When she's able to take care of herself and go out there and be on her own, pay her own way." Dierdre Mears, the self-described ex-hippie, will consider her son an adult "when he graduates from college and is off our medical plan. And, that's not that I'm trying to get rid of him, but the point at which he becomes substantially self-sufficient, that's the criterion." Asked to explain what she means by "substantially," she says, "financially, emotionally, and psychologically self-sufficient."

According to American parents, not being dependent anymore on other people, especially one's parents, is key to being and feeling like an adult.[37] To "feel like an adult sometimes you have to have some money of your own, and if you don't feel like an adult, you don't act like one either," believes Jany Kippen. Alicia Groto concurs, "You never feel completely independent until your parents are no longer supporting you." Nancy Beard will consider her children adults when "they seem to be able to handle their own problems, to be financially independent [and] stand on their own two feet." Depending on parents financially is not being really free, Doreen Lawton explains:

> If you look at kids who can't quite make it every month, and they still have to ask Mom and Dad for money, they're not adults because they're still tied to having to have financial access, and when you have the financial access, unfortunately, there's usually strings attached, so you're not free to be your own person. So you need to be financially independent of your parents.

One of the most passionate articulations of the belief that adult independence requires a radical break from the "ties that bind" comes from Pamela and Brad Fagan, well-to-do business owners who themselves grew up in modest middle-class families. Pamela will consider her daughter, a freshman in college, an adult when she is "a completely independent, self-contained adult . . . when she has graduated from college and is supporting herself." Brad explains: "Sara still needs us and uses us as her emotional sounding board, wants to come home. [Right now, it's] sort of like, leaving the nest but coming back to get recharged and then going out again, and the gaps are getting longer, and I think for Sara probably in another year or two, she'll quit needing us that way."

Although they are well-off, Pamela and Brad have been very clear about the limits of the financial support that their children will be receiving. "The kids are real clear," Pamela says. "They know that this is our feeling. We will support them through college. We want them to get a college education. That's their goals too, but they know that, 'Hey kids, it's up to you. You need to make your own way in the world and that's how you learn and feel good about yourself and figure out who you are and what you're doing and what you'd like to do.'" Brad explains that healthy maturation requires being forced to weather hardship and obstacles on one's own. As a parent he might choose to support his adult children at times, but he is under no obligation to do so:

> I think the analogy is—I heard this—that in Australia there's corals outside the Great Barrier Reef that aren't protected and they're very healthy and vibrant and they grow very rapidly. And then there are corals that live inside where the waves can't hit them and they're not as challenged and it's sort of stunted coral. And that's the way I think life is. It's the challenges and adversity that gives us our character and our uniqueness and that ultimately people thrive on. . . . [My daughters] are going to be on their own. There's going to be a point where, in a catastrophe, they could move back, but there will be a clear message: "You are on your own. And you are to make your way in the world, and I don't participate in giving you money unless I choose to, and you have to make your own way."

American middle-class parents like to see evidence of their children's outward push away from the home, even before they are able to financially support themselves. They are relieved when their children want to go away to college far away from home. Cheryl Tober really hopes both her children will "go away" to college: "I think that they grow up a lot faster when they are away." Jennifer Reed wants her son "to go somewhere else" for college. "That sounded bad. Didn't it?" she adds. Her son is a homebody, and she expects him to go to college in-state, somewhere within driving distance but "hopefully a couple of hours away." Rhonda Fursman is delighted that her daughter Kelly "wants to explore. She is ready to go all the way to the East Coast. . . . She is ready to go." Her son might "be a little more problematic." Unlike her daughter, Sam is a popular and social child. "Because of his attachment to the local community and his friends, he might decide he wants to spend two years at a junior college." But Rhonda says:

> I would like the kids to be gone. I really think they should go away, if it is at all possible, just because Corona is a small town. And it is not the center of the universe. And I think they need to go see other places and see other people. . . . I might kick [Sam] out anyway, because he needs to go.

Although financial self-sufficiency remains for most American parents the ultimate criterion for independence, moving out is a good first step. For middle-class children, many of whom will be financially dependent until their early twenties, demonstrating readiness "to go" is an important marker. Brad Fagan, who spoke so eloquently about the crucial role of financial self-sufficiency in achieving healthy adulthood, conceptualizes his daughter's move to college in similarly dramatic terms. He is not sure whether she will be ready to move out when that moment comes. However, he believes, children "need to move out when they're eighteen. It's sort of a *trial by fire*. I mean, ready or not, there it comes because they need to catch up with the real world."[38]

Preparing the Coffee on One's Own

In sharp contrast to their American counterparts, Dutch middle-class parents do not believe that earning a living is necessary to becoming an adult.[39] "Being an adult does not have to do with money," says Ada Kaptein. Money "does play a large role [in society] these days. But it has nothing to do with being an adult. No." Trudie van Vliet agrees. Being an adult has to do with "how you are mentally, how you deal with the normal situations of life but not whether you make money or not." Both Ada Kaptein and Trudie van Vliet are full-time homemakers. But Jos de Vries, a self-employed business man, also says, "I don't think [working] has anything to do with being an adult."

It is not that earning one's own living is not important eventually, because it is. But it does not constitute the defining feature of adulthood. Karin Meier thinks earning money is important in adulthood, but her son, Berend, will be an adult before he is financially self-sufficient: "Going to university I see as a sort of work. He gets money for that," referring to the student stipend Berend will receive from the government when he starts going to college. A couple of parents stress that they want their children to work rather than rely on government benefits as a long-term way of life: "We don't give [our children] that attitude," says Jacqueline Starring. Her husband Piet adds, "No, I do think that they must work." However, Piet would regard his son as an adult in college even if he were not able to contribute financially since, "Yes, studying is like working." Likewise, Loek Herder believes earning an income "eventually is important," but:

> [Earning one's own income] does not need to happen very early on. You know, if they are in college [they don't earn their own income]. . . . I do hope [my son] will earn his own money, certainly. [I hope] that he would not become unemployed or go on disability benefits or whatever. . . . But it is not like he would not be able to be an adult [just] because [he relies on government benefits], that is another story.

If not earning an income, what then defines adulthood in the Netherlands? Taking care of oneself, say Dutch parents. Though earning a living through employment is not the yardstick, "taking care of oneself" *is* critical to being, and being considered, an adult. Dutch parents articulate a concept of "self-care" which revolves around being able to sensibly regulate one's everyday affairs. Jolien Boskamp says an adult is "someone who can think sensibly. I think that is the most important thing for adulthood— being able to think and act in a sensible manner." Adulthood, Corrine van Zanden explains, is when people "can organize matters well. They can say 'I have time for this then, and time for that then. I do this thing this way and I do the other thing that way.'" Apparently exasperated at being asked to explain what she regards as self-evident, Corinne repeats, "[Being an adult means] being able to organize everything well and regulate everything well." Ria van Kampen articulates precisely what "taking care of oneself" means to her:

> [Adulthood] has to do with whether or not you dare to express your own opinions and how you relate to others, whether you can . . . well . . . take care of yourself. That means eating healthy and eating on time. It means that you keep an eye on things like, "Now I am tired, I should go to bed a little earlier," or, "Now I am having a good time, now I am going to make a night of it." It means you can correct yourself and have your own opinions. [My daughter, Fleur] can take care of herself very well. She can spoil herself and she can also work very hard.

In other words, Dutch parents make the criterion for adulthood exactly the type of autonomous self-regulatory capacity they believe teenagers are developing. But unlike the definition of self-care and autonomy that American parents use as the criterion for independence, the independence that Dutch parents describe does not require *onafhankelijkheid*, or nondependence on others. In fact, a critical part of *zelfstandigheid*, or independence in regulating one's affairs, involves other people—and learning how to independently manage one's own affairs in relationship to the needs of other people.

When they talk about the criteria for moving out of the parental home, Dutch parents do not talk about the need to be driven by strong passions and interests, as do their American counterparts. Instead of the excitement that American parents associate with "striking out on one's own," Dutch parents speak of the mundane. Katinka Holt says that to be ready to move out, one has to be able to take care of oneself: "Eating dinner on time, cooking . . . maintaining things, keeping up your room." Loek Herder says that to move out, her son Paul "needs to be able to regulate his affairs. . . . For instance, he has forms from school that he needs to send in. Right now, we do that together [because otherwise he'll] forget that. He is very messy. He always leaves things lying around." To move out, a person must "be well organized, not be impulsive," says Corrine van Zanden. Her own seventeen-year-old daughter is almost there, she thinks. "She really thinks about things before she does them, like when [her friends] call her and she needs to do her homework first, she'll do her homework first and only go out after."

In fact, the strong passions that American parents believe will lead their children toward the autonomy required for adulthood might well hinder the kind of self-care that Dutch parents believe is necessary for adulthood. Perhaps because it is indicative of the capacity for self-regulation, Dutch middle-class parents are more likely to emphasize the importance of knowing how to spend wisely than knowing how to generate an income. Helen de Beer says her daughter must grow more independent before she can move out, like learn how to "do the small grocery shopping, buy food, [and] keep her finances under control." Being independent has less to do with bringing in money, says Hannie de Groot, than with knowing how to manage expenses, knowing "what can I spend, what can I not spend? I have so much student stipend. What can I do with it, what can't I?"

There is one aspect of the process of children becoming adults for which Dutch parents use dramatic, emotionally loaded language. Compared to their American counterparts, Dutch parents are more likely to talk about anticipating feelings of loss. Dirk de Groot hopes his daughter will elect to study in a city nearby and live at home: "You always hope that they stay home as long as possible." But his wife adds, once that moment comes, "as a parent you must say, 'I step over [my own feelings of loss] and I go along with it.' And then I will really support her, even if you find it really hard and sad." Jolien Boskamp is glad that her daughter Natalie has declared that she wants to stay home while she goes to college. "That is *gezellig*" (cozy), Natalie told her mother. Jolien does not understand why others move out: "Maybe some children don't like it at home—you know, maybe it is *gezellig* and good with their parents, but there is some reason why they don't feel free. Maybe that is why they want to leave." Luckily, her daughters don't feel that way: "I wouldn't mind if they always stay with me."

Children too are expected to miss the *gezelligheid* of home. Loek Herder thinks her son is too messy to move out on his own, but she also doesn't "know whether he is emotionally ready." That is even more important "than all those other things I mentioned because [those practical matters] will turn out all right eventually. Emotionally, I don't think he's ready because, well [laughing], then I won't be able to sit and talk with him any more at night." Anne van Wijngaarden is more confident about her son's capacities. But when her son moves out, Anne says, he will miss his parents' company. "He could leave today," Anne knows. "He can take care of himself. He is so critical of himself already. He would miss the *gezelligheid*, but he loves being alone. [Then] he can regulate everything, he likes that. But he will miss the *gezelligheid*."

Being able to manage the loss of the *gezelligheid* that the parental home provides, and substituting self-generated *gezelligheid* for it, is critical to being able to move out. To make that transition, one needs to be able to manage loneliness. Margo Schutte thinks the main thing her daughter needs to learn before she can leave home is to "accept that you are alone. I think that that will be the biggest problem for her. That is what she is most reticent about. At home you are seldom alone. Sure, when you are in your own room, but there is always someone else around. And I think that is the difficult step of leaving home, and of being independent, that all that [being alone] costs a lot of energy and emotions."[40] Karel Doorman describes poignantly the loneliness he expects his daughter to encounter on the road to adulthood. To move out, Karel says:

> You need to have a good sense of what it means to really be alone . . . to spend a whole week alone: those evenings, when you don't get visitors you know coming by for a cup of coffee. Really, you can't be ready for that. You just need to do it. You need to learn that, experience it. . . . [And I wonder,] "What is she going to do with her laundry, what happens if she has to work, and study, and what time does she come home at night and so forth." But I imagine that just like most children she'll push through that, but also that she'll spend some nights in bed crying, thinking, "It was not quite what I had imagined it would be."

It is exactly when Heidi will have managed to create a "home place" for herself, both practically and emotionally, that Karel will consider her "economically independent" and an adult. Economic independence means not financial self-reliance but mastery over, and comfort within, an independent household. Karel will consider Heidi *zelfstanding* "when, as a twenty-year-old, she has lived for two years in Utrecht on her own." Then, "I will still financially support her in large measure. She will be an adult then, but not financially self-reliant (*onafhankelijk*)." Though not financially self-reliant, Heidi will then surely have learned to make and drink her cup of coffee alone.

Battles that Cannot be Lost

American parents typically report a fair amount of explicit conflict with their teenage children over everyday matters. Thinking back to the time when her daughters were sixteen, Flora Baker says they would have conflicts about "anything: curfew, shopping, if I wouldn't drive them somewhere, if they talked back—and they did, a lot." They attribute these conflicts to the "rebellion" that is a normal part of adolescent development. Flora thinks conflict during the teenage years is inevitable: "To some degree I think everybody experiments. They rebel. They want to do something different, something fun." Looking back at the arguments with her two oldest children, Nancy Beard says she always believed they would "turn themselves around and come back to what they know is right. Jodi and Art have done that. They have done their little teenage rebellious thing, but they have come back and are becoming responsible, loving adults."

If a certain amount of rebellious energy is a natural part of adolescent development, then, American parents suggest, forcefully opposing that energy on critical issues is a key component of properly parenting teenagers. To describe such confrontations, American parents often use the metaphor of the *battle*. Harold Lawton is among the parents who use the most combative language. If, in conflict with Jesse, "the issue was unimportant or we were tired, we would let it slide." However, "if it was important or we had the energy, we would press the issue until he complied with our point of view." This meant "making it progressively more difficult for him not to comply, until he finally realized that we will prevail and it is useless for him to press the issue any further, [and he realized that] it is a continuous *tug of war*. We *win* all the issues we think are important and the other ones, sometimes we don't."

Jennifer Reed's son, Daniel, was "very rebellious" as a young teenager. "He's always been very strong-willed, and he went through puberty at a very young age. . . . He would get these emotional surges of anger; every emotion was this surge and there were times when he was uncontrollable." When Daniel was most "uncontrollable," there were times when she thought, "Okay, *military* academy. There's a reason for those places. Put the boys in there, and let them go through all this stuff." These days, Jennifer sees her son as "a nice young man," but, to get to this point, she had to work through things like, "No, you're not going to get everything you want. Yes, you do have to call if you're out." But when Jennifer held firm, her son came around. "And [now] he's actually very responsible." Her younger sons learned from their older brother's conflict, and know they won't "be able to just run loose, and boys want to do that. They think they should have total control over their lives and that nobody should be telling them what to do."

Like Jennifer, numerous American parents talk openly about feelings of anger and mistrust. When Flora Baker disagrees with her kids, she "yell[s]. I do. It's terrible." Then, her children "yell back." Harold Lawton describes the teenage years as a period when children "start out as vicious animals and end up human beings," but only thanks to their parents' hard work. Deborah Langer has always told her kids, "If I can't trust the choice of friends or I feel that you have told me a lie about something, I thought you were going to be somewhere and you're not—then your privileges are going to get really small." Carole Wood's daughters "have mood swings that are really triggered by something very simple. There are lots of tears that just seem to come out of nowhere. They're very angry about things that are really not, in my mind, a big deal. Very self-centered, especially my girls and especially at fourteen, fifteen, and sixteen."

While more conservative American parents have few qualms about regarding adolescence as a battle where parents must exact obedience through sheer use of force, the more liberal American parents describe trying to reason and compromise. When he disagrees with his son, Calvin Brumfield makes sure Adam "understands our point of view and I want to understand his point of view. And if I understand where he's coming from or how he feels about it, lots of times, it's a compromise, you know, compromise on both parts, you know, instead of being stuck, you know, on a polar position." When Iris DiMaggio disagreed with her son Phillip about his hairstyle, she "finally just turned to him and said, 'Okay, do whatever you want with your hair. Just please humor me and don't make it blue or green.' And he said, 'Okay, fine.'" Then, they "came to that agreement. He could shave it. He could wear it long. He could do whatever he wanted just not color it an odd color, an unnatural color. So we agreed."

But even liberal Americans occasionally use unilateral force and punishment. Asked about conflict resolution, Laurie Williams says laughingly that she and her daughter Margaret "are very good actually." They can discuss conflicts: "We are both very reasonable. I try to see her side, she tries to see mine. We try to compromise. . . . [But] a lot of times, [Margaret] doesn't want to give up her stand, and then I just have to make a decision of what

I feel at that point, if there is no compromise." Rhonda Fursman had made an agreement with her son that his curfew was to be 11:30. But then, "he showed up about 1:00 in the morning, and his curfew got pushed back to ten o'clock for the entire summer, which he did not like at all. But it was. I told him, he violated our agreement and our trust issues." Sometimes, Rhonda worries that she's been too liberal with her son, and whether a stricter approach might have been better. When she grew up:

> You had definite rules that you didn't do, there was a lot of "you didn't do," and things that you were expected to toe the line about. And so it was easier to rebel because you had all these rules of things you weren't supposed to do. You were very daring if you sneaked out for a smoke or something like that. I think that because things have liberalized enough, kids don't have as many clear-cut things that they are not supposed to do. To some extent I see this as escalating. They have got to find new and more shocking things to prove that they are different.

The belief that a certain amount of struggle is necessary for children to prove they are different may explain why even fairly liberal parents often describe their relationship with their teenage children in antagonistic terms. Nancy Beard speaks of having just called a "truce" with one of her daughters. Iris DiMaggio tries to reach agreements when she can: "You have to give them more responsibility, and they have to learn to use that responsibility. It tends to be very difficult: knowing when, as we put it, to *yank the rope*, and when to just let go." Dierdre Mears explains that being out in the country means her children live in *"a wonderful form of prison*. I mean, my kids live in a *beautiful prison*. I can keep them out of the mall. We don't get television reception out here without using a satellite dish. I can actually insulate [them], to a certain degree, to stuff I neither believe in or like." Nevertheless, Dierdre suspects her son recently drank alcohol. She told him:

> "Frankly I don't care what the answer is [with regard to whether or not you drank alcohol]," and I meant that. And I said, "But these are the things that I want you to know, and these are the things that I respect. If you want to know how to get more responsibility and privilege in your life, then this is *how the game's set up*."

With her mix of liberal and conservative attitudes, Jany Kippen articulates well the two approaches that American parents take to conflict with their teenage children. The first stresses the importance of "letting go" of little things; the second stresses the necessity of "winning" the critical battles. Jany disagrees with her son's choice of clothes, but she has learned to respect his choices and keep her opinions to herself:

> He's into that baggy look. I hate it, but that's getting better. He's kind of outgrowing that phase. Actually, we don't disagree that much. I have always been amazed at that, but it may be because we talk a lot. They are pretty free to talk to me, and I try to bite my tongue if I don't like what they are saying and keep my opinions to myself until it's time to give my opinions.

More often than not, Jany and her son resolve conflicts through a compromise. But Jany is not so affable on all matters. Like many American parents, Jany will tolerate baggy clothes and strange haircuts but draws the line at earrings or other forms of piercing. "I pick my battles and *there are certain battles I refuse to lose.*" What other battles might she refuse to lose?

> There will be no smoking in my house. If I ever catch him smoking, he's grounded and *dead meat*. Drugs will never be here. That is not a battle I will lose and, if it requires pulling him out and sending him to a military academy, that's what'll happen. He knows those things. . . . He knows those are non-conditional rules. There's no room for bargaining here. There's no room for argument.

Agreements that Cannot be Forgotten

Like their American counterparts, Dutch middle-class parents say that adolescence is a period of heightened conflict in a family, at least theoretically, that is. In fact, there is a Dutch word specifically meant to describe the contentious teenage child, namely, the *puber*. The *puberteit* technically refers to the early teens when children go through puberty. In practice, however, the term *puber* is used mainly to refer to those teenage children who are especially contentious, as in "real *pubers.*" The term can be applied to a person at any time during his or her youth—or even adulthood. Thus, sometimes a teenager is called a *puber* years after the physical changes of puberty have taken place. Parents may even speak of a twenty-year-old son or daughter who is being extraordinarily disagreeable or impulsive as going through a late *puberteit.*

Asked how one notices that a child is becoming a *puber*, Mieke Aalders says, "Well, that he simply does not listen to you anymore and wants to follow his own mind. . . . To push through their will, that is of course *really* puber." In the *puberteit*, children become "a bit more critical," says Nienke Otten, "a bit more . . . insolent." *Pubers*, Daphne Gelderblom explains, are more "difficult." They have "a more clear own opinion, and at a certain point they push off against you. They start to look at, 'Where are your boundaries? Where are my boundaries? Where are your ideas and where are mine?' And a child that is in the elementary school will do that in a more questioning manner, while a *puber* does that in a more postulating manner." Mariette Kiers, a developmental psychologist, gives her professionally informed take on the *puberteit*:

> Around eleven, twelve, thirteen, fourteen, you have a fairly egocentric period. That makes sense with all the changes in body and being and at that same time changing from elementary to secondary school. . . . Around fifteen, sixteen—if everything is all right—they are more or less back in balance. Twelve, thirteen, fourteen-year-olds are allowed to still be very unreasonable. [Children are] not taken totally seriously when they are in the *puberteit*.

Maybe because of this connotation of "not being taken totally seriously," quite a few Dutch parents insist that neither they nor their children were ever "really *pubers*." Helen de Beer "never really had *pubers*. Measured against what people describe as the *puberteit*, I don't really have that—contrary children, the revolution at home, I don't have that at all." Thinking back to his own adolescence, Karel Doorman does not recall having "a really heavy *puberteit*," nor does he see signs of such a development in his own children. Finally, Barbara Koning never saw her children "as *puber* in the sense of, 'Oh, I have two *pubers*.'" Of course, "they did have that phase both of them, but it was not in that sense. Both boys were reasonably easy. So, even in the time when they started to develop and come into the *puberteit*, I never saw them as *pubers*."

If few Dutch middle-class parents will admit to having *puber* children themselves, many also have trouble naming any conflicts that have occurred in their family. Jolien Boskamp says she has "very few" disagreements with her daughter Natalie. Corrine van Zanden is also hard-pressed to recall disagreements she had with Petra when the latter was sixteen. And Ada Kaptein cannot think of any conflict: "No, absolutely not [any conflicts]. No, knock on wood. No, I don't believe that there are conflicts. No, we don't really argue." Even annoyances do not lead to arguments: "No, we really have a good household. . . . [Ours] is a very close-knit family. . . . We are really very close."

Even those who talk about serious sources of conflict are quick to say conflicts are not *as bad as all that*. Marga Fenning mentions a variety of conflicts in the course of the interview—over alcohol, sex, school—but when asked explicitly to talk about whether or not she had conflicts with her son, she says, "Thomas is an easygoing child. . . . Really, I did not have that many [conflicts] with Thomas." Katinka Holt's daughter Marlies drank excessively at least once and started smoking pot. But when asked what Katinka and Marlies disagreed about, Katinka says, "Well, about the time of coming home, I think. But beyond that, well it really has *not been as bad as all that* with her, I think."

Of course, some Dutch parents do describe their children as "real *pubers*." But when they do, parents tend to attribute their children's *puber-like* behavior to unusual circumstances rather than to "natural" rebellion, as do their American counterparts. Han de Vries says that when his stepdaughters were in their early and mid-teens, there was "an almost permanent conflict situation" about things like what time to come home. His wife, Mia Klant, responded to her daughter's *puberteit* with a lot of anger. It was difficult, Mia explains, to "accept that they have their own opinion." Han elaborates:

> [When they are children] their opinion is our opinion and it almost has to be that way. In the *puberteit*, all that changes and children want parents to have their opinions and ideas. After that, you are again simply individuals who sometimes have the same opinion and sometimes different ones. . . . Now they have become more social, we can have fun together. . . . That is really lucky because we could have just as easily killed them in the *puberteit*.

Looking back, Han believes his strong feelings of anger at the time were wrong. He says he and Mia reacted in "the wrong way" to the *puberteit*: "One could barely speak of any reason, from either side." At the time, Han had just moved in with Mia. Unhappy about the new family configuration, his stepdaughters turned their *puberteit* "into a pretty aggressive attempt to get rid of me again." Mia concurs, "Of course, we were also a bit in love, well a bit, very in love, and all such things. So we were also a bit guilty." Han thinks Mia and he lost their sense of perspective during the conflicts. "In terms of behavior, there may not even have been such a difference between them and us." He thinks "maybe it is possible that [as a parent] you can be a *puber* at the same time that your children are." His daughters have long left behind the *puberteit*. "Not that they don't occasionally have *puber-like* tendencies," Han adds. "But then again so do we."

Han could tell the *puberteit* had passed when "we settled things in a normal manner through exchanging words back and forth, and that [our daughter] took account of our advice when she deliberated [about her own choices]." You can tell that a person has ceased to be a *puber*, Daphne Gelderblom explains, when parents and children find themselves more in the "sphere of consultation: it is no longer two opinions that can oppose one another, but it is more, 'Gee, let's move together in that direction.'" Her friend Margo Schutte concurs: "When children are *pubers*, as parents you make conscious compromises with them. After a while, you don't feel anymore that they are compromises. No, then it is more a question of consulting with one another."

To engage in consultations or *overleg* means to negotiate in a reasonable manner what one wants. But consultation goes beyond the American word negotiation; it requires also the aptitude to "take into account" the (sometimes unarticulated) wishes of others. Moreover, both parties must be willing to stretch. When executed successfully, consultation proves to be a very effective method of soliciting compliance, so many Dutch parents indicate. Anne van Wijngaarden "consults" with her children. "So it gets discussed, 'What time would you like to come home?' What we decide is then acceptable to them, too, and then we average out." Consequently, Anne explains, her children are always on time. Marlies de Ruiter also found consultation to be effective:

> Really, [deciding what time the children must be home at night] happens in consultation. Sometimes we initially don't agree with one another about the time of coming home. . . . But generally it goes fine, so that even if I initially disagree with the time, we can agree about the time in such a way that I think "Well, I would like it if it were an hour earlier." [But] they do keep themselves to that time even if they had to meet me halfway.

Unlike their American counterparts, Dutch parents do not talk about "curfews." Few even use the word "rules." Instead they speak of "agreements" (*afspraken*) which result from mutual consultations. Such agreements may regulate anything from the time a teenager goes to bed to the first vacation he or she takes alone. One the one hand, consultation can involve more external freedom of movement than most American middle-class parents are comfortable granting teenagers. For instance, when her fifteen-year-old daughter Fleur wanted to go to Spain on her own, Ria van Kampen "consulted" with her. They agreed that Fleur would go to Spain with an organization that provided a lot of guidance. This year, Ria and

Fleur agreed that she would be allowed to make the trip on her own and Ria is confident that Fleur will be able to "handle herself just fine."

One the other hand, continuous consultation, whether spoken or unspoken, requires a great deal of consensus-seeking and mutual regulation of a type that seems natural to Dutch middle-class parents but that is itself a formidable form of constraint. Among the most consensus-oriented are Hannie and Dirk de Groot. Hannie says with certainty that in "ninety-nine percent of the cases [of disagreement] we come to an agreement. It is really seldom the case that that does not happen. Maybe sometimes, a half a day goes by that it is not like that, but we always end up agreeing." Moreover, far from "letting go" of the small things, consultation regulates them. The degree to which even mundane household matters were regulated in her host family dismayed the American exchange student who came to stay with Daphne Gelderblom:

> We had agreements that people don't just eat all day long whenever they feel like it. Very simple, that we assumed that you would eat breakfast together and that you discuss things together, you look at what you want to do together. We were on holiday, and then that [kind of consultation] makes quite a difference in terms of your activities. So that it is not like everyone for himself and God for us all, but that when you are with a family, you do things differently.

In a family, you try to harmoniously solve disagreements, says Mariette Kiers. This is the so-called "harmony model," which means "not to act as an authority figure who simply plucks a rule out of thin air." Mariette explains:

> We consult, we explain why—you know, try to demonstrate the reasonableness of our own point of view. . . . That is very Dutch. Yes, avoiding big conflicts yes. "We'll work it out together," you know that slogan. Intuitively, it makes a lot of sense to me. It's also a bit boring. I am not inclined to grab the emergency brake. I do, but only when [a child] has gone very far across the line of our agreements.

Like Mariette, Karel Doorman strives to find compromises with his daughter Heidi. He does so by adapting as a parent but also by requiring adaptation from Heidi herself. Having used that approach all along, Karel feels confident that he will continue to be able to regulate her behavior though consultation:

> At this point, Heidi knows quite well what I will call [our] norms and values, what [my wife and I] want, what we find pleasant, what we find less pleasant. And well, sometimes, she still wants something different. Well, on those points, I think it is very pleasant if we can come to something with which we are both satisfied. And in general, that lies in the middle. Really forbidding things, that we only seldom do at the moment. And really we don't need to.

Karel Doorman intimates, however, that beneath the "harmony model" runs an undercurrent of tension. He talks about how Heidi would like to work in a job between the last day of school and the vacation they will be taking as a family. However, Karel and his wife think that would be too busy. They may say, "That is not going to happen." But that kind of confrontation is rare, Karel says: "[Heidi] feels how strong we are in [some of our opinions]. She no longer looks for those boundaries because she knows that she won't make it. . . . She is getting to know us well. She knows that it is not going to happen without us having to explicitly say, 'It won't happen,' she realizes that." In other words, with the train on certain tracks, grabbing "the emergency brake" is unnecessary.

Cultures of Individualism and Control

This chapter has examined the two distinct individualisms that took shape in post-1960s American and Dutch middle-class families and other institutions. Built on longstanding cultural traditions, the two cultures of individualism forged nationally specific interpretations and experiences of the challenges to traditional sexual, gender, and authority relations. In the United States, the individualism of the post-1960s era built on a tradition of viewing the self as autonomous from others and social ties as matters of choice rather than necessity. Yet, these concepts of self and the social also made self-restraint and social bonds seem fragile when the institutions that had instilled order were changing. In the Netherlands, by contrast, lay individuals, scholars, and commentators could embrace growing self-determination because they still conceived of the self as embedded in a sociality where mutual attunement instills individual and societal order.

The Dutch and American parents who came of age during the 1960s and '70s illuminate these *adversarial* and *interdependent* individualisms that are products of the confluence of change and continuity. They use these different models of individualism and control to explain how they respond to a teenager who drinks alcohol, how they decide when it is time to treat an adolescent like an adult, how some transgressions make a child "dead meat," or how grabbing the "the emergency brake" is usually not really necessary. Each model has an internal logic. It makes sense to occasionally use blatant unilateral parental force if adolescents are impulsive by nature and autonomy can only come from having to struggle. And it makes sense to resolve conflict through consultation—even about small things—requiring all parties to engage in social attunement and self-regulation, when adolescents, like adults, are social by nature and autonomy equals sensible self-regulation and self-expression within a larger sociality.

Insight into these internal cultural dynamics sheds new light on several areas of cross-national variation that have puzzled researchers and social commentators: Americans of the post 1960s-era are in many ways deeply individualistic. Yet they remained more attached to the ideal of marriage, more devout in their religiosity, and more supportive of measures of harsh justice, for instance, than many of their European counterparts, including the Dutch. But the juxtaposition of these different values and attachments are not matters of contradiction, as often assumed: without a concept of self as intrinsically embedded in social relationships and institutions that support them and require restraint from them, Americans may be more inclined to embrace institutions and practices that exert a clearly external control over individuals and their impulses—whether in the form of marriage contracts, religious dictates, or the legal system.

The two models of individualism also make the American and Dutch parents' interpretations and management of adolescent sexuality commonsensical: it makes sense that American parents view teenage sexuality as a potential drama if teenagers are so impulsive that strong external stimulation has the effect of "gasoline on a bonfire." Moreover, if becoming an individual requires struggle, then bonds of love that are forged too early can threaten one's personhood, while the battle of the sexes is just one of many arenas in which a teenager fights for the right—or loses it—to be his or her own person. If healthy adult autonomy is predicated on the eradication of emotional and financial dependencies on others, one's parents in particular, then a sleepover at home—which domesticates new ties before old dependencies have been severed—violates the emotional trajectory required for attaining adulthood. Finally, if parental authority is contingent upon winning the critical battles, then it makes sense that parents forcefully forbid sexual activity they deem wrong rather than negotiate a place for it at home.

Similarly, the Dutch model of modern interdependent individualism makes the normalization of adolescent sexuality possible and plausible. If teenagers learn self-control through their participation in regular social intercourse, then adolescent sexuality, mediated as it is through relationships, need not to be feared for its dangerous consequences. If individuals can reach full adulthood within the social fabric of which they are part, teenage love can coexist with maturation. When adulthood is contingent on self-regulation in the context of ongoing relationships rather than on self-sufficiency, and control is exerted through implicit or explicit consultation rather than use of overt power, then it makes sense for parents to negotiate teenage sexuality in the home and to regard the sleepover not as a threat to the authority of parents nor the autonomy of children.

The two models of individualism not only interpret the behavior of teenagers; they also constitute and control it—though, as we will see shortly, by no means entirely. Each version of individualism permits its own freedoms and calls for its own restraints. The freedom that Dutch teenagers receive to drink and to have sex when they are ready is predicated upon the condition that they behave like the socially oriented and internally regulated individuals that their parents describe them to be. Their freedom not to be subjected to unilateral parental force is predicated upon the expectation that they behave "reasonably" and "take into account" their parents' wishes, of their own doing. That Dutch parents believe neither autonomy nor authority necessitates conflict suggests an expectation and a wish that their children will not be different from them.[41] It is no wonder that Dutch teenagers want to be but also sometimes resist being "normal."

American parents, by contrast, expect and encourage their children to be "different."[42] The centrifugal tendencies which parents hope will take their children, as adults, into the great unknown also induce anxiety and do not give them faith in teenagers' self-regulating capacities. Believing that autonomy requires a radical emotional and financial break between their children and themselves, American parents lack the trust of their Dutch counterparts in the essential similarity and continuity between parents and children. Having neither expected nor instilled the self-regulation and social attunement that Dutch parents require from their children, American parents use more overt forms of power. Yet, even as they insist on winning the important battles—and sexuality is one of those—with force if necessary, parents expect their children to evade and break the rules. No wonder then, that American teenagers spend a great deal of time hiding their sexual and drinking activities—and also getting caught.

FIVE

"I Didn't Even Want Them to Know"
Connection through Control

"I'm the Baby, and the Baby Has to Be a Certain Way"

"If there is a heaven, I'm sure it was just like my childhood," says sixteen-year-old Kimberley. As the youngest of four, in a close upper-middle-class family, Kimberley counts her blessings. "I think a lot about what a wonderful job my family, and the society that I was exposed to, did of keeping me a kid, and unaware of all the horrible things that happen [in the world]. [I experienced] total happiness as a kid." Her parents still try to shelter her. "I have curfews, and I have to always let my parents know where I am. They have to feel comfortable with everything that I am doing." At the same time, Kimberley is getting "some privileges handed that you would as an adult," like driving:

> I'm beginning to get to do things on my own and start to have my own private life away from my family. Sometimes . . . I think my parents have too much control, or they think they should have a lot of license into my personal life, which I really do not agree with. . . . I want to choose things for myself, be my own person.

"Sex is the main thing," says Kimberley when asked about what kind of things she and her parents disagree. "They have different ideas. I mean, I don't know if they disagree with me so much, it's just that they don't want me to do anything." It is not that Kimberley is against all her parents' rules. She thinks rules are important in a family because "it draws a line and when you cross that line, you know you're doing something that hurts another person." And she keeps to the twelve o'clock curfew her parents give her on the weekends because she does not want to worry them. But she has a different attitude toward the rule that she is not allowed to be in a house alone with her boyfriend. "I don't follow that one," she says. "I mean you can make [rules for sex], but you can't always expect them to be followed, if you want to have like an independent kid."

Kimberley has been very independent. When she and her boyfriend had been together for four months, they decided together that they wanted to start having sex. She believes "you have to keep yourself safe and protected and do everything you can to not come across any problems. In my opinion, if you love someone, it's okay to have sex. That's my morals. I've always thought that since I was little and it's come time, I guess." And when that time came, Kimberley took herself to "the clinic to get on the birth control pill." She regards herself lucky that she received a great deal of sex education in school. Her parents never talked to her about sex since, "God no, oh no, it's not going to happen, you know." But at school, "from the time I was like in fourth grade, and we started to get curious," teachers were forthcoming. "They gave us [sex education], and I thought that was great because you're not like running around to try and find out that information."

Sex happens at Kimberley's boyfriend's house when his parents are not home. His parents "wouldn't want it," she says. "But I'm sure they know. Maybe his dad doesn't condone it, but he doesn't say anything against it either, and I think his mom's the same way, just kind of, lets us do our own thing and trusts us." Kimberley cannot imagine her own parents ever giving her the kind of tacit permission to explore sexuality that her boyfriend's parents give him. Nor could she imagine ever being permitted to spend the night with her boyfriend in their home. "Even if I was like twenty-five, it wouldn't happen. . . . Unless you're married, forget it." Her older brothers have been allowed to spend the night with a fiancé, but not with a girlfriend. Not that Kimberley would want her boyfriend spending the night at her parents' house. "I wouldn't want him to stay in my house . . . because that is not something I want to share with my parents."

What Kimberley does mind is that she hides parts of her life from her parents. "I'm not completely open," she says. "I've tried that and it doesn't work." When she and her boyfriend first went out, "it was very bad." There were "lots of rules like about not being in his room and always having a parent around. Lots of control issues. Trying to make sure nothing happened they did not approve of. It got really nasty for a while." When her mother found a letter suggesting Kimberley had lost her virginity, "we had a big fight and she said I was not allowed to see him anymore. I told them I didn't do it and [the letter] was a joke. They finally believed me. But they said, 'It's our business just as much as it's yours until you're an adult.'" Things have calmed down since then:

They've learned a little bit to accept it more and I've learned a little bit how to hide what I'm doing better. Before I wanted to share everything with my parents, but I realized that doesn't really work. For them, it's just easier not to know. So, now I just do my own thing and . . . [just] let them see what makes them happy.

Sex is not the only thing that would make Kimberley's parents unhappy. Kimberley occasionally smokes marijuana. Were her mother to discover the smoking, that "would shatter her image of me as a little princess: 'Do everything right. Just get the A's.' But if it makes her happy, I'm willing to do whatever I can to uphold it." Hoping that "nothing blows up before I'm out of the house, so I don't get caught," Kimberley does not want her parents to be interviewed: "I don't want to start them thinking about sex. . . . They're doing a very good job of being oblivious. . . . I'm not a liar. If they ask me, I can't lie." Still, Kimberley thinks things could be a lot worse. "I have a good relationship with both my parents, in every way except for the fact that I have to hide a few things because I'm the baby, and the baby has to be a certain way."

"Didn't Even Want Them to Know, . . . Didn't Even Want Them to Be in My Life"

Michael liked turning sixteen. "That is the year that you get a lot of freedom." His parents had only a couple of rules: "Grades were a big thing." But being a star athlete—playing football, baseball, and soccer—in a family of outdoorsmen and physical education teachers, Michael was not expected to earn perfect grades. Getting "C's or better, and in P.E. (Physical Education) like A's," was good enough for them. On the weekends, Michael would go out and drink heavily, get "a little rowdy," and come home "looking like crap." After trying to punish him to no avail, his parents switched gears. "Just don't get into trouble. Just don't get arrested," they told him. The deal was, as long as his grades were okay, "they can't really complain about what I'm doing on the weekend." Still, there was tension between his parents and his quest for freedom:

When you're sixteen, they still want to be a big part of your life. You're trying to get out and have more freedom, and they're probably not ready to let you have all the freedom that you'd like. So, they're trying to be a big part, your family. But you are kind of shutting them out. . . . You're kind of like, "Oh well, I'm sixteen now, I've got a lot more freedom. I want to be my own person."

One area in which Michael wanted nothing at all to do with his parents was sex. He got information about sex from his friends. "I never talked to my parents about all that. . . . God, [it] grosses me out, talking to your parents about sex." Asked whether his parents ever discussed contraception with him, Michael responds, "Not a word was said about it. . . . Actually, they just said, 'Don't ever get a girl pregnant,' is the only thing my mom's ever said about that. My dad, he's never said a word to me." When Michael started having sex with his girlfriend during his sophomore year, he first kept it secret:

> It was more about sneaking around type of thing. . . . Because you're still not quite sure how your parents feel about you having a girlfriend. Like I didn't know if they thought I was too young to have a girlfriend. Basically, I just didn't really even want them to know. Just didn't even want them to be in my life.

Not a big fan of "commitment," Michael's ideal is "to have the type of people you can kind of hook up, but not be boyfriend and girlfriend. . . . Like more than one girl, basically." Generally, he does not like to have steady girlfriends because he hates "that lovey dovey stuff" that most girls do: "Where you're holding hands. I hate holding hands in public. They love that stuff: being all close all the time." But Michael is very happy with his current girlfriend. Michael looks forward to having sex with her. "She's never had sex before, so it's a good thing. . . . Because it's better that way, for the guys, it's cool to be the first one. . . . [And] it probably just feels better physically too."

Michael's communication with his parents about girlfriends and sex remained largely wordless. As he grew older, without any further words spoken, Michael shifted from being secretive about his girlfriends to being lackadaisical about the evidence of his sexual activity. "I don't try to hide the condom or nothing. Plus [when they see the condom] they know that I'm being responsible and stuff." Now eighteen years old, Michael simply informs his parents that his girlfriend will be staying the night: "They'll be like 'Okay,'" he says, "Usually, they're in bed by the time we get home":

> I don't think they really want her to sleep over in the same bed or anything, but she's allowed to sleep over, like after prom, she slept over and stuff. And they have no problem with it, because they trust me. It goes back to having a good relationship. . . . They trust me to be responsible and so far I've been responsible.

Connection through Control and the Psychology of Separation

At first sight, Kimberley and Michael tell very different tales about teenage sexuality—she must hide any evidence of her sexual activity even though it occurs in a loving, long-term relationship, and she will not be allowed a sleepover at home until she is married, while he, at eighteen, having sneaked around in his mid-teens, informs his parents that his girlfriend is spending the night and flaunts his condoms at home as evidence of his responsibility. What these narratives—and those of many other American girls and boys—have in common, however, is the notion that to explore sexuality, young people must break away from their families and from the rules imposed on them. Most boys and girls are taught that sex is danger-ous. And those who remain sexually inexperienced often view the dangers as prohibitive to exploration. But those who venture into the wild do so determined to claim their right to pursue their freedom.[1]

In the following sections, we first explore how the management of sexu-ality induces in both American girls and boys a psychology of separation from adult society, and a bifurcation of sexual self and family life. We will see that the toll this process takes is gender-specific, for many American girls have been taught, as Kimberley was at home, that they are not entitled to pursue sexual exploration or intimacy during their adolescence.[2] Even when parents accept that their daughters explore their sexuality elsewhere, American girls fear that should evidence of their sexual activity present it-self at home, they could lose their claim to good daughterhood. Expected to be "bad" by nature of their boyhood, American boys do not confront the same taboo that makes their sexuality a potential affront to the par-ent-child relationship. Even so, they too are taught that sexuality requires "breaking away" from home, psychically if not physically.

Indeed, we will see how sexuality is part of a larger cultural script about coming of age in white, middle-class America. While most of the middle-class girls and boys start adolescence following the rules, when they enter their mid-teens many learn that romance and sexuality, as well as alcohol and drugs, are experiences that one is better off hiding from one's parents. And although they often describe their relationship with their parents as good, the vast majority of American teenagers find that sooner or later they begin "sneaking around" and breaking the rules in order to pursue the truth of their "own person." They may feel sorrow, as does Kimberley, or relief, as does Michael, about the intimacy with parents lost in this process of "sneaking around." But they do not doubt that the loss is a necessary part of growing up. For the process of separation to be complete, however, and for all parties to play their part in it, one more act must follow: "getting caught."

Indeed, the narrative of adversarial individualism becomes psychologically encoded in adolescents when children lose connection with their parents during their teen years and then experience the reestablishment of connection through the exercise of parental control. With sex and drinking among peers forbidden or only tacitly tolerated, many American teenagers often have no choice but to engage in them furtively. Thus, they tend to confront, in exploring these activities, a more profound disruption and disconnection in their relationship with parents than do their Dutch counterparts, even though many enjoyed closeness with their parents as children. One way that the parent-teenager connection is reestablished is for teenagers to get caught. That connection is precarious, since adolescent sexual exploration and alcohol consumption are subject to cultural censure and legal sanction, leaving parents few options other than "not knowing" or adopting the role of the disapproving authority.

"Their Little Girl"

Like Kimberley, many of the American girls I interviewed experience a conflict between their role as good daughters and their sexual selves. How parents and girls approach this conflict ranges. At one end of the continuum are families such as Kimberley's, where parents try to avoid even talking about the possibility that a daughter might have sexual intercourse during her teenage years: Kimberley's experience of not having addressed birth control with her parents at all is shared by half of the American girls. Ashley says her mother never talked about contraception "because I am not like *that*." She explains what *"that"* is: "Well I'm just not . . . I won't have sex until I'm married. So it's never an issue. We're all brought up that way and none of us would." Fiona's mother told her, "if you ever have a question come talk to me," which Fiona has done "many times." Asked whether they have ever discussed contraception, Fiona responds:

> A lot is said without words. She's against anybody experimenting with sex before they are married and she grew up with that and so she passes it along to us, just as that is what she thinks, but she lets us think pretty much what we want to, but I know it would be suicide if I ever got pregnant. *I would be dead, literally dead*, cast out of the family kind of thing. But at the same time,

I know that my parents would be by me and make sure I got through it. But I don't even want to try.

At the other end of the continuum are American girls like Caroline, who says: "[My parents and I] have always had a completely open communication [about the topic of sex], always." Her mother had made clear that "abstinence is the best way to go but . . . she tells me about birth control and all that stuff." About her parents, Caroline says: "They respect my decisions. They know I'm most likely going to make the right decisions." But when Caroline told her mother that she wanted to go on birth control, "She was like, 'Oh wow, I need a cigarette.' . . . She was happy that I told her. . . . At least I'm honest with her and feel comfortable enough to tell my mom." But asked about a potential sleepover, Caroline responds: "No, my parents would kill me." Caroline did spend the night at her boyfriend's house a few times: "My parents don't know about this. Actually they know about one time and they got kind of mad. . . . I told them I was sorry and that I wouldn't do it again." Caroline can sympathize with her parents' reactions:

> They don't want to know that I'm doing it. It's kind of like, "Oh, my god, my little girl is having sex kind of thing." . . . It's just really overwhelming to them to know that their little girl is in their house having sex with a guy. That's just scary to them. . . . [They] won't let me have a guy in my room without the door open.

Indeed, it is among the more socially liberal American households that one bumps up against the limits of what is possible: unlike Kimberley's parents, the more liberal American parents may come to accept their daughter's sexual experiences even if those experiences tend to compromise their ideals. Seventeen-year-old Michelle is unique among the American girls interviewed in that her boyfriend may spend the night in her room. Still, Michelle knows that not being "like this perfect little girl," for instance by having become sexually active, is a source of disappointment to her mother. And like her nineteen-year-old sister's boyfriend, Michelle's boyfriend must sleep on the floor next to her bed rather than with her in it. Explaining the sleeping arrangement, Michelle makes clear that hers is the exception that confirms the rule: "It's just out of respect for my parents. We don't have our boyfriends sleep in our bed." Were they to share the bed, Michelle explains, "All [my parents] think we'd probably do is have sex."

In between are families in which parents, especially mothers, have given some sex education, frequently offering to help girls obtain birth control should the need arise, but where girls do not want to share. Margaret's mother does not know that she has had sex: "[My mother] hasn't asked me and I haven't told her." This suits Margaret: "I'd rather her not ask me straight out." Jill and Laura, both sexually inexperienced "good girls" with close relationships to their parents, do not believe they will take up their mothers' offer to help get on birth control. "We have such a close relationship with other things, not like that," says Jill. "It is just uncomfortable to talk with her about that kind of thing." Laura also describes a close relationship with her parents and thinks "it would be a disappointment" for her parents if she were to have sex as a teenager. If she became pregnant, she would tell her parents, but "unless I *had* to, I probably wouldn't."

Regardless of where the American girls and their parents fall along the communication spectrum, girls' (potential) sexuality appears difficult to integrate for parents and daughters. Girls who imagine their sexual trajectory unfolding in accordance with their parents' wishes—that is, in close conjunction with marriage, in some families, or after having moved out, in others—do not describe conflict between their relationship with their parents and their sexuality. But girls who have had sex or imagine doing so say that such sex, if acknowledged, threatens their parents' image of them as good daughters and could diminish the preexisting closeness between them. They describe two different strategies. One is to avoid disclosure and psychologically separate their relationships with parents from their sexual lives. Another is to disclose but spatially bifurcate outside the home, where girls can exercise a measure of sexual autonomy, and inside the home, where girls respect their parents' rules and uphold the image of "their little girl."

"It's Going to be Your Responsibility"

If for girls sexuality brings to the fore the exacting standard of the "good girl," for boys sexuality brings to the fore the cultural expectations and fears of the "bad boy." Few boys live up to those expectations of the "bad boy" with such gusto as Michael, though many American boys I interviewed have dabbled in some "bad" behavior. Yet, even when boys seem not to be particularly "bad," the primary message they receive about their sexuality is that it could cause them "big trouble" if they do not look out. Andy's mother told him not to have sex and that "it's scary now to have unprotected sex with diseases and everything." Marc describes the lecture he receives from his mother every six months: "'[Use] protection. Don't do it. Don't trust the girl saying she has [protection]. . . . Always carry condoms and that kind of thing." She just does the drugs, alcohol, sex thing. . . . [It is] just like the triple threat and I am just like, 'God, go away.'"

Many boys have been told, as Michael was: "Don't ever get a girl pregnant!" Daniel's mother made it clear to him that he must do "everything possible to stop pregnancy because that would be the worst thing right now, having to take care of a kid [when] you're in high school. No more sports if that happens. You have to get a job and that'd just be the worst." When Jesse's mother asked him whether he was having sex, she was not happy with his answer: "She's really nervous about the fact that sex is something that I do." He understands why: "[Sex] is a really dangerous thing. It's pretty dumb that I do have sex because I am not ready to become a father right now. That's probably like the worst thing that could happen to me right now." Phillip's parents also treat the possibility of sex with foreboding: "Make sure you're ready for it, in case, for some reason, birth control doesn't work," they warned him. He explains what being ready for "it" means:

> "If the birth control isn't working, you're going to have a kid. It's going to be your responsibility." So that kind of conversation happened. . . . They've basically gone over that once, and they've really never brought it up again. And I think they felt better knowing that they got the message across. They feel they don't have anything else to worry about. They hope.

Beyond the mandate to not get a girl pregnant, parents communicate very different messages to boys. Some parents, like Michael's, leave the matter unspoken. But some boys receive encouragement to pursue their desires from their fathers, especially fathers who are divorced. Patrick says, "Most fathers, if their sons tell them [about sex], they're proud." Adam believes that single fathers are an important source of sex education: "Single parents talk about it, like especially dads brag about it." Steve's father was excited when Steve told him about his first date: "He goes, 'Alright, good job!' because I was pretty young." But his father does not give unqualified encouragement. As an interviewee, Steve's father explained that he wanted to see his son preserve his virginity for marriage. However, Steve recalls his father telling him:

> If you're with a girl a long time and you feel comfortable around her. If you're almost positive you're not going to have a baby or something and you have a condom or something, then it would be all right. But if it's a one-nighter [or a] two-week thing then you don't even want to do it.

A few boys whose parents are strongly opposed to premarital sex have been told not to have sex before they marry. Isaac says, "My parents were really strict [about the whole abstinence thing], shaking their fist at me about that." Colin's parents have also made it clear that "they don't want me having sex." There was no talk of contraception: "No. They just said, 'Don't have sex.'" A girlfriend sleeping over is out of the question: "Not in my mom's house." Colin explains: "She doesn't want us having sex until we get married. . . . She knows my brother [has sex], but she doesn't want to know about it. She doesn't want [his girlfriend staying over], like she doesn't want to know like for sure."

But boys, unlike their female counterparts, rarely report being given rules against dating or being alone with girls. Sometimes, however, they inadvertently bump up against unarticulated prohibitions. Marc's mother told him, "I don't want you to do it, but you're probably going to do it because you don't listen anyways." Marc's interpretation of those conversations was, "She's not against it, but she's not for it either. She wants me to be ready . . . doesn't want me to get in over my head." Hence he was taken aback when his mother became extremely angry when she found him half-sitting, half-lying on his bed with his girlfriend, his best friend, and the friend's girlfriend watching television: "She just said, 'No way. Don't you ever do that again or I will kick your butt.' I was like, 'All right. . . . Oh crap.' I was scared for a little while." Marc figures that a sleepover is out of the question:

> I never asked her if my girlfriend could spend the night and I don't think that I would in the future if I want to live. . . . I might try it one of these days just to see her reaction, but probably not. Even at eighteen, she would be like, "Nooooo." She would just shake her head and say, "Hell, no."

For many boys, however, eighteen *is* a turning point, at least in their own minds. This is true both for boys with little and for those with a great deal of supervision. Already relatively free to do as he pleased, once Michael turned eighteen all rules fell away: "Everything was just, 'Do whatever you want.' Right when you turn eighteen, because you're an adult. It's basically, if you get into trouble, you're getting yourself in trouble." Isaac, by contrast, has parents who keep strong tabs on his comings and goings. Isaac's parents had forbidden him to attend a sleepover party after his senior prom because there would be girls at the party. But Isaac would be turning eighteen before prom, and he pushed through a rare confrontation with his parents, saying, "This is my senior prom and I'm making this decision as an adult." Isaac is also relishing the prospect of an unsupervised vacation to Hawaii which he has planned for the day that he turns eighteen.

Asked about the sleepover, many boys think eighteen might be the magical age. Adam says, "I'm going to go with just like eighteen because that's when people say you're legally an adult, like on paper and able to make these decisions." Before then, they would not permit it, "Just because it's been so long that that is not okay, that boys and girls are going to jump on top of each other as soon as they can." If Phillip were to have a girlfriend sleep over, his parents would also "be afraid we would do something that we aren't ready to do, just because it seemed like a good opportunity." Phillip says he is not ready for sex, but he seconds their concern: "I only have one bed, so I am sure that both [sleeping in the same room and having sex] would come in one for the most part." Phillip thinks that his parents might shift their position when he is over eighteen:

> If I was over eighteen and that was something that I felt like doing, my parents would say, "It's your choice, it's your life." That's basically my parents' feeling. After I'm eighteen, *anything you want is up to you*. . . . We're not responsible for you, so if you get into trouble, it's your responsibility. We're not going to call anybody and say, 'Oh can you please just let him off, just this once.'" It's on me.

Two boys—both Corona residents—say it would not be their age but the quality of their relationship that would determine whether a girlfriend could spend the night. Randy lives with his mother and her boyfriend. Randy describes himself as "abstinent and everything," and hopes that it is something he'll "still have" when he gets married. But he believes that even before then, his parents would let a girlfriend spend the night, depending on "who the girl was. . . . Really, it would depend on how well they know her and how our relationship was. . . . They would have to look at the relationship first. They would have to know us. It would be after we'd gone out for a while." Dean lives with his father, who is gay and divorced from his mother. A girlfriend would be allowed to sleep over "if it wasn't like a girl I just brought over one night and said, 'Hey, she's going to spend the night.' . . . If I brought her to the house, if he met her, had dinner with her, not like dinner once, but like you know, brought her around just to hang out, you know."

In most families, however, the sexuality of sons, and the question of how to respond to it as a parent, is assessed in terms of boys' capacity for self-reliance. While they are in their teens, boys' sexuality both foreshadows *and* threatens their impending autonomy. Boys are expected, sometimes encouraged, to pursue their sexual desires. But few boys expect to be given permission to spend the night with a girlfriend before being able to fully live as their "own person," independent from their parents, capable, if need be, of supporting a child. When boys are eighteen or close to that turning point, parents may grant tacit permission for a sleepover. More often, parents feel as Jesse's do. Jesse would "love" to hold his girlfriend with whom he is "totally in love" all night long, but his mother and father, he explains, need "me to break off from them, to be doing my own thing before they can handle . . . that I would be staying with my girlfriend like that."

Sex and the psychology that it requires from American middle-class girls and boys are emblematic for their coming of age process more generally. That process typically starts with a certain degree of closeness between teenagers and their parents. Especially for girls in the more conservative families, this closeness is predicated on "following the rules." But even boys with relatively liberal parents report that to maintain the peace they have to follow their parents' rules.[3] Yet the fun that lies outside those boundaries entices most to, sooner or later, start sneaking around. Many teenagers report a lengthy period during which their parents had very little idea of what they were up to—a furtiveness that was thrilling, isolating, and occasionally very dangerous. Hence, the relief some express in "getting caught." Indeed, it is quite striking how several boys in particular wholeheartedly endorse a strong show of authority as necessary for order.

Following the Rules

Many of the Tremont girls and a few of the Corona girls I interviewed describe themselves as very good and their relationships with their parents, especially their mothers, as genuinely close. Ashley, for instance, has a "really good relationship" with her parents: "I tell them everything usually, unless I forget and it's not a big deal. But I am really close with my mom. If I said anyone was my best friend, I would say it was my mom." However, closeness between a very good girl and her parents typically requires her obedience to their authority. Ashley's parents are "really big on respect to your elders, adults and things like that." She explains that respecting them means "that you don't talk back and things like that, like you would not talk back to your parents."

Jill also has a good relationship with her parents: "We can talk about things and express our feelings and not be afraid to feel judged around them. It is more like a friend than a parent." What makes her parents happy is when she is "getting good grades, making the right choices, listening to them, obeying what they say, and just generally not misbehaving." And when Jill and her parents disagree, she says, "usually I get a punishment, like being grounded or they talk to me about what I did wrong and I apologize. That's basically every disagreement we've ever had, that's how we solve it. That works for me and I know not to do it again." Jill is content with the state of affairs. Yet as she contemplates life after high school, Jill says, she is in no hurry to get married:

> I'd just like to try being my own person for once and just having new experiences and having fun and seeing different things. . . . Because it's always been my parents who have helped me and told me what to do and I how I should do it. So maybe I could get some personal experience and then have my own life without anyone else's help or anything.

Jill has friends who have "chosen to do wrong things," including sex, drinking, and drugs. Some friends have decided to mend their ways because of the "way people look at them . . . think[ing] that they are some dumb bad teenager." The process of regaining social esteem is difficult, more so even for boys than for girls, Jill believes: "I know some girls that have done some bad things and they are disrespected pretty bad. But for boys, I think it is a lot worse because boys get . . . criticized more often." Jill explains: "Most people will say, 'How can you do that with a girl when the risks for her are so much higher than they are for you?'" Recovering from mistakes is easier for girls:

> Girls are portrayed as good and they make mistakes and people just forgive those mistakes more easily than boys because boys are known as bad and they do things without their parents telling them to. . . . [Sex is seen as something that] was more the boy's influence on the girl than that it was the girl's choice.

That "boys are known as bad," explains perhaps why some of the most supervised and apparently "good" teenagers I interviewed are not girls but boys presumed to be bad. There are families where the icon of the "bad boy" does not legitimate "bad boy" behavior, as it does in Michael's family, as much as inspire "preemptive discipline." Isaac's father is a policeman whose "wrath" Isaac fears. He believes it is a lot worse for him than for his younger sister. When she came home drunk one night, "she got into trouble, but I've gotten in worse trouble for doing less. I'm a guy and I think she's daddy's little girl." And his dad's strictness has had its intended effect: "I can't honestly say that I would not have tried alcohol or tried drugs hadn't my dad been who he is and been as strict as he is because my dad is really, really strict." Isaac says, "I'm thankful for it." At the same time, "It is weird because I kind of have a shadow over me all the time."

Adam is not one to give his parents much trouble. He keeps to the curfew his parents give him, and, when he and his parents disagree, Adam says, "I usually go ahead and favor whatever they say." Adam describes his relationship with his parents as "closer than a lot of my friends. I'll talk to them about just about anything because I am home more." Lacking an active social life, Adam has few opportunities to engage in "bad boy" behavior. Instead, he spends a lot of time with his parents. Still, when he does go out with friends, Adam must "check in" every two hours by phone. His parents "want to know like where I am, what I'm doing. . . . [They fear] I might start hanging out with the wrong guys or doing pot or go driving with someone who's a really irresponsible driver and get in an accident or just like get into trouble or get in a fight or something like that."

Phillip takes honors classes in school and works over twenty hours a week at a paid job. But although he has a full plate of responsibilities, which he seems to take very seriously, his parents expect Phillip home at ten o'clock, including on weekend nights. They don't allow him to go "driving around, looking for something to do with my friends" because they "just don't want me out there getting into trouble, for the most part." In cases of conflict, "It usually ends up that they end up winning it and I end up doing whatever they ask. Just because, as they put it, they're older, and until I'm eighteen, they have control over me no matter what." Phillip is generally quite positive about his parents' strictness: "I'm sure I'll be nice and tight on my children when I'm older, and I'll expect them to do this and to do that and be home when I say." But as a teenager, he finds it difficult to be on the receiving end of his parents' rules and authority:

> It feels almost like they aren't listening to me even though I know they are listening to what I say, but they don't care. That is basically what it comes down to. . . . I think it's reasonable [that I am not allowed to go out] but at the same time . . . I would like to go out with my friends and just go find something to do.

The desire to "just go out and find something to do" away from one's parents is fueled by learning to drive, as most American teenagers do when they first turn sixteen. A rite of passage is getting one's own driver's license and sometimes one's own car. Whether they were strictly supervised or given a great deal of latitude to begin with, both girls and boys see driving as their ticket to greater freedom from parental oversight. It is great to be sixteen, says Daniel: "You get a driver's license, a little more freedom from your parents. You can go places, hang out with your friends, your mom's not always following you around." Paula has also loved "getting to drive, getting the chance to get out and be by myself, and having my parents back off me." Having gained new mobility and freedom, Paula knows her final departure from her childhood and home is not far off: "I'll be gone in two years. . . . They're more lenient now that I am sixteen. And [it is good] having them understand that I am growing up and that I am going to be gone."

It is not just driving itself that takes teenagers out of their parents' purview. Many teenagers start working in paid jobs, sometimes up to twenty hours a week, in order to pay for the gas, insurance, and the other costs that are involved in maintaining a car. Though parents may grumble about the long hours, they usually permit their children to work as many hours as they want and are able to without having their schoolwork suffer. What that means is that from age sixteen on, between academic classes, rigorous sports training for some, and long working hours for others, teenagers often spend little time in their parents' company—sometimes not eating dinner together more than a couple of nights a week. Being able to drive also makes it easier for teenagers to spend weekend nights at their friends' houses, as many with active social lives do. All of this distance facilitates an important ritual of American adolescence: "sneaking around."

Sneaking Around

Although many start their teens as "rule followers," few teenagers leave high school without having learned to creatively interpret the rules and sneak around them. And how could it be otherwise if, to paraphrase Kimberley, "you want to be like an independent kid"? Boys and girls both assume that at some point one must break the rules and experiment with forbidden pleasures in order to become one's "own person." Even the most strictly monitored and penalized boys find gray areas in which to hide, so that they appear to be following the rules while getting away with working around them. And even the best of good girls venture into territory that is "bad": they might have friends who experiment with drinking and drugs, they may attend parties themselves, they may meet with boys in secret, or obscure the romantic component of a friendship.

One way to work around the rules is to remain in the dark about their details. Isaac, who says his socially conservative parents have shaken their fist at him as they preached abstinence, has to admit he is not entirely certain whether being abstinent means refraining from vaginal intercourse only or from all sexual intimacy. "I don't know," he says. "I've always wondered that. I don't know what's okay. My parents know that I kiss girls. I don't tell them anything other than that because I will never be comfortable talking with my parents about my relationships with people." Although he is uncertain what is and what is not morally acceptable, Isaac prefers the silence and ambiguity over the alternative: "I don't really want to know. I have never known the answer to that question [of whether it is acceptable to engage in any kind of sexual act] because then I'll feel bad if I've done something wrong, so I just stick with the 'I don't know' thing. It works for me."

Another way to work around the rules is to leave out important details. Daniel, for instance, declined to tell his mother that an opposite-sex friend is, in fact, his steady girlfriend: "I don't even tell her I have a girlfriend. I'm just like, 'She's just my friend.' She'll always just be following me around and stuff, so I don't even tell her that she's my girlfriend." Marc says that when it comes to dating and sex, if it were up to his mother, "I would probably be in a room, a padded room, for the rest of my life." What he means is that "she'd probably lock me up somewhere if she had the choice, but she doesn't." He once kept the fact that he had a girlfriend from her for three months. "She got mad. It turned out that she actually liked my girlfriend." Similarly, Katy told her mother she was going over to "a friend's house" without adding that "the friend" in question was her boyfriend, whom she was not allowed to see unless her mother has phoned his mother.

Several American teenagers have been introduced to alcohol at home and at family celebrations. A few boys even have parents like Marc's, who know he drinks occasionally and are "okay with it, sort of." But many teenagers know their parents do not want them to drink, especially not with their peers. Daniels' parents would "have a cow." And those teens who have drunk typically keep it to themselves. Jesse explains: "I don't like to tell [my parents] I'm going over to my friend's house and drink a little. . . . I don't want to deal with the big old shit fit argument." Kelly puts it more delicately: "I just don't want to worry them. I don't think they really need to know. . . . I don't want to say it's none of their business, because it doesn't sound right." She adds:

They don't need to hear about me getting tipsy, especially my dad. I think my mom would understand, but I think my dad might freak out a little bit. I think he trusts me, but he doesn't trust other people, is kind of the feeling I get. He still thinks of me as being ten sometimes or eight or five, and he thinks of me as his *little princess*. He doesn't want anything to happen to me.

Lisa of Tremont is a "good girl" with a stellar academic record and a precarious place on the edge of "the popular crowd" at her high school. At all the parties she has recently attended, "there's pot and there's alcohol." Lisa does not tell her parents the things her friends do at these parties "because I want them to like my friends and have them over." When Lisa first started going to parties, she tried to test the waters to find out how her parents would respond if she were to tell them about what happens there. A friend of hers had volunteered the information to her parents and after the revelation they allowed her to go to the party anyway, saying that they trusted her. "It sounded reasonable at the time: ask your parents and tell them the truth and be straight up with them and have them trust you," thought Lisa. So, she ran a hypothetical scenario by her own parents "because I thought that was how it could be. And they were like, 'No, we would never let you go to a party where there was drinking.' So I just shut my mouth."

When boys and girls go beyond just happening upon parties where there is drinking and start drinking and smoking themselves, shutting one's mouth is not enough. Andy would "lie and make up stories and try to get out of the house and go [drinking]." When Margaret first started to go out, "I wouldn't want to tell [my mother] what I was doing, so I'd make up some [story]: 'I'm going to a friend's house. . . . I'm going to be there.' I think I ended up, not necessarily lying *a lot*, but just not telling her anything about anything." American teenagers often spend a great deal of the weekends at friends' houses to avoid detection. Steve explains his strategy: "After a party, I either stay the night at my friend's house because people smoke cigarettes around me and cigarette smoke gets on me, and, you know, pot smoke and alcohol could get spilled on me. I want to wash my clothes, you know, just to make it so it doesn't seem like I was part of it."

Melissa has never gotten into "big trouble" even though she goes to parties all the time because she usually sleeps at a friend's house. She looks at her relationship with her parents as "pretty good," but, she says, "I still have to lie. Well, I don't really ever lie. . . . They always think I am . . . they don't really figure [out what is going on]." Melissa thinks being a teenager or a parent of a teenager puts one in a catch-22: "I don't want to be a parent.

It seems like a losing situation. Either your kid sneaks around you or you look like a really bad parent because you let the kid do everything." Lack of closeness between parents and teenagers is inevitable, Melissa thinks, unless parents give up their authority or teens give up the stuff adolescence is made of:

> You can have a good relationship with a parent and then they're pretty much going to have to let you do whatever you want because otherwise you're go- ing to have to sneak around or lie and that's not a good relationship. . . . I don't know how to have a really good relationship with your parents unless you don't do anything.

One solution to the dilemma that Melissa articulates is for parents to knowingly and sometimes explicitly turn a blind eye on their children's forbidden activities. Lisa is not allowed to date until her next birthday, but she hangs out with her boyfriend at home all the time. She knows that her parents know that he is her boyfriend, but they "just don't re- ally say anything. They just let it slide, I guess." When Phillip turned fif- teen, he says, his parents knew they did not want him "out partying with [his] friends at some huge party where the cops were eventually going to show up, almost definitely, and getting in a lot more trouble that way." Phillip tells a story that illuminates how parents are themselves con- strained in their choices. They came up with a plan to keep Phillip *and* themselves out of trouble—he and a friend may drink at the family's yearly camping trip:

> They basically pretend like they don't know what we're doing, but they know we do it and they don't mind as long as we're going to be staying in the im- mediate area, not wandering off. . . . But they don't want the responsibility, like, if we get caught, then it's us who did it, not like they're saying, "Yeah go ahead."

Getting Caught

As they sneak around, sometimes with their parents' complicity, teenagers run the risk that some dread and others blatantly court, namely the risk of "getting caught." "Sneaking around" and "getting caught" can seem a lot like a game of hide and seek, where part of the fun is relishing freedom temporarily gained, whether one gets caught or not. Jeff describes what it was like to go climbing out of the house at night to hang out with friends in the park: "It's kind of boring, but it's fun. It gives you like a rush. . . . If you get caught it's going to be scary, but it will be fun." Katy's sister "snuck out of the house the other night and my mom caught her and that wasn't good." Caroline has cut school a lot over the past year. "I lie to my parents like, you know, trying to cover up for reasons why I didn't go to school or whatever." But then she got caught: "It sort of builds up when they find out. When they look at my report card and they are like, 'Oh my God.'" Caroline is now grounded, but she has few regrets. Before her parents discovered her transgressions, she says: "I had a lot of fun . . . [went to] lots of parties."

Even when parents use advanced techniques to "catch" teenagers and impose heavy penalties if they do, the chase between cat and mouse can appear quite playful. Steve explains how his father has "ways of finding out stuff, like through my brother or sister. Or he just lies and tells me he knows and hopes he'll get a good answer." After Steve came back from parties, "He'd take me in the light and check my eyes to see if I was smoking pot or anything and see how I walk or talk or something like that." When he gets caught, he gets grounded: "In seventh and eighth grade I was grounded for a long time because I snuck out with my friends and I got grounded for that for two years, a year each time." His father is strict, says Steve: "The first time I snuck out, he really didn't stick to the year thing. It was more like six months. The second time, he stuck to it."

According to Melissa, "everyone" at Tremont High gets grounded, for instance, for throwing a party when parents are out of town, though Melissa doubts that parents really are surprised: "They have to know. I mean they can't be that ignorant. . . . It's like common sense that the high-school students get left alone and then throw a party. They always get punished but I don't know if the parents really care that much." Melissa's parents do not punish: "I get lectures. . . . Whenever I do something bad and get caught . . . [my parents] talk to me and I feel bad because I made them disappointed." She thinks her parents' approach is better: "I never end up being mad at them at the end of the conversation like most of the kids because most of the kids never are sorry for what they did. They're just sorry they got caught because their parents are always punishing them."

Illustrative of the social control that prevails in small-town Tremont and the relative anonymity teenagers experience in Corona, Tremont's party-girl Melissa believes that teenagers who throw parties when their parents are out of town usually get caught, while Laura thinks a lot of parents in Corona do *not* find out about parties. Laura recounts a party with a dramatic finale in which the culprit almost manages not to get caught:

I'll tell you, kids will do like the most drastic things. A friend of mine . . . his parents were gone, and he had a really big house and he was going to have a party. . . . He moved all of his furniture out of the house, into the upstairs. . . . [But] so many people were there, the cops ended up coming. Then his sister came home. She was so mad. She was like: "Everybody, get out of my house." And the cops were there and she would not let anyone leave out the back way, which kind of lets out in the woods, so everyone could get away who'd been drinking. But [instead] everybody [had to] go out the front door. People were trying to get out the back, they broke his screen door, tons of his flowers, like from his mom's garden, were all like torn up. His parents wouldn't even have found out, unless his sister told them. [My friend] went out and bought a new screen door . . . and went out and like bought all new flowers, planted them. . . . Kids will like go so far.

And sometimes, they go *too* far. But especially in Corona, where a loose so-cial fabric typical of American suburban communities does not provide the social control typical for small communities like Tremont, young people may never get caught or not care when they are. Several Corona boys de-scribe being undeterred by being caught. Michael, for instance, who tried to shut his parents out when he was sixteen and "didn't even want them in [his] life," simply stopped caring whether he got caught drinking and also stopped complying when he got punished. Having maintained decent grades, not gotten arrested, nor having impregnated a girl, Michael prides himself on his responsibility. Responsible or not, he has come of age, view-ing adulthood as a matter of being able to do "whatever you want" as long as you avoid causing major trouble.

Likewise, when Jesse's parents caught him smoking marijuana as a fourteen-year-old, he says, "that didn't really stop me." Their response did not matter: "It was just something else we fought about." But when Jesse came home with D's, his father gave him "a ton of rules," which Jesse "just hated" because "I'm a kid . . . I want to go out and play and do what I want to do." When he upped his grades, his father let go of control. Looking back a few years later, Jesse says, authority is "totally a necessity" because "if there was not authority, I don't know how we'd get along here. Just terrible, people would be doing whatever they want." Authority got Jesse to improve his grades. But it is his girlfriend, with whom he is "totally in love," whom he credits for turning around his drug habit. He hated being "stoned out of [his] mind" because he was not being himself or able to re-ally connect with her, "so that pretty much got me out of that phase."[4]

If "bad boys" like Jesse and Michael seem at least temporarily to stop caring about what their parents want, good girls like Kimberley seem to have the opposite problem: they care so much about what their parents want that they keep them in the dark about important parts of their lives. Girls may carry around the weight of a secret sex life or dangerous drinking spells, leaving them, in certain fundamental respects, unknown by their own parents. Laura presents herself as a classic good girl: "I just don't have the desire, I guess, to be rebellious and stuff toward my parents. I mean we get in fights every once in a while, but it's just—I've been raised, you're not disrespectful to your parent." Laura can tell her dad "anything" and she is "really honest" with her mom too.

One would never have guessed that Laura began drinking when she was fourteen: "We would just go up to the market and find like some random person [to buy us liquor]." Laura stopped drinking after a close call: "I don't remember throwing up [because] I was passed out." Laura has seen worse: "A friend of my sister's got alcohol poisoning and almost died." Laura has "never been in trouble" for drinking because her parents do not know about it: "I always stay at a friend's house." If they found out, they would be very disappointed. Her mother views teenage drinking as "inappropriate." She has good reason for concern. Her own mother was an alcoholic who died after collapsing in the kitchen, says Laura: "I have the risk of being an alcoholic in my blood."

Getting caught can be a relief, especially when it forces a more open dialogue. Janine's parents used to be working all the time, "So I wasn't really like connected and I hated them for it." Janine kept secret that she was having undesired sex with an older boyfriend. She still keeps sex a secret from her father: "If my dad ever found out, I'd literally be disowned. He cannot find out about that." But her mother did find out, and Janine says, they have become "real good friends" now that her mother supervises her more:

> Kind of a mutual talk [was] going on. [My mother] asked me questions and I gave her an answer and one thing led to another . . . other questions came up and other answers were told. . . . [I felt] nervous. I was like, "Oh, my God." I thought I was going to be disowned. I really thought they would not stand for that. . . . [Instead, my mother said], "Are you being careful? Are you using protection?"

While Janine was able to reconnect with her mother through coming clean, getting caught did not heal Michelle's relationship with her parents. Her premature sexual debut, along with alcohol and drug use, put Michelle squarely in the "bad girl" category. "I went from 12 to 20 in like three years," she says. When her parents stumbled on a box of condoms, "obviously, they probably didn't look at [her] the same way, [like] a little girl." Her mother wants "a straight-A student" and "this perfect little girl." But, says Michelle, "I can't give her that," acutely aware that she is disappointing:

> We've been really close all my life. And after I started doing things and I wasn't a little girl anymore, like I stopped playing soccer. . . . And I wasn't home as much and it's just been really hard for her to handle. I've changed a lot, and like my attitude and everything since I was like a little girl, and they want that back and I can't give it to them. And I don't want to try to lie to them like I'm pretending to.

Connection through Control

Sexuality presents American middle-class girls and boys with different dilemmas: girls must conform to the notion of a little girl who is not sexual, keep sexual activity a secret, or physically and psychologically bifurcate their family and their sexual lives. Boys are expected, and sometimes explicitly encouraged, to feel driven by sexual desire, but they are also taught that sexual activity could end their adolescence and ruin their life. Not unlike their female counterparts, most middle-class boys are taught that sexual activity requires them to command the full social attributes of adulthood. Thus, although the icon of the "good girl" who is untainted by sexual experience, and that of the "bad boy" who is reduced to his sexual drive, exert different pressures, they also have a shared effect: both make sexual activity into a sign, as well as a test, of young people's capacity to separate and maintain themselves independently from parents and home life.

Sexuality is but one among several "bad" things that produce a psychological break between the family togetherness of childhood and the conflict with parents that many American teenagers experience or anticipate upon venturing into adult territory. A common sequence runs through their narratives. Young people typically start their teens not having questioned the received wisdom about "right" and "wrong" behavior. Soon enough, however, that wisdom tends to collide with another certainty, namely, that experimenting with sex, drinking, and drugs is part of claiming one's right to personhood. When, depending on temperament and opportunity, teenagers start breaking the rules and sneaking around, the challenge is to explore without doing major damage in the process. And unless teenagers get caught—as they frequently are but often are not—one of the liabilities of such sneaking around is a disconnection in the parent-teenager relationship.[5]

Through sneaking around, young people who break their parents' rules can and do carve out a significant social and psychological space that is free from adult intervention and norms. Although some may be troubled by having to keep things hidden from their parents or worried about the consequences of getting caught, they often relish the freedom and fun of the furtive and forbidden. As Jeff says about climbing out of the house, "It's going to be scary, but it will be fun." But at the same time that prohibitions and hiding entice young people to pursue adolescent experimentation independently from adult support, they also require that youth "get caught" by their parents so that they can become fully known by them as the persons that they are in the process of becoming. This may be one reason that teenagers sometimes talk about leniency as parents' "not caring" and that boys like Phillip believe it is essential that parenting be "nice and tight."

This strategy of connection through control has its liabilities. For, when the moment of reckoning arrives, it can be disproportionately severe. Alone at the wheel, American teenagers literally and figuratively risk driving off the cliff.[6] With driving crucial to freedom, veering off course becomes all the more dangerous. And with reliable contraception, emergency contraception, and abortion not easily accessible for many teenagers, an unintended pregnancy is, even among middle-class teenagers, a very real risk.[7] Finally, the zero-tolerance policies that have permeated both legal and extralegal institutions, such as schools, impose harsh and consequential penalties even for minor infractions.[8] As significant as the severity of punishment is the fact that teenagers often lack parental support as they learn about the pleasures and dangers of adolescent exploration, leaving them dependent on institutions that, as we will see in chapter 7, rarely serve them well.

SIX

"At Least They Know Where I Am"

Control through Connection

"As Long as I Tell Them, They Allow It"

For seventeen-year-old Karsten, the pleasures of family life and the pleasures of growing up rarely clash. He goes out on the weekend with his
peers for beers, having been introduced to alcohol several years before by
his parents: "They try to teach you, very quietly and carefully." And now
when he goes out on his own, they still say, "Try not to go too far, not to
get drunk." Recently, when Karsten wanted to go out two weekend nights
in a row, his parents were not pleased. Together they negotiated an agreement whereby Karsten was allowed to go out the second night, as long
as he came home early. Karsten spends a lot of time with his parents and
enjoys their company:

> After school, I see my mother. After my father comes . . . we have dinner
> which is *gezellig* and we talk together. . . . Around 9:00 or 9:30 p.m., we are
> together [again] and we can talk, or play games, watch television, whatever
> we feel like doing. . . . We play games at least twice a week for a whole eve-
> ning and have a lot of fun.

Karsten believes his parents have taken "the golden middle road" in raising him. "Our relationship is very free, very open," says Karsten. "We tell
each other everything. . . . If I need to make a decision, my parents will talk
to me about it, but they will not force me to make a different decision." At
the same time, there are expectations. The main one is: "When I have made
an agreement, then I really have to keep myself to it." Karsten's parents always want to know where he is and what time to expect him home: "Especially around dinner. Unless I really call and tell them beforehand, I have
to be home at five o'clock." But Karsten does not feel the agreements he
makes with his parents are impinging on his freedom: "I am allowed to do

a lot, almost everything really, but they do want to know that I am doing it. As long as I tell them, they allow it."

Karsten parents addressed the topic of sex when he was fourteen: "Yes, they explained [contraception] very well. Especially my father, you know it is really a conversation for men among one another. You feel more comfortable." Karsten has no doubt that he has been in love: "On the one hand, it is fun. [But] it is a very strange experience. You think about her almost constantly. You start to wonder: 'What will I say this evening.'" Being in love is "like [having] a warm feeling for someone. . . . [It is] like a special place in your heart." Before having sex, Karsten wants "to have gotten to know [a girl] and we need to come to the conclusion together that we can do that, more or less according to an agreement. I need to really know that she wants to do it too."

Karsten lost his virginity with a girlfriend he was with for two and a half months: "We were talking and at a certain point we got onto the topic and more or less together decided to do it, that she was ready for it too." They spent the night at his house several times, but only after consultation both with his parents and his girlfriend's parents. "Yes, you have to do that," Karsten explains. "I wouldn't want to get into a fight with an angry father. I've heard those kinds of stories from my father. That my grandpa went after him with a shotgun." Nothing so dramatic took place in Karsten's generation. But a careful dance preceded the sleepover:

> We talked about it, kind of very carefully feeling our way: my parents were like, "What exactly do you want?" And I was like, "What would they really allow?" After a while I just asked plainly, would it be allowed? And then they said yes. . . . They'd rather that I am at home when I am going to do something like that, than elsewhere. Because they know: if something is going to happen, it is going to happen. And if it happens at home, at least they know where I am.

"They are Happy that I am Normal"

Getting a courtship (*verkering*) has made sixteen-year-old Natalie very happy. "It is really very wonderful. I am just really happy about it." When she and Rob first began their courtship, three months ago, Natalie told him she did not want to have sex yet. "I wanted to really take the time to get to know each other. . . . It is not that I did not want to do it, but I waited, because I thought, 'If I do it now and things don't work out, that is a shame.' You know, you can only give it away once and that is very special." But

Natalie found that she "was just really happy with [Rob], so . . ." after three months, the couple had their first sexual intercourse. Sex happened "a little early," but that is not a problem, Natalie believes, given the seriousness of the relationship. Indeed, more than a year after their first intercourse, Natalie and Rob are still together (see chapter 2). The first time "did hurt," Natalie recalls, "but I don't regret it in any case. It was pretty fun."

One reason that Natalie has no regrets about her first time is that she used reliable contraceptives. Hence fears of getting pregnant are completely absent in her account of her loss of virginity. When Natalie started menstruating, her mother explained the basics about puberty and sexuality. A few years later, several months before she had her first serious courtship with Rob and her first sexual intercourse, Natalie was reading about the advantages of the pill as a method for regulating menstruation in a magazine for teenage girls: "I had already been thinking about [the pill]. So I showed the article to my mother and I said, 'I want that too.' She said: 'Sure, that is all right. Go to the doctor, tomorrow. Let's go together.' So it was really very easy. [My mother] had no issues with it or anything." Since starting the pill, Natalie has always felt comfortable approaching her mother about taking it: "My mother also takes it—so I could always ask her questions."

Still, when the moment came, Natalie says, "I just did not want to tell them. I don't know why. But at a certain moment, you can't keep it to yourself, you're just really happy. . . . Well, I did not exactly tell them. They discovered it." When a week after Natalie and Rob had their first intercourse—at Rob's house—Natalie's father found Rob in her room late at night, he responded: "Yes, five minutes Rob, and then you have to be out!!" Natalie was furious. In the conversation that followed, Natalie told her parents where things stood between her and Rob. They "weren't shocked. My father said, 'Sixteen is a beautiful age.' . . . My mother thought it was really great. She did not mind because she knows how serious we are." Although, as we learned in chapter 2, it would take her father a while to come around, Natalie is confident that soon her parents will let Rob spend the night with her: "Because they trust me. . . . That is just really important." She looks forward to it: "It is wonderful isn't it, lying next to him at night?"

While trust makes Natalie's parents "tolerant, very tolerant even," such tolerance does not mean Natalie has free rein to do as she pleases. "I know exactly what I need to do to make my mother angry," Natalie says, "really angry. . . . I know what I can do and what I cannot do." One thing she *cannot* do is "bike home alone in the dark." Natalie has to always keep her parents informed of her whereabouts. "If my plans change, I always have to call them. They always want to know where I am." Violating those rules would break down the trust and "if the trust is gone between them and me, that would be terrible." But Natalie takes the rules that her parents expect her to keep to for granted. "Usually I agree with them. . . . I am allowed to do a lot. So I never need to disagree with them." Natalie's agreeableness suits her parents well too, she believes. They are relieved that she does not go "against them like some kids who paint their hair strange colors or stop listening to their parents." Her parents are pleased, Natalie says, "that I am *normal*."

Control through Connection and the Psychology of Incorporation

Natalie's and Karsten's accounts are textbook cases of normalization—they received ample sex education, they initiated premeditated intercourse in respectful relationships, and were—eventually in Natalie's case—able to negotiate permission for a sleepover from their parents. Few Dutch teenagers have experiences that correspond as closely to this tension-free ideal. And yet, these two opening vignettes illustrate broader patterns: unlike Kimberley and Michael in America, Dutch girls and boys do not confront the narrow gender-bifurcated notions of the "good girl" and "bad boy" that deny sexual agency.[1] And like Karsten and Natalie, most Dutch teenage interviewees have received sex education and have been, or project being, allowed to spend the night at home with a steady boyfriend or girlfriend, although such permission is predicated on their negotiating and complying with terms that make a sleepover agreeable to all parties.

In the following sections, we will see that even in families less "free" than Natalie's and Karsten's and in spite of parent-teenager tensions, sexuality becomes a vehicle through which young people are encouraged to develop a psychology of incorporation rather than separation: Boys are encouraged to make their sexuality *gezellig*—to value the integration of sexual and domestic pleasures and to chose partners who can be treated as temporary family members. Girls are encouraged to make their sexuality *normal*—to avoid causing unnecessary disturbances by springing a sexual relationship, let alone a pregnancy, on their parents prematurely or out of the blue, and to be able to discuss emotional issues without letting discomfort get the better of them. But while it is striking how similarly Dutch boys and girls are treated, it is also notable that negotiations around the sleepover are more prolonged and tension-ridden for girls than for boys. Still, both girls and boys illustrate that the choices and constraints they encounter at home encourage them to behave "normally": in close accordance with their parents' norms.

Indeed, as we will see, just as sex and the psychology it requires from American teenagers is embedded in a larger cultural narrative about what it means to come of age in middle-class America, so too is the management of adolescent sexuality in Dutch middle-class families part of an overarching strategy for maintaining connection and control across the fissures of maturation.[2] Dutch teenagers appear, from the perspective of their American peers, to experience extraordinary latitude with regard to sex. But their freedoms are circumscribed by, and predicated on, expectations and taken-for-granted rules that constitute them as *gezellig* family members who exercise the necessary self-restraint, take others into account, show understanding, and seek agreements. These mandates of *gezelligheid* are intended to mitigate the potential disruptive aspects of adolescence, creating continuity in the household and in the self, and exacting control over teenagers by keeping them anchored in relations of interdependence.

This strategy of control through connection is based on a vision of change and the conviction that one is better off sailing forward on its force than left flapping in the wind. Hence, many Dutch parents tolerate experimentation they view as beyond their power to forbid.[3] Instead of the "no sex, no drugs, no alcohol" rules that many American teenagers encounter at home, Dutch teenagers typically describe a form of "vigilant leniency" on the part of their parents, as the latter try to steer them clear of major collisions while permitting them to adjust their own course. Vigilant leniency does keep Dutch teenagers more connected to their parents than their American counterparts, but it does not prevent them from pushing the limits, fudging the truth, and keeping some things secret. And sometimes tolerance begets laxity, with the young failing to demonstrate the self-correcting, especially with regard to alcohol consumption, their parents expect. At the same time, in the process of pushing and fudging, they do not usually veer too far off course from a shared understanding of "what can and cannot be done."

"If My Mother Thinks It's *Gezellig*"

Like Karsten, most Dutch boys say that their parents have made at least a good faith attempt to discuss sexuality and contraception with them. There is a range in how explicit parents are in addressing the topic. All Hans's parents said was, "If you don't understand something, then you should ask us." But it is rare for parents to skirt the topic completely. Erik thinks it is a matter of course that he got sex education from his parents. His father "*gewoon* started a conversation about it, about condoms and things like that. . . . [I think] most parents explain on time how things work and *what can and cannot be done*." Erik explains the expression "can and cannot be done": It means "about being safe and everything. And like general things, like that you shouldn't do it if your girlfriend does not want it." Gert-Jan's father told him about "doing it, contraception and that kind of thing." For Gert-Jan the conversation was "exciting, of course." Berend's father talked with him once "some years ago." Asked what his father told him, Berend says, "Well, *gewoon*, that men can get excited and stuff and about masturbating."

In other families, mothers are the ones to provide sex education, which provokes a variety of emotional responses. While that conversation was "a little strange," says Paul, the information is "kind of nice to know." Frank liked receiving sex education from his mother. She told him, "If you ever want to do something, you need to protect yourself." She offered to buy condoms for her son, or, she said, "We've got some at home too." Thomas's feelings are more mixed about the sex education he received at home. His mother gave him a little book when he was twelve, telling him, "I never got that at home, [but] I want you to have it." His mother would have wanted to talk more with him, but Thomas held off further conversation. A couple of years later, when Thomas had a girlfriend, his mother told him, "You have to do it safely, you know that don't you?" Thomas's response was, "Jesus, mom, I am only fourteen!"

Several Dutch boys say that their parents are more than willing to talk about sex, but boys do not always reciprocate their willingness. Lawrence believes his parents "would like it if I were to talk openly with them, if I were to kind of ask information. . . . They would like to help." Were he to contemplate having sex, Lars says, "I *could* talk about it [with my parents]. Whether I actually would do it, that I don't know." Likewise, Erik says his parents would definitely be available to talk, if he wanted to, "but it wouldn't really be my first choice to talk about" sex with them. Ben's mother would want to [talk more about sex]." And he talks a lot with his mother, he says, "also about that—but not so much. I mean, I am not going to tell her about my sex life!" Ben's mother did come along to purchase emergency contraception the first time that Ben, who is now eighteen, feared that he had impregnated his girlfriend of several years. But when more recently his girlfriend actually *was* pregnant and had an abortion, Ben did not tell his parents.

Other Dutch boys are more positive about the option of talking with their parents about sex, either because they could learn from them or because they want to share their experiences. Sam thinks that when you are trying to figure out whether you are ready, "you should listen to your parents. They have seen you grow up and they probably also remember. . . . They are not the ones making the decision but you should listen to them as well." Gert-Jan is sure he will tell his parents when he loses his virginity: "Yes, you always want to be honest, don't you? Let me rephrase that: I would begin with my sister, then my mother, then my father." Why would he want that? "You'd want to know what they think about it of course," Gert-Jan explains: "Hear their side of the story. You tell them if it felt good or if it didn't feel good. And you want to know how their first time was, that kind of thing." Gert-Jan is pleased that they can talk about sex at home. "You can talk about it during dinner. And then my father joins in and stuff."

In the more liberal families, boys are allowed to bring girlfriends home with few qualifications, and they say they have complete sexual autonomy: Marcel's parents have the attitude that "you should decide that yourself when you do. As long as you are safe, it does not matter to them." Sam thinks his parents "know that if something [sexual] were to happen, that I would be ready for it. They also have enough faith in me . . . that I wouldn't do any stupid things." Berend thinks his mother might "say that we should not do any crazy things. But I think she would permit it. It is [part of] my age. Maybe she would give me advice but she's not going to forbid it or anything." As far as Ben's parents were concerned, his girlfriend "would have been allowed to sleep in my room from the first night." He agrees with them: "Why would [it] not be allowed? That a child goes to bed with someone at a certain point, well, that is going to happen anyway. You might as well let them spend the night. If my mother thinks it is *gezellig*, [then] why not."

At the other end of the spectrum are boys whose parents set stricter limits. Niek suspects he will not be allowed to have a girlfriend spend the night until he is eighteen. If Michiel's parents had known that their son was gay—which they do not—they would not have permitted his boyfriend to spend the night in his bedroom. Peter thinks his mother is "incredibly conservative" when it comes to sex and relationships. Were Peter, who is still a virgin, to bring a brand-new girlfriend home for the night, she would be assigned a guestroom. That could change depending on "lots of things: how often she comes home, how long we've been together, how close we are, how well my parents know her." Peter's older sister sleeps at home with her boyfriend. "But they've been together for like three years. . . . The first year, she did not dare to ask." That means, Peter concludes, that "if I want to make any chance of it being allowed in the short term, then I better start asking for it soon, given the long discussion that I'll have to get about that." Would Peter like the sleepover? Why not, he says, "It would be quite *gezellig*."

Like Peter, Frank describes criteria for the sleepover that are very similar to those articulated by many Dutch girls. He says his parents would "not be easy" about permitting a sleepover, "especially because they would first want to know someone well. I don't think that my father and mother allow [someone] to belong to the family that quickly." He thinks there may be some tensions between his own romantic tastes and his parents' preferences: "I think they want someone who is 'squarer,' but I really don't. [I want] someone with a lot of friends, who is easier, cooler." But once they get to know his girlfriend, and they like her, Frank can see his parents permitting her to stay the night: "And if it went fine the first time, normal, then they think, 'See, it is okay.'" He explains what he means by "normal": "That the sleeping happens in a normal way. . . . That it happens in such a way that it does not bother them at all." Frank likes the prospect: "Yes, I would like it: it is like mom and dad, like when you're married, you also wake up every day next to the person you love. That I do think is beautiful!"

Even in families that boys characterize as "free," there are implicit expectations about self-regulated, relationship-based sexuality with a person with whom parents feel an affinity. Erik's and his girlfriend's parents permitted them to spend the night after three months because "it seemed serious." Gert-Jan's parents would permit the sleepover, no questions asked. But all the same, he says, "My father is always judging, 'That is not a type for you.'" His brother has what his parents consider a "really nice girl. Then they don't mind at all." Thomas is also allowed to spend the night with his girlfriend (with whom he has slept but not had sex). His mother, Marga Fenning (chapter 2) told him, "You have to decide that yourself, [but] you need to think about it before you go to bed with a girl." She urged Thomas to think about "whether you will be continuing to be with her for a long time" and what will happen "if there are problems." Echoing his mother's words, he says, "If the girl becomes pregnant, you should not say, 'Goodbye then!'"

Few Dutch boys describe sexuality as a source of conflict with their parents. [4] While the sleepover can be, as Karsten puts it, a "little awkward," boys usually enjoy or look forward to a girlfriend spending the night with them at home. Unlike their American peers, the Dutch boys do not experience sexuality as a vehicle or symbol of "breaking away" from home. In fact, through the sleepover boys affirm the value of *gezelligheid* and sometimes even identify with their parents. Several boys say explicitly that they value the sleepover not just for its physical pleasures but for the experience of pleasurable togetherness with a girlfriend in the context of their everyday domestic setting. Part of the fun of a sleepover is, as Ben says, that "extra atmosphere." While Thomas and his girlfriend decided against having intercourse when they spent the night together, they did enjoy, he says, the *gezelligheid*. And indeed sometimes, "waking up next to the girl you love" means, as it does for Frank, being just "like mom and dad."

"A Very Intimate Thing to Share"

As Natalie's experience illustrates, girls' sexuality is integrated into Dutch family life in ways that would be unimaginable to most American girls and their parents: three-quarters of the Dutch girls have received some form of sex education at home—including the encouragement, admonishment often, to use contraception and condoms—and they typically report or project being allowed to spend the night with a boyfriend during the second half of their teens.[5] Yet, permission for the sleepover should not be interpreted as an absence of reservations on the part of parents about their daughters' sexual debut or lack of ambivalence on the part of girls about sharing something so intimate. Indeed, contrary to the impression received from Dutch parents, the negotiation of Dutch girls' sexuality is more tension-ridden than that of Dutch boys. At the same time in most families, those tensions are negotiated in such a way that parents and girls remain connected, and the latter can integrate their roles as daughters and as sexual subjects.

There is, of course, a range in home environments. Some girls, like Natalie, project a relatively smooth negotiation in which parents support their daughters' autonomous decision-making and in which girls initiate sex in relationships and at ages acceptable to their parents. Yet, as we know from Natalie's mother (chapter 2), even in those families there can be bumps along the way. Ultimately, the smoothness of the negotiation hinges on accommodations from both sides—daughters' choosing boyfriends that their parents like and parents' honoring their daughter's choices—as well as enough time for everyone to get used to the new situation: were Heidi to want a boyfriend to spend the night, her parents would acquiesce. They believe, she says that "they have no business forbidding me anything in that area. They know I am reasonable enough to make my own decisions." But for her parents to feel comfortable with a sleepover, she knows, they would need to "know [the boy] well and like him, accept him."

The transition is more fraught when there is little communication about sex at home, and when there are strong conflicts between parents' desires and girls' behavior. Margie learned about contraception at school; it was never discussed at home. When in a joint interview with her friend Francine, Margie hears that Francine told her mother about her sexual debut at fifteen, she says, "I would never tell my parents!" Francine's mother was angry when she learned that her daughter had sex at fifteen, but Francine does not regret telling her: "It is something that is yours, but I think you do want to share it with your parents. . . . I mean, I wanted to tell that to my mother. I don't know. It was just on my mind. So I told her, regardless of the consequences." Unlike Margie, who has no desire for a boyfriend to spend the night at home and spends the night secretively at his house, Francine would like her boyfriend to sleep over at home. Now that Francine is approaching seventeen, she thinks she stands a chance that a sleepover will be permitted once her mother gets to know her boyfriend: "I think it will be allowed. I hope so."

But even without overt conflict, several Dutch girls indicate that sexuality can be tension-ridden. Fleur's reaction when her parents gave her a sex education book was, "Get out of here with all those books." Fleur does not fault her parents: "They meant well, but I didn't like it at all. . . . But that is me, not them." Even now, she says, it does not "feel good when I talk about that with my parents." Marjolein is also not eager to discuss sex with her parents. "It is not like I'll think, 'Let me ask a question about that.'" She is not sure she would tell her parents if she were to have sex: "It would depend on what they think of him because if they don't like him then it is a very intimate thing [to share]." But like Fleur, Marjolein is quick to mitigate the strength of her aversion, adding that when the topic of sex and contraception comes up at home, "we deal with that in a very relaxed manner." Thus, rather than validate their initial aversion, both girls demonstrate that they do not view such discomfort around sex as entirely legitimate.

Differences and discomfort notwithstanding, as a daughter's sexual debut moves from the hypothetical to the real, talk about contraception usually intensifies. The intensification of engagement comes from both sides. Petra's parents are more conservative than most. When Petra had a serious boyfriend, they told her that a sleepover at sixteen after three months of courtship was out of the question: "They would rather I not go to bed with him so very quickly." But her father added, "You are allowed to touch," which Petra thought "was sweet of him." And her parents did encourage her to go on the pill. "They thought it would be safer that way." At fifteen, Fleur was deeply repelled at the notion of telling her parents when she was considering having sex. However, as a sixteen-year-old she was, as we learned from her mother, Ria van Kampen, in chapter 2, passionately working to persuade her reluctant parents to let her boyfriend spend the night, insisting that she was ready for sexual intercourse and using the pill.

Several Dutch girls say that although their mothers would accept their own assessment of readiness, they would encourage them to think things over carefully before making a decision. When Elizabeth had her first period, her mother "explained everything," which gave Elizabeth a "safe feeling." She also said: "If you want to go on the pill, I will allow you to. Because I'd rather you go on the pill than come home pregnant really young." Were Elizabeth to tell her mother that she wanted to go on the pill, her mother would "first talk about it with me, give the advantages and disadvantages. She'll say, 'Think about it for a few days.' If [after those days] I reach the same conclusion, she'll say, 'Okay.'" Marleen thinks that if she were contemplating having sex, she would probably tell her parents because, she says, "You'd want to share it with someone. And [your parents] can give you advice." Her mother would probably tell her to "do it safely" and ask, "Don't you want to wait a little longer? Are you sure that you are ready?"

Thus, one way or another, most Dutch girls say their (potential) sexual debut has or will be brought into speech. This communication has both a controlling and an affirming component: girls are subject to ongoing efforts at social control, but they are also able to assert themselves as sexual subjects. Julia wants her parents to stop urging her not to have sex too easily with someone. "They should know," she says, "that I am not someone [who jumps into bed right away or does it unsafely]." Still, Julia foresees that when the moment comes, she will tell her parents about it: "I myself will want to tell them," she says. "Not because they *have* to know, but I myself, I will want to say it." A friend of Julia's did not want tell to her parents, but "they knew." It came up in conversation and was not a problem. "Fun for you" was their reaction. Julia understands, "I also think it would be fun—if I were a parent. [I would also think fun], that you are experiencing all of that when you're in adolescence. After all, it is all very exciting."

The prospect of a boyfriend's spending the night with them at home, like the prospect of sharing that they have initiated sexual intercourse, evokes a variety of reactions in Dutch girls. Elizabeth is confident that her parents would permit a sleepover, and she would quite enjoy having one: "Yes," she says, "I think it would be *gezellig*." But several Dutch girls say that having a boyfriend sleep over at home would NOT be *gezellig*. Pauline has slept at a boyfriend's house but not at home: "Everyone around me . . . I don't think that would be fun." Marjolein's first response is also "Yak no." But as she weighs the options, she switches gears, illustrating how the psychology of incorporation requires a certain cultural and emotional work:

> I think [a sleepover] should be possible if you've known him for a while and your parents have known him. . . . I think sticking him in another room is so extreme in the other direction—with separate doors, hallway in between. . . . No, I don't think I would want that either. Then it would be better [to have him] in my room.

In short, the Dutch girls experience some of the same fears of parental disapproval, desire for privacy, and ambivalence about sharing "a very intimate thing" as do their American peers. But their family cultures give them different options for resolving those fears, desires, and ambivalences. With a clearly demarked cultural space of acceptable sexuality, girls can integrate their sexual subjectivity with their roles as good daughters. That shared space comes with costs and benefits: in the negotiation of the exact parameters of the acceptable, parents are able to exercise some control, which may explain why, unlike their male peers, some Dutch girls do not want sleepovers at home. Normalizing sexuality in speech and practice also takes emotional work, which not all Dutch girls are willing to perform. At the same time, with a shared space for acceptable sexuality, it is easier for Dutch girls to ask for parental support, receive recognition for an emerging part of their lives, and speak about some of its excitement and joys.

The Mandates of *Gezelligheid*

The incorporation of adolescent sexuality into the Dutch middle-class household is part of broader pattern whereby teenagers remain firmly rooted in domestic life—and in the daily rituals that create continuity over time and produce commonality between family members. Thus, even as they become oriented toward life outside the household, they do not view the world of their peers and the pleasures of adolescence as being at odds with the world of their parents and the pleasures of childhood. Like children and adults, Dutch teenagers are expected to participate in *gezelligheid* at home, out of duty *and* desire.[6] The prime form of such participation is the evening dinner. To eat dinner together is a rule that virtually all Dutch teenagers take for granted. Like Karsten's, Frank's parents want him "home on time for dinner, *gewoon* at half past five. . . . I can't just say, 'I don't feel like [eating dinner together]. I'll eat later.'" Karoline does not question dinner: "I live with four people. . . . You have to take each other into account, not that one eats at one moment and another eats at another moment."

Nor is participation in *gezelligheid* viewed by parents or teenagers as a gender-specific duty and pleasure. Regardless of their gender, teenagers are expected home for dinner, and they enjoy the togetherness the shared meal affords. Julia sees the shared dinner "as more social than duty" because "then you see each other." For Monique, household rules foster the feeling of "we belong together. . . . You need to have something to hold the socialness together, to keep a family together in a *gezellig* manner." Ben calls himself "not a family person," but still, he says "eating together is something that needs to happen. It is one of the few times you are together. I have a family. I like them." Lars appreciates the dinner rule. Otherwise, "you could never eat dinner *gezellig* together." Because his parents work at night, Gert-Jan prepares the meal and eats together with his two siblings: "I think it is *gezellig* with the three of us."

As part of being a *gezellig* member of the family, teenagers are expected to make an effort to share events and experiences with siblings and parents. This is true for girls *and* boys. Indeed, Dutch boys are more likely than their American peers to say they talk a lot with their parents.[7] Thomas likes talking with his mother: "Yes, I think that is really *gezellig*: just always talking with her for a little while." Berend, an only child, says he and his mother "know everything about each other, but that is reasonably normal. . . . She's my mother. We've known each other my whole life." Madeleine says it is important that "when something is going on, you need to tell each other, so that you don't become strangers to one another. [You need to] talk often. Not have any secrets from each other." When children fail to participate in *gezelligheid*, panic can ensue. When one of Monique's siblings withdrew from the ritual of talking, it provoked a sense of crisis in other family members: "Oh no, the family is falling apart."

The mandates of *gezelligheid* also require young people to demonstrate a certain amount of consideration for other family members and to take into account their needs. Especially in families with few explicit rules, there are exacting unspoken expectations that children demonstrate attunement to other family members without probing. Dorien's parents raise her in a "free" manner and trust that she will behave in a "social" way, which means, she explains, "Doing things for each other even if you do not like doing it. . . . You help each other." Gert-Jan's parents are not strict at all, but when Gert-Jan's mother returns home after work "you are right away supposed to offer her something to drink" since his mother "pays attention to those small things." Thomas is also "allowed to do a lot," but he explains that leniency has a price: "I have to be nice to [my mother] and help her now and then." When Thomas forgets to take clean laundry upstairs on his own initiative, his mother becomes angry: "I'll say, 'Tell me that I *have* to do it.' 'No that [impulse to help] should come from inside of you,' she'll say."

Some girls say that the mandates of *gezelligheid* can be a bit much, suggesting that these mandates constrain them more than their male peers. Petra's parents would like her to stay home every night: "They think that is *gezellig*, nice at home, together, doing something with all of us. [Our family] is close-knit. . . . [But] I can't be home every evening." Julia enjoys having dinner with her parents, but when they tell her "come and sit downstairs" for a shared breakfast, she says, "I purposively don't say anything. And I hope they notice [that I don't enjoy that]." Fleur is content with her home life: "We have it, *gewoon gezellig*." Her mother would like her to tell her when she is in love: "She is *very* curious." But Fleur does not want to share that much. Monique, now eighteen, says household rules are important: "You need to hold your family together." But when she was sixteen, togetherness did not appeal: "I am myself. I am my own person, my own me. Get away with those rules. I am going my own way."

Tensions notwithstanding, few Dutch teenagers question the premise that sharing experiences and taking other family members into account are important because shared experiences and mutual understanding foster trust and feelings of connection. Sam believes it is important to do things "like celebrating Saint Nicholas. . . . [Doing] the *gezelligheid* things: seeing each other regularly, so you don't grow apart too much." Diana also believes it is important to do things together, like celebrating birthdays: "Otherwise you start living parallel lives. Then you don't know how the other person is thinking. . . . [When] you know how the other person feels and thinks . . . you can trust each other." Parents and teenagers need to know "more or less what is going on inside of another person," says Pauline: "So that you can take it into account if something is going on. [They] also need to show understanding, not hold onto something unilaterally."

The belief that neither parents nor teenagers ought to act "unilaterally" during adolescence results in an exercise of power that blunts its sharp edges, while requiring the young to exhibit a self-motivated "sensibility" and attunement to the household rules. The word "agreement" captures the blunting of power and the demands that come with it. When Heidi was younger, she accepted her parents' rules without questioning them. But now that she is fifteen, her parents no longer tell her what to do. As in Karsten's family, the main rule in Heidi's family is: "keep to your agreements." An agreement, Heidi explains, is "something both parties agree to. Not that one party says: 'You do this.'" Peter's parents changed their approach "now [that] I am becoming more sensible. . . . Now I am getting a say. I never used to have that. But now we first talk about things. It is not like, 'Keep your mouth shut and do it.' Now we first talk about it. That is why I don't speak of 'rules' but of 'agreements.'"

Boys and girls alike speak to the importance of "indulging" one's parents. The significance of indulging each other is not just that it makes possible a system of control that is not unilateral but also that it keeps young people and parents on the same page. Madeleine's parents are not "really indulgent, that they let you just go your own way." Her parents set rules. But they do not tell her, "You HAVE to do this or that. . . . [They don't tell me what I have to do with] my job and hobbies. They are not like that. And I can talk to them about everything. They are open minded. They are not old fashioned. They do stand in this time." For parents and teenagers to relate well, Madeleine says:

> Parents should not be too exacting in the demands they make of their children because at this age that can make certain people contrary. And communicate: when something is going on, you need to tell each other, so that you don't become strangers to one another. Talk often. Not have any secrets from each other. Each side has to indulge the other a bit.

Sam echoes the same theme of the importance of mutual indulgence: "Both [parents and teenagers] need to give in a little bit. So the child shouldn't try to go his own way too much and the parents shouldn't impose too much." Julia says "it is not very handy" when parents simply command, as she has seen happen with some of her friends:

> I think it needs to be discussed, what you yourself think. Not that that means that you need to get it your way immediately. But so that your parents can respond with: "Yes, but this and that [reason]"—so that they can tell you why [what you want] is not good. But they need to know how you see things, I think. Then they can also steer you in the right direction, like [by saying]: "Oh that is strange."

The exercise of control through connection not only assumes the possibility of agreement but also produces a certain essential similarity between parents and children. Indeed, many Dutch teenagers emphasize how much they and their parents agree. Even when she and her parents seem to disagree, says Diana, it turns out that "we all want the same thing anyway. . . . Usually, only one of us thinks differently and then that needs to be set straight." Hans views his family as "sort of average" in how they deal with things. He thinks that parents and children should establish "good rules" together. . . . So the [rules are ones] you both kind of agree with." Tanja has heard of "other [kids] who always have fights with their parents but I always agree with [mine]." When Lars and his parents disagree, "we consult," he says: "Usually something comes out of that which lies in the middle. Then I am able to convince my parents or they convince me." When Niek and his parents fight, they also "talk it out" and eventually move in each other's direction because "if you both want something different, you'll have to."[8]

But sometimes there are undeniable differences and conflicts of interest between parents and teenagers, and the language of agreement becomes a tool in a power struggle. Marleen thinks her parents are too uptight. They do not like it when she comes home late or fails to help around the house. Marleen recounts how her parents communicate their displeasure using the mandates of *gezelligheid*: "[They say] I am not keeping to my agreements. . . . That I am asocial, messy, that I am not taking anyone into account." Berend's mother does not want him drinking and eating as he pleases. Hence, he says, she "had agreements that I was not allowed to take [cookies and soft drinks] except when I asked." But those "were more [a question] of her making an agreement with me, then that I was making agreements with her." There is good reason that his mother thought there was an agreement: sometimes, Berend explains, "I say I agree but later I do it my own way anyway, just out of laziness."

Even when conflicts concern matters weightier than cookies and cleanliness, the mandates of *gezelligheid* can be a way for parents to exert control through connection. In his own words, Peter is not "an easy child." He lacks discipline. Still his parents do not punish as they did when he was younger. They discuss. Well aware that the discussions are aimed at changing his behavior, Peter says, "I do hate those discussions." His parents "don't yell," but, he says, "they say they are disappointed . . . [which is] is one of the worst things." Peter's parents were *very* disappointed when they found out he was selling drugs. Prior to that discovery, Peter had enjoyed a great deal of latitude. But in its aftermath, Peter no longer has the trust or the freedom he once did. To get back to the "old level," Peter says, "I am trying to keep to my agreements as much as possible" and to "do everything my mother asks." Peter says his parents have always considered his needs. Now he is trying to reciprocate, and he has noticed that when "you are not always just doing things for yourself," things "become more fun, more *gezellig*."

"They Will Do it Anyway"

Even as the mandates of *gezelligheid* are a formidable force anchoring young people to home, sexuality and other pleasures of adolescence draw Dutch teenagers, like their American counterparts, toward peers and away from their families of origin. From age fifteen and sixteen on, Dutch girls and boys increasingly want to "go out," which, in the Dutch context, means going out to cafés and discos with groups of friends. In such cafés and discos, which draw a mix of high school and college students as well as working youths, Dutch teenagers usually drink alcohol, sometimes smoke cigarettes, and occasionally smoke marijuana. Such venues for going out are also prime places—next to school and sport clubs—for teenagers to meet potential boyfriends and girlfriends. Because going out lessens parental control and increases exposure to danger, when, where, and how often girls and boys are allowed to go out can be sources of conflict.

However, the notion that, from the mid-teens onward, the young cannot be forbidden from doing what they want inspires parents to let their children remain relatively free. Parents and teenagers alike believe that when the former are too strict the latter do whatever is forbidden—sex, alcohol, or smoking—*secretively*. Thus, blanket prohibitions are viewed as unwise and counterproductive, and Dutch sixteen-year-olds, unlike their American counterparts, rarely encounter rules at home which purport to prohibit their entry into "adult" activities altogether. Instead, parents meet their teenage children's exploration of the pleasures and dangers of growing up with a "vigilant leniency," tolerating exploration within distinct parameters. Part of the bargain of "vigilant leniency" is that the young must meet their parents part way, not keep their activities *stiekem*, and not veer too far off course from what "can and cannot be done."

Not all parents practice "vigilant leniency." A minority of the Dutch teenagers describe their parents as unequivocally "strict." Petra says she has always been taught "that when they say that I have to do something, then I just have to do that." Now sixteen, that lesson about unquestioning obedience to her parents continues unaltered. Strict parents tend to impose nonnegotiable decisions about when teenage children are allowed to go out and what time they must come home. Marcel's father, for instance, decides what time he must come home: "I'll try to make it a little later, but in the end he makes the decision." And when Marcel and his father disagree, "he usually gets his way." Pauline's parents regularly tell her she cannot go out on nights when she wants to. When she is not allowed to go out, Pauline gets "angry. . . . I have a hard time accepting it." Her parents' response to her anger is: "You just have to accept it when we say, 'No.'"[9]

But more commonly parents seek their children's agreement with their decisions about teenagers' going out. When Marjolein was fifteen and first wanted to go out, her parents' initial response was: "Well, no." Eventually, they made "an agreement" with their daughter that she would be allowed to go out once a month. Over time, the agreement loosened, and now that she is sixteen Marjolein's parents are "quite lenient." Marjolein thinks that is good: "[Otherwise] eventually you are going to do it *stiekem* and then you spend all evening feeling a bit . . . No, I think that is bad." It is not often that young people go out *stiekem*, says Marjolein. "You see it occasionally." The other day, Marjolein was at a party "and suddenly, a mother shows up. Oh that is really horrible. She really shows up to pick her daughter out of the crowd, [saying] 'Hey this is not what we agreed to.'" But Marjolein's parents always know her whereabouts. Nor does Marjolein "mind staying home now and then."

While most teenagers are admonished to be careful and not drink too much, few have been told not to drink alcohol altogether. Fifteen-year-old Fleur says her parents "don't like [that I drink], but they have not said, 'I don't want you to drink.' That they have not said at all. They don't forbid me to do it." Her mother has said, "You do have to look out." Her parents have told her about their own experiences: "They don't get drunk now, but they have gotten drunk. I think they think: 'It is part of [life].'" Likewise, Berend is sure he is allowed to drink if he wants to, although his mother "would not really like it." She would not tell him not to drink because "she cannot start to forbid me everything. . . . It is normal to [drink alcohol]." Elizabeth's parents also do not forbid. Instead they encourage her to form and exercise her own judgment:

[My parents] do not say, "You are not allowed to [smoke, drink, do drugs]." They know: if kids want to do it, they will do it anyway. I am free to do it. They give me a lot of information about what drugs, alcohol, and smoking

do to you. Not to disapprove, but . . . to reach your own conclusion that it is
bad for you.

While most Dutch teenagers are allowed to drink in moderation, they
know that their parents do not want them to get drunk, smoke, or start
experimenting with drugs. The first time Hans came home drunk his parents "had to laugh hard." But the second time, "they were angry," and they
made Hans stay home in the evening for a week. Frank's mother has told
him that if he does not smoke tobacco until he is eighteen, he will receive
free driving lessons. But even so, she also said to him: "If you do want to
smoke, don't do it *stiekem* but come and smoke *gezellig* at home." Heidi's
parents "would not object" if she wanted to drink alcohol. Although they
would disapprove of drunkenness or drugs, they would not forbid it. But
"they would forbid it if they *could*," she adds.

Like Heidi, several other Dutch teenagers say parents simply lack the
power to forbid. When Sam started smoking marijuana regularly after
school, his parents "of course did not think that was very great. They said
fairly often that I should not do it too much and that I needed to think
about school." But they never told him point blank to stop: "They know
quite well that if they say that, I will do it anyway." Likewise, Gert-Jan believes that if he wanted to smoke, his parents would have few weapons to
stop him. "They cannot really say: 'You will not smoke.' You are going to do
it anyway, if you feel like it. They cannot hit you anymore. . . . They cannot
do anything really." Of course, parents could tell their children to leave the
house. But Gert-Jan doubts any parent would do that "only because you
are smoking." Still he proclaims with emphasis: "I do have respect for my
parents, of course. I know *what can and cannot be done.*"

Knowing What Can and Cannot Be Done

The language of shared agreement is not always matched by teenage behavior. And vigilant leniency notwithstanding, Dutch teenagers are sometimes *stiekem*. At fifteen, Fleur is angry that she is only allowed to go out
to cafés once a month. Her parents appeal to their agreements with her,
but she thinks "did I really agree to that?" In an effort to change the status
quo, Fleur tells her parents: "Why should I not be allowed to go out more
often? I wouldn't make a mess of things, like coming home really late. . . .
Why are you begrudging me the pleasure of going out twice a month?"
Her parents counter by taking out the family date book and saying: "Look
at how often you have had a party?" But there is a reason Fleur has many

parties: as home-based forms of *gezelligheid*, parties are not subject to the same restrictions. Sometimes, as part of birthday parties, Fleur goes out to a café in town *stiekem*. She also uses a strategy common among her American peers:

> I sleep over with friends [who live one village over] and then I often go out. [My parents] say: "Yes, I do need to be able to trust you." . . . And I say, "You'll just have to trust me." Look, then I am lying, but it is also a little bit their own fault, I think. If they were a little more lenient, then I wouldn't do that. But they are not.

With regard to drinking and smoking, some Dutch teenagers also fudge the truth. When Gert-Jan's father asks him how much he has drunk, he "makes the number smaller." Erik's parents allow him to drink beer when he goes out with his friends. What they don't know is that he also drinks cocktails and started when he was fourteen: "I felt very tough and started to drink whisky. But I also liked how it tastes, that is the problem." Karoline's mother has not forbidden her to drink and smoke, saying "otherwise you're going to do it *stiekem* and that I do not want to have at all." Still Karoline smokes at parties without telling her mother. Her mother also does not know that when Karoline and her friend Lieke go out, they "pre-drink" store-bought alcohol in groups of friends. Lieke realizes "it is actually quite a lot that you drink. Sometimes, you feel quite tipsy, my parents think that I only drink a few glasses, but I drink more than my parents think."

Indeed, parental and peer norms about the acceptability of drunkenness diverge. Unlike their parents, many Dutch teenagers are not troubled by drunkenness per se. But while they do not reject drunkenness outright, those who accept it as part of *gezelligheid* draw telling distinctions between problematic and nonproblematic varieties of being drunk: the first criterion is whether drinkers take into account their social relationships and refrain from causing trouble and disruption. Pauline thinks being drunk "happens sometimes" and that "is fine [as long] as you are not a nuisance to other people." Erik also says that people who are able to drink "normally" are those who "don't bother others."

The second related criterion is that drinking must be motivated by an inner desire and characterized by inner control, even in a state of drunkenness. Madeleine thinks boys drink initially because they are trying to impress others. That is wrong, she says. But, "if you say, 'I am drinking because I think it tastes and feels good,' well, then you should drink. As long as it does not make you aggressive, I don't mind." When you first start drinking, Erik says, "You make mistakes, you keep chugging and you get toasted. After a while, that lessens and you drink because it tastes and feels good to you yourself and because it is *gezellig*." Marjolein also distinguishes between different kinds of drunkenness: "Being drunk is in and of itself not so bad. . . . It is a broad concept. What I don't like is when people can't stand on their legs. Drinking a bit is no problem if that makes your evening more fun, but you need to be aware of how much you can take."

And although they recognize that they go beyond their parents' limits, most Dutch teenagers believe that they still know "what can and cannot be done." Marjolein says, "When I look at myself and my friends, then [how we drink] is *gewoon gezellig*. It is not too much." Marcel also feels he has control: he knows when to switch to soft drinks in time. He does not want to throw up or be unsafe on the bicycle ride home. He does not want to bike in a crooked line at the end of the evening, or else his sister would suspect that he is tipsy. Pauline says "I know what I am doing when I drink. It is not like I am drinking for the first time this year." Her parents are confident she can handle alcohol: "I don't always tell them how much I have drunk because that would just worry them. Sometimes I come home and I am tipsy, but I can keep it hidden from them." Elizabeth also says she can handle alcohol most of the time: "Yes, yes . . . sometimes, not yet. But usually yes."

Several of the older Dutch teenagers report having drunk or smoked marijuana a lot and say that they have since arrived at a place of greater control and self-possession. Ben's parents always said, "You must learn from your mistakes," and he believes he has: "I can keep myself under control. After twenty [half-pint] beers, I am still quiet. You need to know your limits. If it goes over that limit, it will all come out again. But under that, I am fine. I am a calm drinker—I am not aggressive. I talk normally; no one notices it about me." After a period of smoking a lot of marijuana, Sam drastically cut back after coming to the realization one summer, "It really does feel better to be without alcohol and drugs." Monique also has had a learning experience. When she was sixteen, she often had the experience of "really being drunk, which is why later, at age seventeen or so, I really did not do that anymore." Now, she gets a little tipsy but not drunk: "It is a discovery: 'What can I do, what can I not do.' You need to try that out."

In short, vigilant leniency does not prevent the Dutch teenagers from doing things *stiekem* or sometimes going to excess. But although in doing so, they go beyond their parents' viewpoints, their transgressions do not take them completely outside of adult-regulated society. First, for better or for worse, teenagers have access to institutional spaces—the family meal, family celebrations, the café, and the disco—in which they participate in *gezelligheid* alongside adults of different generations. Equally significant, however, are the ways in which young people, even as they discover their individual capacities and boundaries, measure their behavior against shared notions of *what can and cannot be done*. Having gotten drunk once and running rampant through people's gardens in the middle of the night, sixteen-year-old Thomas is unsure about whether he is ready to drink: "On the one hand yes, on the other hand no. I know what can be done and what cannot, I think."

Control through Connection

In contrast to their American counterparts, for whom sexuality is a furtive or segmented experience of coming of age that causes separation in their relationships with their parents, Dutch teenage girls and boys are encouraged to make their sexuality *gewoon* and *gezellig*—integrate it into the self and the household without having it cause unnecessary upheaval and discord. As we have seen, Dutch girls and boys encounter a range of home environments, and the degree to which the negotiation of sexuality matches the ideal of tension-free "normality" also varies. Such variations notwithstanding, being able to discuss sexuality and spend the night with serious girlfriends and boyfriends at home lessens a tension that could grow into a disjuncture between peer and parental culture. The sleepover also creates a bridge between continuity and change. And the Dutch teenagers do generally experience, or foresee, a self-directed sexual development while remaining connected to home and parental support.

This connection goes hand in hand with a sometimes subtle, sometimes not so subtle ongoing control, including the admonishment to use contraception and the explicit or implicit encouragement to engage in a relationship-based sexuality with partners their parents like. Socialized to view sexuality as closely connected to contraception and condom use, most Dutch girls and boys do regard the responsibilities and pleasures of sex as intertwined. With some of the highest teenage contraception and dual protection rates in the world, they largely—though as Ben's experience illustrates certainly not always—practice what they have been preached.[10] Notably, unlike the boys, a few Dutch girls say they would rather sleep over at their boyfriend's house than at home. Their reluctance suggests that these girls want to avoid the parental scrutiny and the emotional work that is involved in bringing a boyfriend home for the night, or to simply bypass the interweaving of middle-aged domesticity and youthful romance.

The psychology of incorporation is embedded in a broader pattern of domestic life, which anchors adolescents to other members of the household in the pleasures and obligations to togetherness. As they move from the relative unquestioned obliging to parents during childhood to the formation of independent positions during adolescence, Dutch teenagers are required to observe the mandates of *gezelligheid* and develop an interdependent conception of their personhood. These mandates include mandatory sharing and mutual attunement among family members, which are intended to produce agreement and commonality and to avoid secrets and alienations. The togetherness that results from the mandates of *gezelligheid* facilitates the "vigilant leniency" that parents practice with regard not just to sex but also to drinking, smoking, and drugs. For folk wisdom, shared by youth and adults alike, has it that the exercise of blatant power through prohibitions and punishments is ineffective, as teenagers will "just do it anyway."

Such "soft power" may work wonders much of the time, but it is not foolproof. Some Dutch teenagers go out at night *stiekem* when they think their parents' "vigilant leniency" is not lenient enough. And some youth move faster sexually than their parents would like or do not use contraception. Many Dutch teenagers who partake in the pleasures of alcohol stretch the truth about how much they drink. Indeed, Dutch teenagers are as likely as their American peers to have been drunk, although they are less likely to have used drugs.[11] Excess comes at a price—Dutch interviewees who say they have drunk or done drugs a lot have often had to repeat a grade in high school. But with a system that gives many second chances to complete high school, with emergency contraception and abortion easily accessible, and without the dangers of driving or harsh legal sanctions for soft drug use, veering off course may take its toll but rarely leads teens into dire straits. Indeed, as those who admit they went too far insist, being able to "discover and try it out" has allowed them to learn from their experience what "can and cannot be done."

SEVEN

Romantic Rebels, Regular Lovers

Throughout the preceding chapters, we have seen many indications that Dutch and American parents and teenagers conceptualize and experience gender differently. The American parents paint a gender-polarized universe in which girls and boys battle over competing aims—but rarely meet on mutual terms. We have seen that for American girls, it can be difficult to reconcile sexual maturation with parents' expectations of them as "good girls," while American boys confront the expectation that they will be "bad." Dutch parents, by contrast, assume that boys and girls both will fall in love and form relationships, and Dutch girls and boys encounter similar preconditions for a sleepover—personal and interpersonal readiness, contraceptive use, and respect for domestic peace. But girls are more likely to encounter tension in negotiating their sexuality and some prefer reducing parental involvement by sleeping at their boyfriends' houses.

This chapter switches gears to examine how girls and boys in the two countries, using the messages they receive in school, from health-care institutions, and in popular and peer culture, conceptualize and navigate dilemmas of gender outside the home. Two issues are at stake. The first concerns the physical risks and dangers of sex which have traditionally been thought to plague girls disproportionately—both in reality and in the discursive construction of sexuality. Indeed, American feminist scholars have argued that sexuality always takes place at a nexus of pleasure and danger, although for teenage girls, the emphasis on danger often outweighs that on pleasure.[1] But what we will see in this chapter is that American girls *and* boys both express little faith in their capacity to control the outcomes of sexual activity, with boys as, if not more, likely to articulate a discourse of danger. The Dutch boys and girls assume, by contrast, that they can proactively prevent the unwanted consequences of sex, although, especially in long-term relationships, much of the work of creating a sense of safety falls to girls.

The second issue concerns the ways teenagers in both countries confront gender-specific expectations and constraints, including the sexual double standard that makes (too much) sex a liability for girls and too little a liability for boys.[2] Notably, Dutch teenagers are more prone to speak of differences and conflicts between girls and boys than are their parents. Indeed, in some respects, the generation of teenagers gives evidence of more cross-national similarity than does the generation of parents.[3] At the same time, how teenagers perceive and experience these shared dilemmas of gender differs depending on their cultural templates. The template of adversarial individualism—with its skepticism about people's inherent relational needs and proclivities—leads American teenagers, especially boys, to construct an oppositional understanding of self. Meanwhile, in accord with the template of interdependent individualism, neither Dutch girls nor their male counterparts view themselves as especially unique for wanting to integrate love and lust.

This chapter starts with two vignettes and additional examples from the interviews with American teenagers to show how both girls and boys have learned that sex carries risks that are beyond their power to fully control. It then examines a gender-specific risk—the slander of being called a slut, which looms much greater for American girls than it does for their Dutch counterparts. American boys, in turn, confront the assumption circulated in same-sex peer culture and the media that they seek "soulless sex," a notion that many fervently resist, articulating an almost "hyper-romanticism." The second half of the chapter examines the same themes using vignettes and segments from interviews with Dutch teenagers. We will see how Dutch boys and girls learn from a variety of institutions that it is possible and necessary to "do it safe." We also see how assumptions about the "normality of love" allow girls to avoid being slandered as sluts and boys to integrate ideals and reality. At the same time, assumptions about the "normality of love" can also obscure important differences between girls' and boys' readiness for love and sex.

"A Big Mistake"

Sixteen-year-old Stephanie is a quintessential "all-American good girl." As she explains, "I get the good grades. I'm obedient; I follow the rules most of the time." But she is also a cheerleader, and in small-town Tremont, people often get the wrong idea: they think "[cheerleaders] are slutty and that they sleep around—probably because they wear such shorts skirts." Getting a bad name has serious and long-lasting repercussions, as one of Stephanie's friends discovered: "She was drinking and, if you drink, then you are automatically easy, so she got a really bad reputation and guys started spreading rumors that, you know, she was a sure thing. . . . One little thing can wreck your whole reputation for all of high school."

Boys don't have to worry about these kinds of mistakes, Stephanie explains, "because . . . [if you are a boy] you are cool if you drink, you are cool if you have sex." Stephanie believes "girls and guys are a lot different." She does not blame boys for the fact that "they always want something physical, it's just the way they are, their hormones or the way that they think. Also, it is peer pressure because I know that if guys do it, then they are considered cool." The whole thing is extremely unfair, according to Stephanie: "Because if guys do it they are looked up to and if girls do it they are looked down upon."

When Stephanie and her boyfriend had been going out for nine months, she started researching birth control options on the Internet. But, as we know from chapter 3, her mother, Cheryl Tober, did not respond positively to the news. "You may think that you are physically ready because your hormones are, but you are emotionally not going to be ready," Stephanie recalls her saying. Shortly thereafter, Stephanie and her boyfriend had their first intercourse, unprotected. Stephanie cannot say why: "[My boyfriend] never pressured me ever to do any of that." Still she felt pressure, "like I was obligated to because we were going out for so long."

While Stephanie has a blurry recall of what came before, the aftermath of her first sexual intercourse is ingrained in her memory: "I was just, like, scared to death. I was a nervous wreck and I told my mom about it because I tell her everything and I just wanted her to know that she was right. I was definitely not emotionally ready. My boyfriend and I were both a wreck." But only Stephanie was shamed at the pharmacy the next day:

> I had to go and get the morning-after pill, which was scary because they just looked at you like, "You stupid teenagers." . . . I had to get counseling to get it, and I was crying the whole way through because they just looked down on you.

Her mother responded as a friend, who helped Stephanie "get over it," and as a disciplinarian, who "shortened [her] chain." Now there are limits to how long Stephanie can spend alone with a boy. Stephanie does not mind. She doesn't want to be put in a position again to do something before she

is ready. She and her boyfriend broke up shortly after their fateful intercourse, but not before hashing over the big mistake at great length:

> [We talked] about how we shouldn't have done it and how it was a big mis-
> take and we were pushing ourselves too hard. After talking about it, you
> know [that helped] like being able to get over feeling really ashamed of my-
> self because I didn't think that I would ever do that because I wanted to wait
> until I was like eighteen or married.

"Screwed for the Rest of My Life"

When Jesse was fourteen, "drunk out of [his] mind," Jesse had sex with a
girl who was also drunk. Without the two knowing each other, Jesse and
the girl "were like 'hey let's go do this.' It just came on spontaneously. The
next thing you know, we were in bed." They had sex without protection
but got lucky. No pregnancy resulted. At that time, Jesse was taking other
risks as well. "The path I was going along was definitely the wrong path,"
he recalls. And for a while, he was smoking marijuana daily and drinking
heavily on the side: "I've gone through the experience of being [kind of]
addicted to a drug," he says. "That was like what I did."

Two years later, Jesse describes himself as radically altered. He is deeply
in love with his girlfriend of ten months. He has had many different girlfriends over the years, but "this is the only one I ever want to have from
now on. . . . We're just so happy together and I couldn't imagine being
with anyone else." Defying his father Harold Lawton's characterization of
boys (chapter 3), Jesse says, "My first priority in life is being in love with
my girlfriend, and giving her everything I can." He thinks he is different
from other teenage boys: "Most teenage guys are pretty much in it for
sex. . . . The only reason they get involved in relationships with girls is to
have sex. . . . I guess it's just a sexual drive or whatever but I can't really
relate to that."

Jesse and his girlfriend use condoms every time they have sex. But measuring his sexual behavior against what he sees as the gold standard, he
comes up short: "The best situation for two people to have sex would be if
they were totally committed to each other, like married," Jessie says. Moreover, like many of his American peers, Jesse views sex as something that
requires readiness for fatherhood. "It's pretty dumb that I do have sex because I am not ready to become a father right now. That's like probably the
worst thing that could happen to me." But, says Jesse: "I guess it is some-

thing that I'm willing to deal with . . . the risk of that, you know." Yet, the risk comes with an emotional cost:

> If you're not looking to have a baby, sex is definitely a risk. . . . I have had a situation where condoms have broken and I was like, flippin' out of my mind, about ready to puke. I was like, "Jesus Christ, we're dead. I'm screwed for the rest of my life." . . . But it turned out okay. . . . Yeah that scared the life out of me.

"The Risk of Ruining My Life"

If one of the lessons in the dramatization of adolescent sexuality is that sex is dangerous, as Jesse and Stephanie illustrate, then the American teenagers I interviewed seem to have taken that lesson to heart. The sense that sex is by definition risky is communicated not just at home but also in the other institutions that teenage girls and boys encounter—schools, pharmacies, and health clinics.[4] Sexual and reproductive education and services are uneven across the United States—with some teenagers receiving relatively easy access to information and services, while others encounter many barriers to clear information about the contraceptive technologies that can protect them against sex's unwanted consequences.[5] With the rise of "abstinence-only" education, even school districts not directly funded under this policy have shied away from teaching about condoms, contraception, and abortion, as well as about the positive aspects of sex and relationships.[6]

The lack of access to basic sexual health information and services is particularly apparent in Tremont, where a "pregnancy crisis center" perches prominently on one of Tremont's hills, and where even the school nurse does not know where Tremont girls go to get contraception.[7] Some Tremont girls are quite enterprising. Stephanie researched the Internet. Laurie checked out books from the library. But another Tremont girl, Ashley, does not recognize the word "contraception." She says that she knows what the pill is, but has not "any idea" where to get it. Contraception "seems like kind of a topic that people just kind of close off on," says Alexandra. And Lisa, an ambitious straight-A student, describes a pregnancy prevention project at school:

> We did a big teen pregnancy thing and everyone had to carry . . . this little doll and it had a key and every time it cried you had to hold the key in it and

it would wake you up in the middle of the night crying and you'd have to turn the key and you got graded on how many neglects it had and it can tell if you would hit it.

Teenagers growing up in Corona, by contrast, receive much more sex education. Caroline says she learned about diaphragms, condoms, and the pill in her health education class. Hence Kimberley, who received no sex education at home, learned at school how to "keep yourself safe and protected and do everything you can to not come across any problems." Yet, despite receiving a great deal more information at school than their Tremont counterparts, several Corona teenagers articulate the notion that sex can be life-ruining. As we saw, Jesse, a Corona boy, is either unaware of emergency contraception or does not know how he and his girlfriend might obtain it to protect themselves more fully against pregnancy. Kelly, a Corona girl, says that fear of AIDS is "probably the main thing that would stop [her] from having sex." "The risk of AIDS alone," she explains would make it hard for her to trust a potential sexual partner. "Because no matter how much I cared about the guy, he may be lying to me. I want to think that he wouldn't . . . but I don't want to run the risk of ruining my life just for that."[8]

Some American boys—from both Tremont and Corona—voice a similar suspicion of potential sexual partners and of the dangers their previous sexual experiences might pose to their health. When Michael considers having sex with a girl, he always wants to know "who she's been with, if anybody at all. Like diseases and stuff, you don't want that." Girls who have had sex are viewed differently from those who are inexperienced because of the risk of contracting an STI, says Steve. Using the language of drug addiction, he explains: "Guys will wonder 'is that guy clean that she's done it with?' Because if I want to get with her in the future or something and I don't know what's happened or if she's going to be pregnant or something, it makes me start to wonder." Given the risk of contracting an STI through sex, Steve would prefer to lose his virginity to a girl who was also a virgin, "unless I was older and it was just between me and her and we had been dating for a while. . . . If I knew she was clean herself."

Nor do the boys seem any less aware of the threat of an unintended teen pregnancy than girls. Like their female counterparts, they talk about teenage pregnancy as a very prevalent and possible outcome of sex. And if anything, several American boys suggest a greater sense of powerlessness than do girls about their capacity prevent it. Like Jesse, they seem to have little faith in condoms or other contraceptives and they see having sex as playing Russian roulette. Adam believes that "no matter how many combinations [of contraceptives you use] you're still not safe." Illustrating a similar sentiment, Phillip says he is certain he does not want to have sexual intercourse any time soon because he does not "want to deal with the responsibilities [of pregnancy] right now." While the fear of impregnating a girl may deter some from having sex, other boys like Jesse "take the risk" and have it hang over them. Donald uses condoms, but:

> I don't do it very often because I always have that feeling in the back of my head, what if I somehow did get her pregnant because I don't want to get someone pregnant this young. . . . You might think, "I am never going to get her pregnant." But you never know. It could happen. And then you are kind of screwed for life.

Indeed it *could* happen. Steve, interviewed a few days after Donald, has two friends who have unintentionally impregnated girls. Donald may be his third. Steve knows Donald just found out that day that his girlfriend had a positive pregnancy test. With the rest of his life hanging in the balance as he awaits a second pregnancy test, Donald is scared, Steve says. If the second one comes back positive, Steve thinks that Donald "would want to name [the child] and he'd want to care for it, but he does not want to have it." If Donald's girlfriend's second test comes back positive, it is more likely than not that she and he *will* have it since American teenage girls are twice more likely to carry a pregnancy to term than they are to terminate it.[9]

Access to abortion services has become increasingly difficult in recent decades in the United States.[10] Abortions are quite economically costly for most American girls. And a common conception of abortion as "killing a baby," even if it takes place in the earliest weeks of fetal development, may, as several of the American teenagers suggest, make it emotionally costly as well.[11] People often ask pregnant girls questions like, "Are you going to have an abortion, or are you going to love the kid, or are you going to give it away," says Steve. The choice, says Dorothy, is life-altering: "The girl has to deal with the fact that she is pregnant, that she may have to abort or give it up for adoption. She has to deal with that for her entire life." Randy echoes a similar sentiment. Sex is "a greater risk" for girls, he says: "If they get pregnant . . . and they decide to have an abortion, it's harder on them. [It will] stay with them forever knowing that they killed the baby. . . . If they do have the baby, that's [also] a lot of like trauma."

Slandered as a Slut

Another potential trauma that American girls face is being slandered as a "slut." The category of the slut is very salient in interviews with American girls: almost half of the girls spontaneously use words, like "slut," "slutty," or "easy" in reference to perceptions of girls' sexuality, or recount examples of girls who have been quite randomly slandered as a slut. Although some accounts that American girls and boys give suggest acceptance in American peer culture of teenage sex in the context of long-term relationships, Stephanie posits that sexual intercourse is "always [viewed as a] negative" in girls.[12] And like Stephanie, Laurie sees an endemic double standard: "If the guy does it, he's like cool or a pimp. The girl does it and she's a slut and everyone thinks of her badly, [which] I think is definitely something that should change but it probably never will." Finally, Kimberley has "seen a lot of girls, like, just made into these bad, horrible images that they can't get out of just for like one dumb [sexual] experience."

What stands out is the randomness of social derogation.[13] Being called a slut for having sex with multiple partners is a sure thing, says Dorothy, but even girls in long-term relationships or those without sexual experience are at risk, since if friends of a girl's boyfriend don't like her, "it will get spread around everywhere that she is a slut." Isaac has "friends who have really cared about someone and had sex with them because they love them and then people called them a slut and that's been very upsetting." Caroline has seen girls "call other girls with big breasts sluts, for no apparent reason, just because they have a bigger cup size." Katy was called "a little whore" by an angry boyfriend who "started like spreading rumors around the school." The rumors had quite an impact: "I was pretty much the talk of the school. Everybody was pretty much looking at me and whispering as soon as I would look over."

One reason the category of the slut remains so salient is that American peer and popular cultures remain profoundly ambivalent about girls' sexual desire and pleasure, alternatively denying girls' desires and viewing them, akin to boys' desires, as indiscriminate. Melissa says, "not very many girls want to have sex" and just go along for the boys' sake. Others suggest that girls use sex, often to their own detriment, as a weapon in the battle between the sexes. Patrick portrays a typical tug of war: "Girls are thinking, 'How can I hold on longer to this guy because I really like him?' And the guy is like, 'How can I get further?'" At the same time, American teenagers are grappling with a competing observation—that it is possible for girls to desire sex or, as Paula puts it, "There are horny women too." Adam has observed girls at school who "joke about [sex] all the time. . . . Guys are just supposed to be more into [sex] than girls are and that is not necessarily the case anymore." Isaac also sees girls being more overtly sexual: "There are a whole lot of girls who would do it anytime, any place, and they don't care."

Yet, dramatizing girls' desires in terms traditionally reserved for boys' desires is not the same as viewing girls' sexual exploration as a normal and legitimate part of their lives. Katy has observed that some girls "are really into like having sex and stuff," but she also believes that "you are either really into going for [sex] or you are not, there is no real in the middle." Caroline has observed that "[you've got] the easy girls or else the girls who are prudes and don't do anything with guys at all [or] the girls who have been in relationships for a long time." The same girl can even go from one extreme to another. Margaret has seen girls get "slutty" after drinking at parties. First, they are "real shy and then all of a sudden they start drinking and they're all on everyone and like they just get with someone. . . . The next day it's like nothing happened." And Laurie went from being "really shy" to making out "with tons of guys," and being called a slut.

A girl Laurie knows claimed the slut label as a badge of honor because "she likes having sex and does it a lot." But for Laurie, the social stigma against girls' sexual experimentation seems to have hampered the sense of entitlement to enjoy sex and communicate her wishes to her partners. She has done "hand jobs" (though not "blow jobs," she says), but, mirroring research on the highly gendered "orgasm gap" in college "hook-ups," Laurie's sexual encounters do not seem to have included reciprocation of pleasure.[14] Having borrowed books from the library, Laurie discovered that "for girls, actual insertion does not do anything unless you know where the G spot is." But she has felt uncomfortable sharing this knowledge with her sexual partners:

> I've had a guy finger bang me and it did nothing and this guy thinks this is happening. I don't know how to tell him that nothing is happening. I've told a couple of guys that they don't have to do that because I don't think you could and it's demeaning. But for girls, most of the time, if the girls want to get anything out of it, you do it on your own. When making out, it's mostly for the guys.

If one reason for the enduring power of "the slut" in American peer culture is a continued ambivalence about girls' desires, another reason is skepticism about whether teenagers can attain the feelings and relationships that legitimate sex. Kimberley disagrees when people say, "You're young.

You can't fall in love." But Margaret thinks "a lot of teenagers who have sex don't love each other. They may care about each other, but they're not in love." Teenagers "think anything is love," believes Dorothy, but it "just may be infatuation." Fiona says that "usually [sex] is with somebody that they didn't know or something that they did at a party." Even girls who are in long-term sexual relationships often describe themselves as exceptional. Caroline, for instance, thinks "there are not many kids who actually have relationships." Most "are just . . . pretty easy." Michelle says she has a good relationship, but she believes that for most teenagers sex "has nothing to do with love." Paula also sees herself as exceptional. For most people she knows "sex is just a frivolous thing," while for herself and her friends, sex is "a very sacred thing."

Many American girls are in romantic relationships, yet they tend to view falling in love as the exception rather than the rule. One reason may be that falling in love remains associated in the cultural imaginary with making a lifetime commitment, a capacity which few teenagers have. Melissa wants to wait to have sex until she knows "that's the person I'll probably want to be with forever." But she has "no clue" how she would know she felt such love. When girls do have sex assuming their boyfriend is the one they are "going to be with forever," as have several girls that Katy knows, they are "devastated" by a breakup.[15] That being in love continues to be measured against the ability to commit in marriage may explain why Alexandra is not sure she is in love with a boyfriend she cares about, and why Lisa is quick to add, "I don't know if it's [like] the love when you get married" after saying she is in love.[16] It may also explain why sex before being "eighteen or married" felt like such a big mistake to Stephanie.

Within the more liberal Corona context, peer culture provides a space—the relationship—within which girls are somewhat safeguarded from the risk of social derogation for having sex. And several Corona girls, who have established relationships in which they feel connected and empowered, describe pleasurable, self-directed experiences of sex.[17] Kimberley, for instance, describes her sexual evolution positively: "Just as we progress in our relationship, it's like, you want to touch this interesting person, and you want to see what they're like." Like Kimberley, Paula had sex with a steady boyfriend, a decision she never regretted. She describes being ready as "more of an issue of self, not somebody else. It's what you want to do, not because you want to give yourself away or because you feel you owe it to the person." Cultural ambivalences about girls' sexual agency and pleasure and their capacity to fall in love notwithstanding, some American girls describe having sex as a positive and enriching choice.

Soulless Sex and the Search for Meaning

American girls and boys both complain about what one might call a culture of "soulless sex." They tend to blame this soulless sex on popular culture and peer group dynamics which have reduced sex to a fad, a consumer item, and something with which to be "cool." Katy believes teenagers have sex "just to try out what it's like, to see what the big [deal is], because it's like all over television and in the movies and everybody's like 'oh, that is so cool.'" Dorothy says that the media have made sex seem as if "it's not such a big thing, you know, it's just, it's like, going to the mall, it's frequent, you know, it's all around you." When Isaac was younger, the norm was "no sex before marriage." Now eighteen, all his friends have sex, which he attributes to the fact that "the world preaches sex." Especially, "MTV is a big thing," he explains. "And they preach sex. Everything is sex in America. If you're not having sex, you're not cool. . . . Everybody talks about it. . . . You see it in movies and on TV and in songs."

But although American girls and boys both bemoan the loss of sex's meaning, it is the American boys who rail most passionately against the soullessness that results, maybe because they confront most acutely a cultural concept of themselves as driven by "raging hormones." In same-sex peer groups at school, in sports, and at work, they are confronted with the notion that they are supposed to single-mindedly and emotionlessly pursue sex.[18] Andy explains that "in the locker room guys will talk about sex and in the halls you will hear certain guys talking about having sex or whatever, their conquest from the weekend." Adam hears the guys he works with "bragging of something [sexual]." He thinks "guys are really into [sex] because . . . it feels like power, like they've conquered something you know. They are supposed to be like the aggressor." Dean sees guys "pretend as though they don't really care about the girl [they are with]. When they're alone, they'll care about them but when they're around [other guys, they pretend otherwise]. . . . I don't know if they're just all talk or if that's really the way they feel. But it's common."

Nor is it only other *boys* who put pressure on them to behave like "real boys." Several American boys have been propositioned by girls who wanted to have sex but not relationships. Patrick relates a situation in which a girl asked him to have sex. "Some girl came up to me and I was like, 'Ah, no!' I couldn't do it. . . . She said I was hella cute and everything." Dean has come to the conclusion that "a lot of girls are out there just to get the pleasure like guys are, and they really don't care very much if the guy has feelings for them or if they have feelings for the guy. It's a matter of physical attraction and instinct, I guess." Isaac had a girlfriend who wanted sex but not an exclusive relationship.[19] In interpreting that situation, he first uses the traditional "battle-of-the-sexes" language: her offer might seem "perfect from a hormonal point of view," because "girls get the whole emotional thing going." But he quickly shifts gears to a different story. He says he "cared about her a lot." So he did not have sex and broke up with her instead.

With the assumption that most boys are just vessels for what Jesse calls "sexual drive or whatever" and that many girls have stopped being the traditional bearers of meaning and relational connection, many American boys believe sex has lost its enchantment and has been reduced to an individualistic, bodily activity devoid of soul and connection. Andy says teenagers generally have sex "at a party atmosphere" or "not really when they care about each other." Adam does not see teenagers around him with meaningful relationships: "It's like strictly physical attraction." He poignantly illustrates a dark worldview in which biology and a ruthless commercial and interpersonal peer culture combine forces to drive teenagers to pursue physical pleasure blindly without exercising any individual agency or constructing any interpersonal meaning: "You see it on TV and you hear it in songs the way people portray it. . . . No one thinks it's like that special a thing. . . . It's like animals do it . . . to . . . increase their population and people . . . like the first two people, they just did it, just programmed to breed."

But what stands out in the interviews with American boys is how much they do not want to be those soulless automatons that have been "just programmed to breed." Several boys make a point of stating, cultural expectations of boyhood to the contrary, that they *do* have control over their sexual impulses. To underscore their capacity for self-control, they relate stories of having had the opportunity to have sex and having decided against it. Adam explains, "I have total control over what I'm going to do. . . . I mean, I've been to an all-night guys and girls sleepover party and nothing happened, so I know I can control myself." For other boys, Dean says, sex is "a matter of physical attraction and instinct." He is different: "Just this weekend, when my dad was out of town, I had a girl in bed with me. . . . We probably could have done anything we wanted to but I didn't feel the need to show that I felt good about being with her, more than just holding her and falling asleep with her in my arms, that was good enough for me."

Not only do boys resist the notion that they cannot control their impulses; many also contest the common perception that boys do not value relationships and love. Michael may want "more than one girl," and Patrick may recall his first sex with a friend as a nice birthday present. But American boys typically describe themselves much as Jesse does: as romantic rebels, aspiring to love and swimming against the tide of hormonally crazed boys.[20] "If you ask some guys, they'll say it's mainly just for the sex or whatever, but with me," says Randy, "you have to have a relationship with the person before you have sex with her. . . . I'd say I'm exceptional." Jeff wants to care about a girl before having sex: "Maybe even love them, know them for a long time, definitely, because most people don't really cherish it as anything. They don't respect it." There are guys whose "whole reason they want to go and find a girlfriend is because they want to have sex," says Phillip. He says he is different: "I want to really fall in love with somebody."

In an effort to distance themselves from the motivations of other teenage boys and to highlight the depth of their own romantic aspirations, some boys also draw distinctions between emotionality and physicality, identifying themselves with the former but not the latter. In doing so, they seem to distance themselves not only from other boys but also from sexual desire and pleasure. Jesse has just said that the most important thing to him is his love for his girlfriend, unlike most guys who just want sex. Asked why he believes guys are like that, Jesse responds, "I don't know. I can't understand. . . . I guess it is just sexual drive or whatever, but I can't relate to that." In a similar manner, Patrick believes he is different from most boys—although, just like Jesse Lawton, he used to have sex without being in love with his partners. Whereas most guys are wondering "how can I get further," he says, "after you think about it . . . if you really care about someone, you don't really care if you have sex or not."

In trying to discern what it means to fall in love, some set the bar very high. Phillip is disdainful of people "who have been going out for a month or so and they *think* they're in love." And even after dating his girlfriend for a year, Daniel is reluctant to say he is in love: "I am not really sure about [whether I am in love], so I'd say I wasn't. I am not a hundred percent sure." One reason for his uncertainty is that in high school "you need to explore different kinds of people." Another reason may be that "being in love," as several American boys describe it, requires an almost superhuman capacity to feel and to give, a heroic relinquishing of self.[21] Jesse, for instance, says that his first priority in life "is being in love with my girlfriend and giving her everything I can." Patrick does not think he has loved any of his previous girlfriends because that would mean "you're willing to give up anything for that person. . . . Love means you're willing to do anything for them no matter what the consequences are."

Like several female counterparts, a number of American boys view marriage as the benchmark for a truly meaningful relationship and the ideal circumstance for sex. However, the marriage ideal may not serve as a useful measure for healthy adolescent relationships. Even Jesse, who is "head over heels" in love with his girlfriend, still says that "the best situation for two people to have sex would be if they were totally committed to each other, like married." Randy struggles to explain the relationship that makes sex right. Finally, he says, "I'd say like when you're married. That would be the best way to put it. I'm like abstinent and everything. . . . I hope it is something I still have when I get married." Phillip wants "to really fall in love with somebody" before he has sex. He elaborates: his partner "has got to be someone where I can't see myself living with anybody else. Possibly even waiting until I am completely married." Yet, since many American teenagers are likely not to marry until almost a decade after they start having sex, this means that they set their ideals very far from the concrete reality of their lives.[22]

In the following vignettes, we meet two Dutch teenagers, Pauline and Erik. In several respects, their experiences resemble those of Stephanie's and Jesse's featured at the start of the chapter. Like Stephanie, Pauline had her first sexual intercourse under conditions that were less than ideal—uncertain, unprotected, and, from what we can ascertain, unsatisfying. And like Jesse, Erik is in a serious relationship with a steady girlfriend with whom he is very much in love. Moreover, in both countries, the girls and boys encounter some similarities in gender constructs and constraints promulgated in peer and popular culture. But despite similarities between the teenagers in both countries, Pauline's and Erik's experiences of themselves as sexual and romantic beings differ notably from their American counterparts, due to the institutional supports they receive and the cultural templates they have available to them.

"Not Completely Behind It"

In her sixteen years, Pauline has been in love plenty of times. She describes the experience as "thinking a lot about that person, feeling comfortable with him, being able to talk well with him. . . . You just feel good with that person. You want to be near him." At this age, Pauline explains, being in love "has a lot to do with your hormones . . . with your sexuality, and what you want. . . . It's the feeling that you can have of being really sexually attracted to that guy or girl, and [figuring out] whether you want to do something with him . . . go to bed with him." She sees boys and girls as more similar than different:

Both boys and girls are thinking about sex and they also want to do it, I think, but maybe don't dare to, [while] with relationships, it is more we'll see how far it goes, and now and then it is serious. . . . Perhaps boys think a little sooner, "Oh, I am going to be stuck with the girl," and boys may want sex a little sooner, but that can also be the reverse, so I don't see a clear-cut separation [between the two].

But probed about whether girls and boys are *viewed* differently, Pauline says:

With boys, it is more seen as "tough" (*stoer*) when they have been to bed with a girl. [And] if they have not lost their virginity by age eighteen, [it is a problem]. And with girls, it is [different]. Everyone is just like, "I am not ready for it, so I am not going to do it," you know. They deal with it differently.

And probed about whether or not girls are looked down upon, Pauline says: "More quickly [than boys], I think. . . . If you kiss with a [different] boy often, then you are more quickly [viewed as] a slut than a boy who kisses a [different] girl each week. And a girl who often has a boyfriend or often goes to bed with a boy will be looked down upon more quickly." Girls are safe, she says, as long "as it doesn't go too quickly."

When Pauline was fourteen, she had a boyfriend for six months with whom she had "gone further [than just kissing] and stuff." She asked her parents whether she could sleep over at his house: "We talked about it well. Of course, I went on the pill—well, I had not started it but I had gotten it. They knew how far things were." But, waiting for her period to begin, Pauline had not started the pill when she spent the night:

He asked me, you know, "Would you like to go to bed with me." And then I did it anyway. It is very strange, how you weigh things in that kind of moment, thinking of the reasons you would and the reasons you would not do it. I thought, at a certain point, well, "Why would I not do it? I want to, but . . ." And what that "but" is, you don't know. But still, you are not standing completely behind it.

The experience was not a success: "The condom slipped off. That is really very shitty! And that for your first time! Well, I was like . . . [to the] hospital for the morning-after pill." She and her boyfriend broke up. All in all, the experience "scared [her] to death." Still, she does not regret it: "Because the boy was really . . . not someone who talks, you know. . . . Because if he had started talking [and telling everyone] then you do start to think, 'Oh, why did I do this?'" Since then, she has kept relationships shorter, "going further" without having intercourse.

Looking back Pauline says, "I was young compared with other girls in my class. But that happens, when you have a boyfriend for six months. He was also older. He was eighteen, and you know, then you come to it sooner." Two years and several short-term relationships with no intercourse later, Pauline says, "I am ready for it. And I would like [to do] it." She is "open to" having sex with her current boyfriend once she really trusts him and is sure she is ready to do it. If she felt that certain, her parents would not stop her, Pauline says, if "I were on the pill and safe"—using condoms and contraception, as "really gets harped on in those commercials."

"In Their Right Mind"

At sixteen, Erik feels that he is given a lot of freedom in society and at home. Of course, there are "moral rules" which dictate that he must not go about his "business in an asocial manner." With regard to sex that means, as his father explained to him, "doing it safe, and general things, like, 'You should not do it when your girlfriend doesn't want to.'" Erik sees nothing unusual in his father's words: "Most parents tell their children on time how everything works and what can be done and what cannot be done."

When Erik and his girlfriend had been together for a few months, his parents and hers decided that the couple would be allowed to spend the night together. Erik explains: "They could see that the relationship seemed kind of serious." Around age sixteen, "it is normal to be allowed to sleep together," says Erik. "I'd let my children do the same." Erik's parents might have been surprised to discover that their son's first sex took place considerably before his first sleepover: "We did it after two weeks, but to tell you the truth, it just felt perfect," Erik says. One reason, Erik says, is that "I really had the idea that I wanted to do it with *her*." He explains, "I had had the idea for a while, 'I want to grow old with you.'" And indeed, a year after first consummation, the relationship is going strong.

Erik sees few gender differences when it comes to sex:

In the past, [there was the idea that] boys were into sex and girls were not. But I think that difference is not really there. Girls think the same about sex. [And] when I was younger, I had the idea about sex, that girls wanted love, but I think that is not really true. I mean, I think that boys are perhaps more likely to do it "just for an evening" and then nothing. A girl won't do [a one-night stand] so quickly. But in principle I think boys and girls think the same about it.

Nor does Erik see himself as an exceptional guy because he has a serious girlfriend: "I think in my circle of friends, most guys think the same about things. You know there are always going to be a few guys who have a big mouth, but I think that in principle, they all want to have a relationship before having sex. . . . I think that everyone wants that, to have a relationship and everything." Nor does wanting a relationship mean that sex is devalued. If anything, the opposite is true. Erik struggles to articulate his belief that sex is important to teenagers and that relationships are normal: "In the beginning, young people have sex to have *sex* . . . but . . . they will [tend to] wait until they have a good relationship, not just after a week. . . . The first time they do it to have *sex*. . . . [But for] those in their right mind, I think, sex happens in a relationship of some sort."

"Doing it Safe"

What distinguishes Pauline and Erik from Stephanie and Jesse is first an assumption that they have the power and the institutional support for "doing it safe." Sex education and health-care practices have made contraceptive use practically as well as conceptually accessible to Dutch youth. Ever since the early 1970s, policymakers and health-care providers have been committed to removing financial and emotional barriers to contraceptive use among teenage girls. Low rates of unintended pregnancies, primarily the result of high rates of contraceptive use—two thirds of sexually active Dutch girls are on the pill—and secondarily, emergency contraception, illustrate how Dutch women and girls have been largely "liberated from the fear of pregnancy."[23]

The message that sex is fun and to be enjoyed by girls and boys equally, combined with the message that both should take responsibility for avoiding unwanted consequences, runs throughout sex education not only at school but also in commercials, magazines for youth, and media sources that youth value for their information.[24] Public health campaigns feature images of both opposite- and same-sex couples playfully holding condoms combined with such slogans as "Take off Your Pants, Put on Your Coat," "Your Condom or Mine," and "I Make Love Safely or Not at All." In the 1990s, such campaigns were stepped up in response to concerns about

AIDS, leading Monique to complain, "It is like they're stoning you to death with all the safe-sex messages."

Like Erik, other Dutch boys say they have been educated to be "in their right mind" and to not behave in an "asocial" manner when it comes to sex and relationships. Frank knows that "of course, you should not be so stupid to [have sex] with a drunken head." Thomas knows that it would not be right "if it went wrong, to not take responsibility for it, like if the girl becomes pregnant, you should not say, 'Okay, goodbye then.'" Peter has heard so much about contraceptives from the "papers, television, and stories" that "it goes without saying that you use them. You really do not need to talk about it." He explains that sex used to be for procreation, but nowadays, he says, "You don't want kids, and over the last few years, all kinds of horrible diseases have entered into the picture, so you also [use contraceptives] for those reasons."

But although Dutch boys have been schooled both at home and at school not to be "asocial" in sexual matters, Dutch girls experience most strongly the imperative to prevent pregnancy. That, like their adult counterparts, Dutch girls do typically use birth control pills effectively explains why Dutch boys do not voice a fear of sex "screwing" them for life.[25] And with confidential and free abortion services available in clinics across the country, even when girls do not follow the mandate to use contraceptives and become pregnant unintentionally, as did Ben's girlfriend, they rarely give birth. For although Dutch girls are far less likely to become pregnant than their American counterparts and less likely to have an abortion, if they do become pregnant they are more likely to terminate their pregnancies.[26] Thus, even when sex "goes wrong," Dutch boys can be fairly confident that they will not become fathers against their will.

Not Taboo Anymore?

While Pauline was able to obtain emergency contraception without shaming, like Stephanie she was nonetheless scared and somewhat scarred by her first time. Yet, the shadows cast by those scares and scars are distinct in their shading. Unable to reconstruct a narrative in which her choices make sense to her, Stephanie looked back on her first time as a terrible personal mistake and gladly relinquished her sexual agency to her mother. Pauline, by contrast, drew the conclusion that she behaved unwisely by not standing completely behind, and not being complete prepared for, sex, but she did not view her experience as a big mistake that diminished her faith in herself. Instead, the experience led her to take subsequent relationships more slowly, experiment with romance and sexuality within parameters that feel comfortable, and remain confident that she would be able to control and recognize her progression to feeling truly ready.

One reason that Pauline is able to maintain her sense of agency in the wake of her first time is that she is less fearful of social derogation for having had sex. Unlike their American peers, Dutch girls do not spontaneously relate stories about "sluts." Certainly the label slut (*slet*) exists, but it does not have the same power in Dutch peer culture as it does in American peer culture, where it is used as weapon against girls who even suggest sexual behavior. One reason for the difference in the potency of the slur is that Dutch girls are unambiguously certain that within a well-functioning, steady relationship, sex is permissible. When a girl has sex with a boyfriend, says Marjolein, "It isn't [looked down upon] at all." Lieke also thinks that having sex is acceptable for girls, when "you're fifteen or sixteen and you have a boyfriend you can trust." Having sex in one or two successive relationships is fine, says Lieke, as long as "they are both in love." Nor do Dutch girls risk being labeled a slut for desiring sex. Indeed, with no apparent qualms about expressing desire, Pauline says, "I am ready for it" and "I would like [to do] it." Consequently, in Dutch peer culture, sex—or more precisely the mere suggestion of sex—is not as readily mobilized in the kind of name-calling and sexualized bullying that permeate American middle- and high-school cultures.

Dutch boys have clearly been schooled in the notions that girls are allowed and supposed to enjoy sex. In today's society, "sex is allowed," Sam explains. "[It is] not like boys are allowed to [have sex] and girls are not. It is not taboo for anyone anymore." Echoing the sex education that Erik received from his father about not doing it unless a girlfriend wants to, Ben says one precondition for having sex is that "she needs to really want it too." Gert-Jan thinks it is stupid when guys go to prostitutes because "for [those women, sex] does not feel pleasurable. I think going to bed with each other is something special. . . . You do really need to enjoy it, in my eyes." Nor do Dutch boys portray female desire in the way that several American boys do, as the same indiscriminate hunger "to do it anywhere, anytime," that is often attributed to them as boys. The unspoken assumption seems to be that desire awakens in relation to a particular partner.

However, the limits of what girls are allowed come into view when girls' sexual desire is directed toward multiple boys simultaneously or in too quick a succession. Pauline had no trouble telling her parents that she anticipated having intercourse with her boyfriend of six months, even though she was only fourteen at the time. But she is careful not to tell her parents how often she falls in love, and kisses boys, preferring to wait until it is "a little more serious" before telling them about the state of her heart. Marjolein thinks it is fine for a girl to have sex with her boyfriend, but, she says, "I would look down on just for one evening."[27] And like Pauline, when Dutch girls are asked *explicitly* about whether girls and boys are perceived differently after sex, the "s" word falls. Fleur echoes Pauline's words when she says "people are quicker to name a girl 'a little whore' than a boy. About boys, people don't say, 'oh, he is going to bed with everyone.' Well, they say it, but it is less problematic. . . . With girls, it is seen as a shame."

Thus, acceptable sexual behavior for girls is both legitimated and circumscribed by steady relationships in which both parties are in love.[28] They may recognize, as does Pauline, that young people sometimes have sex for reasons other than intimacy. Fleur thinks, for instance, teenagers often have sex because "they want to belong or they want to tell stories like, 'I got there earlier than you did.'" But the recognition that the pursuit of status or pleasure sometimes drives sex does not undermine the fundamental assumption that teenagers can and do fall in love and have sex in that context. Heidi thinks most teenagers have sex because they are in love. For Elizabeth, it is a "matter of course" that young people love each other when they have sex. Indeed, Natalie has a hard time imagining that one could have sex with someone with whom one is not in love. And unlike their American counterparts, the Dutch girls have no trouble identifying what the feeling of being in love is like or might be like. Marjolein believes that "love" is too "deep" and "heavy" an emotion for most girls her age. "Being in love," is a more typical experience, which she describes as "being able to count on each other, feeling comfortable with each other," and having the idea that "I can be together with this person for a while. . . . It is fun, it is going well together. You have a good feeling. You like that person a lot."

Still, several Dutch girls do note a tension, namely that boys their age are often not yet interested in the kind of steady relationships in which both parties can be in love and legitimately have sex. Karoline thinks sex usually happens "when you love each other," but she knows that boys sometimes just do it "for a little pleasure." Sarah explains that while "young boys do not [want love]," that changes "when they become more adult-like—eighteen, nineteen, twenty—a little serious." Sixteen-year-old boys are not yet interested in relationships, Dorien concurs. Not that they get the chance, she says: "The boys [girls choose] are really always older. . . . Most of the boys at sixteen are . . . more childish . . . not as far along.

Maybe the younger ones [want to have sex] but girls really always go for the older boys." In choosing older boys, however, girls may get more than they bargained for. Marjolein has friends whose boyfriends "suddenly say, 'I love you.'" Their reaction is: "'Geez, yuk, what is this? Don't say that!'"

In short, there seems to be little anxiety among the Dutch girls about being derided for sexual experience and pleasure, as long as they stay within the parameters of the acceptable. Nor do they dichotomize between the kind of love only a few can attain and the meaningless sex that is pursued by most teenagers. At the same time, the threat of being labeled a slut may exert a more hidden power on the Dutch girls. For several Dutch girls interviewed suggest that although falling in love is normal, the work of being in love and relationships requires negotiating gender and age differences. Especially when girls form relationships with boys who are several years older, as did Pauline, they face the challenge of internally distinguishing being in love from being ready for sexual intercourse. Fifteen-year-old Fleur is aware that she might have trouble drawing that distinction: "I can also imagine that you are not totally ready for it, but that you are so crazy about the guy that you do it anyway. I think that maybe that could happen to me."[29]

The Normality of Love

Like their female counterparts, Dutch boys take for granted that young people fall in love. "Yes, of course," says Berend, when asked whether teenagers can love each other. At the same time, the Dutch boys describe the state of being in love in more modest terms than do their American counterparts. As we saw, Karsten describes being in love as having "a warm feeling for someone, like a special place in your heart." Niek also remembers that being in love "was a good feeling." Ben enjoys spending time with his steady girlfriend, but he is very low-key about how his feelings for her developed: "When I started to go steady with her, I kind of liked it but did not find it that interesting." Then it became, "Yeah, this is fun, but not for really long." And then his feelings about his relationship blossomed. He felt: "Jesus, I want to go on with this much longer. It feels really good the way it is going. This is good—nice and steady."

If Dutch boys use less exalted language to speak of being in love than do their American counterparts—as *good* feelings and relating, rather than as *extraordinary* feelings and commitment—they are also less disparaging about lust, which they tend describe as an integral part of being in love. Thomas says that he discovered sexual pleasure very early on by "playing doctor" with a girl next door: "That is when I discovered that . . . well, not sex, but that we were different and that that was fun." Describing what needs to happen before he wants to have sex with someone, Ben says he wants to "have butterflies in my stomach, I don't have sex with someone just like that. . . . She needs to really want it too. And there needs to really be a lot [of feeling] between us before I have sex with someone." Gert-Jan describes sexual excitement and being in love as closely related when he recounts how he experienced the physical changes of puberty. "I thought [going through puberty] was exciting," Gert-Jan says: "It also has to do with having feelings for someone." Does he mean being in love? "Yes, you're really in love."

While they recognize that young people often approach sexuality in an experimental fashion, Dutch boys tend not to be as harsh as are their American counterparts in judging the joys and follies of youthful experimentation as meaningless. Instead, they describe the sexual experiences of young people as simply less mature versions of what adults do. Thus, before having sex with someone, Sam says, "I have to be really in love, and we both need to want it." But, he says, "I don't have [the idea] that it has to be the right person, or that I should wait until after marriage or something." Paul explains that "most young people have sex because they are physically attracted to the other person. . . . When you get older, what attracts a person changes. You are not only attracted to what a person looks like and exudes but also [to] something deeper." Sam thinks young people have sex "because they are ready and partly also to boast, like to say 'I had sex with someone.' But also just to see what it is like, to discover it." Niek sees differences between older people and younger people: "Older people have more of a relationship with each other; young people need to learn [how to have relationships]."

Like their American counterparts, several of the Dutch boys I interviewed struggle to make sense of received wisdom about gender and sexuality. But like Erik, they tend to interpret those differences as matters of degree rather than kind and to believe it is normal for boys to want a relationship. Paul thinks boys are quicker to want "something . . . a relationship, and, when they're older, sex." Paul, wonders whether "maybe it is because of the movies" that he has the impression "girls want to keep a really steady relationship, but boys want to move on to another girl." His preliminary conclusion is: "I think women are a little more likely to want a steady relationship." Thomas also thinks "there is certainly a difference. . . . [Girls] say usually 'Yes, boys only want sex and girls just want to talk.' So I do think there's a difference." Asked whether he agrees, Thomas responds, "No, no. I don't think so. I think you just, you just want to have fun with each other."

Berend believes evolution made women "a little more faithful" than men and inclined to "want a man for life." But these days, Berend says, "men may also [be looking for that] . . . a lot more than before. [Men are more like women] . . . because of the emancipation (the women's movement)." Marcel states at first that "most boys are much more into the sex than into relating. Girls are much more about talking and all that. . . . Not that it is a big gap." Later on, Marcel says: "I would like to have a relationship. But I think everyone wants that." Asked to reconcile this statement with his earlier words about gender differences, he explains: "Most people [want a relationship]: someone you can talk to about your feelings and such, a feeling of safety. I think everyone—the largest percentage of people—wants a relationship. But within a relationship, boys want sex earlier than girls. But usually [boys] do want a relationship."

In short, the Dutch boys describe continuities where the American boys describe polarities—between themselves and others, love and lust, teenagers and adults. They also see, and seem to experience, more continuity between "what can (and should) be done" and what *is* done. Erik's actual experience of his sexuality closely matches his description of when it is right to have sex. He believes teenage sex results from a combination of curiosity and desire, coupled with the establishment of a relationship within which to express that curiosity and desire. And like Karsten and Ben, the other two boys who have had sexual intercourse, Erik did indeed experience his first sexual intercourse within the context of an ongoing relationship. Their more modest model for being in love and forming relationships integrates rather than polarizes male and female motivations and experiences, love and lust, and responsibility and pleasure. But blurring the boundaries also allows the Dutch boys to overlook behavior that does not actually evidence being "in your right mind"—such as Erik's first sex after two weeks of courtship and Ben's "sloppy" contraceptive use—without questioning the unproblematic nature of their love.

Danger and Safety, Love and Lust

The chapter started with the experiences of Americans Stephanie and Jesse. Like more than a quarter of American girls who initiate sex at sixteen, Stephanie did not use contraception.[30] And like the majority of American teenagers who are having heterosexual intercourse, Jesse and his girlfriend do not use the pill or other hormonal contraception. Equally notable are the two teenagers' emotional experiences. Stephanie found herself shamed at the pharmacy for obtaining emergency contraception. And as do the majority of American teens nationally, she expresses misgivings about her first time.[31] Jesse uses condoms faithfully with his current girlfriend, but he thinks one broken condom can leave him "screwed for life." This fear not only suggests that he and his girlfriend lack access to more reliable contraception and emergency contraception, it also reflects the reality that most American teenage girls carry any given unintended pregnancy to term, so that it *does* usually alter, if not "ruin," their life and that of their partner, forever.[32]

Pauline and Erik introduce the experiences of Dutch girls and boys. In some respects, Pauline's first time was atypical: only 8 percent of Dutch girls nationally initiate sex by age fourteen. And the vast majority of Dutch girls say that they were as eager to have their first sex as was their partner.[33] But like nine out of ten Dutch teens, Pauline did use contraception. She nevertheless berates herself for not "doing it safe," which, she knows, means using both a condom and the pill—as do four in ten Dutch youth their first time.[34] In the long term, however, much of the responsibility of preventing pregnancy falls on sexually active Dutch girls. That Dutch girls generally use the pill effectively and that, even when they fail to do so, they are more likely than not to terminate the pregnancy may explain the notably "missing discourse of danger" among the Dutch boys such as Erik, who not once references sex's risks.[35]

The four vignettes also illustrate some similarities in the gender constructs that teenagers in the two countries encounter—a double standard that penalizes girls for (too much) sexual experience and that places pressure on boys to gain sexual experience. However, the effect of the sexual double standard on girls' and boys' experiences is mediated by cultural beliefs about love and lust, femininity and masculinity. The threat of being slandered as a slut seems much more present and real to the American girls who, unlike their Dutch counterparts, often relate stories of having become or having seen others be the victim of such slander. And while boys in both countries encounter, and sometimes believe, the notion that boys are more out to get sex than girls, the way that they relate to this notion of gendered sexuality differs. American boys describe themselves as unique in their quest for sex with love and a relationship, while the Dutch boys describe their desires for emotional and sexual intimacy more as universal human longings.

The notion common among American teenagers that teenage sexuality usually takes place outside of meaningful interpersonal contexts is one they frequently attribute to the media. The American boys and girls both recurrently and disparagingly speak about how "the media" creates a culture of what one could call "soulless sex," which makes young people "do it" just as they would purchase a consumer item, just to be cool. Dutch teenagers occasionally refer to the media as shaping their perceptions of gender in relationships—indeed, with many Dutch TV programs adopted from the United States, Dutch teens are subject to some of the same cultural influences as are their American peers. However, they are as likely to mention the media as a source of useful information about sexuality, such as about contraception and using condoms. Moreover, unlike their American counterparts, the Dutch teenagers do not attribute teenagers' sexual activity to the influence of the media, perhaps because they have access to cultural scripts in which adolescent sexuality is both self-generated and embedded in meaningful connections.

That Dutch teenagers have access to a widely shared cultural scenario for such a self-directed and relationally embedded adolescent sexuality while American teenagers construct oppositional scenarios is related to their different cultural definitions of love—its requirements and its recognizable features. Dutch girls and boys alike describe being in love in terms that are more earthy than the exalted terms their American counterparts use—as emotions that feel good rather than emotions that are extraordinary, as motivations that are indiscernible from physical attraction and a normal part of life that teenage boys and girls share. While some Dutch teenagers distinguish between the lighter "being in love" and the weightier loving, they do not suggest, as do several American teenagers, that young people cannot know their own feelings, or that discerning the truth of one's love requires passing some kind of heroic test, like being willing and able to give everything up—perhaps even risk one's life—for another person.

The definitions of love and relationships and experiences of gender are interconnected. It may be that marriage has remained for many American girls and boys the benchmark for love and commitment, even though marriage is very far away for teens on a middle-class trajectory, because, as a symbol, it gives them access to parts of the human potential from which they are excluded by narrow definitions of femininity and masculinity—in marriage, a women can be both good *and* sexual, and a man can be both in love *and* masculine. Although most Dutch boys and girls will eventually marry, none suggest that marriage is the ideal context for sex. With more integrated cultural models of love and lust, masculinity and femininity,

Dutch teenagers also have access to models of romantic relationships that are more age appropriate—attachments that are safe and fun but do not require fully matured capacities and commitments.[36] But the "normality of love" sometimes obscures important distinctions—between doing it safe and being ready, and between love and arousal—which are important to draw, especially for teenage girls.

EIGHT

Sexuality, Self-Formation, and the State

The Paradox

We started with a puzzle. Two groups of parents who are similar in terms of the social attributes typically thought to explain differences in parenting practices—education, social class, religiosity, and race and ethnicity—nevertheless differ strikingly: Dutch middle-class parents *normalize* adolescent sexuality, permitting teenagers to spend the night at home with girl- and boyfriends, while American parents *dramatize* adolescent sexuality, and, with few exceptions, oppose teenage couples spending the night together. One reason the two sets of parents view and manage teenage sexuality differently is that they draw on different models of modern individualism: given their different assumptions about (self-) control, autonomy, and authority, it makes sense to American parents to view teenage sexuality as a potential drama in the making, while to Dutch parents the "normality tale" is both plausible and desirable.

However, one cannot assume that just because a cultural logic makes sense to parents, it will make sense to their children as well. Belonging to a different generation and subject to multiple sources of (sexual) socialization, teenagers differ, in certain respects, from their parents in how they describe sexuality and gender. And as subordinates within the family, they are less invested in its rules and regulations and more inclined to resist control. As we have seen, both American and Dutch teenagers do in fact resist such control. But in their resistance they also underscore central cultural tenets: The American teenagers view sexuality as something that requires them to break rules and separate from their families, even as parents must exert control to maintain connection. The Dutch teenagers experience less conflict between sex and the generally accepted rules for social intercourse, rendering rebellion against those rules largely superfluous.

Indeed, what we have is a paradox: the dramatization of adolescent sexuality is predicated on—and stands in service of—an ideal of freedom from social restrictions, while the normalization of adolescent sexuality is predicated on—and produces—a deep disciplinary structure and interconnectedness within a web of social ties and obligations. In this chapter, we begin by deepening our understanding of this paradox by applying four questions drawn from Michel Foucault's work on sexual ethics. Doing so brings to the fore how dramatization and normalization involve different exercises of power, induce different techniques of self-formation, and produce different individuals. Comparing dramatization and normalization— and the different individualisms in which they are based—shows, in turn, how Foucault's argument about the effectiveness of modern power misses critical pieces of the puzzle, namely connection, support, and self-mastery.

The conditions for control, connection, and self-mastery are not produced within the family alone. In fact, there are striking parallels between the constitution of individuals in the household and in the polity. As we will see in the second part of the chapter, there are several ways to understand the parallels between the micro-sociological interactions in the family and macro-sociological state structures. The legal environment and welfare state condition and constrain parents in their choices. Processes of self-formation in the household induce capacities that serve young people's functioning within the polity and economy. And the management of adolescent sexuality illuminates core cultural ideals and contradictions that shape both private and public institutions. The chapter concludes with a discussion of challenges to the interdependent individualism and its concomitant model of governance—with its assumptions of self-regulation and mutual attunement—that prevailed during the 1990s in the middle-class Dutch household, polity, and economy.

Dramatization and Normalization as Sexual Ethics

To fully grasp any system of sexual regulation, Michel Foucault has argued, one must understand its sexual ethics, which is often not as apparent as the code of law.[1] But four questions can illuminate it.[2] The first question is: what about sexuality is of concern or, to use Foucault's words, what is the "part of the individual that becomes the prime material of his moral conduct?"[3] Second, we must ask: what kind of regulation should be exercised over that arena of concern and what reasoning is used to persuade people to conform to it? The third question is: what ethical and emotional work must individuals perform to bring themselves into compliance with the ethical rules about sexuality? And the final question asks: what is the ideal mode of being—both for the individual and for the collectivity at large—that is to result from performing such ethical work on sexuality?

To discern a key difference between normalization and dramatization, we must ask: what aspect of teenage sexuality is of special concern to parents in the two countries? The problem of teenage sex is for American parents the problem of the hormonally driven or impulsive self. The materials on which parents and teenagers are urged to act are "raging hormones." On the one hand, strong impulses and drives are looked upon favorably, as potential passions that will propel teenagers away from the parental home and into the outer world. Indeed, although the parents do not explicitly say so, one gets the sense that they would be troubled when teenagers *lack* "raging hormones," for such a lack might signal the absence of essential life energy and the drive to grow up and move on. One the other hand, they worry about that drive getting out of control and taking their children to places where they make bad and life-altering choices. The key is not to squash or even necessarily to diminish the impulses but to channel them in the right way.

For Dutch middle-class parents the problem of adolescent sexuality is not primarily the problem of the impulsive self; rather it is the problem of new attachments and whether these attachments can be harmonized with existing family attachments. Although Dutch parents are concerned to see their children evidence self-regulation, they do not worry, as their American counterparts do, about sexual impulses getting out of control. They express few concerns about pregnancy or disease ruining their children's lives. They do problematize whether their children will relate in a good way—that is, attach romantically in a solid rather than fleeting manner, choose someone whom they will like, and gradually integrate him or her into the household in a manner that is not disruptive. The horror scenario is not hormones gone wild, but new or wrong boyfriends and girlfriends moving in and out of the household at too rapid a pace.

The second question is: how should the problem be regulated and what reasoning is used to persuade the individual to conform to ethical rules? The sleepover provides a key to the differences in regulation. In American families, parents apply a dual strategy of prohibition and expulsion from the home. It is important to note that this mode of regulation is not a purely repressive one: even the most conservative of American parents seek to channel their teenage children's hormones by providing them a modicum of independent space to date and pursue their sexual interests from age sixteen on. At the same time, even the most liberal among them typically strongly oppose sexual intercourse during the high-school years.

While gender plays a role in many families—girls encounter more explicit prohibitions—even boys who receive tacit approval to engage in sexual activity elsewhere are rarely given explicit permission for a sleepover.

Regulation in Dutch families consists of a dual strategy of consultation and the incorporation of the sexual relations of high-school-aged couples into the home. At first the sleepover might appear to American parents and teenagers as permissive or hands-off, and a sign that parents "don't care." But as we have seen, preparing for and negotiating the terms of the sleepover can, in fact, involve exercising a great deal of oversight. By bringing teenage sexuality into conversation and into household practices, Dutch parents can encourage teenagers to pace themselves in their sexual and emotional development, to treat pleasure and preparation as equally important parts of maturation, and to choose sexual partners who can be integrated in a *normal* way into the household. Indeed, that several Dutch girls say explicitly that they are not interested in bringing a boyfriend home for the night and would rather sleep elsewhere demonstrates that they are well aware of the controlling aspects of consultation and incorporation.

The two modes of regulation aim at different parts of the self. The dual strategy of prohibition and granting a separated space outside the home to date is more external in nature. Control is exercised by limiting, though not entirely eliminating, the times and the external spaces in which young people can explore their romantic and sexual desires. This dual strategy of prohibiting and granting privileges aims to control sexual *behavior* but not the sexual experiences themselves or the relationships in which they take place. By contrast, the dual strategy of incorporation and consultation aims at the inner life of teenagers, that is, at their emotional attachments and their competencies within those attachments. By foregoing the power of prohibition and granting leeway, while encouraging conversation and consultation to reach agreement, Dutch parents aim to shape their teenage children's desires to behave in accordance with the socially acceptable rules.

Regulation of sexuality includes the reasoning meant to elicit compliance with the rules. Here we find a notable difference: American teenagers are asked to comply with the rules against sex at home because they are teenagers, that is, because they are *not* adults. It is their ongoing dependence on parents that defines teenagers' non-adult status. Dutch teenagers by contrast are not asked to comply with the rules because they are non-adults. Rather, they are compelled to comply with the household rules because they are family *members*. Teenagers are expected to "take into account," an expression without an explicit power differential, the needs of other family members and of the family as an institution. Their job is not to keep their sexuality out of trouble and out of sight, as it is for American boys and girls, but rather to tailor their sexual progression and the new attachments they form so that these do not threaten the preexisting household culture.

Thirdly, the two modes of regulation require different types of self-formation from teenagers *and* their parents. Foucault calls this process of self-formation the *ethical work*: the work and the relationship to the self that the individual must develop in order to bring him- or herself into compliance with the ethical rules about sexuality. The American teenagers must engage in ethical work to physically and psychically separate their emerging sexual selves from their home life and relationship with their parents. While they are not forbidden from all sexual and romantic exploration, they are strongly discouraged from progressing toward intimate sexual contact. And since it is the norm for American teenagers to initiate such sex before leaving home, they must perform the ethical work necessary to reconcile their experiences with appearances to the contrary. Externally, this means not "getting caught." Internally, it means erecting a barrier between their sexual self-expression and their roles as members of their family of origin.

Normalization involves the opposite psychological process. Rather than being compelled to hide, Dutch teenagers are exhorted not to behave *stiekem* or secretively. They are expected to let their parents get to know their romantic partners and to inform them of the development of their relationships. If dramatization encourages teenagers to establish a barrier between their roles as family members and their sexual selves, normalization encourages teenagers to accomplish a harmonious internal integration.

Moreover, normalization calls on teenagers to practice a deeply regulated sexuality. American teenagers can attribute not having prepared for, or consciously directed, their sexual activities to having been carried away by their hormones.[4] But Dutch teenagers are expected to use their hearts *and* their heads to recognize internally when they are becoming ready, plan for sex, and then, it goes without saying, use contraceptives.

In both countries, the ethical work is unequally divided among boys and girls: Many American middle-class boys are encourged not to become sexually active in high school, and to hide their sexual activities if they do. But it is girls on whom the burden of the nonsexual "good girl" image weighs most heavily. Whether they struggle to maintain their parents' image of themselves, carefully keeping signs of their sexual exploration and other "bad" activities out of sight, or whether they risk shattering it, sexuality is especially fraught for girls with close relationships with their parents. The burden of self-regulation also weighs more heavily on Dutch girls than on boys, given that girls are ultimately the ones who, especially within long-term relationships, must do the work of preventing pregnancy. Indeed, neither Dutch parents nor Dutch teens tend to question whether teenage girls can or should use oral contraceptives effectively.[5]

Parents too must perform ethical work: even as Dutch parents ask their children to self-regulate, they too must control their impulses to forbid or to surrender to their fears. After all, as one of the Dutch mothers puts it, permitting a sleepover does not mean that she is "jumping up and down with joy outside the bedroom door either." Still, just as Dutch parents ask their teenage children to take into account the needs of the household, they also ask themselves to adjust to, and take into account, their children's sexual maturation and relationships, even when they feel discomfort or wish things were otherwise. Likewise, American parents must hide and separate from their teenage children in much the same way as the latter do from them. They must hide the knowledge they have of their children's sexual activity and separate psychologically by treating their children's sexuality as belonging to physical and psychological spaces into which they are not to intrude.

Why do Dutch parents permit a sleepover that some might rather forbid? Why do American parents stand fast against a sleepover when many know their children are sexually active elsewhere? They do so in service of culturally ideal states of being. Normalization and dramatization valorize different ideal states, neither of which are realistic in the sense of attainability, yet both have tremendous cultural power. The ideal mode of being at the center of the dramatization of adolescent sexuality is total and complete freedom. This is the freedom of total autonomy from others, where one lives by one's own will only, free from the demands of social ties other than those of one's choosing. The ideal mode of being that is at the center of normalization is *gezelligheid*. It denotes freedom of a different kind: not the freedom to do whatever one wants but rather to develop one's individual self within a sociality made up of different parties, essentially benign in nature, that are neither intractably conflicted nor evidently unequal.

Table 8.1 Dramatization and normalization as sexual ethics

	American dramatization	Dutch normalization
What is problematic?	Hormone-driven self	New attachments
How and why is it regulated?	Prohibition and expulsion due to non-adult status	Negotiation and incorporation due to family member status
What self-work regulates the problem?	Separation and hiding	Self-regulation and speaking
What ideal state and individual result?	"Total freedom" and self-sufficient individual	*Gezelligheid* and self-regulated individual

These visions of the ideal state of being suffuse conceptions of adulthood and of the vision of autonomy it represents. American parents describe adulthood as characterized by full financial and emotional self-sufficiency. American teenagers speak longingly of the moment that they will turn eighteen and have access to such "complete freedom," which they too describe as the freedom from parental restrictions to do whatever they want. In the Netherlands, parents do not talk about adulthood as characterized by the financial or emotional self-sufficiency that begets the freedom to do whatever one wants. While autonomy is critical, ultimately, freedom remains bounded, since adults, as teenagers, remain part of a sociality which is essential to humanity. "Why would anyone want to live without *gezelligheid?*" parents and teenagers ask. Hence, the ideal of *gezelligheid* makes it possible to produce order not by extraordinary commitment or by force but by daily acts of mutual adjustment in which individuals freely participate.

In sum, American white middle-class parents problematize the impulsive self. They seek to cultivate and contain their children's individual passions through a dual strategy of prohibition at home and partial permission elsewhere. In the process, they develop in their children and in themselves a psychological capacity to segment and separate. The ethical work serves the ideal of total freedom and of the self-sufficient individual. Dutch parents problematize their children's attachments. By using mutual consultations to talk about sexuality and reach agreements that regulate these new attachments, they cultivate in their children and in themselves the inclination not to hide or behave secretively and the capacity to self-regulate deep emotional impulses. This ethical work stands in service of *gezelligheid*: collectivities free from conflict and explicit use of power where self-regulating and socially attuned individuals peacefully coexist.

Sexuality, Control, and Connection

While Foucault's second volume in *The History of Sexuality* focused on sexual ethics as a source of meaning and agency, his better-known first volume focuses on the ways in which sexuality in the modern era has become a source of disempowerment.[6] Indeed, discourses and disciplinary practices—including the categories that divide individuals according to sexual identities, the restrictions placed on adolescents, the focus on the reproductive lives of couples, and the sexual self-revelations many institutions encourage—all make people easier to govern by public authorities, Foucault argues. Such governance, however, unlike the governance in the premodern era, is not based in hierarchy or blatant show of force. Indeed, modern power is effective because it is hidden, and "tolerable only on the conditions that it masks a substantial part of itself."[7]

The regulation of adolescent sexuality in Dutch middle-class families approximates Foucault's conception of modern power more closely than the regulation of adolescent sexuality in American middle-class families. The admonishment to "say it honestly" and "go on the pill," for instance, incites girls to be forthcoming about their desires and conform to a form of governance that is apparently egalitarian. Indeed, control is generally more hidden: when Dutch teenagers use the language of consultation, agreements, and *gezelligheid*, they participate in the process of obscuring the inequality between parents and teenagers. This does not mean they are oblivious to their parents' power, and when probed, the more adventurous and strong-headed admit to hiding and rule-breaking. For the most part, however, Dutch teenagers are as eager as their parents to view family life as relatively free from conflict and to see themselves as offering consent to household rules rather than being forced to obey against their will.[8]

In American families power is more apparent. Just as American parents are not bashful about stating that they must "win important battles," American teenagers admit without shame to having no choice but to submit to rules they dislike. All but the most timid of American teenagers resist complete submission: they hide their "bad" behavior, "sneak out" of the house to be "bad," and accept punishments when they "get caught." But even as they are being "bad," American teenagers often accept the premise that adult authority is necessary to keep youth on the right track. At the same time, they experience a sense of agency and autonomy by evading or opposing that adult authority. The unspoken contract between American parents and their teenagers is that the former have the duty to be rule-enforcers, while the latter have the right to be rule-evaders and rule-breakers who may hide what they need to and try to get away with what they can.

The sexual behavior of teenagers suggests that "soft" power is more effective. Compared to their American peers, Dutch teenagers, particularly girls, engage in sexual behavior that is more rationalized and in keeping with the stated social norms: unintentional pregnancies and childbearing are not uncommon even for college-bound teenage girls in the United States, while they are extremely rare among Dutch girls on similar trajectories, in large part because of the latter's daily use of oral contraception.[9] And while promiscuity is frowned on in both countries, American teenagers appear more prone to having sex outside of monogamous romantic relationships than Dutch teenagers. Finally, while both Dutch and American adolescents typically initiate sexual contact before they leave their teenage years behind, sexually experienced American adolescents are more likely to have had multiple partners than are their Dutch peers.[10]

When viewed as different forms of power, the normalization and dramatization of adolescent sexuality seem to confirm Foucault's argument that discipline and the encouragement to speak control subordinates more effectively than does hierarchical rule. The normalization of teenage sexuality produces youth who cause less "trouble" in the form of unintended reproductive outcomes or in the form of rebellion against authority. Dramatization, by contrast, involves techniques of control—prohibitions and expulsions based in a hierarchy—which seem to inspire, rather than quell, going against the grain. But to understand why management by consultation works in Dutch households and why prohibitions and silence around adolescent sexuality still have such currency in American ones, we must look beyond social control per se.[11] We must look at the ideals these forms of control invoke and the types of connection and agency they make possible.

To understand why normalization "works" as a form of control, we must see that it valorizes, and creates opportunities for individuals to experience, human connection, and that it makes it easier for teenagers to gain self-mastery through that connection.[12] The normalization of adolescent sexuality makes it easier for *parents* and other adults to support youth as sexual subjects. Teenagers, in turn, self-regulate and speak—following the mandates of *gezelligheid*—not just because they have been disciplined to do so but because they value and want to participate in togetherness. When they are excited to share their first sexual experiences, it is because they believe they are communicating something new and real about themselves and, in doing so, connecting with people who recognize them. And when girls and boys shape their sexualities and selves in accordance with the expectations of normality, by using contraceptives for instance, they are demonstrating to themselves and others that they are competent adults-in-the-making.

By the same token, to interpret the dramatization of adolescent sexuality merely as an outdated and largely ineffective form of social control is also to miss a piece of the puzzle. It is true that in exerting unabashed authority, by insisting on winning important battles while letting go of the small things, American parents embrace elements of what Foucault has termed sovereign power—the power to override and punish subordinates. But this persistence of sovereign power does not signal, as one might initially imagine, simply a "lag" in development toward more modern forms of power and social control. Indeed, to understand why a particular form of power evolves, persists, or becomes reinvigorated over time, it is not enough to consider its technical efficiency and effects. We must also consider, as Foucault does in his work on ethics, visions of the "good life" for the individual and society at large, and the self-formation required to attain that life.[13]

Indeed, the sexual ethics that prohibits teenage sexuality and expels it from the household results, in part, from the celebration of the freedom to do whatever one wants. This celebration of individual volition has a "positive moment" in its prioritization of self-actualization over inextricable obligations to others, and of change, with its potential for creativity and challenge, over continuity.[14] Its "negative moment" comes from the absence of a solid and common ground for the continuation of social relationships. The ideal of total freedom conceives of social ties as matters of choice rather than necessity, and as constraints rather than natural pleasures, constructing "breaking away" as the way that adolescents assert their agency. Yet, without faith in the ties that bind—and in the inalienable human need and desire to form such ties—it becomes difficult to imagine the restraint of individual impulses without reliance on fear of authority or external controls.

In short, to understand why parents use the techniques for control that they do, and how these techniques affect adolescents, we need to look at the cultural ideals they embrace and the proclivities and capacities they seek to develop in their teenage children. These different cultural ideals and cultural capacities do not denote more or less modern forms; rather, they denote two different ways of imagining and giving shape to modern individuals and collectivities. One conditions the creation and enjoyment of harmonious, pleasant togetherness in the absence of sharp power differentials. The other envisions and prepares for the power and pleasure of pursuing one's dreams without being held back by rules or relationships, even as it suspends such power and pleasure for those not deemed ready or deserving. These versions of post-1960s self and society have been produced not only in white middle-class households but also in the polity and economy.

The Politics of Accommodation and Integration

A politics of consultation and accommodation has characterized the Dutch government and economy during the final decades of the twentieth century. The Dutch multiparty government long operated—from the national level down to the local level—according to this "politics of accommodation."[15] The "consultation economy" similarly regulates the branches of industry and service through "collective labor agreements," which result from negotiations between representatives of government, labor, and business—whose presumed shared interests are reflected in the common parlance in which the parties are referred to as "the social partners."[16]

On the one hand, the politics of accommodation and integration have involved "taking into account" the needs of groups with less social and economic power—the working class, women, immigrants, and children—and granting them rights to housing, health care, and other necessities.[17] On the other hand, the "agreements" that result from consultations do not denote full equality. The calls for self-restraint and accommodation that accompany governance by negotiation preclude those in power from exercising it without regard for the humanity and dignity of those below. Rules of representation give subordinates say in all matter of decision-making.[18] However, although all parties make compromises, it is often those with the least economic or political power who are expected to exercise the greatest restraint and forbearance.[19] Thus consultative arrangements do not fundamentally challenge the existing system of stratification—between the classes, the sexes, or the members of different ethnic groups. Much as negotiation in the family effectively elicits consent and prevents rebellion, so too have the politics and economy of accommodation long stifled unrest and prevented protest, whether from the labor, feminist, or gay rights movement.[20]

A hybrid structure, the Dutch welfare state thus supports and "emancipates" the weaker groups in society at the same time that it also solidifies status differences.[21] Its social democratic features, aimed at creating equality among citizens, are expressed in, among others, universal pension benefits. Its corporatist features, aimed at preserving status differentials, have inhibited women from joining the workforce as full-time employees and have tailored unemployment benefits according to previous salaries earned. The policies of the Dutch welfare state prevent any group from sinking into abject poverty and facilitate upward mobility for the working class, *but also* stabilize the class position of the middle class, including that of the upper-middle class.[22]

As a result, for several decades the Dutch welfare state outspent most others.[23] And as it spent on carrots, the Dutch state of the 1980s and 1990s was notoriously averse to using sticks. Much as Dutch middle-class parents hasten to say that "one should never forbid," the post-1960s Dutch state long shied away from prohibition and harsh punishment. In responding to crime, the Dutch criminal justice system often makes use of alternatives to imprisonment, such as fines and community sentences, and prison sentences and conditions are mild in comparison to those in many other European countries and the United States.[24] Finally, the dominant response to drug abuse and prostitution has been to regulate and accommodate within limits rather than to forbid and to punish. This policy of domestication destigmatizes "deviants," making it easier for them to "learn from their mistakes" and participate in normal society, or, if nothing else, to contribute to its social services by paying taxes.[25]

In short, the controlling and supporting dimensions of the Dutch welfare state have gone hand in hand:[26] as is true of governance in the Dutch middle-class family, the disciplining, incorporating, and subduing effects of Dutch state policies depend, in part, on the social supports they provide and the opportunities for self-realization they offer. Thus, just as a Foucauldian analysis of normalization in the Dutch middle-class family misses the significance of interpersonal connection in facilitating the exercise of "invisible" power, so too is such an analysis of the effectiveness of the Dutch welfare state amiss in overlooking the social bonds between people and the self-determination it helps foster.[27] Indeed, authors of a 1998 social and cultural report conclude that in spite of growing individualization, the Dutch welfare state may well have become a "civil" religion: "a symbolic center that gives the Dutch people a feeling of communal identification."[28]

Winning, Losing, and Stepping Out in America

In contrast to the relative stability, continuity, and continuous negotiations established by the Dutch political and economic system, the American economy and polity are characterized by rapid changes, sudden successes, and reversals of fortune. Neither the winner-take-all nature of the executive branch, nor the two-party system of the legislative branch, nor the all-or-nothing legal decisions of the Supreme Court involve the kind of mutual accommodations and compromises required in the Dutch political and legal arena.[29] Thus, from the federal to local level, American politics divides winners, who make most of the decisions, from losers, who either wait by the side for their turn in the seat of power or find themselves structurally excluded.[30]

The American economy too is characterized by more flux and by sharper divisions between "winners" and "losers" than is the Dutch economy. Indeed, the salaries of executives and upper managers are considerably higher in the United States than they are in the Netherlands, while the incomes of Americans in "low-wage" occupations are significantly lower, relative to average incomes, than those of their Dutch counterparts. Their lack of job protection means that American workers move in and out of jobs much more rapidly than do their Dutch counterparts. Further, in the absence of centralized wage-setting institutions, many American middle-class workers are directly responsible as individuals for bargaining with their employers for wages and benefits. Salaries and benefits vary a great deal, even between similarly qualified employees. Thus, the economic fortunes of an individual depend greatly on his or her own ability to "win the important battles."[31]

The American polity and economy thus create circumstances in which individuals experience either a great deal of decision-making power or very little at all. At the same time, the mobility engendered and required by the American economy and polity means that, especially for those in the middle, it is never too late to win *or* lose. The American welfare state does little to temper upward and downward mobility or the antagonism between those with different interests. If anything, the welfare state has exacerbated rather than mitigated the social divisions in American society—between black and white, young and old, and between the poor and working class on the one hand and the upper-middle class on the other.[32] Americans at the bottom experience an intensity of poverty unparalleled in the advanced industrial world.[33] And large holes in the safety net mean that even middle-class families can, at any time, "fall from grace."[34]

The flipside of a government that neither aims for consensus nor offers economic protection, however, is that those citizens who—for reasons of political conviction, ethnicity, or sexual orientation—find themselves on the losing side of the battle are free to "break away" from "mainstream" society and form distinctive communities. The formation of gated communities for the wealthy has been widely noted. Equally notable is that cultural communities—with beliefs, habits, and aims that differ from or are even antagonistic to the mainstream—are given more leeway to go their own way in the United States than they are in the Netherlands. Whereas the Dutch state consults, subsidizes, and requires accommodations from those on the political, economic, and cultural margins, the American state neither subsidizes nor expects equivalent "accommodations" from those in alternative religious, ethnic, and political communities.[35]

But if American society tolerates relatively autonomous ethnic and political communities in its midst, it also issues stricter prohibitions against activities deemed deviant and punishes transgressions more severely. Moreover, prohibitions and punishments are directed disproportionately at the "losers" in society—the poor, minorities, and minors. Thus, rather than tolerate and regulate "vices" such as drug use and prostitution, as has the Dutch state, the American state outlaws these activities and aggressively prosecutes offenders.[36] During the 1980s and 1990s, it has imprisoned an increasingly large proportion of its population, frequently imposing long sentences in response to minor crimes.[37] Although this "culture of control" affects young people of color disproportionately, even in white middle-class communities young people often face intense surveillance practices and police-enforced curfews in schools and public spaces, and they can face severe consequences for drug use, drinking, and sexual behavior.[38]

Constituting Individuals and Collectivities

There are several ways to interpret these parallels between the language and practices at work in middle-class families and broader political and economic institutions in the two countries. First, the American and Dutch welfare and penal states create economic and psychological conditions for the dramatization and normalization of teenage sexuality. As we have seen, American middle-class parents have reason to feel uncertain about their own economic futures and those of their children. Especially among nonprofessional middle-class parents, this sense of uncertainty and lurking danger may well feed the belief that parents must use rules against sex and other temptations to keep their teenage children on the right track.[39] Moreover, parents may fear their children's high-school attachments because they could impede the physical mobility that is often required to obtain a four-year college degree.[40]

The American state also compounds the dramatization of adolescent sexuality by taking a punitive approach to the "mistakes" of those who indulge in "adult" pleasures. Consequently, even if American parents would like to be more lenient about teenage sexuality and drinking, they themselves risk "being caught" by law enforcement.[41] If the American state constrains parents in their ability to negotiate, it also bolsters their capacity to prohibit and punish. Not only does the law typically prioritize the rights of middle-class parents over those of children, but the features of the welfare state also leave teenagers directly dependent on their families for the financial resources necessary to attain and maintain middle-class status.[42] Thus, American teenagers do, in fact, need to attain financial self-sufficiency to be fully emancipated from their parents.

The relative economic security ensured by the Dutch state and economy, by contrast, cushions anxieties about status maintenance for Dutch middle-class parents, reducing both the symbolic potency and real costs of a teenage pregnancy. Few Dutch parents appear worried about their children becoming derailed economically by their sexual or other youthful explorations. Unintended teenage pregnancies carried to term, while uncommon among the native Dutch population, do not threaten economic survival, given the various supports and subsidies available for families and children and the second chances to "make it."[43] Moreover, the preference for accommodation over punishment in the public policies that regulate the use of "pleasures" means that Dutch parents, unlike American parents, are able to negotiate, rather than forbid, adolescent behaviors that are punishable by law in the United States.

Not only does the Dutch state mitigate the risks of raising children; as several Dutch sociologists have argued, the state has also created the ground for a relatively equal relationship between family members. Student stipends, parents' legal obligation to support their children, and the strong rights position granted to minors by Dutch law mean that Dutch middle-class youth have, in fact, a position of relative strength vis-à-vis their parents, such that their negotiations can approximate those of true partnerships.[44] Indeed, without a welfare state that supports middle-class parents as they raise their children *and* bolsters the economic power of young people vis-à-vis their parents, it is possible that Dutch parents might not have the equanimity they do to confront their children's sexuality, and that teenage children would not feel as empowered to negotiate their sexuality.[45]

There is a second way to connect the processes of conceptualization, control, and constitution in the middle-class family with those that operate in the economy and polity: we can see normalization and dramatization as processes by which teenagers acquire skills that will facilitate their thriving and success in their respective political economies. To function adequately within a system of politics and economics that thrives on continuous consultation and compromise, it is of great importance to be the very self-regulating and socially aware individual that the negotiation of sexuality in the family teaches.[46] The higher on the Dutch status ladder one is to climb, the more important is the capacity to exhibit self-control and consideration for others. Indeed, occupying positions of power in a society that so delicately balances equality and inequality requires the capacity to exert authority without gloating or obviously neglecting those below.[47]

American middle-class teenagers, like their Dutch peers, learn to experience themselves as the kind of individuals capable of succeeding in their society. American boys in particular are taught to experience their sexuality as biological urges which originate inside themselves and which propel them into action.[48] Not expected to exert internal control or to socialize such urges to meet the demands of social relationships, they are inadvertently encouraged to experience their sexuality as a potentially exploitative, aggressive force which, when unchecked by external constraints, leads them to take risks. But to do so fully, American boys learn, they must separate from home—furtively at first, and legitimately as soon as they legally and financially can. Experiencing oneself as propelled by strong inner drives which ought to be acted upon aggressively when possible and without undue caution is critical in a society which requires the ability to fight to get ahead and the willingness to take risks in the process.

Indeed, it is economically and psychologically beneficial for young men to be able to separate easily from parents as well as from sexual partners, so as to be as physically mobile as middle-class educational and occupational trajectories often require. At the same time, to succeed in business, American young men need to have the capacity to respond well to rules that are unilaterally imposed from above, at least until they attain more senior positions, and to not feel that this compromises their dignity. Unlike their Dutch counterparts, who typically have considerable input into various aspects of their everyday working conditions through works councils (mandatory in companies with more than thirty-five employees), American young adults in entry-level positions may have very little say over their day-to-day experiences in the workplace.[49] Engaging in a modicum of rule-breaking, without getting caught, is a way young Americans can reconcile subjugation with a self-concept of radical autonomy.

In both countries, the economic and cultural advantages of the capacities and orientations conferred onto the young by the sexual ethics that are practiced in the family are more apparent for boys than for girls. Becoming a member of the middle- and upper-middle class has meant something different for Dutch men than for Dutch women. The latter typically have had only part-time paid employment, especially once they are mothers.[50] The ideology of motherhood has remained extremely strong in the Netherlands, and, outside of government service, women have held little power in the public sphere. But they have been seen, and see themselves, as possessing significant power in the private sphere, excelling in the art of creating *gezelligheid*.[51] For such an arrangement to be satisfactory, however, the domestic sphere must be regarded as socially significant and offer opportunities for the exercise of agency. The sexual socialization of adolescents is one arena in which mothers, who do most of that socialization, find such opportunities.[52]

As we have seen, in their home-based sex education, mothers teach their daughters both that intimate relationships are valuable and that they can and must develop their capacity for agency within them. What the celebration of regulated love does not teach girls, however, is that intimate relationships sometimes conflict with and impede the pursuit of individual potential. While regulated love grants girls sexual subjectivity in the context of the relationship, it does not encourage them to develop their sexuality or their identities outside of the context of intimate relationships.[53] Indeed, non-relationship-based sexuality is not part of being "normal."[54] And as we have seen, when a mother or daughter wants the latter to be less relationship-orientated, the negotiation of a daughter's sexuality in the family can produce more tensions and conflicts than normalization would, at first sight, lead one to expect.[55]

The conception of sex and self as inner struggles barely controlled is more contradictory for American girls than it is for American boys and also less likely to "pay off" emotionally or economically. No longer taken seriously by parents or other adults in their professions of love, American girls are increasingly taught that their romantic longings are the consequence of biological urges which lead them, like boys, to act in ways that are risky. On the other hand, unlike their male counterparts, American girls still learn that acting upon those urges can ruin their reputation and social standing, making it critical that they be able to hide any evidence of sexual activity. Thus, American girls inherit the worst of both worlds—they are expected to uphold the (semblance) of virginity required by the double standard of the old gender order and to demonstrate a male-like heartlessness when they act on the "equal-opportunity" hormones granted to them by the new gender order.

This sexual double bind of American girls reflects the deep ambivalence and sense of unease which American parents, especially mothers, feel about gender relations in contemporary American society and the implications thereof for their daughters' future well-being. With their missing discourse of (adolescent) love, American middle-class parents express pessimism about the possibility of mutuality between men and women. An awareness of the costs that girls and women often incur in intimate relationships seems to have led to a loss of faith in the promise of love. One response to this loss of faith is to reinforce the prescripts of the old gender order—according to which a girl who preserves sex for marriage or at least a "serious commitment" will be rewarded for her patience by protection against sexual exploitation—and even many liberal American mothers express the wish that their daughters could remain virgins until marriage.

But even as they embrace marriage as the only safe place for girls to have sex, American parents are well aware that the rewards of marriage are far from a "sure thing." Thus, at the same time that they want their daughters to maintain (the appearance of) the chastity of the good girl, parents also encourage them to acquire the fighting spirit and the economic independence traditionally befitting bad-boys-become-good men. Even the most conservative of American parents admit that they do not want their daughters marrying in their late teens or early twenties, since settling down too young would compromise their educational and occupational opportunities.[56] Lacking the cultural resources of an ideology of domesticity or a welfare state that supports such an ideology—by giving women (and men) social rights and benefits to engage in caregiving—American parents are all too aware that without credentials and job prospects even their successfully married daughters will be only one divorce away from poverty.

We have seen how the Dutch and American states create conditions for normalization and dramatization. We have also seen how normalization and dramatization confer upon young people, particularly young men, the capacities to thrive in the two societies. We have seen, in other words, the interplay between the conditions created by the institutions of the polity and economy, on the one hand, and the cultural processes at work in the white middle-class family, on the other. This does not mean however that the economic and legal environments determine the cultural ideals, assumptions, and practices through which modern individuals become constituted. After all, there is a third way to understand the parallels we have seen: in both countries, the regulation of sexuality in the family and the regulation of public welfare are shaped by different ways of conceiving, constituting, and controlling individuals and collectivities.

Indeed, we can trace some of the most notable cultural concepts and their concomitant practices back to before the institutionalization of the modern welfare state. In political and religious philosophy and practice, in literature, and in the rituals of everyday life, especially those prominent among the middle classes in the two societies, there has been a history of embracing and seeking to enact the concepts "complete freedom" and *gezelligheid* that white middle-class parents and teenagers articulate today.[57] Indeed, the cultural concepts and modes of reasoning about how people acquire self-restraint, attain autonomy, and exercise and accept authority at work in the regulation of behavior in middle-class families during the 1990s have also shaped the kinds of welfare state programs that were adopted in previous decades.[58] Thus, rather than reduce the cultural processes that shape the management of sexuality in the family to political and economic conditions, we must view culture and state policy as mutually constitutive.

Indeed, I have argued, the core cultural ideal of *gezelligheid*, and its concomitant assumptions and practices, provided the Dutch with cultural resources with which to weather the aftermath of the 1960s and 1970s. It may be that the cultural traditions on which the Dutch middle class drew as it encountered the challenge against traditional authority relations and sexual morality, offered both faith in, and skills for, the constitution of secular and equalized collectivities. The celebration and institutionalization of a "secular religion of the social" in the private and the public sphere may have helped create boundaries and social bonds "without God." By contrast, the belief in, and celebration of, individual autonomy attained in opposition to dependency and society may have ironically left middle-class Americans without the cultural grounds on which to expect or to demand social attunement and self-regulation.

This lacuna in the secular "cultural imaginary" of the American white middle class may explain why in the United States "harsh justice" has been embraced as a means to keep people in check.[59] It may also explain the particular significance of marriage. Finally, one reason that Americans continue to be drawn to religious communities may be that they provide the higher authority and shared moral rules missing from the ideal of freedom that they embrace. Indeed, like marriage, religion allows Americans to reconcile contradictory cultural imperatives, as it is both "perfectly free and perfectly binding."[60] Conversely, that the Dutch formulated a cultural concept of the common good in a secular age and maintained faith in people's tendency to form solid relationships may help explain why, paradoxically, the country in which teenage sexuality had been far from normal in the 1950s would be the one to go through the most dramatic change, and yet also be the one in which that dramatic change would be viewed as not at all extraordinary.

Cultural Continuity, Confrontation, and Change

The cultural processes this book reveals are snapshots of a decade—1991 to 2000. But in the decade since then, several notable shifts have taken place in the Netherlands: the growth of women's participation in the labor force, especially among the middle- and upper-middle class, to "normal" European and North American percentages; the expansion of the governing powers of the European Union and the introduction of the euro; strong cutbacks in spending on social welfare; a more restrictive approach to alcohol and drugs and a more punitive approach to crime—in part a response to "drug tourism" and the increase in organized international crime; growth in the numbers of first- and second-generation immigrants from non-Western countries; and two high-profile assassinations, one of which brought to the fore the conflict between Dutch secularist institutions and culture and Muslim fundamentalism.[61]

At the same time, there has been much continuity: while the majority of Dutch mothers now work, unlike their European and American peers they continue to do so part time.[62] And despite having shrunk the percentage of gross domestic product spent on social programs from one of the largest in Europe to around average, the Netherlands still has a health care system that ranks among the top among industrialized countries in access and provision of equitable care, and it still has some of the lowest poverty rates in the European Union.[63] Dutch poverty rates remain significantly lower than those in the United States.[64] Dutch children remain among those most likely in Europe to grow up in two-parent families, and are far less likely to live in single-parent families than their peers in the United States.[65] Finally, in spite of a more punitive climate, the use and sale of "soft drugs" are still tolerated, though under more restrictive conditions, and prostitution, under certain conditions, is still legal.[66]

Still, if the Dutch middle-class family and state seemed to sail smoothly through the new cultural currents of the 1960s and 1970s, adapting old customs to new needs—maintaining social cohesion and significantly reducing inequality in both the intimate and public sphere—the early twenty-first century appears to have led the country into rougher waters. Some of the challenges are what sociologists call endogenous—they come from within the culture. Dutch youth are proving not always as self-regulating as parents and policymakers of earlier decades expected, for instance with regard to alcohol consumption. And efforts to bolster girls' and boys' capacity to recognize and communicate their readiness and to form mutually respectful relationships have not necessarily, as recent research shows, protected Dutch girls from sexual violation.[67] Attention in research, media, and policy to these personal and interpersonal transgressions, sexual and otherwise, has challenged the premises and optimism of interdependent individualism.[68]

But perhaps the greatest challenges to that interdependent individualism have come from outside the country. Unlike the "emancipated" groups that preceded them, many first- and second-generation immigrants have not cooperated with the culture of consultation and consensus, instead forming bastions of difference and, in instances, of hostility.[69] The responses to problems around immigration, or to what the Dutch call "the question of integration," have exposed internal fissures—including those based on class inequalities—and have contributed to more confrontational and punitive methods of behavior control. They have also illuminated the current of control that runs through normalization. Confronted with groups that do not share the aims or methods of "regulated love," policymakers have tried to impose ideas about love as a form of regulation and exclusion, and for a period required prospective immigrants to view a film with two gay men kissing.[70]

In short, the strains of the early twenty-first century have exposed assumptions and contradictions in the ideal of *gezelligheid*, namely, that some behavior and conflicts do not lend themselves to accommodation and that in the course of creating togetherness in a collectivity, the less powerful parties—youth, women, workers, and ethnic minorities—are often expected to make greater sacrifices than the more powerful parties. Almost half a century after the start of the 1960s, the country is—with people, governing bodies, and cultures that originate from outside its borders—more internally diverse and divided, and less self-governing. How the challenges and opportunities that characterize the current period of societal upheaval and cultural conflict will ultimately shape the family and polity is unclear. But clearly, the present time is a fruitful one to study the interplay of cultural continuity, confrontation, and change, as well as to investigate the different experiences of the relationship between teenage sexuality, self-formation, and the state.

Beyond the Drama

As an adolescent in the Netherlands in the 1980s—where my family had moved from the United States—I never heard of teenagers becoming pregnant during high school. I took for granted the playful public health campaigns on billboards across town, advocating safe sex, and I watched with fascination, though not fear, a three-hour television production about HIV/AIDS, how it was transmitted, and how to protect against it, which was broadcast simultaneously across all Dutch television channels. I noticed the apparent equanimity with which the mother of one of my Dutch friends responded when her youngest daughter announced one evening that she and her steady boyfriend were retiring to her tiny bedroom. Mrs. de Wit would not have left a breadcrumb on the floor of her immaculate, modest middle-class home, which was adorned with signs of her Catholic faith. Yet, she did not blink an eye when her sixteen-year-old daughter made clear that she was taking her boyfriend to her bedroom where sexual relations might occur.

When I visited the United States over the summer and returned to study as a young adult, I learned that unintended pregnancies among teenagers were far from the relics of a past before reliable contraception became widely available, as I had been taught in the Netherlands. I discovered that even among the well-educated, politically liberal friends of my parents, teenagers rarely confided in their parents the state of their sexual affairs. I found myself inadvertently in the role of sex educator when I wrote a long letter to one of my American friends, explaining when during her menstrual cycle she would be most fertile and urging her to talk to her mother about going on the pill. Listening to the radio and reading newspapers in the United States in the early 1990s, I heard commentators attribute societal disarray and poverty to sex among unmarried teenagers—an attribution not corroborated by my experience in the Netherlands, where unmarried youth formed sexual relationships without living in the poverty that I witnessed in the United States.

Two decades later, many of the contrasts I observed remain. Despite a sharp decline in teen births over the past fifteen years, by age twenty almost one in five American women will have given birth.[1] While some such births have been planned, and, once born, many unplanned children are deeply cherished, most births to teenagers are unintended, and they alter the lives of young people in ways that are not of their choosing.[2] American teenagers also have some of the highest rates of STDs—including life-threatening ones like HIV/AIDS—in the industrial world.[3] Equally significant are the ambivalent and negative feelings that American youth attribute to their first sexual experiences, with many young women and men describing a lack of what researchers sometimes call "agency," a sense of full control over their sexual decision-making process. Finally, sexuality and relationships are a source of strain in many American families, especially between daughters and parents, and between parents and non-heterosexual teenagers.[4]

While not without its challenges, adolescent sexual and emotional development remains considerably less problem-fraught in the Netherlands. Even though Dutch youth initiate sex at comparable ages, their birth and abortion rates are eight and two times lower, respectively, than those of their American peers: in 2007, one in twenty-four American girls aged fifteen to nineteen gave birth, versus one in nearly two hundred Dutch girls.[5] And even in low-income immigrant communities in the Netherlands—where births to those under twenty tend to be concentrated—the teenage birth rate remains considerably lower than in low-income communities of color in the United States.[6] HIV rates are also substantially lower among Dutch youth than among their American counterparts.[7] As important: most Dutch youth surveyed report that their first sexual experiences were fun, wanted, well timed, and in their control.[8] Finally, although Dutch parents and teenagers must also negotiate tensions over sex and romantic relationships, teenage sexuality is more integrated into family life than it usually is in the United States.

Why these differences? One answer is simply different public investments in the provision of resources and services. Lacking quality schools and health care, a guaranteed minimum income, and adequate housing, the communities that have the highest pregnancy and STD rates in the United States are characterized by a prevalence and intensity of socioeconomic disadvantage that is unparalleled in the Netherlands.[9] While American teenagers have very uneven access to sexual education and health care,

Dutch policymakers and physicians have committed to make sure that all Dutch minors are educated about and can obtain contraception. And while abortion remains both practically and culturally very difficult to access in the United States, Dutch girls sixteen and older have access, without parental consent, to free abortions. Without easy access to vital resources, services, and education, it is no wonder that in spite of impressive increases in condom use, American teenagers remain much less likely to use the most reliable forms of birth control, use dual protection, or terminate unintended pregnancies than are their Dutch counterparts.[10]

But access to resources and services, essential as it is, constitutes only one piece of the puzzle that explains the international differences in the experience of teenage sexuality. Another piece is the difference in adult approaches, which are, in turn, shaped by different cultural frameworks for understanding what teenage sexuality is, what capacities young people can and should develop, and what the responsibilities of parents and other care providers are.

This book illuminates important differences in those frameworks. In Dutch middle-class families and institutions, adolescent sexuality has been normalized. In contrast, in American middle-class families and institutions, adolescent sexuality has been dramatized. Although differences in adult approaches *within* the two countries deserve further study, there is reason to believe that the cultural differences highlighted in this book shape experiences and attitudes beyond the specific populations studied, not in the least because they disproportionately influence the institutions of government, health care, education, and the media.[11]

What we have seen is that adolescent sexuality has been *normalized* in Dutch families—viewed as a continuum of feelings and behaviors, which are accepted as part of adolescent development and relationships. Youth are expected to possess an internal barometer with which they can pace their sexual progression, within the context of trusting and loving relationships, and discern the point at which they are ready to move toward sexual intercourse. While parents have the responsibility to educate about contraception, the cultural mandates dictate that, in order to stay connected to their children and their relationships, they are wise to accept that from sixteen or seventeen onward adolescents' sexual progression may include intercourse. Normalization also means that most parents permit steady boyfriends and girlfriends to spend the night in their teenage children's bedrooms—usually on the condition that they have gotten to know and like them—even if this means parents must self-regulate their own feelings of resistance.

Adolescent sexuality has, by contrast, been *dramatized* in American families. Although they see them as natural and inevitable, many American parents view sexual desires as spurred by "raging hormones" that are easily out of control. Thus they consider sexual acts—usually thought of in terms of acts of intercourse—undesirable and dangerous during the teenage years. Indeed, not only adolescents' sexual urges but also their emotional longings are viewed askance; parents see a battle between the sexes in which boys pursue sex and girls pursue love and in which both parties can be duped. With adolescent sexuality as an internal and interpersonal battlefield, it is not surprising that few American parents permit high-school-aged couples to sleep together. But opposition to the sleepover stems also from a conviction, shared by liberal and conservative parents alike, that children must establish themselves independently from their parents before it is right to sanction their sexuality or necessary to overcome one's discomfort about it.

Normalization and dramatization are rooted in different ways of understanding what it means to be and become an autonomous individual and form relationships with others—indeed, in different cultures of individualism. One reason that adolescent sexuality is such a drama for both parents and teenagers in the United States is that the culture of "adversarial individualism" dictates that to attain full autonomy a person must first sever his or her dependencies on others. This conception of autonomy, however, leaves adolescents—who are in the process of becoming autonomous selves—without the continuity of social bonds—especially with adults—that provide them with support and with the grounds for exercising self-restraint within an intergenerational sociality. With sexuality culturally coded as symbolic for the break between teenagers and parents, the latter become disconnected from a developmentally important part of their children's lives, and they can often offer little guidance other than to urge them to postpone sex until they are on their own.

One reason that it is possible for Dutch parents and teenagers to normalize adolescent sexuality is that they conceptualize adolescent autonomy as unfolding within continued interdependencies. Rather than requiring the severing of old ties and the establishment of complete self-reliance, this culture of interdependent individualism allows adolescents to attain autonomy in concert with their ongoing relationships with others. While adolescents are expected to develop their independent opinions and self-regulating capacities, they are not required to break with adult society in order to do so. In fact, keeping teenagers integrated in intergenerational social settings—whether in the family, venues for socializing, or schools that span the spectrum from early to late teens—enhances adult support as well as control. Accepting adolescent sexuality—within certain parameters—and negotiating sleepovers at home not only allows young people to develop their emergent sexuality and selves within a larger social fabric but it also gives parents the opportunity to provide guidance and exercise oversight.

The different cultures of individualism also shape perceptions and experiences of gender. The American culture of adversarial individualism exacerbates gender conflicts over sexuality: with autonomy and attachments viewed at odds, the two have been bifurcated and desire for the latter relegated to girls, who are still often seen as the sole keepers of intimacy. At the same time, when girls behave as boys are "supposed" to and pursue sex without relationships, what results, American teenagers report, is a "soulless sex" from which most boys feel alienated.[12] Like their American counterparts, Dutch teenagers confront gender stereotypes and pressures. However, their culture of "interdependent individualism" softens, though it does not eradicate, gender conflicts. With relationships viewed as an unavoidable and desirable part of life, oppositions between girls and boys over love and lust are not as sharply drawn. Nor do Dutch boys feel they are unusual for wanting to be in love, as do many of their American peers.[13]

Cultures emphasize certain aspects of the human potential and downplay others. As cultural constructs, the two versions of individualism thus provide different resources and constraints, and entail different costs and benefits. The American adversarial individualism gives more legitimacy to profound differences—whether between parents and children, or between population groups with different convictions and commitments. It also provides a cultural language for describing and emphasizing conflicts of interest, which may at times exaggerate such conflicts but which also provide important cultural tools to address them.[14] The Dutch interdependent individualism emphasizes similarity over difference—between parents and children, and between girls and boys—and the possibility of consensus over intractable conflict. But it makes it more difficult to recognize—both positively and negatively—the consequential differences within a collectivity. And it can obscure conflict of interest and inequality in power, and leave people without a satisfactory cultural language to address transgression of boundaries.

Neither interdependent individualism nor the normalization of adolescent sexuality that it has facilitated constitutes a panacea. But normalization does offer several advantages in the arena of adolescent sexual health. It makes it easier for adult caregivers and youth to accept that teenagers are sexual beings who, with the right support, have the capacity and responsibility to make decisions about their sexual progression and to prepare for their sexual behavior. The emphasis in Dutch sex education at home and at school on romantic relationships gives teenagers opportunities to learn the interactional skills with which they can better recognize and articulate sexual wishes and boundaries, and negotiate contraception and condoms. Finally, the normalization of adolescent sexuality makes it easier for youth to admit to others, including adults, when they have progressed to the point of wanting or having sexual intercourse, which makes it easier to ask for assistance without fear of causing disappointment or being shamed.

Perhaps the most important lesson to be learned from the Dutch normalization of adolescent sexuality is that while cultures offer resources and impose constraints, culture is not destiny; its applications to actual situations are by no means fixed. For as we have seen, prior to the early 1970s neither the general public nor the major institutions of Dutch society accepted sex between unmarried youth as legitimate.[15] Profound discomfort with their own lack of sexual socialization—and the secrecy and shame that had surrounded sexuality—made large segments of the Dutch population open to change. Dialogue among political, professional, religious, and cultural leaders led to the reassessment of old rules and the development of new guidelines for sexual self-determination and intimacy.[16] The normalization of adolescent sexuality emerged out of this interplay between a widely felt discontent with past ways and conscious deliberations about how better to approach the present.

The potential for a similar synergy exists in the United States today. Awareness that heterosexual marriage neither honors the diversity, nor solves the dilemmas, of sex and intimacy in today's society is growing: after years of stasis, the percentage of the American population that categorically condemns homosexuality has steeply declined over the past decade.[17] Young people are and remain notably more positive about sexual diversity than their elders. Research and the proliferation of parent workshops about sexuality suggest eagerness among parents for effective ways to engage with adolescents around issues of sexuality and relationships.[18] Grassroots organizations advocate for culturally sensitive and empowering sex education in schools as part of the human rights required to foster healthy families and children.[19] An important opportunity has been created by the 2010 health-care reform, which has allocated federal funds for sex education that allows educators to teach about contraception.

But for all the desire and opportunity to change course, lacking in most efforts has been a conception of adolescent sexuality as a normal and potentially positive part of adolescent development. While the potential negative aspects and consequences of adolescent sexuality do, of course, need attention, so too do the potentially pleasurable, connecting, and empowering aspects.[20] For without attention to positive personal and interpersonal experiences, we cannot discern the skills and conditions that foster them. Our current paradigms provide no such discernment: the marriage-only paradigm of recent policies equates refraining from any sexual intimacy with the promotion of sexual health; the sex-as-risk paradigm that prevails in much of public health and education promotes condom and contraceptive use but nevertheless equates adolescent sexuality with a sickness best prevented.[21]

Ironically, lacking from our current paradigms is recognition that teenagers are *adolescents*, neither children nor adults, and that their sexuality exists within that emergent space. The criteria for sexuality during established adulthood are of little use to teenagers in figuring out when to proceed sexually or how to assess the quality of their relationships. At the same time, teenagers *are* capable of learning to develop the skills for discernment and the capacity for self-protection in the arena of sexuality that they are learning in other parts of their lives. But neither the "marriage-only" nor the "facts-only" approach sufficiently supports their psychosocial learning. Adolescent sexuality requires from adults—parents, policymakers, educators, providers, and members of the clergy—the engagement in a precarious balancing act of granting youth the rights they need to embark on that learning process, and of providing ongoing practical, emotional, critical, and ethical guidance to see them through the process of emergence.

Our cultural conceptions of individuality and autonomy have impeded us from that engagement—a joint enterprise in which adults give and take responsibility—and the dramatization of adolescent sexuality is, at least in part, the result of these cultural barriers.[22] Moving beyond the drama of adolescent sexuality thus requires us to engage in a process of cultural innovation. This process of cultural innovation need not involve denying the potentially difficult and dangerous aspects of sexuality. But it does need to start with an acceptance that most youth start their sexual "careers" in their mid-teens, and that they need internal discernment skills, interpersonal communication skills, connectedness with adults, and society-wide resources to transverse adolescence in a healthy fashion. Providing those skills, relationships, and resources will take a change of course in policy, education, health care, the home, and ministry, not just in action but in the language we use to think and talk about teenagers and their sexuality. To aid in this enterprise, I conclude with an ABC-and-Ds framework for adolescent sexuality.

The first component of adolescent sexual health in American society today is the development of the *autonomy* of the sexual self (A). As this book has shown, in American middle-class culture, financial self-sufficiency is upheld as the criterion that defines autonomy and legitimates sexual intercourse. And our sexual education policies of recent decades have also taught students that sexual intercourse is only acceptable after attaining the capacity for self-reliance. However, many middle-class youth do not become fully self-sufficient until their mid-twenties. Financial self-sufficiency is even more difficult to attain for low-income youth who lack the necessary educational and occupational resources and who often face additional discrimination.[23] As important, the current cultural and political definition of autonomy does not encompass the inner qualities and capacities that young people need to exercise autonomy as sexual beings vis-à-vis others, whether in peer relationships, romantic relationships, or as consumers of the media.

Such autonomy of the sexual self involves recognizing one's sexual feelings and desires as separate from the pressures from the desires and needs of others, taking ownership over those feelings, and exercising control over one's sexual behavior and decision-making.[24] To foster autonomy of the sexual self requires thinking of adolescent sexuality not simply as acts of intercourse or even as identities but rather as a continuum of feelings, behaviors, relationships, and identities. Young people must be encouraged to move slowly through this continuum of experience, to pace themselves so that they can assess their comfort levels at each step along the way, communicate their desires and boundaries, and adequately plan and prepare for next steps. Girls and boys face gender-specific barriers to their autonomy of sexual self. Girls must be encouraged to own their capacity for sexual pleasure and use it as one of the criteria for sexual decision-making.[25] We must cease to undermine boys' autonomy with images of them as mere vessels for physical forces and instead bolster their autonomy vis-à-vis detrimental norms of masculinity.[26]

Building relationships (B) is a second vital component of healthy adolescent development. Just as we must recognize that young people begin exploring sexual intimacy in the mid-teenage years—as long as a decade before they are financially self-sufficient—we must recognize that adolescents will form multiple emotional attachments that are significant. Our current paradigms provide two archetypes: the marriage ideal, on the one hand, and the risk of the abusive relationship, on the other. But rather than uphold marriage as the only goal of intimacy, we must validate the need for intimacy during the adolescent years and assist teenagers in building egalitarian and fun romantic relationships that are suited to their life stage. Warning against the exploitative and abusive potential of intimacy is only one component of relationship education. Other important components are discussions of, and exercises to practice, positive relating—including how to show interest, negotiate difference, share enjoyment, and build trust.[27]

Adolescent sexual health also requires *connectedness* with parents and other care providers (C). Connectedness between parents and teenagers is important to healthy development: young people who have close relationships with their parents are more likely to take protective measures in sexual behavior and to thrive in other areas of their maturation.[28] But as we have seen, American middle-class culture, and American culture generally, exacerbate what is perhaps an inevitable field of tension in the parent-adolescent relationship—sexuality—in a way that often leads to secrecy and undermines connectedness between parents and teenagers.[29] Such connectedness is absent altogether for the many teenagers, who for a variety of reasons lack emotional support from their biological parents. Thus other providers of care—professional and kin—play an important role both in helping parents become more effective sex educators and in supplementing their efforts. Medical professionals, educators, and members of the clergy and the media can help promote honest dialogue in their spheres of influence and in the family.

Finally, two D's are critical to adolescent sexual health: *Diversities* and *Disparities*. There is great diversity in the pace of sexual and emotional development, orientations, gender identifications, and cultural values that shape perceptions and experiences of sexuality. Education and health policies must honor those diversities, and teach young people to respect their own distinctiveness and that of others. But respecting differences—individual and cultural—is not the same as accepting disparities. Many of the negative sexual health outcomes in the United States, as elsewhere, result from young people's lack of resources and opportunities for meaningful education and jobs.[30] Our cultural conceptions of autonomy often prevent us from seeing that poor sexual health outcomes result from conditions that supersede individual choices. To advance adolescent sexual health, we need to invest the public resources necessary to remove the disparities in access to the services that foster autonomy and facilitate the formation of relationships.

These ABCDs of adolescent sexuality call for the bridging of oppositions that have characterized the politics of adolescent sexuality in the United States in the post-1960s-era—oppositions that have resulted, in part, from different interpretations of and responses to the changes in the relationships between parents and children, men and women, and citizens and governments since then. To overcome this adversarial political climate, some of which has been driven by a tug of war over whether teenagers are to be treated as children or as adults, we need to recognize that adolescents, like all human beings, need strong social bonds. To provide youth with such bonds—at an interpersonal and societal level—is the work of us all.

Methodological Appendix

In Search of Comparable Samples

Despite several obvious differences between the two countries—in size, in ethnic and racial diversity, and in geographic range—the United States and the Netherlands share some surprising commonalities.[1] Both countries were early republics with a highly decentralized state. In fact, the American and Dutch struggles for independence had much in common.[2] Indeed, it has been argued that the American Declaration of Independence was modeled after the Dutch Act of Abjuration (*Plakkaat van Verlatinge*) from Spain.[3] In addition, the middle classes have historically had a powerful position in both countries. In the absence of a strong aristocracy, commercial elites in the Netherlands and the United States achieved an early and unusually strong hold on the countries' culture and politics.[4] Finally, in both countries Protestants long formed the dominant religion but exerted their influence within the context of religious pluralism, with Roman Catholics constituting a significant religious minority.

Building on these cross-national commonalities, my goal for this research project was to pursue samples consisting of three cells in each country—parents, boys, and girls—that would be as similar as possible in terms of socio-demographic characteristics. I focused on the secular or moderately Christian white middle class, recognizing that in both countries religious conservatism significantly impacts attitudes toward sexuality, and that social class and education also affect childrearing practices.[5] To avoid interviewing only members of the upper middle class, I used a broad definition of middle class—including both those at the "lower" and "higher" end of the spectrum: salespeople, for example, with little or no college education and professionals with advanced training. Avoiding political and geographic extremes, I sought out medium-sized cities and bedroom communities, neither in large metropolitan centers nor in remote rural towns.

Yet, in search of perfectly cross-nationally comparable samples, I learned much about the political, economic, and cultural differences between the two societies. First, it proved extremely difficult to gain access to high schools in the United States—a significant stumbling block since high schools served as the entry to reaching almost all teenagers, and, through them, in turn, many of the parents I interviewed. Describing my study as one about "growing up in the United States and the Netherlands," and listing among the topics "school, work, alcohol, relationships with parents, relationships and sexuality, and adulthood," all of which I covered in the interview, I found few schools, even those located relatively near the San Francisco Bay Area, responsive to my queries. Illustrating poignantly the political battles brewing around teenagers and sex education, one principle said he wanted to avoid all controversy and that "all it takes is one parent."[6]

The second, perhaps more surprising, challenge I encountered was finding a community that would, at least according to its descriptive demographic statistics, promise to render a sufficient pool of "middle-class" interviewees. Using census data, I found that most towns, suburbs, and medium-sized cities either appeared decidedly below or decidedly above "middle-income" if measured in terms of median family income. Especially in Northern California, communities were separated into upper- and lower-income extremes, reflecting the hollowing out of "the middle of the middle" during recent decades."[7] When I gained entry to schools in Corona, a medium-sized Northern California city, I found that interviewees often lived either in spacious upper-middle-class houses or in households with some economic instability.[8] And even in the town of Tremont, where the cost of living was lower by comparison, it was hard to recruit lower-middle-class parents in part because their children seemed more reluctant to refer them.[9]

Third, although I set out to exclude evangelical and fundamentalist Christians from my sample, I was not always successful. As we saw in the book's introduction, this group of Christians differs from the rest of the American population in categorically opposing sex outside of marriage. While a much smaller proportion of the overall population in the Netherlands, conservative Christians also have markedly different sexual attitudes than do the rest of the population. Thus, it made sense to try to exclude them for maximum comparability across nations. But especially in the small town of Tremont, I found that the screening questionnaire failed to adequately identify a potential interviewee's church as "conservative," and only in the course of the interview did I discover that he or she could be categorized as such. Thus, a couple of the American interviewees do, in fact, live in Christian conservative families.[10]

My experience searching for interview sites and soliciting interviewees was quite different in the Netherlands. First, almost all schools that I approached were welcoming. Sometimes through a personal connection and sometimes without, I gained easy access to classrooms. That I was engaged in postgraduate research and affiliated with a major research university in the United States sufficed in vouching for my legitimacy. This easy access bespeaks a feature of Dutch society of the 1990s, which I discuss in chapters 2 and 4, namely a trust in elites, including medical, scientific, and educational elites. This trust—and indeed confusion when confronted with a suggestion of lack of trust—became evident in an interview with a somewhat older and less well-educated Dutch couple. When, after giving me a friendly welcome, they received the consent form describing the research— its "risks" and "benefits," as required by the research protocol—the husband was a little indignant: "We agreed to do it, why do we need to read this?"

The second difference was that it was easy to find the group that proved elusive in the United States. In the Dutch lower-middle-class families in which I did my interviews, at least one parent had typically received some vocational education in addition to a high-school degree and had a white collar job. Parents' educational credentials ranged from high-school degrees with on-the-job vocational training to degrees from vocational (non-academic) colleges. They worked as salesmen, bank clerks, insurance workers, and middle managers. The solidity of the interviewees' class position had perhaps less to do with the specifics of their education and occupation than with the comforts and security that characterized the rhythms of their everyday lives. Fathers typically worked nine-to-five jobs, while mothers were homemakers or worked part-time. Typically, such families would take at least one lengthy vacation a year, often abroad.[11] And while having children in postsecondary education might require some budgeting, it was certainly within reach.

As in the United States, in the Netherlands I also interviewed physicians, teachers, civil servants, upper-level managers, and psychotherapists.[12] But in the Netherlands, parents with university degrees and lower-middle-class parents with little or no college were almost equally represented among the interviewees, whereas in the United States the parents with four-year degrees outnumbered those without by almost three to one. Consequently, the American parents were, on the whole, more likely to be highly educated and hence, one might expect, more liberal. At the same time, the American parents and teenagers were more likely to have some religious affiliation and practice. There were similarities between the Corona and Norwood interviewees and the Dutch interviewees—both were usually Catholic or nonaffiliated. But in Tremont, parents and teenagers were typically Protestant and reportedly active in their church communities.

There were also several common patterns across the two countries. In soliciting interviews, I invited both parents to be interviewed as a couple. But, in practice, fathers were present and participated in only about a third of the interviews, usually with their wives, but occasionally alone. I did not set out to analyze parents by their gender, nor did the small numbers permit any systematic comparison.[13] In keeping with the experiences of previous researchers, I also found teenage boys somewhat more difficult to recruit than their female counterparts—though not necessarily more difficult to converse with.[14] Finally, in both countries, teenagers were somewhat more likely than their parents to live in families in which neither parent had a four–year degree or a professional occupation.[15] One reason for this discrepancy between teenagers and parents is that about half of the of the parents were recruited through informal and formal parent networks such as PTA's, in which highly educated parents were overrepresented. I approached the remainder of the parents after interviewing their children and receiving the latter's permission to contact them. Because I interviewed more teenagers than parents and because I recruited parents through multiple methods, only fourteen of the thirty-six American teenagers and fifteen of the thirty-six Dutch teenagers lived in families in which I also interviewed one or both of their parents.

The Interviews

Most of the recruitment of teenage interviewees took place through schools. In the United States, I selected public high schools which draw a substantial proportion of their students from middle and upper-middle-class neighborhoods. In the Netherlands, most of the high schools I selected included the pre-college tracks (*HAVO* and *VWO*) disproportionally populated by students from lower- and upper-middle-class families, although two Dutch interviewees were students in the vocational track, *MAVO*. I solicited interviewees after entering tenth-grade classrooms and explaining the interview and the topics it included. Usually, about half of the students in a classroom wanted to be interviewed. Interested students filled out the screening questionnaire. They received a consent form for themselves and one for their parents. I interviewed students who met the sampling criteria and whose parents gave permission for the interview.

All interviews were semi-structured and in-depth. For such interviews to be successful and positive experiences, interviewees must feel comfortable talking about personal matters. I took a number of steps to create an atmosphere in which the interviewees would experience such a level of comfort. I asked them to select the place where the interview would take place. Most teenagers chose to be interviewed at home, in a private office at school, or in a café or public library. Virtually all interviews with parents took place in their homes. To give interviewees a sense of what to expect from the interview, the consent form, which they read and signed before the interview, explained the topics that would be covered in each interview and how confidentiality would be maintained. Before each interview—which was tape-recorded—I emphasized that interviewees could decline to answer any question they did not want to answer.

Each person or couple was interviewed once. The interviews themselves were structured to gradually establish rapport. With the teenagers, I started with a number of concrete, easy-to-answer questions on their day-to-day schedules, school, friends, and jobs. Only gradually did I move into topics such as drinking, parental rules, and sexuality, topics which they might find more difficult to address. I concluded each interview by asking teenagers questions of a less personal nature: their ideas about adulthood and their own future plans. After the interview, I asked them permission to contact their parents for an interview. With the parents, I started each interview with a number of open-ended questions about raising children and the adolescent phase in particular, only gradually moving into the more emotionally loaded territory of parent-teenager conflicts, drinking, relationships, and sexuality. Again, I concluded each interview with questions about the parents' wishes for their children's futures, questions intended to be more general and easy to answer.

The interview questions were designed to elicit explicit opinions and attitudes. But equally if not more important were the concepts, expressions, and mode of reasoning which interviewees used, often entirely unselfconsciously, to express implicit cultural assumptions and beliefs. To gauge actual practices—which are sometimes different from stated intentions and beliefs—I asked questions about interviewees' behavior in multiple ways at different times throughout the interview. In an attempt to get as close as possible to actual behavior, I asked interviewees to reflect on what their actions were or would be in concrete situations—either real or hypothetical.

Thus, the interviews sought to establish a number of different "truths": that is, the interviewees' opinions, their taken-for-granted cultural languages and conceptions, their purported behavior, and finally, their actual practices and lived experiences. The tensions and contradictions between these different truths themselves constitute valuable sources of information.

Each sociological interview constitutes a balancing act between accurately establishing the particulars of one individual's perceptions and experiences and eliciting the kind of information that can be meaningfully compared across multiple cases. To balance the objectives of depth and systematic comparison, I sought to flexibly combine different types of interview questions. The first type of question lent itself for open-ended answers in which the interviewees had free rein to use their own language and convey meanings which would allow me to discern qualitative patterns in cultural meanings and practice. The second type of question was concrete and required clear-cut, often yes-or-no answers. For each important substantive topic area—alcohol, parent-teen relationships, sex and relationships, adulthood—I included two or three of the latter.[16] Using the same language, I tried to ask all interviewees these standardized questions.

Theory, Culture, and Practice

The analyses presented in the book chapters are the product of a continuous process of moving back and forth between theoretical and empirical "tracks of analysis.[17] The first stage of analysis took place in 1991–92, in my undergraduate thesis at Harvard University on the cultural construction of adolescence among Dutch and American parents.[18] The analytic and theoretical interpretation I developed then informed the subsequent research I conducted for my sociology Ph.D. thesis at the University of California at Berkeley. This research took me to the Netherlands in 1994, 1995, 1998, and 2000, to Corona in 1998 and 1999, and to Tremont in 2000. After each interview, I wrote memos on notable findings, and how they confirmed, challenged, or developed my hypotheses. As my ideas evolved with new theoretical lenses and empirical observation, I refined the interview questions I used, adding some new questions and dropping others.

As a consequence of these processes of moving back and forth between theory and data, by the time I started the systematic analysis of interview transcripts, I had already developed a fairly clear idea of the critical cultural concepts and practices in the two countries, as well as of the important relationships and dynamics which the data revealed. These ideas refined themselves as I coded the transcripts with the help of QSR's qualitative software programs N5 and NVivo 8 and tabulated the answers to the quantifiable standardized questions. I analyzed the transcripts in the same order as the chapters of the book—moving from the Dutch parents, to the American parents, to the teenagers in the two countries. The analyses of the data evolved from the creative interplay between these tabulations of quantifiable answers and my interpretations of the meanings, causes, and consequences of the critical cultural concepts and practices.

I would be remiss if I did not discuss some important additional tools and sources for my interpretations, analyses, and theoretical propositions. The first is the interpretative lens that I developed as the oldest child of American immigrants, living and fully participating in Dutch society from childhood to young adulthood. Like many second-generation immigrants, I had participant observation or "observing participation" thrust on me from an early age, becoming familiar enough with Dutch culture to see it "from a native's point of view" but not so familiar as to take it for granted.[19] This familiarity gave me access to what Clifford Geertz has called "first-order interpretations": the interpretations that are made by people who share a culture, and that are distinct from the "second-order interpretations" made by cultural analysts.[20] A second source of information has come from interactions with researchers, professionals, policymakers, and advocates in health and education. In 2004, I published an article in an online medical journal. The article's distribution through networks outside of the academic social sciences led to speaking engagements at sexual and reproductive health, policy, and education conferences, at government organizations, and to collaborations with educators and adolescent medicine specialists. These interprofessional exchanges have constituted a different source of learning: the back-and-forth with audiences who spoke as professionals and as parents—and reflecting on their teenage years, as adolescents—greatly enriched my understanding of the cultural, political, and economic factors that shape adolescent sexuality in the United States today. These inspiring exchanges have also attuned me to what appears to be a widely felt desire to see adolescent sexual development become less fraught territory and prompted me to develop the conceptual map for adolescent sexual health with which I close this book.

Tables of Parents and Teenagers

In these tables I count parents who were interviewed together as a couple as one because although they are two people, together they represent one household. In brackets are the numbers counting both parents.

Table A.1   Number of interviewees

	United States	Netherlands
Parents	32 (41)	26 (34)
Girls	20	20
Boys	16	16
Total	68 (77)	62 (70)

Table A.2   American interviewees by place of residence

	Parents	Teenagers
Norwood	12	1
Corona	10	18
Tremont	10	17
Total	32	36

Table A.3   Dutch interviewees by place of residence

	Parents	Teenagers
Western City	15	19
Eastern City	11	17
Total	26	36

Table A.4   American and Dutch parents by education/occupation

	American parents	Dutch parents
Professional[a]	23 (72%)	14 (54%)
Nonprofessional	9 (28%)	12 (46%)

[a]The category "professional" refers to households in which at least one parent has a four-year degree and a professional or an upper-managerial position.

Table A.5   American and Dutch teenagers by parents' education/occupation

	American teens	Dutch teens
Professional	16 (44%)	13 (36%)
Nonprofessional	20 (56%)	23 (64%)

Table A.6   American and Dutch parents by religious affiliation

	American parents	Dutch parents
Protestant	11 (34%)	3 (12%)
Catholic	11 (34%)	12 (46%)
None	10 (31%)	11 (42%)

Table A.7   American and Dutch teens by religious affiliation

	American teens	Dutch teens
Protestant	20 (56%)	3 (8%)
Catholic	9 (25%)	15 (42%)
None	7 (19%)	18 (50%)

The Settings

Corona (population, 130,000) is a county capital and home to a reputable junior college as well as a state university. Although located in the midst of liberal Northern California, the majority of Corona residents identify as moderates. Far enough away from major metropolitan areas to make commuting difficult, close enough to draw many "escapees" from the big cities, Corona is a blend of city and suburb. It possesses a popularly frequented commercial core of cafés and shops, including a Barnes & Noble, which, true to its Northern Californian location, features extensive sections on spirituality, astrology, and gay and lesbian studies. Much of the city's life, however, takes place in the stretched out, suburban neighborhoods that lie a car-ride away from the city's center. While Corona's residential neighborhoods are segregated by income and ethnicity—over 10 percent of the city's residents are Hispanic—the city is not as polarized economically as are many of its counterparts across the country.

For the parents who reside in the green, spacious, middle- and upper-middle-class neighborhoods that lie sprinkled within the city's boundaries, it probably comes as no surprise that Corona ranks high on a number of measures of the "good life." Corona parents are typically part of married couples, in which both spouses have at least a two-year, if not four-year, college degree and are employed as professionals in health care, engineering, and business. Most inhabit sizable, detached homes, found at the end of cul-de-sacs, perched along hillsides, or half-hidden among woodsy growth. While few would characterize themselves as particularly wealthy, none would deny being relatively "comfortable."

And yet, if Corona parents have gone a long way toward attaining the "American dream," they are acutely aware that an entirely different world lies beyond their own secluded streets. One way parents confront that world is through their own children. The teenage children of most Corona parents attend two of the city's five public high schools. Like its residential neighborhoods, Corona's high schools are economically and ethnically segregated. However, the dividing lines between schools are less rigid. Corona's steadily growing gang problem, for instance, has become a defining feature of even one of Corona's most economically and educationally advantaged public schools. Corona high schools give evidence of "diversity" in other ways as well. On the one hand, there is a wide array of student cliques and organizations—including a group for gay and bisexual teens at one school. On the other, a sizable proportion of students have parents with serious substance abuse problems. And it is not uncommon for Corona's high-school students to move back and forth between parents, or to live for extended periods with grandparents.

Tremont (population, 10,000) lies a short plane flight away from Corona in Washington State. The flight north, however, feels like a move across time as well as space. In many respects, Tremont approximates the mid-century, small-town America featured in many sociological classics. Tremont was long a thriving blue-collar town with strong egalitarian sentiments—millworkers and lawyers met on their walk down the hill to work in the morning—and a firm civic culture organized around church, school, and voluntary associations. Those social and political traditions are still evident even as profound economic changes are underway: as Tremont's population grew by almost one half, its productive center of gravity moved from the mill in town to the high-tech firms out of town, as has much of its commercial activity. Downtown still houses a movie theater and a supermarket, but many locals now shop and entertain themselves in the newer developments and malls that lie ten or fifteen miles out of town.

The residential patterns of the Tremont interviewees mirror the town's character. Half of the parents are natives or long-time residents of Tremont. The other half are relatively recent transplants, mostly from other regions in the Pacific Northwest. The majority of parents live outside of the "old town"—in the new developments on the other side of the hill or in the rural areas beyond the town's limits. Tremont parents are more educationally and occupationally diverse than their Corona counterparts. Half of the Tremont interviewees were only in college for a year or two, while the other half hold four-year degrees. Their occupations range from customer service provider and postal clerk, on the one hand, to engineer and company president, on the other.

If Tremont is changing, the high school does not yet show visible signs of change. With seven hundred students, Tremont's only high school is significantly smaller than any of the Corona schools. The calm and highly regulated way in which students and teachers move about in the former—discipline in and outside of class is tight—is a far cry from the chaotic atmosphere of the latter. The sea of fair-haired boys and girls—most Tremont residents are of Northern European heritage—demonstrate the student body's ethnic homogeneity. The student groupings of Tremont High also lack the diversity of Corona high schools. But sports, the mainstay of Tremont's extracurricular life, are strongly supported by the community. And it is common to see groups of adults and teens congregated on lit fields on early spring evenings, taking joint pleasure in cheerleading, running track, and playing ball.

As its name suggests, Eastern City is located in the east of the Netherlands, a region which has long functioned as the semi-periphery to the more densely populated and commercially developed West. Although it lies at some distance from the country's main political and economic center, Eastern City nonetheless constitutes an urban area of some substance. With 130,000 inhabitants and two vocational colleges as well as an internationally renowned soccer facility, the city has its share of urban charms and problems. One of Eastern City's undeniable assets is its downtown, a conglomeration of cafés, restaurants, and small shops housed in centuries-old buildings along windy, cobblestone roads. On Friday and Saturday nights, the main plaza draws youths, including children of the parents interviewed, from all over the city and beyond.

About half of the Dutch interviewees, and most of the lower-middle-class interviewees, live in the Eastern City's outskirts or in the bedroom communities that surround them. They mostly inhabit the relatively new developments (*nieuwbouw*) built on the ever-expanding border between city and farmland. In these developments, families typically occupy tidy and comfortable houses of moderate size that, like the vast majority of dwellings in the country, are attached on both sides to other houses. Most homes are adorned with small, well-kept gardens, or, at the very least, with a plant box or two, that serve to distinguish each from its otherwise identical neighbors. Little brooks and tree-lined paths for pedestrians, dog-walkers, joggers, and cyclists of all ages crisscross the blocks of pale-tinted brick structures. The modern design, the orderliness, and the sheer number of housing units planted amidst the green pastures with their black-and-white dairy cows render that blend of tranquility and population density that is so typical of Dutch life outside the city centers.

Two hours away by train, on the other side of the country, lies Western City. With its 110,0000 inhabitants and its world-renowned university, Western City marks the heart of the *Randstad*, the corridor of large and medium-sized cities which have long shaped Dutch politics, economics, science, and art. Despite the students and faculty it draws from all over, its proximity to the excitement of Amsterdam and the political power of The Hague, and its increasingly multi-ethnic character, Western City remains oddly quaint. Outside of its centuries-old center, the city's streets quickly become completely residential, blending gradually into neighboring bedroom communities. In the center of Western city lies the School for Classical Education, one of city's oldest public secondary schools with a reputation for academic excellence. At its southern border lies Ferdinand College, drawing a more economically and ethnically diverse population.

Most Dutch parents who live in or near Western city are parents of SCE children. They belong to professional middle-class households where at least one parent has a master's degree or equivalent. More likely to be employed in the professions—science, architecture, medicine—than in commerce, these parents are part of the country's cultural, rather than economic, elite. Even so, mothers rarely work more than twenty-five hours a week. The Dutch teenagers attend both the SCE and Ferdinand College. Neither set of Dutch teenagers is likely to live in Western city itself—although a few do inhabit charming, turn-of-the-century red-brick houses in the vicinity of the school. Indeed, most Western City families live in the upper-middle-class neighborhoods of the surrounding bedroom communities. Consequently, twice a day, the Western City teenagers join the steady stream of cyclists who make their way to and from school alongside city traffic, highways, and canals.

CHAPTER ONE

1. All names of people and places, and some occupations, have been changed to preserve anonymity. All translations from Dutch are mine.

2. The words "sexuality" and "sex" have multiple meanings: The word "sexuality" can be used to refer to the wide range of feelings, experiences, identities, and behaviors that are part of one's experience of oneself and relationship to others. In a second definition, the words sex and sexuality are used interchangeably to refer more narrowly to sexual behaviors and experiences per se, which one engages in with another person or alone. The final meaning is the narrowest, and it refers exclusively to acts of (vaginal) intercourse. In this book, when I talk about "adolescent sexuality" and sexual experiences, I am referring to teenagers' sexual feelings and the range of sexual behaviors in which they do or will engage. However, when I use demographic data on having "sex" and being "sexually active" or "experienced," unless I specify otherwise, I will be referring to heterosexual vaginal intercourse. (Although surveys in both countries are increasingly collecting data on multiple sexual behaviors and on same-sex partners, data on experiences with heterosexual intercourse are typically the most internationally comparable.) And when, in discussing the interview material, I use the expression, "having sex" or "going to bed with," I am referring to vaginal intercourse, since this is what interviewees usually mean.

3. Michaud 2006.

4. This is especially true for classical (psychoanalytically informed) developmental psychology and evolutionary developmental psychology, in which separation from parents is a critical element of the individuation process. See also notes 55 and 56.

5. Sociological classics on adolescent peer groups and status hierarchies include Waller 1937 and Coleman 1961. Contemporary sociological studies of adolescent networks and peer groups include Bearman and Brückner 2001; Bearman 2004; Anderson 1999; Eder, Evans, and Parker 1995; Bettie 2000; and Pascoe 2007.

6. See for instance Bettie 2000; Fine 1988; Nathanson 1991; Tolman 2002; Tolman, Striepe, and Harmon 2003; Vanwesenbeeck, Bekker, and van Lenning 1998; and Armstrong, Hamilton, and Sweeney 2006.

7. Abma et al. 2004; de Graaf et al. 2005; Darroch, Singh, and Frost 2001; and Mosher, Chandra, and Jones 2005. More than half of American and Dutch seventeen-year-olds (both girls and boys) have had oral sex with a same-sex and/or opposite-sex

partner. Among seventeen-year-olds, a little under half of American girls and boys, 45 percent of Dutch boys, and six out of ten Dutch girls have had vaginal intercourse (Mosher, Chandra, and Jones 2005; de Graaf et al. 2005).

8. Bozon and Kontula 1998.
9. Jones et al. 1986; Berne and Huberman 1999; and Rose 2005.
10. Laumann et al. 1994, 198 and 326.
11. Finer 2007.
12. The Gallup poll statistics come from Smith 1994.
13. Petersen and Donnenwerth 1997.
14. Abma, Martinez, and Copen 2010; Abma et al. 2004; 2010.
15. Kost, Henshaw, and Carlin 2010.
16. In 2007, the birth rate was 5.2 for Dutch teenage girls and 42.5 for American girls (Garssen 2008; Hamilton, Martin, and Ventura 2009). The table below shows abortion and pregnancy rates for the latest available year.

Table 1.1   Pregnancies, births, and abortions per 1,000 women, ages 15–19

	US (2006)	NL (2006)
Pregnancy rate[a]	61.2	14.1
Birth rate	41.9	5.3
Abortion rate	19.3	8.8
Abortion ratio[b]	31.5	62.4

Sources: Kost et al. 2010; van Lee et al. 2009.
[a]Pregnancy rates exclude estimations for fetal losses.
[b]The abortion ratio is the percentage of pregnancies (excluding those resulting in fetal losses) that are terminated.

In both countries, teenage pregnancy rates are higher among economically disadvantaged groups. In the United States, non-Hispanic white girls, and in the Netherlands, girls who are themselves and whose parents are native-born have lower rates of socioeconomic disadvantage, and they also have lower pregnancy rates. By comparing these two groups, we still see a strong difference between the two countries. Note that the two groups are not strictly comparable because Dutch rates are grouped by immigration status rather than by race and ethnicity.

Table 1.2   Pregnancies, births, and abortions per 1,000 white/native-born women, ages 15–19

	US (2006)[a]	NL (2007)[b]
Pregnancy rate[c]	37.6	11.1
Birth rate	26.6	5.2
Abortion rate	11.0	5.9
Abortion ratio[d]	29.3	53.2

Sources: Kost et al. 2010; van Lee et al. 2009.
[a]Non-Hispanic white women.
[b]Includes all races and ethnicities, but woman and both her parents must have been born in the Netherlands.
[c]Pregnancy rates exclude estimations for fetal losses.
[d]The abortion ratio is the percentage of pregnancies (excluding those resulting in fetal losses) that are terminated.

During the early 1990s, Dutch teenage pregnancy rates were comparable to those in recent years (van Lee and Wijsen 2008). But early 1990s American rates were significantly higher than those in recent years, and the contrast between the two countries in teenage pregnancy rates was even starker than in the tables above. During the second half of the 1990s, the Dutch teenage pregnancy rate increased, before steadily decreasing again after 2002. But in 2000, the Dutch teenage pregnancy rate was still approximately four times lower than the American rate.

17. Evert Ketting (1983; 1994) has attributed the low Dutch teenage pregnancy rate to the use of the pill primarily and to emergency contraception secondarily. In 1995, 63 percent of Dutch secondary school students always used the pill with their last sexual partner, and 42 percent always used condoms (another 31 percent sometimes used condoms) (Brugman et al. 1995). That same year, a quarter of American females and a third of American males, ages fifteen to nineteen, who had sex three months prior to being interviewed by the National Survey of Family Growth, used the pill at last intercourse. Thirty-eight percent of American females and 64 percent of American males used a condom. Since then, condom use among sexually active youth has increased in both countries. Indeed, as the table below shows, condom use at first vaginal intercourse is relatively high in both countries. However, pill use and dual protection (condoms and hormonal methods combined) are much higher among Dutch teens than they are among American teens. International comparisons of contraceptive behavior at last vaginal intercourse among sexually active fifteen-year-olds have found a similar pattern (Currie et al. 2008; Santelli, Sandfort, and Orr 2008; Godeau et al. 2008).

Table 1.3   Use of contraception at first vaginal intercourse among males and females, ages 15–19

	Dutch females, %	American females, %	Dutch males, %	American males, %
Condom	78	68	75	82
Pill[a]	59	20	53	22
Dual methods	43	14	38	19

Sources: Abma et al. 2010 for U.S. rates; Ferguson, Vanwesenbeeck, and Knijn 2008, who used de Graaf et al. 2005 to calculate Dutch rates.
Note: U.S. data collected between 2006 and 2008 and Dutch data collected in 2005.
[a]For the Dutch teens, the percentages of "pill" use also include other hormonal methods and diaphragms. However, only 1% of females and 0.2% of males categorized as pill users use a method other than the pill. For American teens, the percentages of "pill" use also include other hormonal methods *and* emergency contraception. Almost a quarter of the American females and one in ten males categorized as pill users use methods other than the pill.

18. See tables 1.1 and 1.2 in note 16.
19. See Thompson 1990; Thompson 1995; Martin 1996; Tolman 2002; Carpenter 2005; and Pascoe 2007.
20. Abma et al. 2004.
21. Albert 2004.
22. Meier found that the majority of teenagers do not experience negative mental health effects after first sex. However, some groups of girls do experience such effects, which depend on their age and relationship status during and after their first intercourse

(Meier 2007). On the relationship between first romance and conflict with parents, see Joyner and Udry 2000.

23. In the late 1960s and early 1970s, Dutch policymakers and the organization of family physicians, who provide the bulk of primary care in the Netherlands, made a concerted effort to make contraception easily accessible to unmarried women, including teenage women (Ketting 1990). During that same period, Constance Nathanson argues, the majority of American physicians shied away from the issue of teenage sexuality and pregnancy prevention. Indeed in 1970, Nathanson reports, the American Medical Association's House of Delegates, the organization's principal policymaking body, rejected the recommendation by its Committee on Maternal and Child Health to adopt a policy "permitting physicians to offer contraceptive advice and methods to teenage girls whose sexual behavior exposes them to possible pregnancy" (1991, 39). Policymakers also struggled with the issue: Nathanson argues that "neither Nixon in 1972 nor Carter in 1978 was prepared publicly to endorse birth control for unmarried adolescent women" (57). And teenagers' legal right to access contraception was, according to Kristin Luker, "very ambiguous" in the mid-1970s (Luker 1996, 65). Individual health-care providers and pharmacists were often hesitant to provide contraceptive services to minors because it interfered with traditional notions of parental authority (Luker 1996, 66). Meanwhile, starting in 1972, Congress began advocating for the inclusion of minors in the population served by federally funded family planning clinics, and when in 1977 it reauthorized Title X, which provides most of the federal funding for public contraceptive services, it made explicit that minors were a group eligible for funding (Luker 1996, 69). Today, many states permit minors twelve and up to consent to contraceptive services. However, concerns about confidentiality and costs still constitute barriers to adolescents' obtaining reproductive health care (Lehrer et al. 2007; Ralph and Brindis 2010; Guttmacher Institute 2010).

24. D'Emilio and Freedman 1988, 342.

25. See Ward et al. 2006 and Steele 2002.

26. See Irvine 2002 and di Mauro and Joffe 2007.

27. Kantor et al. 2008. While the recent health-care reform act has included federal funding to schools that teach about contraception and contraception, it also allocated funds to support abstinence-only programs.

28. See Lindberg, Santelli, and Singh 2006; Darroch, Landry, and Singh 2000; and Fields 2008.

29. Since the mid-1970s, the General Social Survey has found that at least four out of five Americans support sex education in schools.

30. *Sex Education in America* 2004.

31. See *Sex Education in America* 2004. Using 2002 NSFG data, Mosher and colleagues (2005) report that by age sixteen, the majority of American teenagers have engaged in some sexual contact—which could include oral sex or intimate touching—with another person (either same or opposite sex).

32. See Ravesloot 1997.

33. Centraal Bureau voor de Statistiek 2003.

34. Bozon and Kontula 1998; Ravesloot 1997; and Wouters 2004.

35. Kooij 1983.

36. Ketting 1990; Ketting and Visser 1994. See also note 23. Schnabel (1990) has argued that there was wide support among the Dutch population for the changes of

the sexual revolution, and that change was certainly not confined to a small group of students.

37. Jones et al. 1986, 178. Historian James C. Kennedy has also argued that during the 1950s and 1960s, Dutch religious leaders, especially within the Catholic Church, went much further than bishops in other countries in fundamentally changing doctrine and practice, replacing a morality based on individual compliance with an ethics based on universal human compassion and service to others (Kennedy 1995). The Dutch sociologist Kooij (1983) has also pointed toward the role of religious leaders in opening up discussions around sexuality in Dutch society of the 1960s and 1970s. It is notable that the new moral discourse did not only pertain to heterosexual couples. In his "De Kracht van de Moraal: De Doorbraak in het Emancipatieproces van Nederlandse Homoseksuelen" ("The Power of Morality: The Breakthrough in the Emancipation Process of Dutch Homosexuals"), Dutch sociologist Bram van Stolk (1991) argues that the remarkable progress in the position of homosexuals in Dutch society between 1960 and 1975 can be in large part attributed to the moral claims made first by progressively minded psychiatrists and religious thinkers and later adapted by members of the (mainly male at that time) gay movement itself. Van Stolk argues that it was the power of the moral claims rather than movement activism that was responsible for the breakthrough in the "emancipation" of homosexuals. But while religious leaders, intellectuals, psychologists, and medical professionals helped shape the new cultural climate, the changes in sexual morality were supported by broad segments of the Dutch population, argues Paul Schnabel (1990).

38. One group that played an important role was the Dutch Association for Sexual Reform (NVSH), which in the mid-1960s had more than 200,000 members. The NVSH was a strong advocate for family planning and sex education—including through the media—and it helped shape government policy as well as public opinion (Ketting and Visser 1994; Hekma 2004a).

39. Dutch policy long kept commercial radio and television broadcasting illegal, and allocated air time to different political and religious nonprofit groups—whose membership roughly corresponded to the political, class, and religious population segments into which Dutch society through the 1960s was divided. Even as the segmentation of Dutch society broke down in the 1970s and 1980s, the Dutch government followed the policy of supporting "a pluralistic public broadcasting system built along social and cultural lines," write Kees van der Haak and Leo van Snippenburg (2001). They note moreover that even after the legalization and expansion of commercial broadcasting in the 1980s and 1990s, the government was "intent on keeping the public part of the whole broadcasting system as strong as possible in a context of national and international competition in commercial broadcasting" (2001, 210).

40. Jones et al. 1986, 154. Survey research in the 1980s did not find strong effects of factors such as gender, class, religion, or urbanization on attitudes toward sexuality among the Dutch population (Van Zessen and Sandfort 1991).

41. Ketting 1994.

42. Ketting and Visser 1994 and Hardon 2003. Hardon describes the legal parameters and public sentiment: "Over age 16, patients are considered autonomous in decisions on health care, including contraception. Between ages 12 and 16 parental consent is needed, but if parents do not give consent and the minor wants treat-

ment (e.g. contraception), a doctor can provide it if not doing so would have serious, negative consequences for the minor. The extent to which the Dutch respect the autonomy of minors is reflected in a recent survey in which 75 percent of respondents thought a doctor should prescribe contraception without parental consent if that is what the minor needed and wanted" (61).

43. That confidence was challenged when Dutch teen pregnancies and abortions rose notably between 1996 and 2002. But the Netherlands' role as "guide country" with regard to teenage births and abortions remained intact, writes Joop Garssen, and was strengthened by a sustained decrease in those rates between 2002 and 2007. Especially notable were declines in the birth rates of first- and second-generation immigrant girls and young women (Garssen 2008).

44. Brugman et al. 1995 and Vogels and van der Vliet 1990.

45. Cremer 1997 and Ravesloot 1997. Vanwesenbeeck and colleagues (1998) found that gendered patterns had persisted among Dutch college students of the 1990s: girls were likely to take a defensive approach to sexual interactions, while males were more likely to take an active, "go-get-it" approach.

46. Rademakers and Ravesloot (1993), for instance, state: "Sexual contact is a situation of negotiation in which both partners have an equal position [*gelijkwaardige uitgangspositie*]. . . . Youths must learn that they are not victims of circumstances. Particularly, for traditionally oriented girls it is important to emphasize more clearly the shared responsibility in sexual relationships. Sexual education ideally has an emancipatory character, such that teenage sexuality is discussed in an open and matter-of-course manner. That way the threshold for girls is lowered as much as possible to take their own initiatives in sexual behavior and contraceptive use. Moreover, it is important that sex education orients itself to the interactive competencies of youths. Learning to talk about sex and contraception is particularly important, but also learning to negotiate in general" (277).

47. De Graaf et al. 2005.

48. Lewis and Knijn 2002; 2003.

49. Lewis and Knijn 2002, 687. But curricula are also adapted for religious audiences. An example of such adjustments included the emphasis on faithfulness over condoms and the exclusion of passages on masturbation and orgasm for a textbook used in schools of the Dutch Reformed Church (SOAIDS 2004).

50. In their analysis of fifteen nations, Kelley and de Graaf (1997) use a variety of measures for religiosity. They characterize the United States as an extraordinarily devout modern society and the Netherlands as a relatively secular one.

51. Goodin et al. 2000.

52. Singh, Darroch, and Frost 2001.

53. All of the American parent interviews informed the analyses and calculation of parents' answers to the question of the sleepover. However, only Corona and Tremont parents are quoted in this book. For quotes from the interviews with Norwood parents, see Schalet 2000.

54. Michaud 2006 and Nathanson 1991.

55. Steinberg 2004.

56. American psychoanalytic developmental theory places a great emphasis on separation and on sexual development as one of the motors of separation (Erikson 1950; Freud 1958). For a fascinating analysis of how American psychoanalytic developmental psychology has been shaped by Anglo-American cultural traditions that emphasize, among other things, self-reliance, resulting in an emphasis on separation

as the marker of psychological health, see Kirschner 1990. Socio-biological evolutionary perspectives also place an emphasis on the necessity for separation between parents and adolescents (Collins, Welsh, and Furman 2009, 634).

57. See, for instance, Risman and Schwartz 2002, and Carpenter 2005.

58. Martin 1996. The term "antagonistic gender strategies" comes from Thorne 1993.

59. See Fine 1988 and Fine and McClelland 2006.

60. See also Tolman 2002.

61. Foucault 1977; 1978.

62. This critique of Foucault has been partly inspired by the work of Norbert Elias, who offers an alternative and more optimistic view of the relationship between sexuality and control in the modern world (Elias 1994, 177; Smith 1999). Norbert Elias' *The Civilizing Process*, published in 1939, argued that since the late Middle Ages people became increasingly dependent upon one another, which, in turn, has required them to be more considerate of others and to exercise greater restraint over their emotional impulses. For Elias, this gradual "civilizing process," while taking its toll, also had benefits, one of which is greater self-mastery.

63. Williams 1976.

64. For a useful overview of the different concepts of culture that have informed sociology and anthropology, see Sewell 1999.

65. Swidler 2001 and Archer 1985.

66. Bourdieu 1984 and also Lamont 1992; 2000.

67. See for instance, McRobbie 1991; McRobbie and Garber 1993; Willis 1977; Hebdidge 1979; and Wilkins 2008.

68. This synthetic approach draws on the Geertzian paradigm of culture as webs of meaning (Geertz 1973; 1983), the Foucauldian attention to the controlling and constitutive consequences of discursive constructions and practices (Foucault 1977; 1978; 1985), and is sensitive to the ways in which cultural practices serve as means of drawing status distinctions (Elias 1994; Bourdieu 1984; 1990). My approach is synthetic in a second respect: it combines attention to the systematic and structuring properties of cultures, with recognition of the way in which individuals use the cultural tools and templates available to them (Swidler 1986; 2001).

69. The concept of "emotion work" comes from Hochschild (1979). It refers to the active attempts on the part of individuals to shape their feelings according to the social rules about the appropriate emotions in a given situation.

70. The concept of a "cultural language" comes from Bellah et al. (1985), who have argued that Americans have primary and secondary cultural languages. The first cultural language of individualism is most readily available to middle-class Americans. The second cultural language, which promotes commitments to others, is less easily accessible. For an extension of this argument in a cross-cultural analysis of middle-class American and Hindu men, see Steve Derné 1994.

71. Swidler 2001, 19.

72. See Lamont 1992; 2000; Biernacki 1995; Dobbin 1994; Kremer 2007; Griswold 1987; and Spillman 1997.

73. Kremer 2007 and Steensland 2008.

74. Weber 1958.

75. Nor are national cultures without contradiction or contestation over the application of their components.

76. See Collins 2004; Bettie 2000; and Carpenter 2005.

77. Röling (2003) notes the irony that sex education became acceptable in the Nether-

lands right around the time that large populations of immigrants started arriving with a very different sexual culture and values.

78. My argument about the two individualisms builds on two strands of scholarship. The first is that of Robert Bellah and colleagues (1985), who have discerned several different traditions of individualism in the United States. Uniting them is a voluntaristic conception of the self as the origin of social action and ties (see also Varenne 1977; Swidler 2001). For my argument about interdependent individualism I draw on the work of Dutch sociologists, who in turn build on Norbert Elias' theory of the civilizing process (de Swaan 1981, 1988; Elias 1994; Goudsblom 1987, 2000; Wilterdink 1995; and Wouters 1986, 1987, 2004). Following Elias, Wouters and de Swaan have argued that an increase in the structural interdependencies between different social groups within society has led to a growing awareness of interdependence and mutual pressures toward greater self-restraint among citizens of advanced industrial societies. I depart from this perspective in several respects. First, while in keeping with Elias' "structural" perspective, Wouters and de Swaan attribute cultural processes to underlying structural changes and differences, I credit cultural traditions and meaning-making processes with a "semi-autonomous" role in shaping social institutions and selves. Second, and more specifically, I argue that while the vision of modern societies advanced by sociologists such as Wouters and de Swaan may accurately describe Dutch middle- and upper-middle-class institutions and culture in the post-1960s era, it does not capture the culture of American private and public institutions during that period (Schalet 2000; 2001; see also Stearns 1994).

79. This plays on the title of Jane Collier's *From Duty to Desire: Remaking Families in a Spanish Village* (1997).

80. See Garland 2001; Whitman 2003; Western and Petit 2002; Starr 1986; and Solinger 2005.

81. The term "politics of accommodation" comes from Lijphart 1975. See also Hemerijck and Visser 1999; Outshoorn 2000; and Schuyf and Krouwel 1999.

82. Freeman 1994 and Hemerijck and Visser 1999.

83. "Harsh Justice" comes from Whitman 2003; Bernstein 2007; and Buruma 2007.

84. The age of consent in the Netherlands is sixteen. During the 1990s, consensual sex with someone between the ages of twelve and sixteen was not prosecuted if neither party nor the parents or guardians filed a complaint. David Evans (1993) referred to this legal situation as one in which young people were granted "conditional rights of consent" which recognized that they could potentially exercise sexual self-determination but needed protection against potential abuse. A 2002 law removed this conditional right of consent but has left the prosecution of consensual sexual relations with someone between twelve and sixteen at the discretion of the courts. The "Children's Telephone," an organization which is part of the government-subsidized Bureau of Youth Care (*Bureau Jeugdzorg*) explains this legal gray zone as follows: "According to the law, it is forbidden to have sex with each other when you are under sixteen. Sometimes, it is not seen as wrong, namely, when the difference in age is not so great, when you both want it and/or you have a relationship on the condition that it happens without force, violence, or deceit and outside of a relationship of dependence (so it can't be your teacher or your coach). Under twelve, it is always punishable!! Even if you're both the same age and you both want it!!"

85. Bernat and Resnick 2009.

CHAPTER TWO

1. "Going to bed with" is the most common Dutch expression for having sexual intercourse.

2. An expression often cited to illustrate the cultural premium placed on acting "normally," that is, without excessive emotionality or drawing attention to oneself, is *"Do maar gewoon, dan doe je al gek genoeg"* which translates as, "Behave normally [because] then you are already crazy enough!"

3. Dutch sociologist Paul Schnabel has argued that the sexual revolution led Dutch society to a widely felt need to order and arrange "a new polder of civilization" (Schnabel 1990, 27). The metaphor is an apt one for the Dutch, as polders—land reclaimed from the sea or other bodies of water—make up a large part of the Netherlands. The cultural frame of normal sexuality—with its concomitant practices of open discussions and rational negotiation—expresses the assumption that the polder can successfully be ordered and constitutes a means by which to do so.

4. These are the findings of Lewis and Knijn's (2003; 2002) review of Dutch sex education curricula in the 1980s and 1990s. For a review of recent Dutch sex education curricula, including a content analysis of "Long Live Love," the widely used, government-funded sex education program, see Ferguson, Vanwesenbeeck, and Knijn 2008.

5. Lewis and Knijn 2003, 120.

6. Lewis and Knijn 2003, 121.

7. Lewis and Knijn 2002, 687.

8. As we saw in chapter 1, a remarkably quick shift in attitudes toward sexuality took place in the Netherlands between the mid-1960s and mid-1970s. The changing attitudes about parents and children taking showers together—and hence being nude in each other's presence—illustrate this rapid shift. In 1968, 28 percent of men and 21 percent of women said parents and children taking showers together was "always acceptable." In 1981, six out of ten of men and women agreed that such a practice was "always acceptable" (Kooij 1983).

9. In their interview study of lower- and upper-middle-class Dutch parents, the Dutch researchers Yolanda te Poel and Janita Ravesloot (1997) found similarly that parents of the 1990s looked back on their youth with misgivings about the sex education they received. The parents they interviewed remembered silences, warnings, and evasions, which though not terribly troubling to them as teenagers, were seen in retrospect to have left them ill-prepared for sex during their engagement and marriage: "The taboo on sexuality and physicality, and the negative evaluation of this as adults, strengthened their intentions to do it 'differently' with their own children" (58). Although mothers are the primary sexual educators at home, fathers too want the topic to be "the most normal matter in the world" (60).

10. See Berne and Huberman 1999. SOA/AIDS, a government-sponsored organization in charge of AIDS- and STD-prevention, publicized the new edition of this popular sex education curriculum with an online blurb that demonstrates the desired sequence—from making contact to making love: "Safe Sex is, in this new curriculum, 'Long Live Love,' the central theme. Attention is devoted to the existence of HIV, other STDs, and unwanted pregnancies. Other themes are going over your own boundaries and those of others. In addition to the transmission of knowledge about safe and unsafe sexual behavior, the curriculum stimulates a positive, responsible attitude toward sexuality. Of course, we deal with the fun, exciting, but also the vul-

nerable feelings that are part of making contact, being in love, getting a courtship, and making love."

11. Lewis and Knijn 2003, 123. The authors found that sex education curricula typically place teenage sexuality in the context of being in love, and emphasize the interplay between self-reliance and mutual respect. Speaking about sexual attitudes in Dutch society more generally, Paul Schnabel (1990) contends that in the post-sexual-revolution era, sexuality remained closely tied to relationships and love among broad sectors of the population.

12. In a qualitative study, published under the title "Problems? No Problem! Becoming Homo/Lesbo in a Tolerant Social Climate" (my trans.), Picavet and Sandfort (2005) report that the parents of their interviewees were very accepting of their homosexuality. De Graaf and colleagues (2005) found that the twenty-four Dutch homosexual youth with whom they spoke in focus groups had had different home environments, ranging from supportive and accepting parents, to families in which fathers and brothers (but not mothers or sisters) made negative comments about homosexuality.

13. Characterizing the shift in attitude among Dutch family physicians in the early 1970s, Evert Ketting writes: "The newly available (and first really effective) possibilities to prevent unwanted pregnancies must be utilized. . . . It makes little sense to try and stop young people from having sexual relations together, because they will do that anyway; but you can prevent the problems that follow from it" (Ketting 1990, 78).

14. The metaphor of the "web" which I use in this chapter is of course a reference to Clifford Geertz's famous definition of culture as the "webs of significance [man] himself has spun" (Geertz 1973, 5).

15. Other studies have also found that the sexual activity of their teenage children is not a matter of overt concern for Dutch parents (te Poel and Ravesloot 1997; Ravesloot 1997; Brinkgreve and van Stolk 1997). The Dutch political scientist Jan Willem Duyvendak has argued that, in response to the emergence of AIDS in the 1980s, the Dutch government, alone among its industrial peers, strove to counteract the possible stigmatization of gay and bisexual men (Duyvendak 1996). Thus, AIDS, although prompting new public health campaigns that emphasized "safe sex" and condom use, did not lead to a moral panic about sex itself, gay or straight.

16. In 1995, the American teenage birth rate was 54.4 per 1,000 girls, ages fifteen to nineteen. At 5.8, the Dutch teenage birth rate (per 1,000 girls, ages 15–19) was nine times lower. In addition, the Dutch teenage abortion rate was one of the lowest in the world (Singh and Darroch 2000; Garssen 2008). A cross-national study of sexually transmitted diseases (STDs) among teenagers in developed countries found that in the mid-1990s, U.S. rates dwarfed those of almost all other countries. Dutch rates were far below those reported for American teens—especially with regard to gonorrhea: 7.7 per 100,000 versus 571.8. However, since in the Netherlands fewer than 70 percent of diagnosed cases were estimated to be reported, the rates were not fully comparable (Panchaud et al. 2000). In recent years, the tracking and reporting of STDs has improved in the Netherlands. Rates of reported incidences of STDs remain considerably lower than in the United States. But studies of chlamydia *prevalence*— which measure the proportion of a given population that is infected—have found less stark differences between the two countries. Van Bergen et al. found that 2 percent of a Dutch study group, ages fifteen to twenty-nine, was infected with chlamydia, while Miller et al. found that 4.2 percent of their nationally representative

sample of American young adults, ages eighteen to twenty-six, were infected (Miller et al. 2004; van Bergen et al. 2005). In 2007, youth in the United States were more than three times as likely to be living with HIV—rates were estimated at .7 percent for young men, ages fifteen to twenty-four and .3 percent for young women, respectively, as compared to .2 percent and .1 percent for men and women in the Netherlands (UNAIDS 2008). As is true for teenage pregnancies, HIV and other STI's are disproportionately concentrated among low-income teens.

17. In a mixed-methods Ph.D. thesis, Maria Brugman (2007) found that American female college students were far more likely to have known someone who became pregnant in high school than their Dutch counterparts.

18. Like nudity among family members, acceptance of homosexuality became, in post-sexual revolution Dutch society, a way to demonstrate the normality with which one deals with sex. Historically speaking, the broad-based acceptance of homosexuality in the Netherlands today is a rather unexpected development, Bram van Stolk (1991) has argued, since as of 1960 homosexuals were still among the most derided individuals in Dutch society.

19. Reviewing his own writings about the sexual revolution and its aftermath, Dutch sociologist Paul Schnabel notes that what he calls "guilty sexuality," defined as "abuse of power and authority relationships," did not receive much attention until 1989. "Abundantly late," he concludes (Schnabel 1990, 49).

20. Despite great efforts on the part of the Dutch government to promote upward mobility through education, many children from working-class backgrounds—including the vast majority of ethnic minorities—still enter the lower-level tracks of secondary education (Driessen and Mulder 1999). Only a small percentage of the children who enter the HAVO or VWO, the two college-preparatory tracks of Dutch secondary schools, come from working-class families (Bakker, Bogt, and de Waal 1993, 98). But although young people's socioeconomic background does effect the kind of secondary school into which they are tracked, it has relatively little effect on their subsequent transition from secondary to tertiary education (De Graaf and Ganzenboom 1993).

21. Te Poel and Ravelsoot (1997) find that Dutch parents of the 1990s try hard to be "modern sexual educators," though they do not fully succeed in conquering their shame and embarrassment. Indeed, the management of sexuality in Dutch middle-class families can be viewed as a vehicle in the "civilizing" of parents, as much as of children, through the tempering of strong emotions and their subjection to reason (Elias 1994; 1998).

22. Lewis and Knijn (2002) cite a Dutch informant who makes the controlling aspects of permission quite clear: "We give freedom [for adolescent sexuality] because we can control it (679)."

23. In Dutch, *vertrouwen* means both "trust" and "faith."

24. That the Dutch parents feel less under assault by the commercial media than their American counterparts has a basis in reality. Throughout the 1980s, commercial broadcasting was illegal in the Netherlands. Government policy regulated both the distribution of airtime to different cultural and political interest groups and the distribution of program content (educational and cultural versus entertainment). It set and continues to set parameters around the programs that can be broadcast during hours when children typically watch television. But in the 1990s, commercial television became legal though restricted. In 2000, domestic commercial networks—which tend to favor entertainment programs over educational and cultural

ones—commanded almost half of the primetime market share (van der Haak and van Snippenburg 2001, 218). Moreover, as has been the case in the United States, the internet has greatly increased young people's exposure to unregulated media content, especially with regard to sexuality.

CHAPTER THREE

1. A recent study found that "cervical cancer screening continues to limit prescription of routine and emergency contraception by many U.S. obstetrician/gynecologists" (Schwarz et al. 2005), despite the fact that in 1993 the Food and Drug Administration voted to allow physicians to prescribe oral contraception without performing a pelvic examination. One year earlier, Planned Parenthood changed its medical standard to allow a three-month deferral between prescription and exam. This change was "based on a nationwide survey done in 1986 that revealed a 60% rate among teenagers who considered the exam a barrier to family planning service use" (Revised Oral Contraceptive Labeling: FDA Approves Recommendation Allowing Delay of Pelvic Exam 1993).

2. See Mosher et al. 2005 and de Graaf et al. 2005.

3. See, for instance, Luker 1975 and Nathanson 1991.

4. The absence of a language of love to refer to adolescent sexuality in American public education and health campaigns is particularly notable when compared to several European countries. As noted in previous chapters, a publicly financed and widely used Dutch sex education program is entitled "Long Live Love." In France and Germany, themes of adolescent love have also been integrated into prevention campaigns (Berne and Huberman 1999). However, in an exploratory comparison between the United States and Denmark, Rose (2005) suggests that Danish girls are less inclined to use the word love in relation to their sexual relations than American girls.

5. The vision of sexuality as an arena in which adolescents can easily lose control of themselves is common in American social scientific writing as well (Griffin 1993).

6. See also Michaud (2006) for the dominance of the risk paradigm in public health research and Fine (1988), Fine and McClelland (2006), and Fields (2008) for its prevalence in American sex education.

7. Kirsten Rickets and her husband seem to have a similarly gendered dynamic. When their fifteen-year-old son went to a sleepover party together with some female friends, Kirsten's husband Gary was hoping that he had sex. "You think he'll get some tonight?" he asked Kirsten. Her husband "loved his teenage sex years and so he wants my son to have the same thing." Kirsten Ricketts' response to her husband's musing was, "it's like, 'GARY!!!'"

8. Brad Fagan believes kids are ready once they are eighteen: "Out of our house, out of sight, do what you want." However, were his daughters to come home and say, "By the way, we're sleeping together anyway and we'd like to share the same bed here," he would consider it. His wife is skeptical, but Brad insists: "If they wanted to fight their way through it, and if they're adult enough to talk about it, then I'm adult enough to respect that." One could interpret Brad's criterion for adult recognition as an application of what Robert Bellah and colleagues (1985) call "expressive individualism": individual personhood is determined by the capacity to express oneself.

9. In a book first published in 1968, anthropologist David Schneider (1980) argued that in the symbolic logic that defined family and kinship roles in America, sexual

intercourse was something that should only happen between parents. More than four decades later, there is still considerable symbolic power in this definition of kinship roles.

10. Bellah et al. 1985. See also Derné 1994.

11. In articulating romantic and realistic conceptions of love and commitment, the American parents illustrate the two languages of love that Ann Swidler has argued middle-class Americans draw on: the "heroic" language of love, which corresponds to the experience of the institution of marriage which requires a life-altering choice, and the "prosaic" language of love that "helps people be the kinds of persons, with the kinds of feelings, skills, and virtues, that will sustain an ongoing relationship" as marriage has become a less stable institution (Swidler 2001, 131).

12. This is a common theme. Many American parents do not want their children to repeat or to know about their "wilder" days—whether those concern sex, drugs, or alcohol. For similar accounts of regret regarding one's experiences during the 1960s, see Tipton 1982.

13. By contrast, Henry Martin, who grew up in a working-class environment, describes having had fewer resources.

14. See for instance, D'Emilio and Freedman 1988.

15. Duyvendak 1996.

16. In his study of American culture, the French sociologist Hervé Varenne (1977) found that adolescent love too is conceived as a drama in American families.

17. During the 1950s, many young Americans established their own families in their teens and very early twenties. In 1951, the average age of marriage was 22.6 for men and 20.4 for women (Bailey 1988, 43), although as Frank Furstenberg (2007, 9) has pointed out, early marriage did not necessarily equate postponing sex until after marriage, as throughout the 1950s a large proportion of teenagers who married were pregnant.

CHAPTER FOUR

1. Garssen 2008; Kost et al. 2010; and van Lee et al. 2009. These differences are based on a comparison of 2006 rates. See also chap. 1, n. 16. The differences between the two countries were even greater during the 1990s when American teenage pregnancy rates were higher.

2. The available data suggests that sexual intercourse outside of monogamous romantic relationships is more common among American teenagers than it is among Dutch teenagers, but it is not possible to draw firm conclusions since the surveys ask different questions. De Graaf and colleagues (2005) found that 80 percent of sexually active Dutch girls and women and 68 percent of sexually active Dutch boys and men, ages twelve through twenty-five, had their last intercourse in a steady, monogamous, romantic relationship. (Native-born Dutch boys and men were significantly more likely than first- or second-generation immigrants to have had their last sex in a monogamous romantic relationship.) There were also differences by age: two-thirds of fifteen- to seventeen-year-olds, versus three-quarters of eighteen to twenty-year-olds, had their last intercourse in a steady monogamous relationship. Most American teenagers have their first sexual intercourse in the context of a dating relationship. However, a recent study found that once sexually experienced, half of girls and two-thirds of American boys have intercourse outside a dating relationship, usually with a friend or acquaintance. More than half of those in non-dating sexual relationships, and four out of ten of those in dating sexual relationships, say

one or both partners is "seeing someone else" (although not necessarily having sex with them) (Manning, Giordano, and Longmore 2006).

3. For descriptions of gender roles and authority relations in American middle-class families of the 1950s, see, for instance, Coontz 1992. For descriptions of gender roles and authority relations in Dutch families of that time, see van der Kamp and Krijnen 1987 and du Bois-Reymond 1990.

4. Brinkgreve and Korzec 1978; du Bois-Reymond 1993b; du Bois-Reymond, Peters, and Ravesloot 1990; Alwin 1989; and Lareau 2003.

5. Bellah et al. 1985, 142.

6. See also Wright 1977 and Hewitt 1989.

7. Bellah et al. 1985, 144.

8. Bellah et al. 1985, 146. See also Swidler 2001.

9. Swidler 2001, 157.

10. Cherlin 2009.

11. An indicator of the social security net is the "unemployment benefit replacement rate." In 2000, this OECD-calculated summary measure of benefits was at least 25 in most of continental Europe. In the Netherlands, this summary benefit measure ranged from 48 to 57 between 1965 and 2000. In the United States, by contrast, it ranged from 9 to 14 during that same period (OECD 2009). Even those government programs that have lifted segments of the population out of poverty in the United States—such as Social Security—are commonly conceptualized in terms of individual earners and savings even though, in fact, they involve intergenerational redistribution (Fischer et al. 1996).

12. Whitman 2003.

13. The culture of control that has permeated American legal and extralegal institutions disproportionately affects poor and minority youth but also affects the white middle class (Garland 2001). One Corona boy, interviewed in 1998, for instance, complained that police surveillance was becoming increasingly strict.

14. Stephenson 1989, 232. Stephenson also notes the high value in Dutch culture placed on *gezelligheid* and on spending time together, even if that means spending time together in very close quarters, a value which he contrasts with that placed on getting away from others in North American cultures.

15. Stephenson 1989, 244.

16. Schama 1988. Others have also argued that the geography of the Netherlands has shaped Dutch culture. Robert Kaplan (2010) has argued that as colonialists in Indonesia, the Dutch "were the most utilitarian of imperialists," as a consequence of their struggles with water in their own home land, much of which lies below sea level: "You could 'manage' water but could not 'force' it. Thus, there developed the supreme need for tolerance within their own community, out of which such coordination and cooperation could emerge. It was a culture of 'consensus'" (264).

17. Kickert 2003. Lijphart (1975) coined the term "politics of accommodation." Until the 1960s, Dutch society was organized according to "pillars" (one Catholic, two Protestant, one Liberal, and one Socialist), resulting in a "segmented" pluralism that kept members of the pillars largely separated from one another. The pillars, perhaps best envisioned as silos, had elaborate political infrastructures which included not only political parties but also unions, newspapers, sports clubs, and other institutions of public life. Membership in a pillar was determined by religious affiliation or politics. Because none of the pillars could attain a majority status, elite members of the pillars had to form coalitions and broker agreements with one another in

order to govern, although lower down the social ranks of each pillar the population was expected to be quite passive (see also Ellemers 1984). During the heyday of pillarization, between 1920 and the 1960s, movement between the pillars was minimal. However, with the secularization and social mobility of the 1960s and 1970s, the pillars lost much of their grip on Dutch society. Today, the shell of the older pillar structure can still be found in politics, the names of clubs and newspapers, and in the organizations of schools.

18. New interest groups included, for instance, gays and lesbians (Schuyf and Krouwel 1999; Duyvendak 1996) and recent immigrants (Soysal 1994). In her 1980s study of immigration policies in Europe, Soysal found "consultative arrangements" with immigrant groups to be taken for granted at all levels of Dutch policymaking.

19. The emphasis in Dutch social theory of 1970s and '80s on interdependence and the strengthening, rather than loosening, of commitments was preceded by such an emphasis in Dutch political rhetoric of the 1960s. The Dutch, writes historian James C. Kennedy (1995), became convinced that "solidarity, unity, and integration were *necessary* developments" (my translation and emphasis). The Dutch queen illustrated this conviction when she stated in her speech of 1963 that "in this time of dynamic developments the awareness of mutual dependence grows and the desire for cooperation increases as well." The belief in interdependence did not just extend to intranational social relations but also to international ones. In donating aid to non-Western nations, the Dutch were among the most generous (Kennedy 1995).

20. This scholarship accepted as a given premises of Norbert Elias' civilizing process thesis. Abram de Swaan (1981) coined the term "management by negotiation" to describe the new ways in which behavior became regulated in intimate and public relationships, a form of behavior control that created greater latitude but also required greater mutual consideration and self-control. Cas Wouters (1986; 1987) argued similarly that as people became more interdependent, it meant that their behavior could become more informal and diversified, but also that they experienced greater pressures to control themselves and identify with the needs of others. Dutch family sociologists echoed the same sentiments. In 1990, Dutch family scholars stated authoritatively that "the modern household" was based on "individualization and negotiation" (du Bois-Reymond, Peters, and Ravesloot 1990): modern parents must develop critical capacities such as the ability to rein in their aggressive tendencies and refrain from physical punishment, and to communicate effectively and reach solutions agreeable to all parties. The shifting balance of power makes the relationships between the sexes and generations more equal and also more emotionally intimate. Surveying family research of the preceding twenty-five years, a report by a national Dutch research and policy institute observed in 1997 that the emotional bonds between parents and children had "strongly increased," and it asked, only partly tongue in cheek, whether the Netherlands might be able to stake a claim to the Nobel prize for childrearing (Praag and Niphuis-Nell 1997).

21. On the unusual equalization in the Netherlands in the 1960s, 1970s, and 1980s, see De Graaf and Ganzenboom 1993 and Szirmai 1988. For the history of the Dutch welfare state, see Engbersen et al. 1993. Writing in the early 1990s, the latter authors state that in relation to the American one, the Dutch policy style is "informal, flexible, cooperative, and consensual rather than adversarial, relying more on persuasion than on coercion, and willing to take account of specific circumstances of individual clients" (20).

22. Tonry and Bijlenveld 2007.

23. Although it goes beyond the scope of this study, I suspect that other cultural and philosophical traditions also played an important role in facilitating this transition, including religious traditions that emphasize self-discipline, notably Calvinism (see also Gorski 2003). Historian James C. Kennedy (1995) suggests that Dutch interpretations and experiences of the 1960s were shaped by German idealism and romanticism. From that tradition, they took the notion that society is like an organism that grows according to its own rhythm, a notion, Kennedy points out, that is reflected in the Dutch expression "society develops itself." Echoes of that same sentiment can of course be heard in Dutch parents' discussions of *er aan toe zijn*.

24. James C. Kennedy (1995) argues that by taking a flexible, accommodating approach, authorities largely maintained order in the Netherlands. Garland (2001, 202) also argues that the Netherlands, along with several other countries, does not fit his account of the emergence of a culture of control in the post-1960s era.

25. Drug use was more common among American youth who were high-school aged in the early 1970s than among Dutch youth of that time. In 1975, more than 40 percent of American twelfth graders had ever used cannabis (marijuana or hashish) versus (an estimation of) less than 20 percent of Dutch eighteen-year-olds (MacCoun and Reuter 1997). International comparative data for more serious drugs is not available for that time period. However, a recent international survey by the World Health Organization found much higher lifetime use of both cannabis (42 percent) and cocaine (16 percent) in the United States than in almost any other country. Dutch lifetime use was 20 percent for cannabis and 2 percent for cocaine (Degenhardt et al. 2008). Comparing cannabis users in San Francisco and Amsterdam, Reinarman and colleagues (2004) found that the former were more likely than the latter to also use "hard drugs."

26. The expression is a play on Barbara Ehrenreich's *The Hearts of Men: American Dreams and the Flight from Commitment* (1983). While Ehrenreich argues that American men's flight from commitment to the family started before the sexual revolution, Kristin Luker (1975) and others have contended that the sexual revolution loosened the gender bargain between men and women that had previously provided women both emotional and economic security.

27. Knijn 1994a; 1994b; and Kremer 2007.

28. As wages fell behind the cost of living in the late 1970s, Claude Fischer (2010, 54) argues, one way middle-class families could maintain their lifestyles was by having mothers work a greater number of hours. In her 1990s study, Hochschild (1997) found that while middle-class mothers generally embraced their working hours, working-class mothers preferred to work less but could not afford to do so.

29. Drawing explicit comparisons with the United States, James C. Kennedy (1995) argues that Dutch public administrators responded sympathetically, rather than hostilely, to the youth protests of the 1960s. Choosing an accommodating, nonviolent exercise of authority in order to channel new developments in a socially acceptable direction, public administrators of the 1960s prefigured a philosophy that would inform the Dutch policy in the following decades. Historian Beth Bailey (1999) comments by contrast on the aggressive—both verbal and physical—reactions to student protests and rebellion in the United States.

30. Interestingly, Dutch youth and American white youth move out from their parents' home at roughly the same age. Among twenty to twenty-four-year-olds, a little over

a third of young women in both countries live in their parental home. In that age group, 65 percent of Dutch young men and 52 percent of white American young men still live at home (Iacovou 2002).

31. In Tremont, a high-school student who is caught at a party at which alcohol is served is, by high-school statute, automatically suspended from playing sports. Such suspensions carry not only social repercussions in a town where playing and watching high-school sports constitutes a treasured pastime, but they can also carry economic repercussions for those who would otherwise be eligible for college athletic scholarships.

32. Until the mid-1990s, these student stipends were unconditional for those participating in higher education. Since then, "basic stipends," which can be supplemented by needs-based stipends, have become conditional on successful completion of a degree within ten years. Otherwise they are converted into loans.

33. Despite their greater dependence on parents, American young adults cannot make a legal claim to ongoing parental financial support, as can Dutch young adults whose parents are required to continue to support their adult children up to age twenty-one, if they can afford to do so.

34. A few American parents, who were typically raised Catholic, are more open to the idea that a sixteen-year-old could be ready to drink. Kirsten Rickets, for instance, says, "I was raised Irish. Everybody drinks from the time you're little. You don't drink copious amounts; you just have a drink with dinner."

35. Several parents comment on ways in which legal constraints and culture shape their responses to the question of whether or not a sixteen-year-old is ready to drink alcohol. Bonnie Oderberg, for instance, says that most are not ready to drink: "As our laws stand now, no. In this culture, as this culture is now, no."

36. The standard Dutch beer glasses are about half the size of the pint-sized mugs that have become popular in American bars and restaurants.

37. Several American parents acknowledge that a person who is unemployed or a homemaker might not be financially self-sufficient for a period, but they tend to view these situations as exceptional.

38. In *Habits of the Heart: Individualism and Commitment in American Life*, Robert Bellah and colleagues argue that "breaking away" from the parental home is critical to American understandings of individualism and independence, and that parents actively encourage children to indeed "break away." They write: "While it sometimes appears to be a pitched battle only the heroic or rebellious wage against the parental order, more often the drive to get out in the world on your own is part of the self-conception Americans teach their children." The adults the authors interviewed "describe their coming of age in terms of breaking away from dependency on parents and relying on themselves, though in many cases, they continue to have close relations with their parents" (Bellah et al. 1985, 57). The sociologist Derek Phillips (1985) was also struck by how Americans viewed their children's leaving home as a radical break.

39. For a similar finding among parents of Dutch college students in the 1980s, see de Regt 1988.

40. Dutch university students who do not live with their parents typically inhabit "rooms": they eat, sleep, study, and entertain in a room that is part of a house or apartment which they share with other students. Such living arrangements lack the supervision or structures for eating and socializing that typically characterize dormitory life at American colleges.

41. Indeed, when I told a Dutch psychologist that American parents expect their children to be different, she looked astonished. No, she said, Dutch parents really don't want their children to be different; they want them to be normal.

42. French anthropologist Hervé Varenne (1977) notes that American children are taught by educators, and especially by their parents, to differentiate themselves.

CHAPTER FIVE

1. The expression "into the wild" comes from Jon Krakauer's nonfiction book by the same title about a college graduate who undertakes an extended and ultimately fatal trek into the wilderness.

2. There is an extensive qualitative literature documenting and theorizing the ways in which institutions such as schools, the media, and the medical establishment have denied sexual subjectivity to girls in the United States. See for instance Fine 1988; Fine and McClelland 2006; Nathanson 1991; and Tolman 2002.

3. Psychological research has found that American teenagers typically deal with conflicts with their parents by disengaging or giving in (Smetana, Campione-Barre, and Metzger 2006).

4. The positive effects of Jesse's relationship on his well-being may be part of a larger pattern. There is evidence that adolescent love relationships reduce the likelihood that those with criminal records offend again (McCarthy and Casey 2008).

5. International studies have shown that American teenagers are among the least likely to feel they can talk to either parent about something that is really bothering them (Currie et al. 2008 and Currie et al. 2004).

6. I am indebted to Greggor Mattson for suggesting this metaphor.

7. In an international comparative analysis based on data from the mid-1990s, Singh and colleagues (2001) found that even young American women (ages twenty to twenty-four) with medium and high levels of education were more likely than their similarly educated peers in other developed countries to have given birth before age twenty. And middle- and upper-income American teenage women (ages fifteen to nineteen) were less likely than their counterparts in Great Britain to not have used contraception at last sex. Since the mid-1990s, the contraceptive use of American teenagers has improved considerably, an improvement which accounts for a large proportion of the decrease in teen pregnancies (Santelli et al. 2007). However, even with contraceptive use greatly improved, in 2006–8, American women, ages fifteen to twenty-four, whose mother had attained some college or more (an indicator of middle-class status) still had a one in ten chance of giving birth by age twenty (Abma, Martinez, and Copen 2010).

8. See Garland 2001.

CHAPTER SIX

1. As we saw in the introduction, Ravesloot (1997) also did not find strong differences by gender. Girls and boys were equally likely to feel controlled by their parents. Also, a national survey by the Central Bureau voor de Statistiek (2003) found girls and boys as likely to be permitted a sleepover with a steady girl- or boyfriend.

2. International comparative research that shows that Dutch teenagers are among those most likely to feel comfortable discussing something that troubles them with their fathers and mothers, indicating that most Dutch teenagers do indeed feel relatively well connected with their parents (Currie et al. 2008; Currie et al. 2004).

3. This logic of argumentation mirrors the one that historian James C. Kennedy found among Dutch elites in the 1960s. He argues that one reason Dutch politicians, unlike their American counterparts, acquiesced and actively contributed to the changing of the guard is that they interpreted these changes as part of an inevitable process of modernization. Asserting that "one cannot, no one should not, go against the times," the Dutch elites of the 1960s took on a flexible, consensus-oriented, and "anticipating" approach to change (Kennedy 1995; 1997).

4. Research by Joep de Hart (1992) also finds that Dutch boys experience fewer conflicts with their parents over sexuality than do Dutch girls. And Ravesloot (1997) finds that although girls and boys are equally likely to feel controlled by their parents with regard to sexuality, the former experience greater pressure from parents than the latter to only have sex in the context of relationships.

5. The proportion of Dutch girls interviewed who have talked with their parents about contraception is in keeping with other research. A national survey found that 71 percent of Dutch girls have talked to their parents about pregnancy and contraception before age sixteen (de Graaf et al. 2005).

6. This is a play on the title of Jane Collier's *From Duty to Desire* (1997).

7. This difference between the countries is corroborated by large-scale survey research: 91 percent of Dutch fifteen-year-old boys, versus 68 percent of American boys, find it easy or very easy to talk to their mothers about things that really bother them; 83 percent of Dutch boys, versus 60 percent of American boys, say they find it easy to talk to their fathers (Currie et al. 2008).

8. While many of the Dutch teenagers I interviewed emphasize their lack of conflict with their own parents, they often note that many other teenagers have conflicted relationships with theirs. This suggests that, like their parents, Dutch teenagers are eager to see themselves as having a harmonious parent-teenager relationship, and even that it may serve as a source of pride and distinction, much as not being "old fashioned" does for their parents.

9. Of these three teenagers, two live in lower-middle-class families. Research in both countries shows that working- and lower-middle class parents are more likely to embrace more hierarchical relationships with their children (du Bois-Reymond 1992; Rispens, Hermanns, and Meeus 1996; and Lareau 2003).

10. Godeau et al. 2008, and Ferguson, Vanwesenbeeck and Knijn 2008.

11. Hard drug use is rare among Dutch youth. The 2001/2002 Health Behavior in School-Aged Children Survey found that about a quarter of Dutch fifteen-year-olds versus a little over a third of American fifteen-year-olds had ever used cannabis. The percentages of fifteen-year-olds who have been drunk more than twice are similar in the two countries: one in five girls and about one in three boys (35.3 percent of Dutch boys and 30.4 percent of American boys). But American boys have their first drunken episode substantially earlier than Dutch boys: right before turning thirteen versus right before turning fourteen. For girls, first drunkenness occurs, on average, right after turning fourteen in the Netherlands and right before turning fourteen in the United States (Currie et al. 2004).

CHAPTER SEVEN

1. Classic works on the pleasure/danger nexus in women and girls' experiences of sexuality include Fine 1988 and Vance 1984. For a review of how such themes have been taken up in more recent scholarship, see Schalet 2009.

2. For discussion of how girls and young women navigate the potential threat of being

called a slut, see for instance Armstrong, Hamilton, and Sweeney 2006; England, Shafer, and Fogarty 2007; Martin 1996; and Tolman 2002.

Interview and ethnographic studies have suggested that boys are subject to pressures to gain early sexual experience and to avoid or disown emotional attachments to their sexual partners; see Carpenter 2005; Martin 1996; and Pascoe 2007. However, several studies have found that boys are more emotionally invested in relationships than assumed; see Giordano, Longmore, and Manning 2006 and Tolman et al. 2004. Indeed, Dutch boys in their mid-teens have typically been in love and in a relationship. In a recent national survey of Dutch youth, 92 percent of boys ages fifteen to seventeen said they had been in love. Seventy-eight percent had experience with being in a "courtship" *(verkering)* (de Graaf et al. 2005).

3. One source of convergence may be their shared exposure to American popular culture, which has become increasingly prevalent in Dutch media since the introduction of commercial television in the 1990s.

4. On the history of how the medical discourse of sexual risk became appropriated by the abstinence-only movement, see Irvine 2002.

5. About half of the teenagers surveyed by Kaiser said they needed more basic information on birth control. A similar percentage did not know that minors can get the pill without parental permission or that emergency contraception is an option. Three-quarters of the surveyed teens said they talked with their parents about sex, but less than half had talked about contraception. Of those who are already sexually active, about one-third still need to learn more about how to use birth control and where to get it (Henry J. Kaiser Family Foundation 1996). The 2002 NSFG found that by age eighteen half of American girls have talked to their parents about contraception (Abma et al. 2004). A recent study (Beckett et al. 2010) found that many American parents do not address the topic of contraceptives until after their children are sexually involved. More than 40 percent of the teenagers in this study had had intercourse before having had any discussions with their parents about condoms or birth control.

6. For accounts of the history and impact of the abstinence-only sex education movement, see di Mauro and Joffe 2007; Fields 2008; Irvine 2002; and Lindberg et al. 2006.

7. Crisis pregnancy centers, which have received federal funding, do not provide counseling about abortion (Kantor et al. 2008; di Mauro and Joffe 2007).

8. Kelly illustrates how the risk discourse permeates thinking and talking about adolescent sexuality (see also Fine 1988 and Fields 2008).

9. Kost et al. 2010.

10. See di Mauro and Joffe 2007 and Joffe 2003.

11. For a discussion of the language of the fetus as child and of abortion as killing a baby in American abortion rhetoric, see Myrsiades 2002.

12. Tolman (2002) and Martin (1996) found a similar duality: on the one hand, a relationship seems a protective factor against being labeled a slut. On the other hand, girls still rightly fear being called sluts. That sex even within a relationship remains unacceptable to many American teenagers is suggested also by the 2002 National Survey of Family Growth, which found that a majority of American youth do not approve of sixteen-year-olds who have a strong affection for each other having intercourse (Abma et al. 2004).

13. See also Tanenbaum 2000.

14. See England et al. 2007.
15. Sharon Thompson (1995) and more recently Laura Carpenter (2005) have argued that girls who have sex with a strong emotional investment are especially likely to be emotionally distraught after a break-up (see also Meier 2007).
16. See also Ann Swidler (2001) on marriage as the cultural reference point for love in American culture.
17. Others have noted that girls are more likely to report gratifying sexual experiences, and less likely to report negative emotions, when sex happens in committed romantic relationships (Meier 2007; Carpenter 2005).
18. On the role of same-sex peer groups on boys' experience of relationships, see Giordano et al. 2006. On the role of sports culture in particular, see Foley 1994. For the historical evolution of same-sex peer culture and its effect on definitions of masculinity, see Kimmel 1996 and Carpenter 2005.
19. A recent representative survey found that a quarter of American girls who are in dating relationships in which they are having sexual intercourse are also "seeing someone else." Among sexually active boys in dating relationships, almost half are seeing someone else (Manning, Giordano, and Longmore 2006).
20. Several other studies have also found boys more emotionally invested in relationships than assumed. See Giordano, Longmore, and Manning 2006; and Tolman et al. 2004.
21. These views of love correspond to what Ann Swidler (2001) has called the "heroic" love myth.
22. See, for instance, Finer 2007 and Cohen 2004.
23. De Graaf et al. 2005; Hardon 2003; Ketting 1983; 1990; and Ketting and Visser 1994.
24. De Graaf et al. 2005 and Lewis and Knijn 2003.
25. Their effective use of contraceptives led a well-known population researcher to call the Dutch the "perfect contraceptive population" (Ketting and Visser 1994).
26. About a third of all teenage pregnancies in the United States result in abortion, versus two-thirds in the Netherlands (Garssen 2008; Kost et al. 2010).
27. De Waal (1989) found also that once a girl was in a steady relationship, she was protected against being called a slut.
28. Survey data show that four out of five Dutch youth believe that sexual intercourse is legitimate if a girl and a boy feel a lot for each other (de Graaf et al. 2005, 30).
29. This might explain why even though the vast majority of Dutch girls and young women, surveyed in a national study, say that they are (very) satisfied by the sexual pleasure and contact they feel with their partner, a majority also said that they experience pain during sex, at least sometimes, and a quarter often have trouble reaching orgasm.
30. One out of four American girls who first have sex at age sixteen do not use contraception (Manlove et al. 2009).
31. In a national poll, conducted by The Campaign to End Teen Pregnancy (see Albert 2004), a majority of sexually active American girls and boys said they wished they had waited longer to have sex. The National Survey of Family Growth found that among young women who had their first intercourse between fifteen and seventeen, in retrospect only a third said they "really wanted it." One in ten women said they did not really want it. The majority had mixed feelings. See Abma et al. 2004.
32. Two out of three pregnant American women, ages fifteen to nineteen, carry their pregnancy to term (Kost et al. 2010).

33. Hanneke de Graaf and colleagues (2005) found that 86 percent of Dutch girls say about their first intercourse: "We both were equally eager to have it."

34. De Graaf and colleagues (2005) found that among twelve to twenty-four-year-olds surveyed in 2005, 64 percent of girls and women were on the pill or another form of hormonal contraception at first sex. Forty-one percent of males and 46 percent of females report having used condoms and the pill (or having gone "double Dutch") at first vaginal intercourse.

35. This is a play on words, referring back to Michelle Fine's concept of the "missing discourse of female desire" (Fine 1988; Fine and McClelland 2006).

36. Several scholars found more gender-stereotypical attitudes about sex among Americans surveyed than among Dutch surveyed (VanYperen and Buunk 1991; Hofstede 1998; and Brugman 2007). Rose (2005) also argues that American youth hold more gender-stereotypical ideas about teenagers than Danish youth, especially about boys.

CHAPTER EIGHT

1. In the introduction to *The Use of Pleasure*, Foucault distinguishes sexual ethics from sexual codes. While the latter tell one what is forbidden and prescribed, the former tell one why, how, and to what end individuals are "urged to constitute themselves as subjects of moral conduct" (1985, 28).

2. In making use of these four questions to deepen my analysis, I largely use my own words rather than Foucault's. For instance, rather than use the term "ethical substance" to refer to the aspect of sexuality that is of concern, as Foucault does, I refer to that which is considered problematic about adolescent sexuality.

3. Foucault 1985, 26.

4. Not just hormones are blamed for sexual acts and their unintended consequences. In the mid-1990s, more than half of the teenagers surveyed by the Kaiser Family Foundation said that unplanned pregnancies happen because teens have sex when they are drunk or on drugs (Henry J. Kaiser Family Foundation 1996).

5. In fact, 64 percent of Dutch girls and young women, ages twelve through twenty four, said they were using the pill at the time of their first intercourse (de Graaf et al. 2005, 74).

6. In segments of the first volume of *The History of Sexuality*, where Foucault discusses how the upper middle class uses sexuality—its "repression" and liberation of "repression" as a mode of distinction vis-à-vis other classes—he places greater emphasis on the ways individuals can exercise agency with regard to sexuality.

7. Foucault 1978, 86.

8. De Hart (1992) also found a lack of overt conflict and power between parents and older teenagers.

9. Singh et al. 2001. It is not just American high schoolers who often fail to use contraceptives effectively. American adults have also been poor contraceptive users (Glei 1999). Indeed, almost half of all pregnancies in the United States are unplanned (Finer and Henshaw 2006). A recent report found that magical thinking, misperceptions, and ambivalences contribute to poor contraceptive use among young adults (Kaye et al. 2009).

10. For a discussion of teenage sex outside of monogamous romantic relationships in the two countries, see chapter 4, n. 2. By age eighteen, the majority of Dutch and American youth have experienced vaginal intercourse. But sexually experienced American teenaged men and women are more likely to have had multiple

partners: among American women, ages eighteen and nineteen, who have experienced vaginal intercourse, 37 percent have done so with four or more men. Among Dutch women, ages eighteen to *twenty*, who have experience with vaginal and/or anal intercourse, 26 percent have had four or more partners. Likewise, 42 percent of American eighteen- and nineteen-year-old men, who have had heterosexual intercourse, have had four or more female partners, while 34 percent of Dutch men, eighteen to *twenty*, who have had vaginal and/or anal intercourse, have had four or more partners (of either sex). Among eighteen- to twenty-year-olds, two-thirds of Dutch women and half of Dutch men are in steady relationships, lasting on average over a year (Mosher, Chandra, and Jones 2005; de Graaf et al. 2005; Abma, Martinez, and Copen 2010).

11. Dutch sociologist Abram de Swaan (1981) coined the term "management by negotiation" to describe the form of behavior regulation in which previously unequal parties negotiate their needs and come to mutual agreements based on relatively equal terms with the exercise of mutual self-restraint and consideration.

12. Indeed, the desire for and the fulfillment of human connection—between parents and children, between lovers, between citizens—does not seem to factor into Foucault's analysis of sexuality and subjectivity.

13. It is notable that while Foucault gives attention to issues of what we might call "meaning" and "agency" in his work on sexual ethics, these are not foci of his earlier work on discourses of sexuality and power.

14. In their study of sexuality and relationships in a mixed-class public university, Laura Hamilton and Elizabeth Armstrong (2009) find that middle- and upper-middle-class students see hook-ups as more consistent with their class-based notions of independence than are "traditional" romantic relationships.

15. Lijphart 1975.

16. See Bosch 2009; Green-Pedersen, van Kersenbergen, and Hemerijck 2001; Hemerijck and Visser 1999; and Freeman 1998. One significant feature of the Dutch collective labor agreements is that they tend to be "inclusive": they cover workers within a given sector, regardless of whether they are members of the unions who negotiate the agreement (Bosch 2009).

17. For a discussion of the consultative approach to immigration, see Soysal 1994.

18. Rogers and Streeck 1994.

19. Hemerijck and Visser (1999) argue, for instance, that the "voluntary pay restraint" on the part of representatives of labor throughout the 1980s was a critical component in creating the so-called "Dutch Miracle," the remarkable rebound and growth of the Dutch economy in the late 1980s and 1990s.

20. Just as in the family, consultation in politics has costs and benefits. For an argument about how the consultation and compromise approach of the Dutch government depoliticized gay activism, see Duyvendak 1996. For a critique of the effects of accommodation politics on the gay movement in the Netherlands, see Hekma 2004a and b. For an argument about how the compromise character of the Dutch welfare state appeased feminists' concerns *and* kept women with children effectively relegated to the domestic sphere throughout the 1970s and 1980s, see Knijn 1994. More recently Kremer has argued that the "sharing" policy ideal—in which men and women both combine part-time work and childcare—pursued by Dutch policymakers has, in practice, resulted in women doing most of the sharing: Dutch men, especially upper-middle-class men, work fewer hours than their peers elsewhere, but Dutch women still do most of the part-time work *and* childcare work. While

this arrangement appears in keeping with women's stated preferences, Kremer argues that it puts them at a financial disadvantage (Kremer 2007).

21. See Esping-Anderson 1990; Goodin et al. 2000; Knijn 1994a; and Kremer 2007.

22. See Engbersen et al. 1993; De Graaf and Ganzenboom 1993; Goodin et al. 2000; and Kremer 2007. The National Assistance Act of 1965 made receipt of benefits to cover basic life needs (housing, food, clothing) a right rather than a privilege. Throughout the 1990s and 2000s, this law was repeatedly revised to curtail benefits and tie them more closely to work (or for youth, to education). Renamed "Law Work and Assistance" (*Wet Werk en Bijstand*) in 2004, this law still "guarantees a minimum income for people who are not able, without the help of others, to provide for their livelihood. . . . The Dutch system of assistance is based on the principles that citizens should be able to provide for their own livelihood without the help of others. Those who cannot do so receive income supports and help in finding work as long as that is necessary" (Blommesteijn and Mallee 2009, 4). When combined with supplemental benefits, receiving assistance benefits theoretically prevents people from being categorized as poor. But in 2009, between one fifth and one third of people who lived on some type of social benefits were categorized as poor, in part, it has been speculated, because they do not know about and fully utilize the available supplemental benefits (Blommesteijn and Mallee 2009).

23. Engbersen et al. 1993; OECD 2009.

24. Although the Netherlands has moved towards a more punitive legal climate, including increased sentences, legal scholar Peter Tak (2003, 13) writes: "The relative mildness of the Dutch criminal justice system is built into the system itself as a core element of Dutch criminal policy."

25. Since 1976, the Dutch government has followed a policy of "decriminalizing" the use and sale of cannabis products such as marijuana and hashish (Buruma 2007). While the Netherlands has long been known for its famous red-light districts, running a brothel—and profiting from others' prostitution—was not legalized until 2000. Interestingly, one of the clearest examples of the principles of *gezelligheid* informing policies around prostitution comes from the time when prostitution was legal but brothels were not. In her international comparative study of prostitution, Bernstein describes how the drop-in center of a zone for street prostitution, designed by the Dutch government in 1997, is called a *huiskamer* (living room); this "seems to bespeak the government's attempt to normalize and domesticate commercial sexual exchange: open from 9:00 p.m. to 5:00 a.m., the *huiskamer* provides all variety of medical and social services to street workers, including free coffee and tea, affordably priced condoms and sandwiches" (Bernstein 2007, 156–57).

26. This combination of discipline and social support on the part of authorities has a historical antecedent in Dutch society. In his analysis of the "disciplinary revolution" in the early modern Netherlands, Philip Gorski describes how local Calvinist consistories imposed social and moral order: "In their campaigns to achieve congregational purity, the elders often went beyond their formal roles as moral policemen. In their efforts to enforce sexual morality, for example, they sometimes found themselves attempting to reunite married couples, reform abusive husbands, or locate missing fathers. Similarly, in their attempts to maintain social order, they might seek to counsel and rehabilitate alcoholics, reconcile estranged friends and relatives, mediate disputes between employers and workers. . . . They served a preventative as well as punitive function and often behaved more like modern day social workers than early modern policemen" (Gorski 2003, 58).

27. This is where an analysis inspired by the work of Norbert Elias is more satisfying than a Foucauldian one, because the former makes space for people's capacity to exercise control over their actions under favorable conditions (Smith 1999).

28. The authors note broad support not only for a national welfare state but also for transnational welfare. They believe the welfare state may embody a "biblical and secular ideal: a Dutch, a Western, and a global symbol of solidarity between strangers" (Sociaal en Cultureel Planbureau 1998, 117). Even after a decade of privatization and cutbacks, two-thirds of the Dutch surveyed in the 2000 European Values Survey expressed considerable confidence in their system of social security (Inglehart et al. 2004). Official government rhetoric has also maintained a language of care and connection, even as it has incorporated a greater emphasis on incentives and individual responsibility. A 2006 report, issued by the scientific counsel for government policy (WWR), for instance, describes the functions of the welfare state—which is called the "care state" or *verzorgingsstaat*—as to care, to insure, to elevate, and to connect (WRR 2006).

29. See Glendon 1991.

30. See Weir 1995.

31. For statistics and arguments on the differences in wages, job security, and the role of wage-setting institutions in the United States and Europe, see Freeman 1994, 1998; and Bosch 2009. In the mid-2000s, the wage of a full-time low-wage worker in the United States was about a third of that of the average full-time worker, but almost half in the Netherlands (Bosch 2009, 345).

32. See Esping-Anderson 1990; Goodin et al. 2000; Fischer et al. 1996; Quadagno 1994; Howard 1993; and Misra, Moller, and Budig 2007.

33. In the mid-2000s, the percentage of the American population whose income was less than 40 percent of the median income in the United States was 11 percent (versus 4 percent in the Netherlands and a little over 5 percent in all the OECD countries) (Source: OECD.StatExtracts). Goodin and colleagues (2000) point out that many Americans live in intense poverty over longer periods of time. See also Rank 2003.

34. The term "falling from grace" comes from Newman 1999. And indeed many families do fall from grace: two-thirds of all Americans spend at least one year in poverty or near poverty by the time they reach the age of seventy five (Rank 2003).

35. The Dutch have long subsidized the social and cultural activities of religious and ethnic minorities, and have recognized their rights to sovereignty within their own circles, which followed from the Dutch system of pillarization (*verzuiling*); see also chapter 4, n. 17. For instance, the Dutch state supports religious schools, including Islamic schools, and it subsidizes broadcasting companies with religious (including Muslim and Hindu) affiliations. At the same time, there has been an expectation that ethnic minorities integrate into Dutch society. When it became apparent that, among certain segments of ethnic minorities, the desired integration was not occurring, several laws were introduced to make integration mandatory. Evelyn Ersanilli (2007, 8–9) concludes: "It is clear that there is a consensus on forced integration that was unimaginable ten or fifteen years ago. . . . There is now an almost parliamentary-wide consensus that immigrants can—and should—be obligated to learn Dutch and accept certain liberal-democratic values." Indeed, the Dutch government now requires new immigrants and some noncitizen residents to take a civic integration exam.

36. On drug policy, see Bewley-Taylor 1999 and Reinarman, Cohen, and Kaal 2004. On prostitution policy, see Bernstein 2007.

37. See Garland 2001 and Western and Pettit 2002.

38. Many high schools prohibit and punish "displays of affection" between teenagers. Bringing police officers into school to enforce order is common and was being considered even in small-town Tremont.

39. In my own data, I saw the connection between financial insecurity and sexual control most clearly in my interview with the Woods, who say multiple times throughout the interview that they are counting on their daughter's professional success to help them through the retirement years. The Woods are also among the most anxious about their daughter's virginity. For other arguments on the relationship between economic insecurity and concerns about sexuality, see Ehrenreich 1989.

40. This is not only true for romantic attachments. Rhonda Fursman, for instance, worries that her son's attachment to his high-school peer group will inhibit his leaving home and the local community for college.

41. This is why even the DiMaggios, who have made a self-conscious choice to permit their son to drink alcohol on summer vacations, must "pretend not to know" in case he "gets caught."

42. In addition to needing parental support to afford higher education, American adults often need parental assistance to afford housing in middle-class neighborhoods (Rubin 1994). Also indicative of the relative financial fragility of the adolescent maturation process in the United States is the fact that, as young adults, Americans are much less likely to have medium or high incomes, and to be able to support a family of three, than are their Dutch counterparts (Smeeding and Phillips 2002).

43. Sociologists Christien Brinkgreve and Bram van Stolk noted with some surprise how little the Dutch middle-class parents they interviewed in the early 1990s seemed to be concerned about the future economic positions and well-being of their children (Brinkgreve and van Stolk 1997). However, given that welfare reforms have significantly trimmed welfare benefits, especially for youth under the age of twenty-one, it is possible that anxieties about teenage childbearing have since increased, especially in working-class and poor families.

44. Dutch law dictates that parents are required to help provide for their children's livelihood and education until they are twenty-one, even though children become legal adults at age eighteen. Thus, while parents are required to help support their adult children's education, they do not have the right to dictate their (educational) choices. Research has estimated that the average university student derives half of his or her income from government subsidies, a third from parental contributions, and one fifth from work (Dieleman 2000). On the strong rights position of Dutch adolescents in health care and education, see Abbing 1996.

45. Indeed, in the 1980s and 1990s, many Dutch scholars argued that the provisions of the modern Dutch welfare state had equalized intimate relationships, by diminishing the power of parents and husbands and increasing the power of children and wives. Ali de Regt (1988), for instance, argues that, throughout the 1980s, Dutch students experienced their government stipends as a right, which diminished the dependence of children on their parents. Bram van Stolk and Cas Wouters (1983) have argued that government benefits increased the power of women to leave abusive marriages. Moreover, among broad segments of the population there arose what van Stolk and Wouters call the "equanimity" of the welfare state—the profound sense of well-being that people experience when they are protected by income maintenance programs. (For a critique of van Stolk and Wouters' argument,

see Kremer 2007.) Based on their research among Dutch parents and teenagers, Manuela du Bois-Reymond and colleagues (1990) conclude that "modern" parents live together with their teenage children in peaceful coexistence based on negotiations. Echoing the opinions of a number of Dutch boys I interviewed, the authors note that parents have few ways to force their children to do things. Parents, they write, "are aware that they have only a few powerful sanctions to force their children into certain behaviors, particularly once those sons and daughters have passed the age of sixteen or seventeen live at home and probably will continue to do so for many years because they have a long education ahead of them. Youths are in many ways 'partners' of their parents and cohabitants of a common household. Decisions about family matters are no longer made by one person but are the outcome of talking and searching for compromises such that each member of the family will have his or her needs met" (du Bois-Reymond, Peters, and Ravesloot 1990, 69). In recent years, welfare state reforms have repeatedly curtailed a variety of benefits for youth, and future research will have to bear out whether, and if so, how, these changes in the welfare state have changed family dynamics.

46. Brinkgreve and van Stolk (1997) find also that Dutch parents of the 1990s are especially interested in developing the social-emotional skills of their children.

47. In his ethnographic observations of Dutch society in the 1980s, anthropologist Peter Stephenson (1989) observed a strong disliking of obvious hierarchies in the workplace and in public spaces. More recently, the online resource "Expat Focus" describes Dutch workplace culture as follows: "Egalitarianism is one of the key principles underlying Dutch society, and this extends to the workplace and business relationships. There is little formal hierarchy, people at all levels of an organisation are likely to be on first-name terms, and will expect to be involved in decision-making, while managers and supervisors typically discuss work with their staff rather than just giving orders or instructions. Working practices usually include many meetings, called *overleg*, which means consultation. These meetings are chaired, with papers and an agenda distributed in advance. Everyone who is invited to an *overleg* is expected to attend and to contribute their views and suggestions on the issues being discussed; the goal is for participants to compromise as necessary until a decision is reached that everyone is content with. This consensual approach to decision-making also characterises management/labour relations in the Netherlands, and has been institutionalized in the form of works councils which all companies employing more than 35 people are required to have under Dutch law. Worker representatives sit on these councils and are consulted by management regarding any issues likely to affect the employees of the company. As a result, the Netherlands has historically had a low rate of industrial action compared with other European countries." The authors of the article note, however, that the principle of workplace equality has not been extended to women who rarely occupy positions of leadership in business. See http://www.expatfocus.com/expatriate-netherlands-holland.

48. See also Fields 2008.

49. In their international review of workplace representation, Rogers and Streeck note that "approaching the twenty-first century, the United States effectively stands alone among the developed nations, on the verge of having *no* effective system of worker representation and consultation" (Rogers and Streeck 1994, 98; see also Wood 1998). Survey data also suggest that the Dutch are more likely to value and measure freedom in terms of having a say in their everyday working conditions than are Americans (Hofstede 1998 and Inglehart 1990).

50. In 1994, women worked full-time in only one quarter of all Dutch couples under the age of 65 (van Praag and Uitterhoeve 1999). Throughout the 1990s, women's labor participation rate was considerably higher among the middle- and upper-middle classes than among the working class (Fortuijn 1996; Kremer 2007).

51. The "public" power of Dutch women is somewhat contradictory: in business and education, including higher education, the percentage of leadership positions occupied by women is very low. In politics, women are relatively well represented—more than a third of the members of parliament are women. Rosi Braidotti, an Italian-born professor of women's studies at the University of Utrecht, speaks of the Dutch paradox: women are well supported by government-funded feminist institutions; their well-being and levels of satisfaction are high; however, other than as politicians and mothers, Dutch women posses very little power in society (Pruin 1998). Despite a strong increase in female labor-force participation, a decade and a half later, outside of parliament and government, Dutch women still occupy relatively few leadership positions, especially in academia, business, and civil service (EUROSTAT 2008).

52. Te Poel and Ravesloot (1997) find also that mothers, rather than fathers, feel responsible for, and do the emotional work of, normalizing teenage sexuality by making it a topic of discussion with their children.

53. In a study of the meaning of work in the life plans of one hundred and twenty Dutch secondary-school students, conducted in the late 1980s, Frans Meijers (1991) found that 50 percent of the girls planned to stop working outside the home altogether once they had children. Only 3 percent of girls aspired to work full-time while mothers. As this cohort of girls came of age, their perspective changed. In 1998, seven out of ten Dutch women with children under the age of six preferred a care-sharing arrangement whereby the man works full-time and the women works part-time. Only one in ten did not want to work outside the home at all (Kremer 2007, 218).

54. In her 1980s research, Janita Ravesloot (1997) found general acceptance of sexual experience on the part of girls, but not of sex outside of steady relationships. In 2005, four out of five sexually experienced Dutch girls and young women had their last intercourse in a monogamous relationship. But having sex within relationships is not the same as making lifetime commitments. Indeed, six out of ten of the Dutch girls and young women surveyed have had two or more sexual partners (de Graaf et al. 2005).

55. It is instructive that when Ria van Kampen and her daughter Fleur were arguing about whether Fleur could have her boyfriend sleep over (see chapter 2), Fleur asked her mother defiantly, "Would you rather I had looser affairs?" It is possible that Ria, who wishes her daughter were not so attached to a local boyfriend, would indeed prefer her daughter to have looser affairs, but the taboo on non-relationship-based sexuality would have kept her from saying so and so she was effectively silenced.

56. In an interview with *The New Yorker*, Christian conservative Mike Huckabee says, for instance, that although he himself married young, "If my kids had come to me and they were eighteen or nineteen and said we're getting married, I'd have said you're crazy" (Levy 2010).

57. See Bellah et al. 1985; Gorski 2003; Stephenson 1989; Kickert 2003; van Elteren 1990; Schama 1988; and Engbersen et al. 1993.

58. Reviewing the Dutch welfare state policy style during the early 1990s, Engbersen and colleagues write that, in comparison with the American policy style, it is "informal, flexible, cooperative, and consensual rather than adversarial, relying more on

persuasion than on coercion, and willing to take account of specific circumstances of individual clients" (Engbersen et al. 1993, 20). A decade later, after substantial shifts in the Dutch welfare state, crucial elements of this flexible approach remain (see note 66). On the role of cultural concepts in Dutch and American welfare state policies, see also van der Veen 1996; Knijn 1994a; Levine 1988; Zvesper 1996; Fraser and Gordon 1997; and Steensland 2008.

59. The term "social imaginary" comes from Charles Taylor (2007). "Harsh justice" is the term James Whitman (2003) uses to describe the particularly harsh penal climate that is the "dark side of the nation's much vaunted individualism."

60. Swidler 2001, 157.

61. Between 1996 and 2006, the proportion of young people (fifteen to twenty-nine) who were themselves, or whose parents were, born in a country categorized as non-Western, increased from one in ten to one in six. Immigrants of Turkish or Moroccan descent—who constitute of the bulk of the Muslims living in the Netherlands—make up about 40 percent of the non-Western immigrant population (Garssen 2006; 2008; and Ersenalli 2007).

62. In 1994, 51 percent of Dutch women were employed. By 2007, that percentage had risen to 68 percent, very similar to the percentage of American women who are in the workforce (66 percent). However, six out of ten Dutch working women do so part-time versus only 18 percent of American women (Kremer 2007, 86; OECD 2008b). Indeed, even single mothers—who, following what Monique Kremer calls a 1996 paradigm shift in policy, were no longer supported unconditionally but were rather required to work once their children were over five—were not required to do so full-time. The consensus in recent debates, Kremer asserts, is that all political parties and social organizations oppose requiring single parents to work full-time: "In the new 2003 law municipalities are allowed to place work requirements on lone mothers of children up until the age of 12, but they have to take into account the wishes of lone mothers and make sure enough childcare is available" (Kremer 2007, 128). Knijn and van Wel (2001) also found that following the 1996 welfare reform, local officials preferred to carefully stimulate rather than harshly pressure single mothers to move from the home into the workplace, and they often accommodated mothers' wishes to continue to care for their children by exempting them from full-time work obligations.

63. The Commonwealth Fund recently ranked the Dutch health-care system first among seven industrial nations on a variety of items, including on access and equity of care (Davis, Schoen, and Stremikis 2010). On Dutch 2008 poverty rates in European perspective, see Eurostat 2010.

64. On the Dutch and American poverty and public investment rates compared, see OECD 2008a and OECD 2009. The Dutch "replacement rates" (the average unemployment benefits) declined steeply from 53 percent in 2000—which was the highest among all OECD nations—to 34 percent in 2007. Despite this strong decline, the Dutch replacement rate has remained in keeping with those in several Scandinavian countries and other Northern European countries, and is more than twice as high as in the United States (14 percent). Moreover, the percentage of the Net National Income (NNI) spent on income supports to the working-age population remained relatively high in the Netherlands—in between that of the social democratic Scandinavian welfare states and the corporatist welfare states of Germany and France. At 7 percent, it is more than three times as high as the percentage in the United States (2.2 percent) (OECD 2009).

65. In 2001, 88 percent of Dutch children fourteen and under lived in two-parent families. Italy was the only country in Europe with a higher percentage of children living in two-parent families. One in nine Dutch children fourteen and under lived in a one-parent family. By comparison, in 2005, a quarter of American children seventeen and under lived in a one-parent family (OECD 2010). In both countries, children in single-parent families are much more likely to experience poverty than children in dual-parent families (Misra, Moller, and Budig 2007).

66. See Buruma 2007. Elizabeth Bernstein has argued that, ironically with the legalization of brothels in 2000, a legal distinction was drawn between documented and undocumented sex workers, which significantly worsened conditions for the latter. A Dutch legal scholar she interviewed described the Dutch regulation of prostitution in the following terms: "It involves self-regulation, enforced if necessary through administrative rules, but always with the criminal law as threat in the background" (Bernstein 2007, 162). In the wake of legalization, more informal arrangements became more complicated. Indeed, Bernstein reports that the *huiskamer* or "living room," described in note 25, was closed several years later. Incarceration rates quadrupled between 1990 and 2004 in the Netherlands. The reasons for the rise remain debated. Among the factors to which this rise has been attributed are increases in serious offenses, harsher sentencing practices, and more vigorous enforcement of hard-drugs laws. Immigrant populations, especially from non-Western countries, are overrepresented among those incarcerated (Tonry and Bijlenveld 2007). Scholars have noted the growth in Dutch incarceration rates with some astonishment. While a more severe climate—both among officials and the public at large—is indisputable, it should also be noted that prison conditions appear to remain relatively humane: prisoners typically serve sentences of under a year. They have their own individual cells and the right to weekly visits, regular sport activities, and daily outdoor time. They may also purchase televisions, keep small pets, and have spaces for sexual relations when serving longer sentences. But prisoners are also required to work and spend leisure time together. Notably, the principle informing Dutch prison policy is not, Peter Tak (2003, 94) writes, one of "separation" but one of "association."

67. To the surprise of many Dutch researchers, a 2005 study found that among twenty-one to twenty-four-year-old women, almost a quarter had ever been forced to do or permit sexual things against their will. "Sexual things" was purposively left undefined, the authors of the study wrote, so that respondents could interpret it to include a forced kiss or manual or oral sex (de Graaf et al. 2005, 107–8). Sexualization and female objectification in the traditional media—which has been increasingly commercialized since the early 1990s—and in the new media have also become causes for concern to researchers and policymakers.

68. In 2000, the Netherlands still ranked number five on a list of eighty-one countries in terms of their overall levels of trust. But even then there were notable differences by education: Almost eight out of ten Dutch people with high levels of education (compared to only four out of ten highly educated Americans) said most people could be trusted. Three out of five Dutch people with medium levels of education agreed, but only four out of ten with low levels of education did (Inglehart et al. 2004). But since then, public confidence in tolerance as effective government policy and in people's tendency to "do the right thing" has waned.

69. Sniderman and Hagendoorn (2007, 28) report, for instance, that a large majority of immigrants of Turkish and Moroccan descent surveyed in the late 1990s agreed

at least somewhat with the statements "Western European women have too many rights and liberties" and "Western European youth have too little respect for their parents." Over the past decade, there have been increased expressions of mutual hostility between immigrants of Moroccan and Turkish descent and members of the native Dutch population. Since September 11, 2001, and the murder of Dutch filmmaker and author Theo van Gogh by a member of a radical Muslim group, anti-Muslim prejudice has intensified, as has right-wing violence (Ersenalli 2007; Veldhuis and Bakker 2009). But Veldhuis and Baker (2009) have concluded that although many Muslim-identified youths have become alienated from Dutch society, perceiving a lack of respect from the dominant (opinion) leaders, radicalization and the embrace of political violence is rare among them. Among political elites, moreover, there are signs of increased integration. In 2007, eleven of the one hundred and fifty members of parliament were of non-Western immigrant descent. One member of the cabinet was of Moroccan descent and one was of Turkish decent (Ersenalli 2007).

70. This film was introduced in 2006 as part of educational materials for an entry exam that certain prospective immigrant groups to the Netherlands (those seeking family unification) were required to pass. These course materials are no longer mandatory, although strict cultural "integration" and language criteria remain.

CONCLUSION

1. Abma et al. 2010.

2. Unintentional pregnancies are not confined to teenagers. In 2001, eight in ten pregnancies among American women, ages fifteen to nineteen, were not intended. Among twenty to twenty-four-year-olds, six in ten pregnancies were unintended (Finer and Henshaw 2006). The extent to which having a child as a teenager has adverse economic consequences for poor women has been debated, given their already bleak economic prospects (Furstenberg 2007).

3. UNAIDS 2008.

4. First romantic relationships increase conflicts between parents and daughters (Joyner and Udry 2000). For a discussion of strains in the parent–adolescent relationship for non-heterosexual teens, see Diamond and Savin-Williams 2009 and Savin-Williams 2000.

5. Hamilton, Martin, and Ventura 2009; Garssen 2008.

6. Garssen 2008; van Lee et al. 2009; Kost et al. 2010. Among immigrant groups to the Netherlands there is a strong drop in teenage births between the first and second generation. Among Turkish and Moroccan immigrants, the teenage fertility rate among the second generation is now similar to that of girls of indigenous Dutch descent. In other groups, including Surinamese and Antillean immigrants, teenage fertility rates, while decreasing between first and second generations, remain two to three times as high as the national averages. While high for Dutch standards, in 2006 teen fertility rates among second-generation Surinamese and Antillean teenage women—14.4 and 17.2 per 1,000 respectively—were less than half those among all American teenage women and less than a third of those among nonwhite American teenage women—41.9 and 54.6, respectively (Garssen 2008; Kost et al. 2010).

7. UNAIDS 2008. As we saw in chapter 2, n. 16, comparing rates of other sexually transmitted diseases is complicated by different systems for tracking, treating, and reporting. But chlamydia prevalence studies suggest American youth have higher rates than their Dutch peers (Van Bergen et al. 2005; Miller et al. 2004; and Datta et al. 2007).

8. De Graaf et al. 2005.

9. See Singh et al. (2001) on the role socioeconomic disadvantage plays in shaping sexual health outcomes in the U.S. and Europe. A report from the Centers for Disease Control and Prevention points toward poverty as the single most important predictor of HIV/AIDS in the United States (Centers for Disease Control and Prevention 2010). Dutch cities have neighborhoods with concentrations of low-income residents (both minorities and indigenous Dutch), although "there are no residential areas equivalent to the urban ghettos of the United States or the *banlieus* of Paris" (Tonry and Bijlenveld 2007). However, in communities where socioeconomic disadvantage approximates "American" conditions, adolescent sexual health outcomes are concomitantly a great deal poorer (Van Lee et al. 2009).

10. Abortion is available free of cost and without parental consent to Dutch girls over fifteen. Dutch law does require a five-day waiting period, for women of all ages, between the first appointment and the performance of an abortion. In 2005, 87 percent of U.S. counties, in which more than a third of all women aged fifteen to forty-four live, did not have an abortion provider (Jones 2008). For international comparisons of contraceptive use among teenagers, see Currie et al. 2008; Godeau et al. 2008; Santelli, Sandfort, and Orr 2008; and Ferguson et al. 2008. For a discussion of the factors promoting easy access to contraception among youth in the Netherlands, see Hardon 2003 and Ketting and Visser 1994. For a review of changes in sex education in the U.S., including the decline in education about contraception, see Lindberg, Santelli, and Singh 2006.

11. Elliott's (2010) qualitative study of sexual socialization among a group of socioeconomically and racially diverse American parents in the South corroborates many of the findings of my study. At the same time, there are important intranational cultural differences: studies have shown that African-American parents report significantly more communication with their teen children about sex and birth control than parents of any other race or ethnic group (Regnerus 2005).

12. Giordano, Longmore, and Manning (2006) also find that, counter to stereotypes, American boys are as emotionally invested in their romantic relationships as girls.

13. It is not surprising that the Dutch boys interviewed do not feel unique for having been in love. De Graaf et al. (2005) find that 90 percent of Dutch boys in their early teenage years say they have been in love.

14. This does not mean that all conflicts or inequalities can be easily seen or discussed. Class inequality is very difficult for Americans to recognize and discuss. For an excellent discussion of how inequalities of class are often conflated with those of race and ethnicity and mapped onto adolescent sexuality, see Bettie 2000.

15. Kooij 1983.

16. See Kooij 1983; Jones et al. 1986; Ketting 1994, 1990; and Ketting and Visser 1994.

17. Smith's review of attitudes toward sexuality among American adults shows very little change in attitudes toward homosexuality between the early 1970s and early 1990s (Smith 1994). However, the General Social Survey has found that between 1990 and 2006, the percentage of Americans who agreed that sex between two people of the same sex was "always wrong" dropped from 76 to 56 percent. The World Values Survey found an even more spectacular drop. In 1990, 57 percent of American respondents agreed that homosexuality was "never justified." In 2000, that percentage had decreased to 32 percent (Inglehart et al. 2004).

18. Gloria Gonzalez-Lopez (2003) found Mexican-American mothers eager to provide

their daughters with better and more empowering sex education than they themselves had received.

19. See Ross 2005; Mayes and Mguni 2009; Ip 2009; and Jiménez 2007.

20. Within the social sciences—especially psychology—and public health, there have
been efforts in recent years to conceptualize adolescent sexuality in more positive
terms, and to show how pleasure and connection factor into understanding and
promoting adolescent sexual health (Russell 2005; Ott et al. 2006; Dennison and
Russell 2005; Higgins and Hirsch 2007; Horne and Zimmer-Gembeck 2005; Impett
and Tolman 2006; Tolman 2002).

21. See Michaud 2006.

22. In her study of sex education in three different American schools, Jessica Fields
(2008) found that teachers do not have the leeway or training to effectively intervene during sex education courses. She argues that teachers must take (and be given
the freedom to take) the responsibility of creating sex education classrooms free
from the sexual harassment that often takes place. Likewise, Martin (1996) and Tolman (2002) call on adult women to bolster girls' sexual subjectivity by giving them
the tools to recognize their internal bodily knowledge and deconstruct harmful media messages and interpersonal dynamics.

23. See Pager et al. 2009.

24. For a review of the concepts of sexual "agency" and "subjectivity," see Schalet 2009.

25. See also Horne and Zimmer-Gembeck 2005; Martin 1996; Hogarth and Ingham
2009; Tolman 2002; and Impett and Tolman 2006.

26. For the detrimental effect of masculinity norms on boys' sexual and emotional well-
being, see, for instance, Pleck, Sonnenstein and Ku 1993; Pascoe 2007; and Marcell,
Raine, and Eyre 2003.

27. Several studies have found that greater commitment, more intimacy, and/or good
communication in relationships increase pleasure, wantedness, and/or protective
behavior at first intercourse (Sprecher et al. 1995; Smiler et al. 2005; Widman et al.
2006; Houts 2005; and Stone and Ingham 2002). At the same time, researchers have
also found an association between being in longer relationships and poorer contraceptive use (Ford et al. 2001; Ku et al. 1994; Manlove et al. 2003).

28. See Bernat and Resnick 2009. In their mixed-methods study, developmental psychologist Jill Denner and colleagues (2001) found that Latina girls who are strongly
integrated in families and communities through shared norms and social capital
tend to have lower birth rates.

29. It is notable that in cross-national studies asking youth whether they find it easy to
talk with their mothers or fathers about "things that really bother you," American
thirteen- and fifteen-year-olds consistently rank among those least comfortable talking with parents of either gender, and their Dutch peers among those most comfortable (Currie et al. 2008; Currie et al. 2004). For instance, while 63 percent of Dutch
fifteen-year-old girls find it easy or very easy to talk to their fathers about things that
bother them, only 43 percent of American girls feel that it would be easy or very
easy (Currie, Gabhainn, and Godeau 2008, 27).

30. See Singh et al. 2001; Imamura et al. 2007; and the Centers for Disease Control and
Prevention 2010.

METHODOLOGICAL APPENDIX

1. In 2000, a quarter of the American population identified themselves as belonging
to a racial or ethnic minority (U.S. Census Bureau). The Dutch collect population

statistics based on immigration status and country of origin. Adults and children living in the Netherlands are categorized as *allochtoon* or "originating from another country" if either they or at least one of their parents were born outside the country. Using that definition, in 1996, almost one in eight Dutch children fourteen and under was categorized as a non-Western immigrant—typically Turkish, Moroccan, or Surinamese. By 2006, one in six children in the Netherlands was categorized as a non-Western immigrant (Garssen 2006).

2. Gorski 2003; Goudsblom 1967; Lipset 1963; Motley 1855; and Engbersen et al. 1993.

3. Stephen Lucas (1998, 164) has argued that "of all the models available to Jefferson and the drafting committee, none provided as precise a template for the Declaration as did the Plakkaat van Verlatinge."

4. According to Wouters (1998), in both countries commercial elites sought to establish themselves as a type of aristocracy. Brinkgreve and van Stolk (1997) write that the Dutch nobility has played a less prominent part in shaping the nation than in almost any other European country. Their marginality was due to the dominant position of the cities and their governments during the Dutch republic (late sixteenth through late eighteenth centuries). Also, the Protestant character and internal doctrinal battles of the Dutch church did not permit a consolidation of aristocratic power, as the Catholic Church did in many other European nations.

5. Since surveys in the United States have shown that Jews tend to be considerably more liberal with regard to sexuality, I focus on the Christian and secular populations.

6. See Irvine (2002) for a description of the battles over sex education. Remnants of those were felt even when I did gain access to a school in Northern California: before I addressed my first class of prospective interviewees, a teacher took me aside and told me there was a word I should never use: "condom."

7. Fischer et al. 1996.

8. Like all the other names for research sites, and schools within those cites, Corona is a pseudonym, and has no relation to the actual city in Southern California, called Corona.

9. Especially in Corona, the American teenagers whose parents are not professionals often come from families in which divorce, substance abuse, and (mental) health problems are common. I think that one reason teenagers declined to have me approach their parents is that they did not want to add to their burdens. Another reason that American teenagers, especially girls, declined to have me interview their parents is because the topics about which I had interviewed them—sex and alcohol—are cause for considerable conflict, and avoiding discussion about these topics is one way girls and parents manage these tensions.

10. In recent years, the proportion of Americans for whom "pro-family" (and sexually conservative) values are important has grown significantly (Brooks 2002). Since these Americans often join churches not explicitly affiliated with national organizations, it is not surprising that their position is not as easy to detect.

11. Throughout the 2000s, three quarters of the Dutch population participated in "long vacations," which lasted an average of twelve days. Most long vacations involve travel abroad. More than a third of the population also participated in a short vacation away from home, which lasted, on average, three days (Centraal Bureau voor de Statistiek 2009).

12. In keeping with national trends, in such upper-middle-class Dutch families mothers were likely to work.

13. However, drawing on the parent and teenage data, a notable gender pattern did emerge in the United States, which is discussed in chapters 3 and 5.

14. Both Thompson (1995) and Martin (1996) talk about the difficulty of recruiting and interviewing boys. Indeed Thompson found the process so vexing that she switched to interviewing only girls. My experience was that it *was* indeed more difficult to get boys to sign up for an interview, but once we were in conversation, boys seemed to me as comfortable and forthcoming as their female counterparts.

15. Indeed, one or two boys and girls in each country come from what one might call "blue collar" families.

16. Thanks to Robert LeVine for suggesting that I pursue this strategy.

17. Alford 1998, 28.

18. The Norwood interviews, conducted in 1991/1992, informed the analyses of the American parent chapters and were used to calculate the numbers on American parents' answers to the sleepover question, but the examples are drawn from the Corona and Tremont interviews, conducted in 1999 and 2000. The socio-demographic make-up of the Norwood sample was very similar to that of the Corona sample. For quotes from the Norwood interviewees, see Schalet 2000.

19. Geertz 1983.

20. Geertz 1973.

REFERENCES

Abbing, Henriette D. C. Roscam. 1996. Adolescent Sexuality and Public Policy: A Human Rights Response. *Politics and the Life Sciences* 15 (2): 314–16.

Abma, Joyce C., Gladys M. Martinez, and Casey E. Copen. 2010. Teenagers in the United States: Sexual Activity, Contraceptive Use, and Childbearing, National Survey of Family Growth 2006–2008. *Vital and Health Statistics*, ser. 23, no. 30. National Center for Health Statistics.

Abma, Joyce C., Gladys M. Martinez, William D. Mosher, and Brittany S. Dawson. 2004. Teenagers in the United States: Sexual Activity, Contraceptive Use, and Childbearing, 2002. *Vital and Health Statistics*, ser. 23, no. 24. National Center for Health Statistics.

Albert, Bill. 2004. *With One Voice 2004: America's Adults and Teens Sound Off About Teen Pregnancy*. Washington, DC: National Campaign to Prevent Teen Pregnancy.

Alford, Robert R. 1998. *The Craft of Inquiry: Theories, Methods, Evidence*. New York: Oxford University Press.

Alwin, Duane F. 1989. Changes in Qualities Valued in Children in the United States, 1964–1984. *Social Science Research* 18 (3): 195–236.

Anderson, Elijah. 1999. *Code of the Street: Decency, Violence, and the Moral Life of the Inner City*. New York: W. W. Norton & Company.

Archer, Margaret S. 1985. The Myth of Cultural Integration. *British Journal of Sociology* 36 (3): 333–53.

Armstrong, Elizabeth A., Laura Hamilton, and Brian Sweeney. 2006. Sexual Assault on Campus: A Multilevel, Integrative Approach to Party Rape. *Social Problems* 53 (4): 483–99.

Bailey, Beth L. 1988. *From Front Porch to Back Seat: Courtship in Twentieth-Century America*. Baltimore: The Johns Hopkins University Press.

———. 1999. *Sex in the Heartland*. Cambridge, MA: Harvard University Press.

Bakker, Kees, Tom ter Bogt, and Mieke de Waal. 1993. *Opgroeien in Nederland*. Amersfoort: Academische Uitgeverij Amersfoort.

Baldwin, Peter. 1990. *The Politics of Social Solidarity: Class Bases of the European Welfare State, 1875–1975*. Cambridge: Cambridge University Press.

Bearman, Peter S., James Moody, and Katherine Stovel. 2004. Chains of Affection: The Structure of Adolescent Romantic and Sexual Networks. *American Journal of Sociology* 110 (1): 44–91.

Bearman, Peter S., and Hannah Brückner. 2001. Promising the Future: Virginity Pledges and First Intercourse. *American Journal of Sociology* 106 (4): 859–912.

Bergen, J. van, H. Götz, J. Richardus, C. J. Hoebe, J. Broeren, and A. Coenen. 2005. Chlamydia trachomatis-infecties in 4 regio's in Nederland: Resultaten van een Bevolkingsonderzoek via de GGD en Implicaties voor Screening. *Nederlands Tijdschrift Voor Geneeskunde* 149 (39): 2167–74.

Beckett, Megan K., Marc N. Elliott, Steven Martino, David E. Kanouse, Rosalie Corona, David J. Klein, and Mark A. Schuster. 2010. Timing of Parent and Child Communication about Sexuality Relative to Children's Sexual Behaviors. *Pediatrics* 125 (1): 34–42.

Bellah, Robert N., Richard Madsen, William M. Sullivan, Ann Swidler, and Steven M. Tipton. 1985. *Habits of the Heart: Individualism and Commitment in American Life*. Berkeley and Los Angeles: University of California Press.

Bernat, Debra H., and Michael D. Resnick. 2009 Connectedness in the Lives of Adolescents. In *Adolescent Health: Understanding and Preventing Risk Behaviors*, edited by R. J. DiClemente, J. S. Santelli, and R. A. Crosby. San Francisco: Jossey-Bass.

Berne, Linda, and Barbara Huberman. 1999. *European Approaches to Adolescent Sexual Behavior and Responsibility*. Washington, DC: Advocates for Youth.

Bernstein, Elizabeth. 2007. *Temporarily Yours: Intimacy, Authenticity, and the Commerce of Sex*. Chicago: University of Chicago Press.

Bettie, Julie. 2000. Women Without Class: *Chicas, Cholas*, Trash, and the Presence/Absence of Class Identity. *Signs: Journal of Women in Culture and Society* 26 (1): 1–35.

Bewley-Taylor, David R. 1999. *The United States and International Drug Control, 1909–1997*. New York: Pinter.

Biernacki, Richard. 1995. *The Fabrication of Labor: Germany and Britain, 1640–1914*. Berkeley and Los Angeles: University of California Press.

Blommesteijn, Marieke, and Luuk Mallee. 2009. *The Netherlands. Minimum Income Scheme: Work and Social Assistance Act*. European Commission.

Bosch, Gerhard. 2009. Low-wage Work in Five European Countries and the United States. *International Labour Review* 148 (4): 337–56.

Bourdieu, Pierre. 1984. *Distinction: A Social Critique of the Judgment of Taste*. Translated by R. Nice. Cambridge, MA: Harvard University Press.

———. 1990. *The Logic of Practice*. Translated by R. Nice. Stanford: Stanford University Press.

Bozon, Michel, and Osmo Kontula. 1998. Sexual Initiation and Gender in Europe: A Cross-Cultural Analysis of Trends in the Twentieth Century. In *Sexual Behaviour and HIV/ AIDS in Europe: Comparisons of National Surveys*, edited by M. Hubert, N. Bajos, and T. Sandfort. London: UCL Press.

Brinkgreve, Christien, and Michael Korzec. 1978. *'Margriet Weet Raad': Gevoel, Gedrag, Moraal in Nederland, 1938–1978*. Utrecht: Het Spectrum.

Brinkgreve, Christien, and Bram van Stolk. 1997. *Van Huis Uit: Wat Ouders Aan Hun Kinderen Willen Meegeven*. Amsterdam: Meulenhoff.

Brooks, Clem. 2002. Religious Influence and the Politics of Family Decline Concern: Trends, Sources, and U.S. Political Behavior. *American Sociological Review* 67 (2): 191–211.

Brugman, Emily, Hans Goedhart, Ton Vogels, and Gertjan van Zessen. 1995. *Jeugd en Seks 95: Resultaten van het Nationale Scholierenonderzoek*. Utrecht: SWP.

Brugman, Maria Johanna Elisabeth. 2007. Emerging Adolescent Sexuality: A Comparison of American and Dutch Women's Experiences. Ph.D. diss., University of Maine.

Buruma, Ybo. 2007. Dutch Tolerance: On Drugs, Prostitution, and Euthanasia. *Crime and Justice* 35:73–113.

Carpenter, Laura M. 2002. Gender and the Social Construction of Virginity Loss in the Contemporary United States. *Gender and Society* 16 (3): 345–65.

———. 2005. *Virginity Lost: An Intimate Portrait of First Sexual Experiences*. New York: New York University Press.

Centers for Disease Control and Prevention. 2010. Press Release: New CDC Analysis Reveals Strong Link Between Poverty and HIV Infection. Washington, DC: CDC, NCHHSTP Newsroom.

Centraal Bureau voor de Statistiek. 2003. *Jeugd 2003: Cijfers en Feiten*. Voorburg/Heerlen: Centraal Bureau voor de Statistiek.

———. *Vakanties van Nederlanders 2008*. Voorburg/Heerlen: Centraal Bureau voor de Statistiek.

Cherlin, Andrew J. 2009. *The Marriage-Go-Round: The State of Marriage and the Family in America Today*. New York: Alfred A. Knopf.

Cohen, Susan A. 2004. Delayed Marriage and Abstinence-until-Marriage: On a Collision Course? In *The Guttmacher Report on Public Policy*. New York: The Alan Guttmacher Institute.

Coleman, James S. 1961. *The Adolescent Society: The Social Life of the Teenager and its Impact on Education*. New York: The Free Press of Glencoe.

Collier, Jane Fishburne. 1997. *From Duty to Desire: Remaking Families in a Spanish Village*. Princeton: Princeton University Press.

Collins, Patricia Hill. 2004. *Black Sexual Politics: African Americans, Gender, and the New Racism*. New York and London: Routledge.

Collins, W. Andrew, Deborah P. Welsh, and Wyndol Furman. 2009. Adolescent Romantic Relationships. *Annual Review of Psychology* 60:631–52.

Coontz, Stephanie. 1992. *The Way We Never Were: American Families and the Nostalgia Trap*. New York: Basic Books.

Cremer, Stephan W. 1997. Kwetsbaar en Grenzeloos: Experimenteren in Seks en Omgaan met Grenzen vanuit het Perspectief van Jongens. *Comenius* 17:325–37.

Currie, Candace, Saoirse Nic Gabhainn, Emmanuelle Godeau, Chris Roberts, Rebecca Smith, Dorothy Currie, Will Picket, Matthias Richter, Antony Morgan, and Vivian Barnekow Rasmussen, eds. 2008. Inequalities in Young People's Health: International Report from the 2005/2006 Survey. In *Health Policy for Children and Adolescents*, no. 5. Copenhagen: World Health Organization.

Currie, Candace, Chris Roberts, Antony Morgan, Rebecca Smith, Wolfgang Settertobulte, Oddrun Samdal, and Vivian Barnekow Rasmussen. 2004. Young People's Health in Context: Health Behaviour in School-Aged Children (HBSC) Study: International Report from the 2001/2002 Survey. In *Health Policy for Children and Adolescents*, no. 4. Copenhagen: World Health Organization.

D'Emilio, John, and Estelle B. Freedman. 1988. *Intimate Matters: A History of Sexuality in America*. New York: Harper and Row.

Darroch, Jacqueline E., David J. Landry, and Susheela Singh. 2000. Changing Emphases in Sexuality Education in U.S. Public Secondary Schools, 1988–1999. *Family Planning Perspectives* 32 (5): 211–65.

Darroch, Jacqueline E., Susheela Singh, and Jennifer J. Frost. 2001. Differences in Teenage Pregnancy Rates among Five Developed Countries: The Roles of Sexual Activity and Contraceptive Use. *Family Planning Perspectives* 33 (6): 244–50 and 281.

Datta, S. Deblina, Maya Sternberg, Robert E. Johnson, Stuart Berman, John R. Papp,

Geraldine McQuillan, and Hillard Weinstock. 2007. Gonorrhea and Chlamydia in the United States among Persons 14 to 39 Years of Age, 1999 to 2002. *Annals of Internal Medicine* 147 (2): 89–96.

Davis, Karen, Cathy Schoen, and Kristof Stremikis. 2010. *Mirror, Mirror on the Wall: How the Performance of the U.S. Healthcare System Compares Internationally*. New York: Commonwealth Fund.

De Graaf, Paul M., and Harry B. G. Ganzenboom. 1993. Family Background and Educational Attainment in the Netherlands for the 1891–1960 Birth Cohorts. In *Persistent Inequalities: A Comparative Study of Educational Attainment in Thirteen Countries*, edited by Y. Shavit and H.-P. Blossfeld. Boulder, CO: Westview Press.

Degenhardt, Louisa, Wai-Tat Chiu, Nancy Sampson, Ronald C. Kessler, James C. Anthony, Matthias Angermeyer, Ronny Bruffaerts, Giovanni de Girolamo, Oye Gureje, Yueqin Huang, Aimee Karam, Stanislav Kostyuchenko, Jean Pierre Lepine, Maria Elena Medina Mora, Yehuda Neumark, J. Hans Ormel, Alejandra Pinto-Meza, José Posada-Villa, Dan J. Stein, Tadashi Takeshima, and J. Elisabeth Wells. 2008. Toward a Global View of Alcohol, Tobacco, Cannabis, and Cocaine Use: Findings from the WHO World Mental Health Surveys. *PLoS Med* 5 (7): e141.

Denner, Jill, Douglas Kirby, Karin Coyle, and Claire Brindis. 2001. The Protective Role of Social Capital and Cultural Norms in Latino Communities: A Study of Adolescent Births. *Hispanic Journal of Behavioral Sciences* 23 (1): 3–21.

Dennison, Renee, and Stephen Russell. 2005. Positive Perspectives on Adolescent Sexuality: Contributions of the National Longitudinal Study of Adolescent Health. *Sexuality Research and Social Policy: A Journal of NSRC* 2 (4): 54–59.

Derné, Steve. 1994. Cultural Conceptions of Human Motivation and Their Significance for Culture Theory. In *The Sociology of Culture: Emerging Theoretical Perspectives*, edited by D. Crane. Cambridge, MA: Blackwell.

Dieleman, Arjan. 2000. Individualisering en Ambivalentie in het Bestaan van Jongeren. *Pedagogiek* 20 (2): 91–111.

di Mauro, Diane, and Carole Joffe. 2007. The Religious Right and the Reshaping of Sexual Policy: An Examination of Reproductive Rights and Sexuality Education. *Sexuality Research and Social Policy: A Journal of NSRC* 4 (1): 67–92.

Diamond, Lisa, and Ritch Savin-Williams. 2009. Adolescent Sexuality. In *Handbook of Adolescent Psychology: Individual Bases of Adolescent Development*, edited by Richard M. Lerner and Laurence Steinberg. Hoboken, New Jersey: John Wiley & Sons.

Dobbin, Frank. 1994. *Forging Industrial Policy: The United States, Britain, and France in the Railway Age*. Cambridge: Cambridge University Press.

Driessen, Geert W. J. M., and Lia W. J. Mulder. 1999. The Enhancement of Educational Opportunities of Disadvantaged Children. In *Enhancing Educational Excellence, Equity, and Efficiency: Evidence from Evaluations of Systems and Schools in Change*, edited by R. Bosker, B. Creemers, and S. Stringfield. Dordrecht and Boston: Kluwer Academic Publishers.

du Bois-Reymond, Manuela. 1990. Huiselijkheid en Onderhandeling. In *Nuchterheid en Nozems: De Opkomst van de Jeugdcultuur in de Jaren Vijftig*, edited by G. Tillekens. Muiderberg: Dick Coutinho.

———. 1992. *Jongeren op Weg naar Volwassenheid*. Groningen: Wolters-Noordhoff.

———. 1993a. Jeugd en Gezin. In *Jeugd in Meervoud: Theorieën, Modellen en Onderzoek van Leefwerelden van Jongeren*, edited by A. J. Dieleman, F. J. v. d. Linden, and A. C. Perreijn. Utrecht: De Tijdstroom; Heerlen: Open Universiteit.

———. 1993b. Pluraliseringstendensen en Onderhandelingsculturen in het Gezin. *Amsterdams Sociologisch Tijdschrift* 19 (3): 113–44.

du Bois-Reymond, Manuela, Els Peters, and Janita Ravesloot. 1990. Jongeren en Ouders: Van Bevelshuishouding naar Onderhandelingshuishouding. Een Intergenerationele Vergelijking. *Amsterdams Sociologisch Tijdschrift* 17 (3): 69–100.

Duyvendak, Jan Willem. 1996. The Depoliticization of the Dutch Gay Identity, or Why Dutch Gays Aren't Queer. In *Queer Theory/Sociology*, edited by S. Seidman. Cambridge, MA: Blackwell.

Eder, Donna, Catherine Colleen Evans, and Stephen Parker. 1995. *School Talk: Gender and Adolescent Culture*. New Brunswick, NJ: Rutgers University Press.

Ehrenreich, Barbara. 1983. *The Hearts of Men: American Dreams and the Flight from Commitment*. Garden City, NY: Anchor Press/Doubleday.

———. 1989. *Fear of Falling: The Inner Life of the Middle Class*. New York: Pantheon Books.

Elias, Norbert. 1994. *The Civilizing Process*. Translated by E. Jephcott. Oxford: Blackwell.

———. 1998. The Civilizing of Parents. In *The Norbert Elias Reader*, edited by Johan Goudsblom and Stephen Mennell. Malden, MA: Blackwell.

Ellemers, J. E. 1984. Pillarization as a Process of Modernization. *Acta Politica* 19 (1): 129–44.

Elliott, Sinikka. 2010. Parents' Constructions of Teen Sexuality: Sex Panics, Contradictory Discourses, and Social Inequality. *Symbolic Interaction* 33 (2): 191–212.

Elteren, Mel van. 1990. 'Roaring Twenties' in a Cozy Society. Paper presented at the International Conference, "Within the U.S. Orbit: Small National Cultures vis-à-vis the United States: Belgium, Canada, Denmark, the Netherlands," June 6–8, Roosevelt Study Center, Middelburg, the Netherlands.

Engbersen, Godfried, Kees Schuyt, Jaap Timmer, and Frans van Waarden. 1993. *Cultures of Unemployment: A Comparative Look at Long-term Unemployment and Urban Poverty*. Boulder: Westview Press.

England, Paula, Emily Fitzgibbons Shafer, and Alison C. K. Fogarty. 2007. Hooking Up and Forming Romantic Relationships on Today's College Campuses. In *The Gendered Society Reader*, edited by M. Kimmel. New York: Oxford University Press.

Erikson, Erik H. 1950. *Childhood and Society*. New York: W. W. Norton & Co.

Ersanilli, Evelyn. 2007. Country Profile "Netherlands" for Focus Migration. http://www.focus-migration.hwwi.de/uploads/tx_wilpubdb/CP11_Netherlands.pdf

Esping-Andersen, Gøsta. 1990. *The Three Worlds of Welfare Capitalism*. Princeton: Princeton University Press.

EUROSTAT. 2008. *The Life of Women and Men in Europe: A Statistical Portrait*. Luxemburg: European Communities.

Eurostat Press Office. 2010. 17% of EU27 Population at Risk of Poverty: Higher Risk of Poverty Among Children and Elderly. http://epp.eurostat.ec.europa.eu./cache/ITY_PUBLIC/3-18012010-AP/EN/3-18012010-AP-EN.PDF

Evans, David T. 1993. *Sexual Citizenship: The Material Construction of Sexualities*. London: Routledge.

Ferguson, Rebecca M., Ine Vanwesenbeeck, and Trudie Knijn. 2008. A Matter of Facts . . . and More: An Exploratory Analysis of the Content of Sexuality Education in the Netherlands. *Sex Education: Sexuality, Society and Learning* 8 (1): 93–106.

Fields, Jessica. 2008. *Risky Lessons: Sex Education and Social Inequality*. New Brunswick, NJ: Rutgers University Press.

Fine, Michelle. 1988. Sexuality, Schooling, and Adolescent Females: The Missing Discourse of Desire. *Harvard Educational Review* 58 (1): 29–53.

Fine, Michelle, and Sara I. McClelland. 2006. Sexuality Education and Desire: Still Missing After All These Years. *Harvard Educational Review* 76 (3): 297–338.

Finer, Lawrence B. 2007. Trends in Premarital Sex in the United States, 1954–2003. *Public Health Reports* 122 (January-February): 73–78.

Finer, Lawrence B., and Stanley K. Henshaw. 2006. Disparities in Rates of Unintended Pregnancy in the United States, 1994 and 2001. *Perspectives on Sexual and Reproductive Health* 38 (2): 90–96.

Fischer, Claude S. 2010. *Made in America: A Social History of American Culture and Character*. Chicago: University of Chicago Press.

Fischer, Claude S., Michael Hout, Martín Sánchez Jankowski, Samuel R. Lucas, Ann Swidler, and Kim Voss. 1996. *Inequality by Design: Cracking the Bell Curve Myth*. Princeton: Princeton University Press.

Foley, Douglas E. 1994. *Learning Capitalist Culture: Deep in the Heart of Tejas*. Philadelphia: University of Pennsylvania Press.

Ford, Kathleen, Woosung Sohn, and James Lepkowski. 2001. Characteristics of Adolescents' Sexual Partners and Their Associations with Use of Condoms and Other Contraceptive Methods. *Family Planning Perspectives* 33 (3): 100–5, 132.

Fortuijn, Joos Droogleever. 1996. City and Suburb: Contexts for Dutch Women's Work and Daily Lives. In *Women of the European Union: The Politics of Work and Daily Life*, edited by M. D. García-Ramon and J. Monk. London and New York: Routledge.

Foucault, Michel. 1977. *Discipline and Punish: The Birth of the Prison*. Translated by A. Sheridan. New York: Vintage.

———. 1978. *The History of Sexuality: An Introduction, Volume One*. Translated by R. Hurley. New York: Vintage.

———. 1985. *The Use of Pleasure: The History of Sexuality, Volume Two*. Translated by R. Hurley. New York: Vintage.

Fraser, Nancy, and Linda Gordon. 1997. A Genealogy of 'Dependency': Tracing a Keyword of the U.S. Welfare State. In *Justice Interruptus: Critical Reflections on the "Postsocialist" Condition*, edited by N. Fraser. Routledge: New York.

Freeman, Richard B. 1998. War of the Models: Which Labour Market Institutions for the 21st Century? *Labour Economics* 5 (1): 1–24.

Freeman, Richard B., ed. 1994. *Working Under Different Rules: A National Bureau of Economic Research Project Report*. New York: Russell Sage Foundation.

Freud, Anna. 1958. Adolescence. *Psychoanalytic Study of the Child* 15:255–78.

Furstenberg, Frank F. 2007. *Destinies of the Disadvantaged: The Politics of Teenage Childbearing*. New York: Russell Sage Foundation.

Garland, David. 2001. *The Culture of Control: Crime and Social Order in Contemporary Society*. Chicago: University of Chicago Press.

Garssen, Joop. 2006. Demografie van Nederland, 2006. *Bevolkingtrends* 54 (4): 14–33.

———. 2008. Sterke Daling Geboortecijfer Niet-westers Allochtone Tieners. *Bevolkingstrends* 56 (4): 14–21.

Geertz, Clifford. 1973. *The Interpretation of Cultures*. New York: Basic Books.

———. 1983. From the Native's Point of View: On the Nature of Anthropological Understanding. In *Local Knowledge: Further Essays in Interpretive Anthropology*. New York: Basic Books.

Giordano, Peggy C., Monica A. Longmore, and Wendy D. Manning. 2006. Gender and the Meanings of Adolescent Romantic Relationships: A Focus on Boys. *American Sociological Review* 71 (2): 260–87.

Glei, Dana A. 1999. Measuring Contraceptive Use Patterns among Teenage and Adult Women. *Family Planning Perspectives* 31 (2): 73–80.

Glendon, Mary Ann. 1991. *Rights Talk: The Impoverishment of Political Discourse*. New York: Free Press.

Godeau, Emmanuelle, Saoirse Nic Gabhainn, Céline Vignes, Jim Ross, Will Boyce, and Joanna Todd. 2008. Contraceptive Use by 15-year-old Students at Their Last Sexual Intercourse. *Archives of Pediatrics and Adolescent Medicine* 162 (1): 66–73.

Gonzalez-Lopez, Gloria. 2003. De Madres a Hijas: Gendered Lessons on Virginity Across Generations of Mexican Immigrant Women. In *Gender and U.S. Immigration: Contemporary Trends*, edited by P. Hondagneu-Sotelo. Berkeley and Los Angeles: University of California Press.

Goodin, Robert E., Bruce Headey, Ruud Muffels, and Henk-Jan Dirven. 2000. The Real Worlds of Welfare Capitalism. In *The Welfare State: A Reader*, edited by C. Pierson and F. G. Castles. Cambridge, MA: Polity Press.

Gorski, Philip S. 2003. *The Disciplinary Revolution: Calvinism and the Rise of the State in Early Modern Europe*. Chicago: University of Chicago Press.

Goudsblom, Johan. 1967. *Dutch Society*. New York: Random House.

———. 1987. The Sociology of Norbert Elias: Its Resonance and Significance. *Theory, Culture & Society* 4 (2): 323–37.

———. 2000. Norbert Elias and American Sociology. *Sociologicia Internationalis* 38 (2): 173–80.

Graaf, Hanneke de, Suzanne Meijer, Jos Poelman, and Ine Vanwesenbeeck. 2005. *Seks onder je 25ste: Seksuele Gezondheid van Jongeren in Nederland Anno 2005*. Utrecht and Amsterdam: Rutgers Nisso Groep/Soa Aids Nederland.

Green-Pedersen, Christoffer, Kees van Kersbergen, and Anton Hemerijck. 2001. Neo-Liberalism, the "Third Way" or What? Recent Social Democratic Welfare Policies in Denmark and the Netherlands. *Journal of European Public Policy* 8 (2): 307–25.

Griffin, Christine. 1993. *Representations of Youth: The Study of Youth and Adolescence in Britain and America*. Cambridge, MA: Polity Press.

Griswold, Wendy. 1987. The Fabrication of Meaning: Literary Interpretation in the United States, Great Britain, and the West Indies. *American Journal of Sociology* 92 (5): 1077–1117.

Guttmacher Institute. 2010. *State Policies in Brief: An Overview of Minors' Consent Law*. New York: Guttmacher Institute.

Haak, Kees van der, and Leo van Snippenburg. 2001. Broadcasting in the Netherlands: The Rise and Decline of Segmentation. In *Western Broadcasting at the Dawn of the 21st Century*, edited by L. D'Haenens and F. Saeys. Berlin and New York: Mouton de Gruyter.

Hamilton, Laura, and Elizabeth A. Armstrong. 2009. Gendered Sexuality in Young Adulthood: Double Binds and Flawed Options. *Gender & Society* 23 (5): 589–616.

Hamilton, Brady E., Joyce A. Martin, and Stephanie J. Ventura. 2009. Births: Preliminary Data for 2007. *National Vital Statistics Reports* 57 (12). National Center for Health Statistics.

Hardon, Anita. 2003. Reproductive Health Care in the Netherlands: Would Integration Improve It? *Reproductive Health Matters* 11 (21): 59–73.

Hart, Joep de. 1992. Jongenswereld—Meisjeswereld? Jongeren over de Relatie met Hun Ouders en Leeftijdgenoten. *Comenius* 48:430–49.

Hebdidge, Dick. 1979. *Subculture: The Meaning of Style*. London Methuen.

Hekma, Gert. 2004a. The Decline of Sexual Radicalism in the Netherlands. In *Past and Present of Radical Sexual Politics*, edited by G. Hekma. Amsterdam: Mosse Foundation.

———. 2004b. Queer: The Dutch Case. *GLQ: A Journal of Lesbian and Gay Studies* 10 (2): 276–80.

Hemerijck, Anton, and Jelle Visser. 1999. De Opmerkelijke Revitalisering van de Over-legeconomie. In *De Herverdeelde Samenleving: Ontwikkeling en Herziening van de Nederlandse Verzorgingsstaat*, edited by W. Trommel and R. v. d. Veen. Amsterdam: Amsterdam University Press.

Henry J. Kaiser Family Foundation. 1996. *The 1996 Kaiser Family Foundation Survey on Teens and Sex: What They Say Teens Today Need to Know, And Who They Listen To*. Menlo Park, CA: Henry J. Kaiser Family Foundation.

Hewitt, John P. 1989. *Dilemmas of the American Self*. Philadelphia: Temple University Press.

Higgins, Jenny A., and Jennifer S. Hirsch. 2007. The Pleasure Deficit: Revisiting the "Sexuality Connection" in Reproductive Health. *International Family Planning Perspectives* 33 (3): 133–39.

Hochschild, Arlie Russell. 1979. Emotion Work, Feeling Rules, and Social Structure. *American Journal of Sociology* 85 (3): 551–75.

———. 1997. *The Time Bind: When Work Becomes Home and Home Becomes Work*. New York: Metropolitan Books.

Hofstede, Geert. 1998. *Masculinity and Femininity: The Taboo Dimension of National Cultures*. Thousand Oaks, CA: Sage Publications.

Hogarth, Harriet, and Roger Ingham. 2009. Masturbation Among Young Women and Associations with Sexual Health: An Exploratory Study. *Journal of Sex Research* 46 (6): 558–67.

Horne, Sharon, and Melanie J. Zimmer-Gembeck. 2005. Female Sexual Subjectivity and Well-Being: Comparing Late Adolescents with Different Sexual Experiences. *Sexuality Research and Social Policy: A Journal of NSRC* 2 (3): 25–40.

Houts, Leslie. 2005. But Was It Wanted? Women's First Voluntary Sexual Intercourse. *Journal of Family Issues* 26 (8): 1082–1102.

Howard, Christopher. 1993. The Hidden Side of the American Welfare State. *Political Science Quarterly* 108 (3): 403–36.

Iacovou, Maria. 2002. Regional Differences in the Transition to Adulthood. *The Annals of the American Academy of Political and Social Science* 580 (1): 40–69.

Imamura, Mari, Janet Tucker, Phil Hannaford, Miguel Oliveira da Silva, Margaret Astin, Laura Wyness, Kitty W. M. Bloemenkamp, Albrecht Jahn, Helle Karro, Jørn Olsen, and Marleen Temmerman. 2007. Factors Associated with Teenage Pregnancy in European Union Countries: A Systematic Review. *European Journal of Public Health* 17 (6): 630–36.

Impett, Emily, and Deborah Tolman. 2006. Late Adolescent Girls' Sexual Experiences and Sexual Satisfaction. *Journal of Adolescent Research* 21 (6): 628–46.

Inglehart, Ronald. 1990. *Culture Shift in Advanced Industrial Society*. Princeton: Princeton University Press.

Inglehart, Ronald, Miguel Basáñez, Jaime Díez-Medrano, Loek Halman, and Ruud Luijkx, eds. 2004. *Human Beliefs and Values: A Cross-Cultural Sourcebook Based on the 1999–2002 Values Surveys*. Mexico: Siglo XXI editores, S. A. de C. V.

Ip, Diana. 2009. A Toolkit to Transform API communities. *Collective Voices: Sistersong Women of Color Reproductive Health Collective* 4 (10): 13.

Irvine, Janice M. 2002. *Talk About Sex: The Battles over Sex Education in the United States*. Berkeley and Los Angeles: University of California Press.

Jiménez, Laura. 2007. Let's Talk About Sex! Women of Color, Choices, and Reproductive Justice. *Collective Voices: Sistersong Women of Color Reproductive Health Collective* 2 (6): 1–2.

Joffe, Carole. 2003. Roe v. Wade at 30: What Are the Prospects For Abortion Provision? *Perspectives on Sexual and Reproductive Health* 35 (1): 29–33.

Jones, Elise F., Jacqueline Darroch Forest, Noreen Goldman, Stanley Henshaw, Richard Lincoln, Jeannie I. Rosoff, Charles F. Westhoff, and Deirdre Wulf. 1986. *Teenage Pregnancy in Industrialized Countries. A Study Sponsored by the Alan Guttmacher Institute*. New Haven: Yale University Press.

Jones, Rachel K., Mia R. S. Zolna, Stanley K. Henshaw, and Lawrence B. Finer. 2008. Abortion in the United States: Incidence and Access to Services, 2005. *Perspectives on Sexual and Reproductive Health* 40 (1): 6–16.

Joyner, Kara, and J. Richard Udry. 2000. You Don't Bring Me Anything but Down: Adolescent Romance and Depression. *Journal of Health and Social Behavior* 41 (4): 369–91.

Kamp, Trix van der, and Henk Krijnen, eds. 1987. *Dagelijks Leven in Nederland: Verschuivingen in het Sociale Leven na de Tweede Wereldoorlog*. Amsterdam: De Populier/IPSO.

Kantor, Leslie M., John S. Santelli, Julien Teitler, and Randall Balmer. 2008. Abstinence-Only Policies and Programs: An Overview. *Sexuality Research and Social Policy: A Journal of NSRC* 5 (3): 6–17.

Kaplan, Robert D. 2010. *Monsoon: The Indian Ocean and the Future of American Power*. New York: Random House.

Kaye, Kelleen, Katherine Suellentrop, and Corinna Sloup. 2009. *The Fog Zone: How Misperceptions, Magical Thinking, and Ambivalence Put Young Adults at Risk for Unplanned Pregnancy*. Washington, D.C.: The National Campaign to Prevent Teen and Unplanned Pregnancy.

Kelley, Jonathan, and Nan Dirk de Graaf. 1997. National Context, Parental Socialization, and Religious Belief: Results from 15 Nations. *American Sociological Review* 62 (4): 639–59.

Kennedy, James C. 1995. *Nieuw Babylon in Aanbouw: Nederland in de Jaren Zestig*. Amsterdam: Boom.

———. 1997. New Babylon and the Politics of Modernity. *Sociologische Gids* 44:361–74.

Ketting, Evert. 1983. Contraception and Fertility in the Netherlands. *Family Planning Perspectives* 15 (1): 19–25.

———. 1990. De Seksuele Revolutie van Jongeren. In *Het Verlies van de Onschuld: Seksualiteit in Nederland*, edited by G. Hekma, B. v. Stolk, B. v. Heerikhuizen and B. Kruithof. Groningen: Wolters-Noordhoff.

———. 1994. Is the Dutch Abortion Rate Really that Low? *Planned Parenthood in Europe* 23 (3): 29–32.

Ketting, Evert, and Adriaan P. Visser. 1994. Contraception in the Netherlands: The Low Abortion Rate Explained. *Patient Education and Counseling* 23 (3): 161–71.

Kickert, Walter J. M. 2003. Beneath Consensual Corporatism: Traditions of Governance in the Netherlands. *Public Administration* 81 (1): 119–40.

Kimmel, Michael. 1996. *Manhood in America: A Cultural History*. New York: The Free Press.

Kirschner, Suzanne R. 1990. The Assenting Echo: Anglo-American Values in Contemporary Psychoanalytic Developmental Psychology. *Social Research* 57 (4): 821–57.

Knijn, Trudie. 1994a. Fish without Bikes: Revision of the Dutch Welfare State and Its Consequences for the (In)dependence of Single Mothers. *Social Politics* 1 (1): 83–105.

———. 1994b. Social Dilemmas in Images of Motherhood in the Netherlands. *The European Journal of Women's Studies* 1 (2): 183–205.

Knijn, Trudie, and Frits van Wel. 2001. Careful or Lenient: Welfare Reform for Lone Mothers in the Netherlands. *Journal of European Social Policy* 11 (3): 235–51.

Komter, Aafke. 1989. Hidden Power in Marriage. *Gender & Society* 3 (2): 187–216.

Kooij, G. A. 1983. *Sex in Nederland: Het Meest Recente Onderzoek naar Houding en Gedrag van de Nederlandse Bevolking.* Utrecht/Antwerp: Het Spectrum.

Kost, Kathryn, Stanley Henshaw, and Liz Carlin. 2010. *U.S. Teenage Pregnancies, Births and Abortions: National and State Trends and Trends by Race and Ethnicity.* Washington, DC : Guttmacher Institute.

Kremer, Monique. 2007. *How Welfare States Care: Culture, Gender and Parenting in Europe.* Amsterdam: Amsterdam University Press.

Ku, Leighton, Freya Sonenstein, and Joseph Pleck. 1994. The Dynamics of Young Men's Condom Use During and Across Relationships. *Family Planning Perspectives* 26 (6): 246–51.

Lamont, Michèle. 1992. *Money, Morals and Manners: The Culture of the French and the American Upper-Middle Class.* Chicago: University of Chicago Press.

———. 2000. *The Dignity of Working Men: Morality and the Boundaries of Race, Class, and Immigration.* Cambridge, MA: Harvard University Press, and New York: Russell Sage Foundation.

Lareau, Annette. 2003. *Unequal Childhoods: Class, Race, and Family Life.* Berkeley and Los Angeles: University of California Press.

Laumann, Edward O., John H. Gagnon, Robert T. Michael, and Stuart Michaels. 1994. *The Social Organization of Sexuality: Sexual Practices in the United States.* Chicago: University of Chicago Press.

Lee, Laura van, and Cecile Wijsen. 2008. *Landelijke Abortus Registratie 2007.* Utrecht, Netherlands: Rutgers Nisso Groep.

Lee, Laura van, Ineke van der Vlucht, Cecile Wijsen, and Franka Cadée. 2009. *Fact Sheet 2009: Tienerzwangerschappen, Abortus en Tienermoeders in Nederland: Feiten en Cijfers.* Utrecht: Rutgers Nisso Groep.

Lehrer, Jocelyn A., Robert Pantell, Kathleen Tebb, and Mary-Anne Shafer. 2007. Forgone Health Care among U.S. Adolescents: Associations between Risk Characteristics and Confidentiality Concern. *Journal of Adolescent Health* 40 (3): 218–26.

Levine, Daniel. 1988. *Poverty and Society: The Growth of the American Welfare State in International Comparison.* New Brunswick: Rutgers University Press.

Levy, Ariel. 2005. *Female Chauvinist Pigs: Women and the Rise of Raunch Culture.* New York: Free Press.

———. 2010. Prodigal Son: Is the Wayward Republican Mike Huckabee Now His Party's Best Hope? *The New Yorker*, June 28.

Lewis, Jane, and Trudie Knijn. 2002. The Politics of Sex Education Policy in England and Wales and the Netherlands since the 1980s. *Journal of Social Policy* 31 (4): 669–94.

———. 2003. Sex Education Materials in the Netherlands and in England and Wales: A Comparison of Content, Use and Teaching Practice. *Oxford Review of Education* 29 (1): 113–50.

Lijphart, Arend. 1975. *The Politics of Accommodation: Pluralism and Democracy in the Netherlands.* 2d ed. Berkeley and Los Angeles: University of California Press.

Lindberg, Laura D., John S. Santelli, and Susheela Singh. 2006. Changes in Formal Sex Education: 1995–2002. *Perspectives on Sexual and Reproductive Health* 38 (4): 182–89.

Lipset, Seymour Martin. 1963. *The First New Nation: The United States in Historical and Comparative Perspective*. New York: Basic Books.

Lucas, Stephen E. 1998. The Rhetorical Ancestry of the Declaration of Independence. *Rhetoric & Public Affairs* 1 (2): 143–84.

Luker, Kristin. 1975. *Taking Chances: Abortion and the Decision Not to Contracept*. Berkeley and Los Angeles: University of California Press.

——. 1996. *Dubious Conceptions: The Politics of Teenage Pregnancy*. Cambridge, MA: Harvard University Press.

MacCoun, Robert, and Peter Reuter. 1997. Interpreting Dutch Cannabis Policy: Reasoning by Analogy in the Legalization Debate. *Science* 278 (5335): 47–52.

Manlove, Jennifer, Suzanne Ryan, and Kerry Franzetta. 2003. Contraceptive Use Patterns within Teenagers' First Sexual Relationships. *Perspectives on Sexual and Reproductive Health* 35 (6): 246–55.

Manlove, Jennifer, Erum Ikramullah, Lisa Mincieli, Emily Holcombe, and Sana Danish. 2009. Trends in Sexual Experience, Contraceptive Use, and Teenage Childbearing: 1992–2002. *Journal of Adolescent Health* 44 (5): 413–23.

Manning, Wendy, Peggy Giordano, and Monica Longmore. 2006. Hooking Up: The Relationship Contexts of "Nonrelationship" Sex. *Journal of Adolescent Research* 21 (5): 459–83.

Marcell, Arik V., Tina Raine, and Stephen L. Eyre. 2003. Where Does Reproductive Health Fit into the Lives of Adolescent Males? *Perspectives on Sexual and Reproductive Health* 35 (4): 180–86.

Martin, Karin A. 1996. *Puberty, Sexuality, and the Self: Girls and Boys at Adolescence*. New York: Routledge.

Mayes, La'Tasha D., and Bekezela Mguni. 2009. Mission (Im)Possible! *Collective Voices: Sistersong Women of Color Reproductive Health Collective* 4 (10): 21.

McCarthy, Bill, and Teresa Casey. 2008. Love, Sex, and Crime: Adolescent Romantic Relationships and Offending. *American Sociological Review* 73 (6): 944–69.

McRobbie, Angela. 1991. *Feminism and Youth Culture: From Jackie to Just Seventeen*. London: Macmillan.

McRobbie, Angela, and Jenny Garber. 1993. Girls and Subcultures. In *Resistance through Rituals: Youth Subcultures in Post-War Britain*, edited by S. Hall and T. Jefferson. London: Routledge.

Meier, Ann M. 2007. Adolescent First Sex and Subsequent Mental Health. *American Journal of Sociology* 112 (6): 1811–47.

Meijers, Frans. 1991. De Betekenis van Arbeid in het Levensplan van Jonge Mannen en Vrouwen. *Sociologische Gids* 38 (5): 308–23.

Michaud, Pierre-Andre. 2006. Adolescents and Risks: Why Not Change Our Paradigm? *Journal of Adolescent Health* 38 (5): 481–83.

Miller, William C., Carol A. Ford, Martina Morris, Mark S. Handcock, John L. Schmitz, Marcia M. Hobbs, Myron S. Cohen, Kathleen Mullan Harris, and J. Richard Udry. 2004. Prevalence of Chlamydial and Gonococcal Infections among Young Adults in the United States. *JAMA* 291 (18): 2229–36.

Misra, Joya, Stephanie Moller, and Michelle J. Budig. 2007. Work-Family Policies and Poverty for Partnered and Single Women in Europe and North America. *Gender & Society* 21 (6): 804–27.

Mosher, William D., Anjani Chandra, and Jo Jones. 2005. Sexual Behavior and Selected

Health Measures: Men and Women 15–44 Years of Age, United States, 2002. *Advance Data from Vital and Health Statistics*, no. 362. National Center for Health Statistics.

Motley, John Lothrop. 1855. *The Rise of the Dutch Republic*. New York: Harper and Brothers.

Myrsiades, Linda. 2002. *Splitting the Baby: The Culture of Abortion in Literature and Law, Rhetoric and Cartoons*. New York: Peter Lang.

Nathanson, Constance. 1991. *Dangerous Passage: The Social Control of Sexuality in Women's Adolescence*. Philadelphia: Temple University Press.

Newman, Katherine S. 1999. *Falling from Grace: Downward Mobility in the Age of Affluence*. Berkeley and Los Angeles: University of California Press.

OECD. 2008a. *Growing Unequal? Distribution and Poverty in OECD Countries*. Paris: OECD.

———. 2008b. *OECD Employment Outlook 2008*. Paris: OECD.

———. 2009. *OECD Society at a Glance 2009—OECD Social Indicators*, chapter 6: Equity Indicators. Paris: OECD.

———. 2010. *OECD Family Database*. Paris: OECD.

Ott, Mary A., Susan G. Millstein, Susan Ofner, and Bonnie L. Halpern-Felsher. 2006. Greater Expectations: Adolescents' Positive Motivations for Sex. *Perspectives on Sexual and Reproductive Health* 38 (2): 84–89.

Outshoorn, Joyce. 2000. Abortion in the Netherlands: The Successful Pacification of a Controversial Issue. In *Regulating Morality: A Comparison of the Role of the State in Mastering the Mores in the Netherlands and the United States*, edited by H. Krabbendam and H.-M. Ten Napel. Antwerpen-Apeldoorn: E. M. Meijers Institute/Maklu-Uitgevers.

Pager, Devah, Bruce Western, and Bart Bonikowski. 2009. Discrimination in a Low-Wage Labor Market: A Field Experiment. *American Sociological Review* 74 (5): 777–99.

Panchaud, Christine, Susheela Singh, Dina Feivelson, and Jacqueline E. Darroch. 2000. Sexually Transmitted Diseases among Adolescents in Developed Countries. *Family Planning Perspectives* 32 (1): 24–32 and 45.

Pascoe, C. J. 2007. *Dude, You're a Fag: Masculinity and Sexuality in High School*. Berkeley and Los Angeles: University of California Press.

Petersen, Larry R., and Gregory V. Donnenwerth. 1997. Secularization and the Influence of Religion on Beliefs about Premarital Sex. *Social Forces* 75 (3): 1071–88.

Phillips, Derek. 1985. Het Nederlandse Volkskarakter: Enige Notities. In *De Naakte Nederlander: Kritische Overpeinzingen*, edited by D. Phillips. Amsterdam: Bert Bakker.

Picavet, Charles, and Theo Sandfort. 2005. Problemen? Geen Probleem! Homo/lesbo Worden in Een Tolerant Sociaal Klimaat. *Tijdschrift voor Seksuologie* 29:28–35.

Pleck, Joseph H., Freya L. Sonenstein, and Leighton C. Ku 1993. Masculinity Ideology: Its Impact on Adolescent Males' Heterosexual Relationships. *Journal of Social Issues* 49 (3): 11–29.

Poel, Yolanda te, and Janita Ravesloot. 1997. Seksualiteit als Opvoedings- en Ontwikkelingsdomein: Nieuwe Oriëntaties en Dilemma's? *Comenius* 17 (1): 55–65.

Praag, C. S. van, and M. Niphuis-Nell, eds. 1997. *Het Gezinsrapport: Een Verkennende Studie naar het Gezin in een Veranderende Samenleving*. Rijswijk: Sociaal en Cultureel Planbureau.

Praag, Carlo van, and Wilfried Uitterhoeve. 1999. *25 Years of Social Change in the Netherlands: Key Data from the Social and Cultural Report 1998*. Nijmegen: SUN.

Pruin, Frieda. 1998. Nederlandse Vrouwen Hebben Geen Enkele Macht. *Opzij* (December): 10–16.

Quadagno, Jill. 1994. *The Color of Welfare: How Racism Undermined the War on Poverty.* New York: Oxford University Press.

Rademakers, Jany, and Janita Ravesloot. 1993. Jongeren en Seksualiteit. In *Jeugd in Meervoud: Theorieën, Modellen en Onderzoek van Leefwerelden van Jongeren*, edited by A. J. Dieleman, F. J. v. d. Linden and A. C. Perreijn. Utrecht: De Tijdstroom.

Ralph, Lauren J., and Claire D. Brindis. 2010. Access to Reproductive Healthcare for Adolescents: Establishing Healthy Behaviors at a Critical Juncture in the Lifecourse. *Current Opinion in Obstetrics and Gynecology* 22 (5): 369–74.

Rank, Mark R. 2003. As American as Apple Pie: Poverty and Welfare. *Contexts: Understanding People in Their Social Worlds* 2 (3): 41–49.

Ravesloot, Janita. 1997. *Seksualiteit in de Jeugdfase Vroeger en Nu: Ouders en Jongeren aan het Woord.* Amsterdam: Het Spinhuis.

Regnerus, Mark D. 2005. Talking about Sex: Religion and Patterns of Parent-Child Communications about Sex and Contraception. *The Sociological Quarterly* 46:79–105.

Regt, Ali de. 1988. Geld in Intieme Relaties: Afhankelijkheden tussen Studenten en Hun Ouders. *Amsterdams Sociologisch Tijdschrift* 15 (3): 377–413.

Reinarman, Craig, Peter Cohen, and Hendrien Kaal. 2004. The Limited Relevance of Drug Policy: Cannabis in Amsterdam and in San Francisco. *American Journal of Public Health* 94 (5): 836–42.

Revised Oral Contraceptive Labeling: FDA Approves Recommendation Allowing Delay of Pelvic Exam. 1993. *Contraception Report* 4 (5): 4–7.

Risman, Barbara J., and Pepper Schwartz. 2002. After the Sexual Revolution: Gender Politics in Teen Dating. *Contexts: Understanding People in Their Social Worlds* 1 (1): 16–24.

Rispens, J., J. M. A. Hermanns, and W. H. J. Meeus, eds. 1996. *Opvoeden in Nederland.* Assen: Van Gorcum.

Rogers, Joel, and Wolfgang Streeck. 1994. Workplace Representation Overseas: The Works Councils Story. In *Working Under Different Rules*, edited by R. B. Freeman. New York: Russell Sage Foundation.

Röling, Hugo. 2003. The Problem of Sex Education in the Netherlands in the Twentieth Century. *Clio Medica/The Wellcome Series in the History of Medicine* 71:243–63.

Rose, Susan. 2005. Going Too Far? Sex, Sin and Social Policy. *Social Forces* 84 (2): 1207–32.

Ross, Loretta. 2005. Reproductive Rights are Human Rights. *Collective Voices: Sistersong Women of Color Reproductive Health Collective* 1 (3): 16–17.

Rubin, Lillian B. 1994. *Families on the Faultline: America's Working Class Speaks about the Family, the Economy, Race, and Ethnicity.* New York: HarperCollins.

Russell, Stephen T. 2005. Conceptualizing Positive Adolescent Sexuality Development. *Sexuality Research and Social Policy: A Journal of NSRC* 2 (3): 4–12.

Santelli, John S., Laura Duberstein Lindberg, Lawrence B. Finer, and Susheela Singh. 2007. Explaining Recent Declines in Adolescent Pregnancy in the United States: The Contribution of Abstinence and Improved Contraceptive Use. *American Journal of Public Health* 97 (1): 150–56.

Santelli, John S., Theo G. Sandfort, and Mark Orr. 2008. Transnational Comparisons of Adolescent Contraceptive Use: What Can We Learn From These Comparisons? *Archives of Pediatrics and Adolescent Medicine* 162 (1): 92–94.

Savin-Williams, Ritch C. 2000. *Mom, Dad, I'm Gay: How Families Negotiate Coming Out.* Washington DC: American Psychological Association.

Schalet, Amy T. 1994. Dramatiseren of Normaliseren? De Culterele Constructie van

Tienerseksualiteit in de Verenigde Staten en Nederland. *Amsterdams Sociologisch Tijdschrift* 21 (2): 113–47.

———. 2000. Raging Hormones, Regulated Love: Adolescent Sexuality and the Constitution of the Modern Individual in the United States and the Netherlands. *Body and Society* 6 (1): 75–105.

———. 2001. Geciviliseerd of Gestigmatiseerd: Afhankelijkheid en Lichaamsbeheersing in de Nederlandse Figuratiesociologie en Amerikaanse 'Welfare'-debatten. *Amsterdams Sociologisch Tijdschrift* 28 (3): 321–49.

———. 2004. Must We Fear Adolescent Sexuality? *Medscape General Medicine* 6 (4).

———. 2009. Subjectivity, Intimacy, and the Empowerment Paradigm of Adolescent Sexuality: The Unexplored Room. *Feminist Studies* 35 (1): 133–60.

Schama, Simon. 1988. *The Embarrassment of Riches: An Interpretation of Dutch Culture in the Golden Age*. New York: Alfred A. Knopf.

Schnabel, Paul. 1990. Het Verlies van de Seksuele Onschuld. In *Het Verlies van de Onschuld: Seksualiteit in Nederland*, edited by G. Hekma, B. v. Stolk, B. v. Heerikhuizen and B. Kruithof. Groningen: Wolters-Noordhoff.

Schneider, David M. 1980. *American Kinship: A Cultural Account*. 2d ed. Chicago: The University of Chicago Press.

Schuyf, Judith, and André Krouwel. 1999. The Dutch Lesbian and Gay Movement: The Politics of Accommodation. In *The Global Emergence of Gay and Lesbian Politics: National Imprints of a Worldwide Movement*, edited by B. D. Adam, J. W. Duyvendak and A. Krouwel. Philadelphia: Temple University Press.

Schwarz, Eleanor Bimla, Mona Saint, Ginny Gildengorin, Tracy A. Weitz, Felicia H. Stewart, and George F. Sawaya. 2005. Cervical Cancer Screening Continues to Limit Provision of Contraception. *Contraception* 72 (3): 179–81.

Sewell, William H., Jr. 1999. The Concept(s) of Culture. In *Beyond the Cultural Turn: New Directions in the Study of Society and Culture*, edited by V. E. Bonnell and L. Hunt. Berkeley and Los Angeles: University of California Press.

Sex Education in America: An NPR/Kaiser/Kennedy School Poll. 2004. Washington, DC : National Public Radio, Kaiser Family Foundation, Harvard University Kennedy School of Government.

Singh, Susheela, and Jacqueline E. Darroch. 2000. Adolescent Pregnancy and Childbearing: Levels and Trends in Developed Countries. *Family Planning Perspectives* 32 (1): 14–23.

Singh, Susheela, Jacqueline E. Darroch, and Jennifer J. Frost. 2001. Socioeconomic Disadvantage and Adolescent Women's Sexual and Reproductive Behavior: The Case of Five Developed Countries. *Family Planning Perspectives* 33 (6): 251–58 and 289.

Smeeding, Timothy M., and Katherin Ross Phillips. 2002. Cross-National Differences in Employment and Economic Sufficiency. *The Annals of the American Academy of Political and Social Science* 580 (March): 103–33.

Smetana, Judith G., Nicole Campione-Barr, and Aaron Metzger. 2006. Adolescent Development in Interpersonal and Societal Contexts. *Annual Review of Psychology* 57: 255–84.

Smiler, Andrew P., L. Monique Ward, Allison Caruthers, and Ann Merriwether. 2005. Pleasure, Empowerment, and Love: Factors Associated with a Positive First Coitus. *Sexuality Research and Social Policy: A Journal of NSRC* 2 (3): 41–55.

Smith, Dennis. 1999. *The Civilizing Process* and *The History of Sexuality*: Comparing Norbert Elias and Michel Foucault. *Theory and Society* 28 (1): 79–100.

Smith, Tom W. 1994. Attitudes toward Sexual Permissiveness: Trends, Correlates, and

Behavioral Connections. In *Sexuality Across the Life Course*, edited by A. S. Rossi. Chicago: The University of Chicago Press.

Sniderman, Paul M., and Louk Hagendoorn. 2007. *When Ways of Life Collide: Multiculturalism and Its Discontents in the Netherlands*. Princeton: Princeton University Press.

Sociaal en Cultureel Planbureau. 1998. *Social en Cultureel Rapport 1998: 25 Jaar Sociale Verandering*. Rijswijk: Sociaal en Cultureel Planbureau.

Solinger, Rickie. 2005. *Pregnancy and Power: A Short History of Reproductive Politics in America*. New York: New York University Press.

Soysal, Yasemin N. 1994. *Limits of Citizenship: Migrants and Postnational Membership in Europe*. Chicago: The University of Chicago Press.

Spillman, Lynette P. 1997. *Nation and Commemoration: Creating National Identities in the United States and Australia*. Cambridge: Cambridge University Press.

Sprecher, Susan, Anita Barbee, and Pepper Schwartz. 1995. Was it Good for You, Too? Gender Differences in First Sexual Intercourse Experiences. *Journal of Sex Research* 32 (1): 3–15.

Starr, Jerold M. 1986. American Youth in the 1980s. *Youth & Society* 17 (4): 323–45.

Stearns, Peter N. 1994. *American Cool: Constructing a Twentieth Century Emotional Style*. New York: New York University Press.

Steele, Jeanne R. 2002. Teens and Movies: Something to Do, Plenty to Learn. In *Sexual Teens, Sexual Media: Investigating Media's Influence on Adolescent Sexuality*, edited by J. Brown, Jeanne Steele, and Kim Walsh-Childers. Mahwah, NJ: Lawrence Erlbaum Associates.

Steensland, Brian. 2008. *The Failed Welfare Revolution: America's Struggle over Guaranteed Income Policy*. Princeton: Princeton University Press.

Steinberg, Laurence. 2004. Risk Taking in Adolescence: What Changes, and Why? *Annals of the New York Academy of Sciences* 1021:51–58.

Stephenson, Peter H. 1989. Going to McDonald's in Leiden: Reflections on the Concept of Self and Society in the Netherlands. *Ethos* 17 (2): 226–47.

SOAIDS. 2004. *A Delicate Balance: The State of Affairs of HIV and other STIs in the Netherlands*. Amsterdam: STI AIDS Netherlands.

Stolk, Bram van, and Cas Wouters. 1983. *Vrouwen in Tweestrijd: Tussen Thuis en Tehuis. Relatieproblemen in de Verzorgingsstaat. Opgetekend in een Crisiscentrum*. Deventer: Van Loghum Slaterus.

Stolk, Bram van. 1991. De Kracht van de Moraal: De Doorbraak in het Emancipatieproces van Nederlandse Homoseksuelen. *Amsterdams Sociologisch Tijdschrift* 18 (1): 3–34.

Stone, Nicole, and Roger Ingham. 2002. Factors Affecting British Teenagers' Contraceptive Use at First Intercourse: The Importance of Partner Communication. *Perspectives on Sexual and Reproductive Health* 34 (4): 191–97.

Swaan, Abram de. 1981. The Politics of Agoraphobia: On Changes in Emotional and Relational Management. *Theory and Society* 10 (3): 359–85.

———. 1988. *In Care of the State: Health Care, Education, and Welfare in Europe and the USA in the Modern Era*. New York: Oxford University Press.

Swidler, Ann. 1986. Culture in Action: Symbols and Strategies. *American Sociological Review* 51 (2): 273–86.

———. 2001. *Talk of Love: How Culture Matters*. Chicago: University of Chicago Press.

Szirmai, Adam. 1988. *Inequality Observed: A Study of Attitudes Towards Income Inequality*. Avebury, U.K.: Aldershot.

Tak, Peter J. P. 2003. *The Dutch Criminal Justice System: Organization and Operation*. Meppel: Boom Juridische Uitgevers.

Tanenbaum, Leora. 2000. *Slut: Growing Up Female with a Bad Reputation*. New York: HarperCollins.

Taylor, Charles. 2007. Modern Social Imaginaries. In *A Secular Age*. Cambridge, MA: Harvard University Press.

Thompson, Sharon. 1990. Putting a Big Thing into a Little Hole: Teenage Girls' Accounts of Sexual Initiation. *The Journal of Sex Research* 27 (3): 341–61.

———. 1995. *Going All the Way: Teenage Girls' Tales of Sex, Romance, and Pregnancy*. New York: Hill and Wang.

Thorne, Barrie. 1993. *Gender Play: Girls and Boys in School*. New Brunswick: Rutgers University Press.

Tipton, Steven M. 1982. *Getting Saved from the Sixties: Moral Meaning in Conversion and Cultural Change*. Berkeley and Los Angeles: University of California Press.

Tolman, Deborah L. 2002. *Dilemmas of Desire: Teenage Girls Talk about Sexuality*. Cambridge, MA: Harvard University Press.

Tolman, Deborah L., Meg L. Striepe, and Tricia Harmon. 2003. Gender Matters: Constructing a Model of Adolescent Sexual Health. *The Journal of Sex Research* 40:4–12.

Tolman, Deborah L., Renée Spencer, Tricia Harmon, Myra Rosen-Reynoso, and Meg Striepe. 2004. Getting Close, Staying Cool: Early Adolescent Boys' Experiences with Romantic Relationships. In *Adolescent Boys: Exploring Diverse Cultures of Boyhood*, edited by Niobe Way and Judy Y. Chu. New York: New York University Press.

Tonry, Michael, and Catrien Bijlenveld. 2007. Crime, Criminal Justice, and Criminology in the Netherlands. *Crime and Justice* 35 (1): 1–30.

UNAIDS. 2008. HIV and AIDS Estimates and Data, 2001 and 2007. In *2008 Report on the Global AIDS Epidemic*. Geneva, Switzerland: Joint United Nations Programme on HIV/AIDS (UNAIDS).

Vance, Carole S. 1984. Pleasure and Danger: Toward a Politics of Sexuality. In *Pleasure and Danger: Exploring Female Sexuality*, edited by C. S. Vance. Boston: Routledge and Kegan Paul.

Vanwesenbeeck, Ine, Marrie Bekker, and Akeline van Lenning. 1998. Gender Attitudes, Sexual Meanings, and Interactional Patterns in Heterosexual Encounters among College Students in the Netherlands. *Journal of Sex Research* 35 (4): 317–27.

VanYperen, Nico W., and Bram P. Buunk. 1991. Equity Theory and Exchange and Communal Orientation from a Cross-National Perspective. *The Journal of Social Psychology* 131 (1): 5–20.

Varenne, Hervé. 1977. *Americans Together: Structured Diversity in a Midwestern Town*. New York: Teachers College Press.

Veen, Romke J. van der. 1996. Social Solidarity: The Development of the Welfare State in the Netherlands and the United States. In *Social and Secure? Politics and Culture of the Welfare State: A Comparative Inquiry*, edited by H. Bak, F. v. Holthoon and H. Krabbendam. Amsterdam: VU Amsterdam University Press.

Veldhuis, T., and E. Bakker. 2009. *Muslims in the Netherlands: Tensions and Violent Conflict*. MICROCON Policy Working Paper 6. Brighton: MICROCON.

Vogels, Ton, and Ron van der Vliet. 1990. *Jeugd en Seks: Gedrag en Gezondheidsrisico's bij Scholieren*. The Hague: SDU Uitgerverij.

Waal, Mieke de. 1989. *Meisjes, Een Wereld Apart: Een Etnografie van Meisjes op de Middelbare School*. Meppel and Amsterdam: Boom.

Waller, Willard. 1937. The Rating and Dating Complex. *American Sociological Review* 2 (5): 727–34.

Ward, L. Monique, Kyla M. Day, and Marina Epstein. 2006. Uncommonly Good: Exploring How Mass Media May Be a Positive Influence on Young Women's Sexual Health and Development. *New Directions for Child and Adolescent Development* 112:57–70.

Weber, Max. 1958. *The Protestant Ethic and the Spirit of Capitalism*. Translated by T. Parsons. New York: Charles Scribner's Sons.

Weir, Margaret. 1995. Poverty, Social Rights, and the Politics of Place in the United States. In *European Social Policy: Between Fragmentation and Integration*, edited by S. Leibfried and P. Pierson. Washington, DC: Brookings Institute.

Western, Bruce, and Becky Pettit. 2002. Beyond Crime and Punishment: Prisons and Inequality. *Contexts: Understanding People in Their Social Worlds* 1 (3): 37–43.

Whitman, James Q. 2003. *Harsh Justice: Criminal Punishment and the Widening Divide between America and Europe*. Oxford and New York: Oxford University Press.

Widman, Laura, Deborah P. Welsh, James K. McNulty and Katherine C. Little. 2006. Sexual Communication and Contraceptive Use in Adolescent Dating Couples. *Journal of Adolescent Health* 39:893–99.

Wilkins, Amy C. 2008. *Wannabes, Goths, and Christians: The Boundaries of Sex, Style, and Status*. Chicago: University of Chicago Press.

Williams, Raymond. 1976. *Keywords: A Vocabulary of Culture and Society*. New York: Oxford University Press.

Willis, Paul E. 1977. *Learning to Labour: How Working-class Kids Get Working-class Jobs*. Farnborough: Saxon House.

Wilterdink, Nico. 1995. Civilisatie en Cultuur Opniew Bezien. *Amsterdams Sociologisch Tijdschrift* 22 (2): 350–67.

Wood, Ann Marie. 1998. Omniscient Organizations and Bodily Observations: Electronic Surveillance in the Workplace. *International Journal of Sociology and Social Policy* 18 (5/6): 136–74.

Wouters, Cas. 1986. Formalization and Informalization: Changing Tension Balances in Civilizing Processes. *Theory, Culture, and Society* 3 (2): 1–18.

———. 1987. Developments in the Behavioural Codes between the Sexes: The Formalization of Informalization in the Netherlands, 1930–85. *Theory, Culture & Society* 4 (2): 405–27.

———. 1998. Etiquette Books and Emotion Management in the Twentieth Century: American Habitus in International Comparison. In *An Emotional History of the United States*, edited by P. N. Stearns and J. Lewis. New York: New York University Press.

———. 2004. *Sex and Manners: Female Emancipation in the West, 1890–2000*. Edited by M. Featherstone. Thousand Oaks, CA, and London: Sage Publications.

Wright, Will. 1977. *Sixguns and Society: A Structural Study of the Western*. Berkeley and Los Angeles: University of California Press.

WRR. 2006. *De Verzorgingsstaat Herwogen: Over Verzorgen, Verzekeren, Verheffen, en Verbinden*. The Hague/Amsterdam: WRR/Amsterdam University Press.

Zessen, Gertjan van, and Theo Sandfort, eds. 1991. *Seksualiteit in Nederland: Seksueel Gedrag, Risico en Preventie van AIDS*. Amsterdam: Swets & Zeitlinger.

Zvesper, John. 1996. Liberty, Property, and Welfare: America's Lockean Welfare State. In *Social and Secure? Politics and Culture of the Welfare State: A Comparative Inquiry*, edited by H. Bak, F. v. Holthoon, and H. Krabbendam. Amsterdam: VU University Press.